Religion and Politics
in Latin America

Religion and Politics in Latin America

THE CATHOLIC CHURCH IN
VENEZUELA AND COLOMBIA

Daniel H. Levine

PRINCETON UNIVERSITY PRESS
PRINCETON, NEW JERSEY

Copyright © 1981 by Princeton University Press
Published by Princeton University Press, Princeton, New Jersey
In the United Kingdom: Princeton University Press, Guildford, Surrey

All Rights Reserved
Library of Congress Cataloging in Publication Data will be
found on the last printed page of this book

This book has been composed in Linotype Times Roman

Clothbound editions of Princeton University Press books
are printed on acid-free paper, and binding materials are
chosen for strength and durability

Printed in the United States of America by Princeton
University Press, Princeton, New Jersey

For Kalman H. Silvert

Contents

List of Tables and Figures   ix
Acknowledgments   xi

PART I: THE PROBLEM AND THE CONTEXTS

1   *Religion and Politics: The Nature of the Problem*   3
2   *Religion and Politics, Politics and Religion: General Perspectives*   18
3   *Settings for Change: Venezuela and Colombia*   56

PART II: THE BISHOPS AND THEIR WORLDS

4   *The Bishops: A Collective Portrait*   99
5   *Visions of the Church: Authority and Its Problems*   142
6   *The Church and the World: Perception and Action*   171

PART III: CASE STUDIES IN STRUCTURE AND STYLE

7   *Structure and Style: National Organizations*   213
8   *Structure and Style: Two Case Studies*   240
9   *Structure and Style: Six Dioceses*   255

PART IV: CONCLUSIONS

10   *Further Reflections*   289

Bibliography   317
Index   337

List of Tables and Figures

TABLES

3.1	Population and Urbanization in Venezuela and Colombia	61
3.2	Ordination of Priests in Venezuela and Colombia	72
3.3	Selected Data on the Church in Venezuela and Colombia	73
4.1	Personal and Social Characteristics of the Bishops	101
4.2	Age and Education of the Bishops	104
4.3	Career Patterns of the Bishops	106
4.4	Contacts with Government	109
4.5	Relations in the Local Church	111
4.6	Uses of $10,000 in the Diocese	114
4.7	Major Problems of the Church	115
4.8	Major Problems of the Church, by Country and Education	116
4.9	Typologies of Church Elites	141
5.1	Dimensions of Change in the Church	156
5.2	Dimensions of Change in the Church, by Education	157
5.3	Most Important Changes in the Venezuelan (Colombian) Church	157
5.4	Indices of Authority Compared	159
5.5	Context of Discussions of Future of the Church	164
5.6	Ecclesial Dimensions of Change	165
6.1	Structuralism Index	175
6.2	Church Role Indices	181
6.3	Dialogue and Cooperation with Marxists	185
6.4	Dialogue and Cooperation with Marxists, by Education	186
6.5	Dialogue and Cooperation with Marxists, by Career	187
6.6	Dialogue and Cooperation with Marxists, by Church Role Indices	189
6.7	Activation and Career	202
6.8	Dialogue and Cooperation with Marxists, by Changed Authority Relations Since the Council	203
6.9	Dialogue and Cooperation with Marxists, by Changes in Authority Relations in the National Church	203
6.10	Dialogue and Cooperation with Marxists, by Social Progress in the Church Since the Council	204
6.11	Dialogue and Cooperation with Marxists, by Social Progress in the National Church	205

TABLES AND FIGURES

6.12	Dialogue and Cooperation with Marxists, by the Context of Discussions of the Future of the Church	207
6.13	Ecclesial and Sociopolitical Dimensions of Change	208
7.1	Most Important Lay Organizations	219
7.2	Most Important Areas of Lay Activity	219
9.1	Selected Data on the Church in Six Dioceses	257
9.2	Six Dioceses: Summary Characteristics	280

FIGURES

5.1	Processes of Change in the Church	166
6.1	Processes of Change in the Church (continued)	209
9.1	Processes of Change at the Local Level	281

Acknowledgments

MANY things of great personal and intellectual value have come to me in recent years through getting to know the people of the Latin American Church. I admire their courage, dedication, and hope for a better future; and I am happy to have had the chance to know them. I am particularly grateful to the men and women of the Catholic Church in Venezuela and Colombia who gave so freely of their time. Bishops, priests, religious, and lay people were, almost without exception, helpful and encouraging—willing both to talk and listen. In Venezuela, I am especially indebted to Alberto Gruson of CISOR and to Miguel Torres Ellul for helping me get started and for providing many introductions. In Colombia, Roger Vekemans, S.J., of CEDIAL and Francisco Zuluaga, S.J., of CIAS were invaluable sources of insight and orientation.

Research was financed by grants and fellowships from the Horace H. Rackham School of Graduate Studies of the University of Michigan, the Social Science Research Council, and the Joint Committee on Latin American Studies of the Foreign Area Fellowship Program. Kathleen Durham helped with the coding and initial data analysis, and María Sánchez helped make further data analysis a manageable task. I am grateful for the help, support, and collaboration of these institutions and individuals.

I also owe a debt to the several scholarly journals in which parts of various chapters of this book were first published. Specifically, I want to acknowledge previous publication of the following: portions of chapter 2 in "Religion and Politics, Politics and Religion: An Introduction," *Journal of Interamerican Studies and World Affairs* 21:1 (Feb. 1979); portions of chapters 3, 4, and 6 in "Church Elites in Venezuela and Colombia: Context, Background, and Beliefs," *Latin American Research Review* 14:1 (Spring 1979); portions of chapters 3, 5, 7, and 9 in "Authority in Church and Society: Latin American Models," *Comparative Studies in Society and History* 20:4 (Oct. 1978); portions of chapters 3 and 6 in "The Catholic Church, 'Politics,' and Violence: The Colombian Case," *The Review of Politics* 39:2 (Apr. 1977); and portions of chapter 6 in "Democracy and the Church in Venezuela," *Journal of Interamerican Studies and World Affairs* 18:1 (Feb. 1976).

The entire manuscript received a careful critical reading from Thomas Bruneau, Michael Dodson, and Thomas Sanders. I am grateful for their comments, as well as for those made on specific chapters or sections by Phillip Berryman, Leslie Dow, Kathleen Durham, Shepard Forman, Zvi Gitelman, John Kingdon, John Langan, S.J., Phyllis Levine, David Myers, Robert Putnam, María Sánchez, Brian Smith, and Alexander Wilde. In general, I have learned a great deal over the years from conversations with Thomas Bruneau, Margaret Crahan, Thomas Sanders, Brian Smith, Alexander Wilde, and William Wipfler; and I am grateful for their friendship and insight. I owe special thanks to John Harrison for his sustained help and encouragement.

The research and writing of this book began in Ann Arbor, Michigan, and spread through numerous cities and towns in Venezuela, Colombia, and Guatemala. I am grateful to my family for enduring and even enjoying with me the gypsy life style such an undertaking implies.

Finally, this book is dedicated to the memory of Kalman H. Silvert, friend and teacher. I hope he would have liked it.

Ann Arbor, Michigan
January 1980

Religion and Politics
in Latin America

Part I

THE PROBLEM AND THE CONTEXTS

1

Religion and Politics: The Nature of the Problem

RELIGION and politics grow and change together in all societies and cultures. Common structures of meaning and action knit the two domains into one, as notions of authority, hierarchy, and community (to name only a few points of contact) bring religious and political activists together—often in mutual support, often in conflict. This general phenomenon has peculiarly Latin American aspects as well; for in Latin America, religion and politics have been closely intertwined since the Conquest, providing ideological, material, and institutional support and legitimation to one another. But this relation, so central to the historical ethos of Latin American institutions and social processes, is now undergoing profound transformation. Sharp and often bitter conflict has become visible throughout the region. Changes in both religion and politics have led to a struggle to control the direction and to shape the meaning of an emerging new relation between religious and political beliefs, attitudes, and actions.[1]

In this book we shall examine these general processes in their particular Latin American context, through an analysis of changes in the relation of the Catholic Church, and of Catholicism in general, to politics in Venezuela and Colombia. Before going into the origins and structure of this book, however, it may be well to reverse the normal order of things and begin with a broad statement of conclusions; for many readers will wonder why religion deserves the attention of students of politics in the first place. Consciously or unconsciously, we often remain wedded to the nineteenth-century liberal view that, with scientific, technological, and economic progress, religion inevitably loses its popular influence. Moreover, with the spread of Marxist categories of thought, social

---

[1] This process has been extensively documented in recent years. Two good general studies are O'Dea, *The Catholic Crisis*, and Hebblethwaite, *The Runaway Church*. The Latin American scene has been surveyed in general terms in Sanders, "The New Latin American Catholicism," and in Brian Smith, "Religion and Social Change."

scientists have searched for the "roots" of political phenomena in social and particularly in economic processes, taking attitudes, values, and belief structures as products of other, more concrete activities. Liberal evolutionism and the Marxist stress on economics as somehow more "real," more dynamic, together lead to the view that older, supposedly more "traditional" institutions, and especially religious ones, are survivors—static, unchanging structures held over from the past, whose day is rapidly drawing to a close.

But clearly, this view will not do. In theoretical terms, it ignores the fact that religion, like all human institutions, grows and changes, transforming its doctrines, structures, and styles of action in response both to new inner understandings and to challenges and changed conditions in society as a whole. To treat religious institutions as mere survivors is to miss completely their dynamic growth and transformation, and their continuing vitality everywhere. Moreover, as an empirical matter such views gloss over the enormous changes in Catholicism over the last few decades, particularly in Latin America. Few institutions in all of Latin America have changed as rapidly and profoundly as the Catholic Church has; and the intensity, scope, and meaning of this change demand careful and systematic attention.

The "problem" of religion and politics is thus both universal and particular—visible in all cultures, and of special importance in Latin America. Given the dual nature of our subject matter, the conclusions advanced in this book are also both general and particular. Stated briefly, and in general terms, people who are religious place the activities of daily life (be they economic, cultural, social, or political) in a far-reaching context of transcendental significance. The activities of daily life are thus infused with meanings deeply rooted in religious belief and experience, and in the felt nature of the religious community to which believers belong. As an intimate part of everyday life, both in conscious and in subtle and elusive ways, religion thus motivates believers to particular areas and styles of action, generating deep and long-lasting commitments.[2]

---

[2] This perspective remains valid even in contemporary "secular" society, for "secularization" involves more than the mere separation of the institutions of Church and State. Indeed, such separation means that the sacred is to be seen less in institutional terms (i.e., less identified with "churchly" things)

Of course, no person, group, culture, or institution is religious, sacred, secular, or political purely in the abstract. These types of relationships are indeed universal, but it is precisely the richness of human variation which gives direction and meaning to the general patterns.[3] Analysis and understanding must therefore shuttle continuously between the general and the specific, rooting universal processes in particular cultural, historical, and social contexts. Only in this way is it possible to assess the sources and meanings of the patterns which emerge, and to chart their likely future paths with some accuracy. For these reasons, a major conclusion of this book is that, as we move from the general to the particular (that is, from abstract formulae to orientations which guide behavior in the concrete situations of everyday life), national and contextual differences become ever more prominent. The Venezuelans and Colombians studied here profess a common faith and belong to the same Church; but they do this in notably different ways, and their specific orientations reflect the kind of institution and the sort of society in which they were raised and now live.

In working through the theoretical, methodological, and empirical bases of these conclusions, I hope in this chapter to give the reader a sense of the origins and the structure of this book. In my case, this is perhaps more important than usual; for to me

---

than as a trait of life in general. From this perspective even the most "secular" person can find religious significance in the activities of daily life. As Rosemary Reuther points out, "if the church is a community of the new creation, it is not basically a special ecclesiastical world of its own raised up in a sacred social structure beyond the life and destiny of creation; it is simply creation and human society considered from the point of view of where God's activity is renewing the world. We must define the authentic theological distinction between church and world and differentiate this distinction of theological principles from the institutional line between ecclesiastical organizations and those nonecclesiastical or so-called 'secular' organizations that encompass the greater part of life" (*The Radical Kingdom*, pp. 159-60).

[3] As Clifford Geertz puts it, "To be human here is thus not to be Everyman but to be a particular kind of man, and of course men differ: 'other fields,' the Javanese say, 'other grasshoppers.' . . . We must, in short, descend into detail, past the misleading tags, past the metaphysical types, past the empty similarities to grasp firmly the essential character of not only the various cultures but the various sorts of individuals within each culture if we wish to encounter humanity face to face" (*The Interpretation of Cultures*, p. 53).

religion presents a personal and intellectual problem of considerable dimensions. After all, this is a study of Catholicism and politics in Latin America by a Jewish, North American professor of political science. The obvious and somewhat jarring incongruities visible here demand more than the normal perfunctory introduction. Hence, an intellectual and personal history of this project is in order, to clarify the kind of problem that the study of religion poses for any secular social scientist.

ORIGINS AND ORIENTATIONS

This book grew out of my general concern with problems of ideology, social structure, and institutions—their dynamic interrelations, and the implications of the entire process for action. Two key questions underlie the whole approach: first, How do ideas take form, or crystallize, in regular patterns of action? and second, How do institutions develop characteristic styles of action, which spill over from within the institutions to shape the activities of members in their more general social relations? Looked at in this way, religion and politics each constitutes, in Berger's terms, a "package . . . an empirically given combination of institutional processes and clusters of consciousness" which fit together and influence one another continuously.[4]

Religion and politics are useful and important examples of this general process; for each, in a different way, deals with broad questions of the meaning of life, offering symbolic models and organizational structures to articulate and shape it. Politics, after all, deals at the most general level with the organizing principles and symbols of the entire society, giving form to the human community here and now. Religion, in turn, provides values and symbols giving general meaning to human existence, placing any given set of social or political arrangements in broader frameworks of significance. Religion and politics thus necessarily impinge on one another; their goals and structures overlap and run together as a matter of course.

Specifically, this book grew out of my own dissatisfaction with the rather simple-minded evolutionism of much contemporary work on "modernization." My earlier research on Venezuela sug-

[4] Berger, Berger, and Kellner, *The Homeless Mind*, p. 18.

gested that attempts to build simple scales of attitudes, behavior, or institutions running from "traditional" to "modern" were unsatisfactory.[5] They ignored the dynamics of the process of change itself and glossed over the rich possibilities for accommodation, change, and conflict it contains. Thus, quite apart from the obvious difficulty of locating any particular behavior on such a scale, the theory of modernization as commonly used was itself inadequate as a model for understanding change.

Furthermore, my initial look at the Catholic Church in Venezuela, in the context of conflicts over educational policy, showed me that Venezuelan political parties and groups had changed profoundly; but, more surprising, I found that the same was true of the Church.[6] Moreover, it was apparent that such changes could not be dismissed as mere short-term tactical readjustments. Rather, they grew out of the complex process of transformation then underway in the Catholic Church worldwide. The Church's changing style of relating to politics in Venezuela could thus be traced to a more general redefinition of the Church's own sense of self, a reorientation which led Catholic leaders to try to redefine the proper relation between the Church and society at large, and to explore new areas of concern and innovative styles of action for Catholic groups involved in social and political affairs.

After completing my initial work on Venezuelan politics, I began to consider research specifically concerned with the social and political role of the Church. Since I already knew Venezuela well, I decided to begin there. But as we shall see, the Venezuelan Church is poor and weak; it plays only a minor role in a highly secular and pluralistic society. To get a better view of the sources, processes, and meanings of change in the Catholic Church, I needed a comparative frame of reference. Comparative study protects against the possibility that findings are idiosyncratic in ways that would not be apparent were analysis to remain within the bounds of a single culture or political system. It thus provides a more complete test of any propositions or conclusions advanced. Ideally, one would want to match the poor and weak Church of Venezuela with one more rich, powerful, and socially prominent. The neighboring republic of Colombia, famous throughout Latin America

---

[5] Levine, *Conflict and Political Change in Venezuela.*
[6] Ibid., especially chapters 4 and 5.

for its powerful Catholic Church and its pervasive religiosity, admirably filled the bill. Moreover, aside from these differences on religious measures, Venezuela and Colombia also diverge widely on a broad range of social, economic, and political dimensions. Hence, research in these two countries promised to provide a solid basis for comparative analysis.

Despite the many differences between Venezuela and Colombia (to be explored in detail in chapter 3), it is important to realize that these two nations share one trait which makes them special in Latin America today: they are the only consistent electoral democracies in South America. The recent surge of authoritarianism in the region and the growing conflict of such regimes with the Church in nations as varied as Chile, Brazil, El Salvador, or Nicaragua have led many observers to center their attention on the Church's present and future role under authoritarian regimes, and particularly on the development of its "prophetic" stance as a critic of injustice and a defender of human rights. The difficulties involved in charting a course between revolutionary violence and the growing pressures of military governments have thus absorbed much of the attention and energies of Church leaders and scholarly observers of the region.[7]

But Venezuela and Colombia, albeit for different reasons, have resisted the general trend to authoritarian rule. There, political openness survives, and the Church (along with most other groups) retains considerable room to maneuver, with extensive freedom of speech and action. Thus, for all their marked differences from one another, Venezuela and Colombia comprise together a unique example of the potential role of the Latin American Church in an open, pluralistic political system. The Church in these nations has a special opportunity to contribute to change in the framework of an open society—a possibility increasingly denied it in the bleak political landscape of today's Latin America.

The choice of nations as units of analysis deserves a word here.

[7] The literature here is enormous, and the following studies are particularly useful: Antoine, *Church and Power in Brazil*; Bruneau, *The Political Transformation of the Brazilian Catholic Church*; Sanders and Smith, *The Chilean Catholic Church During the Allende and Pinochet Regimes*; Calvo, "The Church and the Doctrine of National Security"; Brian Smith "Churches and Human Rights in Latin America"; and Roncagliolo and Reyes Matta, *Iglesia, prensa, y militares*.

The Catholic Church's popular image of monolithic unity masks its great heterogeneity and its decentralized structure. Until recently, the relevant social unit for most Church operations was the diocese, each governed independently by a bishop who was subject only to the authority of the pope. While dioceses remain important,[8] in recent years the nation-state has become a major focus of Church life. The Second Vatican Council recognized the need for greater communication among bishops and for more elaborate planning at the national level, and it encouraged the formation of national episcopal conferences to achieve this end. Although these conferences have little formal authority, they do facilitate contact and collaboration among bishops and enhance the national development of each Church organization. The growing national identity of each Church thus compels those interested in the relation of religion to society and politics to examine the impact of national differences in a systematic fashion. The logic and the structure of this book both respond to this need.

Having decided to explore the relation of religion, the Catholic Church, and politics, I still faced many basic theoretical and methodological questions. It is no easy task for the secular social scientist to study religion with anything approaching objectivity and understanding. As Clifford Geertz has pointed out, "One of the major methodological problems in writing about religion scientifically is to put aside at once the tone of the village atheist and that of the village preacher, as well as their more sophisticated equivalents, so that the social and psychological implications of particular religious beliefs can emerge in a clear and neutral light."[9]

As Geertz here suggests, many studies of religion betray the lingering effects of positivism in the social sciences. A positivist approach brings the observer close to the position of the "village atheist" to the extent that it predisposes one to concentrate on the externals of behavior, fitting these into the observer's own categories of analysis with little or no attention to the meaning or signification of action to those involved. In the case of the Catholic Church, a positivist approach is very tempting. The extremely

[8] Cf. Vallier, "Comparative Studies of Roman Catholicism"; Bruneau, *The Political Transformation*, chap. 8; and Bruneau, "Religiosity and Politicization in Brazil."

[9] Geertz, "Religion as a Cultural System," p. 39.

visible structures of the Church—its complex and many-tiered bureaucracy, its highly specific codes of law and regulation, and the like—have predisposed numerous scholars and observers to treat the Church as simply another institution, albeit a uniquely widespread and long-lived example of its genre.[10]

Although my own research began with a dissatisfaction with evolutionism and a desire to explore the processes of change within "established" institutions, it remained initially within a positivist frame of reference. Thus the Church was seen as reacting to changes in the surrounding society, and the attitudes and values of Church elites, which I derived from their responses to questions on social and political issues, were taken as valid measures of the Church's disposition to act in society. But as my research progressed, this positivism became increasingly untenable: Catholic elites (most notably bishops) simply do not consider issues in strictly social or political terms. Instead, their answers are couched in religious concepts and metaphors, which flow from their understanding of the requirements of religious faith, their view of the Church as an institution, and their conclusions about its proper relation to society at large—not from purely social analysis alone. At the very least, then, one needs to know the language of Catholicism in order to make sense of its references to society and politics. Yet knowledge of the language alone is not enough; for, as we shall see, an increasing number of Catholic leaders and activists use a "sociological" vocabulary to describe society, employing terms and concepts which at times give their social views a surprisingly "radical" look, at least in the abstract. But this interpretation is misleading, for there is a wide gap between general attitudes and particular actions. Thus, only weak and ambiguous connections emerge between the social views of Catholic leaders and the kinds of roles and actions to which they are willing to commit the Church.

[10] Daniel Berrigan chides many studies of the Church: "What is most precious to us are the elements in our faith which sustain us, and those elements are very mysterious and very difficult to talk about. I often feel that to be asked what is essential to you in your faith is almost as delicate and secret a matter as to be asked what are the elements of a good marriage. And by the same token I am often appalled by the superficiality and vulgarity of mind that is revealed in those discussions of 'what Jesus means' and 'what the Church means' and on and on" (Coles and Berrigan, *The Geography of Faith*, p. 130).

Perhaps this is not a fruitful way to approach the problem in the first place. To get inside the minds of Catholic leaders, to see the world with their eyes, it is clearly not enough to look at behavior and attitudes only on dimensions of interest to social scientists. Rather, as already mentioned, one must learn and appreciate the categories that religious leaders themselves use for sorting out reality; moreover, one must distinguish between the different kinds of concepts they use and the roles they see as appropriate to particular fields of action. This is a complex task because bishops are complex men. They are fully capable of seeing the world in secular terms, of using the current sociological jargon, and in general of displaying an up-to-date awareness of trends in social and political analysis. But in the last analysis their views in these areas are grounded not in sociological analysis or in political opinion, but rather in a deeper commitment to religious world views which set society (the "temporal world") in a transhistorical perspective.

Their views of religion and of the nature of the Church have a major, independent impact, not so much on how they see the world, as on the meaning they accord to what they see, and thus on the kinds of imperatives for action they draw from their social analysis. In particular, as we shall see in later chapters, different views of the nature of religion and of the Church as a community of the faithful are closely associated with very divergent understandings of the Church's proper relation to society and politics as a whole, and have led to the evolution of notably different styles of action for dealing with the world.

I give such stress to meaning and inner understandings because differences here lie at the heart of the issues addressed in this book. Meaning is of central importance; for, as Max Weber points out,

> The external courses of religious behavior are so diverse that an understanding of this behavior can only be achieved from the viewpoint of the subjective experiences, ideas, and purposes of the individuals concerned—in short, from the viewpoint of the religious behavior's "meaning" [*Sinn*].[11]

This argument will be explored in greater detail in subsequent chapters. I mention it here simply to show how my research came into focus. As work progressed, I more and more attempted to understand the images of the Church and of religion itself, all of

---
[11] Weber, *The Sociology of Religion*, p. 11.

which inform the social attitudes, policies, and programs of Catholic leaders and activists. These images and visions of the Church, added to the sense of what being religious is all about in the first place, are taken here as central links between religious belief and commitment, on the one hand, and attempts to understand and deal with the secular world, on the other.

The problem, of course, is how to select the best approach for reliable analysis. A mechanical application of categories derived from politics and social life is inadequate because it ignores the essentially transcendental goals of the Church. Classifying religious groups or leaders simply as "reactionary," "moderate," or "revolutionary," for example, misses much of the point; for, by concentrating on political outcomes and ignoring the way in which political orientations are rooted in religious beliefs and concepts, this approach cannot assess the intensity of motivation or the characteristic style of action of such groups. For a reliable understanding of contemporary processes and likely future patterns, more than simple political labeling is needed. Rather, I would argue that a fresh look at change in the Church itself, a look based on a more phenomenological approach, is a necessary step to fuller understanding.

A phenomenological approach demands that we take religion seriously as a source of guiding concepts and principles, instead of merely subsuming religious phenomena under secular rubrics. Once we take religion seriously, our analysis can then work with religious ideas, exploring their roots, evolution, and impact on society. The main advantage of such an approach lies in its capacity to work with the concepts and categories that people use in their everyday lives, and thus to avoid the temptation to reduce action and meaning to an externally imposed logic.[12] Of course, the relation between secular and religious beliefs and activities

---

[12] This approach, grounded in the Weberian tradition, has recently been developed in the works of anthropologists, and most notably in Geertz's analyses of religion and of "thick description" and in the studies of Cicourel and others on ethnomethodology (the methodology of everyday life). For Geertz see "Religion as a Cultural System," *Islam Observed*, and "Thick Description" in his *Interpretation of Cultures*. A useful introduction to ethnomethodology is Roy Turner, *Ethnomethodology*; see also Rabinow and Sullivan, *Interpretive Social Science*. A good statement of the perspective taken here is Forman, "The Significance of Participation"; see also Forman's comments on peasant religion in *The Brazilian Peasantry*, chap. 6.

cannot be traced deductively from either side of the equation. Rather, it is necessary to work out carefully, and in a dialectical fashion, the sociological links between religious and secular themes. With a firm grounding in religious concepts, we can then look closely at the relationships (the "elective affinity," to use Weber's term) between certain kinds of religious self-images and specific values, organizational patterns, and styles of action in society at large. Working "out" from religious concepts, rather than "in" from sociopolitical ones, is thus a prerequisite to a much-needed reconceptualization of the whole question of the social role of religion and of the Church.

The Church influences social and political behavior in many ways. Of course, the Church is not *primarily* an agent of social, economic, or political action. As an intermediary between people and God, its central mission remains the diffusion of the message of salvation and service. Thus, one cannot simply expect the Church to assume social and political positions, nor may one judge it solely by criteria appropriate to secular institutions, like political parties or public bureaucracies, without considering its transcendental and eschatological goals. Nevertheless, it is clear that the social role of religion and of the Church cannot be adequately addressed in terms of a rigid dichotomy—it is not an all-or-nothing choice. The Church is made up of people and exists in concrete historical situations. Thus religious positions inevitably have temporal consequences, and temporal problems have an impact on the lives of believers. For this reason it is important to realize that the social impact of religion is carried in vehicles more extensive than a limited attention to preaching, exhortation, or specific positions on public issues alone would indicate. At another level, religion shapes actions through images of itself, and of good and proper behavior in general, which are expressed in the daily life of the religious community. Systematic attention to these implicit models, and to the religious motivations of secular actions, allows us to take account of the fact that actions which appear identical when seen from the outside often spring from quite diverse motivations, and hence may be pursued with widely varying styles of action and intensities of commitment.

This discussion foreshadows the arguments of the book in such detail because it is important that the reader understand how and why my research, which began as an analysis of the response of the Church to change, evolved into something more akin to the classic concerns of the sociology of knowledge, with an interest in the interplay between concepts and forms of action, their social and institutional settings, and forms of social and political action.

Reflecting this evolution, the analysis presented here has a double goal. First, it presents concepts and language intended to express the inner structures of significance that orient and give meaning to the actions of the individuals involved—elites, activists, and ordinary members of the Catholic Church in Venezuela and Colombia. This analysis of inner structures is combined with more general concepts which examine the process of action as a whole—putting it in more general terms. Such a combination of internal and external perspectives, which matches meaning to observed behavior and structures, is central to the whole approach taken here.[13]

For these reasons, the reader will note throughout the book a deliberate attempt to frame arguments in mixed analytical and historical terms, with consistent attention to the theories and actions of concrete groups and institutions. It is vital to be specific about historical and institutional contexts, for they provide the matrix through which individual understandings and abstract commitments gain ordered social power. Religious faith and beliefs thus gain socially valid expression only when worked through the parallel and overlapping institutions of the Church and national political life and traditions. I take this historical-institutional approach because, with C. Wright Mills, I see the goal of social science to be

> to take up substantive problems on the historical level of reality, to state these problems in terms appropriate to them; and then, no matter how high the flight of theory, no matter how painstaking the crawl among detail, in the end of each completed act of study, to state the solution in the macroscopic terms of the problem. The classic focus, in short, is on substantive problems.[14]

---

[13] This combination of external verification with inner understanding is central to the Weberian perspective on sociology. For Weber see particularly the essays collected in *The Methodology of the Social Sciences*. The implications of this approach are further explored in Rex, *Key Problems of Sociological Theory*, especially chapter 9.

[14] Mills, *The Sociological Imagination*, p. 128.

Structure and Form

This book is based primarily on original field research carried out in Venezuela and Colombia from 1971 to 1973. The structure of both book and research reflects a particular understanding of the way the Catholic Church operates in Latin America today. Because the Church is such a vast and complex institution, it is important to avoid confusing any single kind of information (be it drawn from interviews, documents, organizational plans, or well-publicized incidents) with "reality." To get a complete picture, data of several different kinds are needed. In addition, it is vital to reach beyond the national level to assess carefully the impact of change in the dioceses and parishes, where much of the Church's daily life is played out.[15]

With these considerations in mind, several different kinds of data were collected at various levels in the two nations. At the national level, structured interviews were conducted with sixty auxiliary bishops, bishops, and archbishops—in effect, with the entire ecclesiastical hierarchy of each country at the time.[16] The interviews were built around a common set of questions, to make codification and quantitative analysis possible, and ranged over many areas dealing with the church and with national and local affairs.

In addition to the bishops, at the national level I also interviewed a large number of leaders of national Catholic bureaucra-

---

[15] Cf. Vallier, "Comparative Studies," and Bruneau, *The Political Transformation*, chap. 8.

[16] In Venezuela, 22 interviews were conducted; one bishop refused, and three bishops were unavailable because of sickness or travel. Of these interviews, 3 were with auxiliary bishops, 14 with bishops, and 5 with archbishops. In Colombia, 38 interviews were completed, with six auxiliary bishops, twenty-five bishops, and seven archbishops. There were five refusals, and three bishops were unavailable because of sickness or travel. For all practical purposes, the interviews cover the entire group of bishops in each country at the time excepting those in charge of mission territories, who were excluded because they are almost entirely foreign. Those in charge of mission territories, of which there are four in Venezuela and seventeen in Colombia, do not generally play a major role in the episcopal conference of either nation. In any case, most mission territories have a lower ecclesiastical rank and status than dioceses; they are commonly apostolic vicarates, apostolic prefectures, and prelatures. The greater number of mission jurisdictions in Colombia reflects the vast extension of sparsely populated territory under mission control in that country.

cies and organizations, ranging from religious orders like Jesuits or Salesians to members of the Church's national bureaucracy, Church-sponsored or affiliated research centers, and officers and advisers to various lay organizations. Particular attention was paid here to the evolving organizational strategies of the Church and its affiliated groups and to the key issues they saw before them. Finally, extensive documentary research was undertaken in both countries in order to understand the evolution of "official" (as well as opposition) thinking within the Church, as well as to clarify the record of action that was derived from interviews.

Information was also collected on changes in local and neighborhood settings. National structures are relatively new; although their importance is surely growing, much of the day-to-day life of the Church takes place in more circumscribed arenas—dioceses and parishes remain the central organizational units of the Church. To assess local change more completely, three dioceses from each country were selected for more intensive analysis. Here, data comparable to those collected on the national level were gathered on diocesan organizations, institutions, and programs. In addition, three parishes were visited in each diocese, and each parish priest was interviewed.

In this way, the research generated data of several different kinds and levels, which together throw light on the sources and processes of change in religion and politics. The combination of perceptions of Church elites with independent data on organizational resources, strategies, and dilemmas provides a rich vein of information; it enables the observer to set general attitudes in the context of actual plans and programs, locating all this firmly in the relevant social and institutional contexts. The combination of comparative analyses within and between nations also provides a further check on the validity of any generalizations advanced.[17]

So far, I have outlined the origins and structure of the research. The structure of the book itself warrants separate attention. I have organized the book in a way which facilitates a gradual, deliberate

[17] Some works in which intranational variation is considered to great effect are Allardt, "Implications of Within-Nation Variations and Regional Imbalances for Cross-National Research," and Linz and De Miguel, "Within-Nation Differences and Comparisons." The case for studying intranational and intrainstitutional variations in the Catholic Church is made persuasively in Vallier, "Comparative Studies."

unfolding and elaboration, from chapter to chapter, of its themes and ideas. Each discussion works out of preceding analyses, incorporating earlier materials in a different context and looking at them from a new perspective. The overall process is much like a continual reexamination, reformulation, and reconsideration of a complex problem from many points of view. The result, I believe, is a more complete and accurate portrait of the processes under study than would be rendered by a more conventional, straight-line narrative approach.

The next chapter in Part I explores the relation of religion and politics directly, both in general and with particular reference to Latin America. Chapter 3 then looks closely at Venezuela and Colombia as settings for change in the Church, examining in detail the evolution of current institutions and issues in each country. Shifting the focus to individuals, Part II lays out an analysis of the leaders of the two churches, with special attention to their goals, orientations, and styles of action. In this part, chapters 4, 5, and 6, respectively, provide a "collective portrait" of the bishops; an analysis of their views on authority and their visions of the Church; and an examination of their social and political stance, and its relation to views of the Church. Part III moves from the hierarchy to other institutional levels. Chapters 7 and 8 examine the development and orientation of Catholic organizations, with in-depth case studies of several different kinds of programs; and chapter 9 assesses change in the Church from the perspective of the dioceses, elaborating and refining the analysis of styles of action at the local level. Finally, a concluding part, with one chapter, takes another look at the process of change in religion and politics alike. The theoretical and methodological implications of the analyses are explored, the likely future of each church is examined, and these patterns are set in the broader context of Latin America as a whole.

2

Religion and Politics, Politics and Religion: General Perspectives

LISTEN to the villagers of Solentiname, Nicaragua, discussing why the Angel of the Lord announced Jesus' coming to the shepherds in the fields:

> FELIPE: The angel came to them because they were working men, and I find this very important for us. Because they were poor little men who were working. They were watching over their sheep which is like taking care of cattle today. They were workers, laborers, poor people. The Angel of God could have gone to the king's palace and said to him: "The Savior has been born." But the angel didn't go where the king was, but where the poor people were, which means that this message is not for the big shots but for the little guys, which means the oppressed, which means us.[1]

Later, while talking about the meaning of the "good news which Jesus says he has come to give," they continue:

> And his good news is for the poor because this new kingdom is the triumph of the poor and the humble. And this is truly good news, not like the others, which were false.
>
> And it's a joyful announcement for the whole people, one that deserves to be celebrated.
>
> And it's news that we can believe in or not.
>
> One of the women says: "What he read in the book of that prophet is prophecy of liberation. And it's a teaching that a lot of Christians haven't learned yet, because we can be in a church singing day and night, tra-la-la-la, and it doesn't matter to us that there are so many prisoners and that we're surrounded by injustice, with so many afflicted hearts, so many people without education who are like blind people, so much unfairness in the

[1] Cardenal, *The Gospel in Solentiname*, pp. 52-53.

country, so many women whose eyes are filled with tears every day."[2]

These discussions, transcribed by the poet and priest Ernesto Cardenal, are but one sign of the dramatic changes in Latin American Catholicism in recent years. The core of these changes lies in a struggle to redefine the meaning of Christian concepts and symbols, and in this way to refashion the entire relation between religion and society. The change has been remarkably rapid and profound. Not long ago, the Church was generally considered to be a monolithic pillar of the established social order, an ally of the powers that be in the economy and in culture, society, and politics alike. Now, by contrast, the same institution has been the source of some of the most revolutionary ideas and individuals in the entire region. In the process, the Church has suffered internal divisions, and has often found itself in sharp conflict with social groups and political authorities of varying ideological persuasions.

Although change has been swift, continuous, and often confusing, a concern for the evolving relation between religion and politics runs throughout the tangled web of events. The two are closely related in Latin America now as in the past, but the problem is new and different because the meaning of both "religion" and "politics" has undergone considerable rethinking in recent years. For religion, the meaning of the Church both as an institution and as a community of believers, as well as the implications of religious faith for social action, have come under consideration. Meanwhile, throughout the region, the scope of actions considered "political" has itself expanded. Once limited to small groups of elites working in narrow institutional settings, "politics" is now widely taken to include mass activities (and their repression) in new and hitherto nonpolitical settings. Indeed, recent ferment within the Church has strongly resonated with broader changes in Latin American society. This confluence of changes—a dominant Church in the midst of change with societies themselves undergoing rapid marches and countermarches—makes for a regional setting especially geared to innovation, conflict, and self-questioning.[3] Of

[2] Ibid., pp. 128-29.

[3] As Geertz has pointed out, when established visions of both society and religion are reworked, change is likely; but there is little consensus as to its proper scope, direction, and expression. Thus, the legitimacy of both established and new patterns is thrown into question, as concepts and symbols no

course, the dynamic relation of religion and politics is not unique to Latin America. Rather, it has a long history in the Western tradition, in which Latin America shares. The next section takes a look at the general ties between religion and politics, laying the ground for a closer analysis of recent Latin American experience.

Religion and Politics: The General Problem

In most cultural traditions, religion and politics have been closely related. Indeed, as anthropologists and historians often remind us, the very idea that they should (or could) be separated at all is a recent notion, rooted in the development of Western societies since the Protestant Reformation. Before the emergence of the idea of "secular" society and its subsequent spread around the globe, the ultimate goals of religion and politics were generally indistinguishable. Of course, disputes occasionally erupted between the respective authorities in each sphere (kings and priests, emperors and popes), but such conflict was typically joined over the question of who should control and orient the totality of life. Questions of dividing and delimiting two spheres of life, secular and sacred, were not at issue.[4]

This pervasive fusion of religion and politics can take many forms: it may be expressed in the form and content of law; in the structures of education; in the nature of approved sanctions and mechanisms for resolving social conflict; and, of course, in the accepted processes for legitimating authority. All these manifestations and others are expressions of a belief that the values which orient individuals and inform the structure of institutions cannot be separated from those which relate individuals to the transcendental or divine. The world is thus a seamless web, and religion knits it all together by infusing each act with transcendental meaning.

Looking more closely at the Catholic tradition, one finds a striking duality. A general downgrading of the importance of earthly life, and a concomitant tendency to treat this world as simply a stage on which eternal principles are played out in prep-

---

longer fit the societies in which they are lived out. Cf. *Islam Observed*, pp. 102-3.

[4] Cf. the very useful discussion in Ullman, *A History of Political Thought in the Middle Ages*.

aration for salvation, is combined with a strong tradition of institutional stability, which requires that the Church recognize and deal with temporal matters on a long-term basis. Both emphases share a view which rather sharply distinguishes "spiritual" from "temporal" matters. Although the temporal sphere has its own rules and integrity, spiritual matters are more important: the former are subordinate to the latter as the body is subordinate to the soul. In medieval Europe this view was translated directly into politics. As Ullman notes, the body-soul metaphor was constantly used "to show the inferiority of the laity and the superiority of the clergy, to show that just as the soul ruled the body, in the same manner the clergy ruled the laity."[5]

Of course, religion and politics were distinguished in institutional terms. This is the source of the famous "two swords doctrine," according to which the Church and political authorities divided tasks of rulership, with the spiritual sword wielded by bishops and priests, and the temporal sword in the hands of kings and princes. In this arrangement, secular power is separate from, but clearly subordinate to, the Church: temporal power is obliged to serve and protect the Church, and its exercise is subject to ecclesiastical judgement. In any case, the very notion of an ideal society, a notion embodied in the idea of Christendom, required that all social questions be infused with principles of Christian doctrine, as authoritatively laid out by the Church.[6] The very idea of dividing human activity according to its function or sphere was quite foreign to medieval thought.

> That one and the same activity could be viewed from a moral and a religious and a political angle was not a way of thinking with which medieval man had been acquainted. What counted then was the undifferentiated Christian: religion was not separated from politics, politics was not separated from morals, and so on. What mattered was the Christianity of man, and not his social or moral conduct.[7]

The traditional Catholic position thus emphasizes the closeness of spiritual and temporal authorities. Since the Protestant Reforma-

---

[5] Ibid., p. 101.

[6] As subsequent chapters will show, the idea of Christendom, and the related goal of re-Christianization of society, remains a powerful undercurrent of much Catholic thinking about society.

[7] Ullman, *Political Thought*, p. 16.

tion, however, Western experience has taken a different path. While Protestant positions on the proper relation between spiritual and temporal authorities differ widely, the Reformation and the subsequent proliferation of independent sects threw the whole question wide open.[8] In any case, the general trend of Western societies since the Reformation has been to separate, not fuse, religion and politics, and by separating them to mark off distinct and relatively autonomous spheres of competence for each. Conflict between Church and State became a continuous thread in Western history, as each institution sought to preserve and extend the scope of its authority.[9] The pattern of conflict has been remarkably persistent. Until recently, it has centered on the question of who is to provide the general orientations and socially valid values for the entire society. This pattern of conflict helps explain the continued attention given to issues dealing with control over the key stages in individual and community life cycles: registration of births, education, sanctification of marriages, provision of social assistance, and burial.

As such conflicts evolved and became a regular part of the Western scene, religion and politics became problems for one another in fairly predictable ways. In politics, religious institutions often appeared to be fighting a rear-guard action to preserve existing privileges and to revive past understandings. This was especially true in areas where traditional Catholicism was strong, for throughout the nineteenth century (and well into the twentieth in some

[8] Sanders, *Protestant Concepts of Church and State*, provides a useful discussion of different Protestant positions and their historical development.

[9] As Reuther notes, "Historically secularization arose in the West as something experienced by the church as a losing rear-guard battle against the rising tide of rebellion that deposed the church from one sphere of influence after another. Economics, politics, education, culture, and finally even the family were secularized by a process of deposing the influence of the ecclesiastical institution and pushing it back step by step until finally it appeared primarily in the privatized form of personal relationship with God that lay in the realm of subjective feeling, having lost contact not only with the social structures that surround the remainder of life but with the larger intellectual world as well. This is what is popularly called churchgoing in modern society" (*The Radical Kingdom*, p. 161). A useful review of these issues in Western Europe is in the introduction to Lipset and Rokkan, *Party Systems and Voter Alignments*. K. H. Silvert's analysis is also relevant here; see his "Conclusions" in Silvert, ed., *Churches and States*, especially pp. 216-17.

cases) the Catholic Church continued to reject the validity of the very notion of a secular and religiously neutral State. In Berger's words, "Throughout the nineteenth century, while Protestant liberalism carried on its great love affair with the spirit of the age, the basic temper of Catholicism can be described as a magnificent defiance."[10]

Religion thus became a problem in politics as an institution to be dealt with and controlled, and further, as a potentially dangerous source of opposition if threatened. From the point of view of religion, politics posed no less a problem. The most obvious kind of problem came from the intrusion of the State into areas formerly left to the Church, such as registry, education, marriage, and the like. But at a deeper level, politics also posed a challenge to the general authority of the Church. Where once the priest or bishop had been the generally accepted guide in each community, now social and political leaders arose to offer secular alternatives to Church guidance. The challenge was twofold: first, secular groups defined alternative paths of action, independent of the sanction or authority of religious leaders; and second, the groups competed openly with the Church for members. The most notable illustration, of course, is the development of trade unions and of a whole socialist subculture among industrial workers.

As a result of this process of conflict and threat, the Catholic Church withdrew, by the end of the nineteenth century, into a closed and rigid set of ideas and institutional structures. These were intended to deny the validity of recent changes in European society and to insulate the faithful from their influence, so far as possible. The Church thus entered the twentieth century in latent conflict with the structures of European society—conflict that erupted from time to time on issues of normative orientation and the regulation of behavior.

In looking at general and particularly at Latin American developments from this point on, I want to stress again the importance of keeping religion and politics in a dynamic and dialectical balance, giving full and equal weight to each. Both religion and politics must be taken seriously as general sources of motivation and guiding ideas. Their particular roles, however, are empirical questions; it is necessary to trace out the sociological links between

[10] Berger, *A Rumor of Angels*, p. 15.

religious and political elements in particular contexts and problems. The transformation of religious ideas poses new problems and dilemmas for politics; at the same time, the pattern of political change raises new problems and dilemmas for religion.

Religion and politics are thus related both analytically and empirically—the two cannot and should not be separated. This position differs considerably from that taken in much recent work on "development," "modernization," and the role of religion in these processes.[11] In general, the authors of such writings see increasing functional specialization and institutionalization as both inevitable and good. In their view, no single institution can embrace all human activity, or provide a valid framework to explain its significance. Rather, spheres of competence are marked off, and the whole is best represented by the metaphor of a marketplace—an arena in which different interests compete and work out changing codes of mutual coexistence.

This view of society has deep roots in the individualism and rationalism which emerged from the Protestant Reformation, and their aftermath in liberal and utilitarian thought. The bias toward increasing secularization and differentiation often leads to the conclusion that religious institutions and leaders should be stripped of most activities and functions not "explicitly religious" (e.g., not concerned with cult, ritual, or salvation). To put it crudely, in this view preachers should preach, leaving politics and the care of the social order to the "experts."

This perspective is a poor guide to any study of religion and politics. In the specific case of Latin America, these authors totally failed to anticipate and understand the dramatic reemergence of political themes in Catholicism, especially (although not only) on the "left." By arguing for a neat separation of spheres of action, their approach assumes that a parallel separation is possible in the minds of the actors themselves. But if religion really *is* a source of powerful motivations and lasting orientations in many areas of life, then the problem for analysis is to trace out the real links between religion and those actions—not simply to seek a dividing line.

[11] Two quite different examples of this tendency are Vallier and Silvert. For Vallier see *Catholicism, Social Control, and Modernization in Latin America*; "Radical Priests and the Revolution"; or "Extraction, Insulation, and Re-entry." For Silvert see *Churches and States*.

In any case, the line which separates religion and politics is not so clear and sharp as these theories would have us believe. Everything depends on what is meant by the terms. So far, I have used both "religion" and "politics" in a conventional way, with no attempt at more precise definition. "Religion" has referred to those activities surrounding Church institutions (centered on cult and ritual), while "politics" has been identified implicitly with government or with actions affecting government in some way. But these conventional usages will not quite do; for, as I suggested earlier, an important part of the dynamic relation between religion and politics in contemporary Latin America rests on the expanded and altered meanings of the terms themselves.

For our purposes, a working definition of religion should help isolate a set of beliefs and motivations and shed light on the way they generate regular patterns of action. We need a concept linking beliefs to action.[12] "Pastoral action" provides such a concept. The idea of pastoral action of course derives from the biblical metaphor of a shepherd caring for his flock, and traditionally this care has been centered on charity, moral suasion, and tending to the needs of the sick and lonely. For the majority of bishops, pastoral action clearly continues in this vein. But in speaking of pastoral action, it is important to distinguish this kind of religious action from others, and further to note that even pastoral actions undertaken for the most conventional motives (charity or aid to the sick, for example) can take on political character and consequences, especially in highly divided or repressive situations. Pastoral action can mean many things, and in Latin America today it is an open question just how far, and in what direction, it extends. Is it limited to the provision of comfort, solace, and charity? May it encompass testimony, bearing witness to and sharing the conditions of peoples' lives as a sign of human solidarity? Need it include denunciation of those social conditions which make a fully human and moral life impossible, such as extreme poverty and oppression? Or must it be developed even further, to provide a theory for social action, making religious communion a part of social and political reconstruction? These issues are all alive in the Church today.

In much of Latin America, the Catholic hierarchy has responded

[12] One useful attempt at a general definition of religion may be found in Geertz, "Religion as a Cultural System."

to pressures for greater political involvement by emphasizing that the bishops' responsibilities are "pastoral" (and hence, in their eyes, nonpolitical).[13] But if the scope of "pastoral" duties is expanded along the lines suggested above, such actions can hardly be kept out of politics, especially as the meaning of politics itself is stretched beyond the confines of government or of partisan conflict alone. For, like pastoral action, "politics" can also be broadened to include denunciations of injustice, which bring new issues to the agenda of national life, or to massive community actions such as land invasions, which seek to redress grievances and change the structure of power and opportunity in daily life. Such activities, while not political in a narrowly partisan or official sense, are nonetheless political in essence: they raise basic issues of power, authority, legitimacy, and distribution.[14]

Now if both pastoral action and politics are expanded in this way, they flow easily together, and the distinction between the religious and the political loses much of its presumed sharpness. Moreover, when these evolving concepts are tied to institutions, the potential for new and complex forms of action is enormous. This is particularly so in the Catholic Church, whose extraordinary development of hierarchical structures linking local, national, and international actors and resources provides a uniquely dense and

[13] In this vein, Msgr. Alfonso López Trujiilo, now President of CELAM (the Conference of Latin American Bishops), argues that political neutrality is an essential precondition for the Church's pastoral independence. He refers above all to neutrality in partisan politics. See his "El compromiso político del sacerdote."

[14] See Levine and Wilde, "The Catholic Church, 'Politics,' and Violence," for a full discussion of the various meanings of pastoral action. As suggested in the text, pastoral action can have unanticipated consequences. One example, to be considered in detail in these pages, involves the consequences of pastoral actions which bring people together to act in new ways. The creation of more open, egalitarian forms of association and interaction to replace the traditional authoritarian and hierarchical structures of the Church has a subtle impact on members' perceptions of authority and on the models the Church itself puts forward of the proper form and content of authority in general. Lessons learned here spill over to affect members' views of society as a whole. These themes are developed further below, in terms of praxis (later in this chapter), styles of action and authority relations (chaps. 4, 5, and 6), organizational structures (chap. 7), and evolving strategies of action at the local level (chap. 9).

complex religious context for social action. Here, activities undertaken out of "pastoral" motives at the local level may be funded by international agencies, with considerable repercussions on the national political scene.[15]

In this regard, it is important to distinguish individual choices from social consequences. The dilemmas of individuals become, in the aggregate, social choices with major political impact. For religion and for politics, whether the original choice be neutrality or activism, the result is equally political. Neutrality, in effect, commits one to work within the status quo; activism may require a commitment to change. But both are political positions. Peter Worsley puts it well, noting that no matter how "spiritual" a believer's goals may be, "he will produce political action simply through acting, even if as unintended consequences. Political action is thus an immanent dimension or aspect of all social action, whether the ends of this action, as far as the actor is concerned, are the worship of God, earning one's bread, caring for one's children, etc."[16]

The preceding discussion suggests that politics and religion present one another with problems of different kinds. As Worsley indicates, in a certain sense everything is political. Hence all religious action necessarily has political consequences. Of course, from another point of view, everything is religious; and politics, along with all other fields of human action, may be judged in terms of transcendental significance. The point, of course, is not to argue which is primary, but rather to realize the degree to which action in either sphere has consequences in the other.

I want to lay particular stress here on the fact that, while religion has long been considered a problem for politics, politics presents no less a problem for religion. Traditionally, the problem religion poses to the political order in Latin America has been seen in terms of "Church-State conflict," especially sharp over control of schools, regulation of marriage and divorce, birth control, and the like. The traditional problems politics has posed for religion are the mirror image of these—the threat of growing secularization and the expansion of the State into areas previously left to religious

[15] This becomes particularly visible in cases where the Church has become, for all practical purposes, the only public voice of opposition to authoritarian rule. Smith, "Churches and Human Rights," offers a full discussion.
[16] Worsley, *The Trumpet Shall Sound*, pp. xxvi-xxvii.

guidance and control. While such conflicts persist in many areas, they are no longer of central importance, especially in Latin America. Rather, with the changes noted above, religion now poses a problem for politics above all as a source of motivations for radical action and as an institutional shield for dissent from authoritarian rule. This new role of the Church implies that politics, and social life in general, are bringing new problems to religion.

The next sections explore these new problems. After a brief overview of Latin American developments in this century, the basic issues currently at hand are explored. These are: first, changing images of the Church and their impact on the way religious faith leads to social and political activism; second, new perspectives on change and transformation, as opposed to static models for understanding the world; and third, in this context, the meaning of power, force, and violence, and the related issue of the Church's stance toward social division and class conflict in general.

These issues take form in the development of a series of groups concerned with the proper relation of the Church, and of religion in general, to social and political change. Three broad positions— left, right, and center—will be discussed below:[17] on the left, there is the example of Camilo Torres and the development of Liberation Theology, combining new theological positions with a commitment to social and political revolution; on the right, there are emerging groups like the Societies for the Defense of Tradition, Family, and Property (TFP), which combine an extremely traditional religious stance with reactionary social and political positions that are closely tied to the ideologies of national security being elaborated by military regimes; and finally, in the center, there is a growing group of bishops and key Catholic institutions striving to maintain the unity of the Church against fierce pressures from right and left alike, while still hoping to respond in some creative way to the demands of contemporary social and political life.

[17] Since they are derived from political alignments, terms like left, right, and center often fail to capture the dimensions of religious orientation which underlie a given political position. I use the terms here in accord with conventional understandings, but with full awareness of their ambiguous and sometimes misleading character. The text should make the meaning of these terms clear in each particular case. The question of terminology is taken up again in chapter 10, below, from a somewhat different point of view.

GENERAL PERSPECTIVES

Religion and Politics: The Latin American Experience

Religion and politics have depended on and influenced one another since the first Spaniard set foot on what we now know as Latin America. Their relation is both mutual and multifaceted: mutual because religion and politics have evolved together, taking material and symbolic support from one another; multifaceted because it embraces interinstitutional conflict and accommodation (e.g., the "Church-State relations" which dominate earlier scholarship) as well as more subtle and elusive exchanges whereby religious and political orders gave legitimacy and moral authority to one another. In this process, religious notions of hierarchy, authority, and obedience reflected and reinforced the existing social and political arrangements to such an extent that the two orders, sacred and secular, often seemed indistinguishable.

Historically, Catholic influence (both material and symbolic) has reinforced existing social arrangements in Latin America.[18] But surely this is not a necessary relation. For religion per se is not necessarily conservative; but, given a particular set of historically determined concepts, traditions, and organizational commitments, it will be.[19] As these change, however, we may expect new models of social and political action to arise. In the same measure, changes in the political order, leading to new concepts and forms of political action, necessarily alter the impact of politics on religion, providing new pressures, problems, and models for action.

---

[18] For example, Míguez Bonino attributes much of the failure of revolutionary propaganda in Latin America to the impact of religion. Revolutionary groups, he argues, have not understood "the depth to which Christianity —as a sociological entity—has penetrated and still moulds the Latin American consciousness, at a visceral level where theoretical, rational explanation fails to make an impact.... People 'live' their economic and social alienation in a world of mythical representation which political ideology is not able to pierce" (*Christians and Marxists*, p. 26).

[19] Worsley makes this point well: "But religion, it ought to be said, is neither intrinsically conservative nor revolutionary. It can be infused with any kind of social content, notably political; there are both religions of the oppressed ... and the kinds of religions that have been summed up in the label given to the Church of England as 'The Conservative Party at prayer.' The relationship of religious beliefs, let alone movements and organizations, to the established power-system thus varies, and is not a matter for metaphysical pronouncement disguised as sociological generalization. It requires empirical investigation to see what the case is" (*The Trumpet Shall Sound*, p. xxix).

Now, as in the past, religion and politics are closely related in Latin America. Indeed, a great deal of the conflict so visible in Latin American Catholicism in recent years has centered precisely over this relation: it has been a struggle to redefine the meaning of religious symbols, and in this way to redirect the social and political thrust of the Church as an institution and of Catholicism as a set of religious beliefs, practices, and motivations. The intense concern for politics, which lies at the heart of this process, has in fact brought religion and politics into a closer and more dynamic relation than ever before.

Thus the issue of politics and religion in Latin America, relegated until recently to the province of the nineteenth-century historians, is very much alive today. On the one hand, the Church as an institution is engaged in public controversy with repressive regimes from Paraguay to El Salvador, from Brazil to Chile. When it serves as a shelter for social and political dissent, it is accused by secular authorities of a "new clericalism." But at the same time, the hierarchy is assailed by critics within the Church for being wed to the powers that be. Radical critics among clergy and laity see the Church's presence as inevitably political, and therefore want to change its alliances to promote the interests of the poor and the dispossessed. New theories and concepts, and new ways of combining religious and political action, are springing up all over the region.

How has this about-face occurred so rapidly? How did the Latin American Church move, in only a few decades, from a position of general support of and identification with the social order to one of massive internal division and multifaceted conflict? Of course, stated so baldly, the portrait is too sharply drawn. Radicals remain a minority in most churches; and, in each particular case, changes which appear sudden turn out, on closer examination, to have long and tangled roots in national history. Nevertheless, as an overview, this image of change and turmoil is not far off the mark. How did it come about?

At the beginning of this century, the general situation was clear. Catholicism was unchallenged as the dominant religion in Latin America, and generally appeared as the ally of conservative forces and established powers. The late Ivan Vallier[20] attributed these

[20] Cf. Vallier, *Catholicism*, and "Extraction, Insulation, and Re-entry."

close ties to the structural nature of the Church. He argued that the Church organization was weak, and hence depended on civil authorities and powerful individuals for support. Thus, its "established" status in many countries was due less to its predominance than to its capture by others. The Church thus "fit" the structures of the stable, mostly agrarian societies of the time, and most people were at least nominally Catholic. In such a situation, Church leaders rarely felt moved to develop autonomous resources and informed participation; this simply was not necessary.

At the turn of the century, much of Latin America was still rural, and in each small town or region, going to church was part of the natural rhythm of life. But the quiet harmony of this situation began to break apart.[21] Increased urbanization, better transport, and the development of dynamic export industries spurred economic and social changes which began to transform the social and political landscape in many nations. Comfortable and dependent, and attuned to the images and rhythms of traditional rural life, the Church hierarchy suddenly felt the ground being cut from under its feet. A first and most visible response was defensive: the pernicious moral consequences of change (especially urbanization and industrialization) were denounced, Catholic education was reinforced, rudimentary Catholic political groups were put together, and in some extreme cases, like Mexico after the revolution, open and occasionally violent conflict erupted between the Catholic hierarchy and political leaders.[22]

These ad hoc responses were soon replaced by a long-range strategy. Beginning in the 1930s, many Latin American churches imitated the Catholic Action movements then in vogue in Europe. They attempted to develop explicitly Catholic organizations in many fields, particularly among organized labor and students, in order to combat the potential "loss" of these elements from the

[21] Of course, this image of the harmony of rural life is in many respects mythical, but nonetheless from the point of view of the Church it offered an attractive model of social relations. For a review of some of the arguments about social and cultural harmony in Latin America, see Levine, "Issues in the Study of Culture and Politics."

[22] See the three-volume study by Jean Meyer on the *cristero* wars in Mexico: *La cristiada. 1: la guerra de los cristeros, 2: el conflicto entre la iglesia y el estado—1926/1929*, and *3: los cristeros*. The term *cristero* comes from the battle cry "¡Viva Cristo Rey!" (Long Live Christ the King!). Cf. also Bailey, *¡Viva Cristo Rey!*

Church. These defensive reactions were meant to resolve the immediate problems created by social change. But Catholic Action did not exhaust the Church's efforts. In addition, two ideologies then current in Europe made their way to Latin America, with considerable impact on later organizational developments: corporatism and neo-Thomism. Let us review these in turn.[23]

The corporatist ideologies and fascist movements that flourished in Europe between the wars had a considerable impact on Latin America. There, as in Europe, corporatist notions of social order proved quite attractive to many Catholic thinkers. Corporatists basically argued that societies have a natural harmony and hierarchy. In this view, different social classes are bound together by ties of loyalty and common interest in the functions they perform together. Thus, for example, instead of setting workers against employers, corporatist thinkers group them together, emphasizing their unity within what are seen as the natural "corporations" of society. This stress on interclass unity, harmony, and hierarchy is reflected politically in a rejection of individualism and the political schemes it generates (e.g., "one man, one vote"). These are replaced by representation through the national corporations or institutional orders of society: the family, industry, agriculture, and the like. The whole package is tied together by a state inspired by Catholic social doctrine.[24]

Within each particular institutional order, and in the system as a whole, hierarchy is thus preserved. Hence, corporatism provided a convenient solution to the conceptual problems posed by development and change, by reaffirming unity and social order. The corporatist ideological response was coupled, in some areas, with strengthened alliances between the Church and conservative political forces, which were seen as its natural defenders. A good example is the "Social Platform" adopted by the 1939 Convention of the Conservative party of Colombia, which brought these various strands together in this way:

on the road to the elaboration of a social structure which avoids

[23] Sanders, "The New Latin American Catholicism," offers a very useful discussion of these developments.

[24] Corporatist notions of social and political organization have had broad appeal in the Catholic world, with concrete examples ranging from Austrian Catholicism in the 1930s and Mussolini's Italy to Vichy France, Franco's Spain, and the Portugal of Salazar.

class struggle and opens more scientific paths toward the development of national production, its equitable distribution, and the defense of common professional interests, the Conservative party will lend all its support to the study of formulae or initiatives leading to the organization of a system of corporations which, ensuring social peace, maintain a perfect harmony with the democratic institutions of the nation and with the principles of Catholic social philosophy.[25]

While corporatism was gaining considerable influence within the Church and among conservative political groups in general, the seeds of what would later be Christian Democratic parties were also being sown, in numerous study circles held throughout the region. Here, the ideas of other Catholic thinkers, particularly Jacques Maritain, became important. Maritain's work has had an enormous and long-lasting influence in Latin America, and so it may be useful here to sketch the main lines of his thought.

The importance of Maritain and of other French thinkers of the time, like Emmanuel Mounier and Pierre Teilhard de Chardin, lies in their provision of a logic and a justification for Catholic advocacy of democracy, pluralism, and social, economic, and political reform.[26] Drawing inspiration from a new look at basic Thomist ideas and a new reading of the major papal encyclicals, Maritain argued that a commitment to democracy and pluralism was both possible and necessary for Christians. Further, he was concerned with social justice and the need to reform society on more communitarian lines. But his thought goes beyond mere corporatism, which includes many of these elements, in its concern for pluralism and openness in the social order.

Maritain sought a means by which Catholics could work to transform society in accord with their faith and their understanding of Catholic doctrine, without imposing their beliefs in an authoritarian manner. His position is therefore often referred to as "neo-Christendom." Christendom, you will recall, was the medieval

[25] Cited in Bernal Jiménez, *La cuestión social y la lucha de classes,* pp. 175-76.

[26] On Maritain see Moreno, "Jacques Maritain y la America Latina." Pierce offers a useful discussion of Mounier in his *Contemporary French Political Thought,* especially chapter 3. For discussions of Teilhard see Reuther, *The Radical Kingdom,* pp. 200-212, and Sanders, "The Priests of the People."

ideal of a society organized along Christian principles. Neo-Christendom differs; for, although it also looks to the transformation of the world in accord with Christian ideals, these are to be promoted by individual Christians, each acting in his or her own capacity as a believer and citizen—not as a subordinate member of a dominant Church or a corporate state.[27]

The further influence of writers like Teilhard or Mounier lay in their stress on history, context, and the need for action. Teilhard's research introduced notions of historical change and transformation as normal and continuous phenomena, and placed them in a framework of Christian eschatology. The very recognition of change as normal, in a Church attuned for centuries to static modes of thought, is of major significance. At the very least, it freed Catholics from identifying any particular social or political order with the will of God. Teilhard also stressed the importance of seeing religious significance in *all* secular values, communities, and developments. Mounier, the philosopher of "personalism," added an emphasis on the need for authenticity, which is to be found in large measure by carrying out one's ideas through direct personal action.

If we add these dimensions of a concern for historical change and a stress on the need for action to Maritain's interest in providing ideas and vehicles for a new Christian transformation of society, we have the basic orientation underlying what later emerged as Christian Democracy in Latin America, coming to power in Chile and Venezuela in the mid and late 1960s.

Despite these stirrings, it is fair to say that in the period running approximately from the end of World War II to the time of the Second Vatican Council, the Latin American Church as a whole devoted most of its energies to resisting the continued threats of the secular state and the infiltration of Protestant or Marxist groups among its rank-and-file clientele. Within the worldwide context of Roman Catholicism, the Latin American Churches were generally viewed as stolid and unimaginative. Moreover, the rare attempts at innovation which were undertaken at all were mostly derivative—imitations of earlier currents in Western Europe.

The Second Vatican Council, held in several sessions from

---

[27] This distinction is examined more fully in chapter 6, below, in the context of its implications for political action.

1962 to 1965, of course marked the opening of a period of deep change for the Church as a whole, but its impact on Latin America was perhaps even more profound. In the most obvious sense, the council was a new experience in that more Latin American bishops probably met and talked there than ever before. Many bishops told me that the simple fact of meeting and comparing notes with colleagues from other Latin American countries was a moving and often eye-opening experience. In the various sessions of the council, they came to see themselves more as a group within the Church, a group with special interests and problems given the fact that Latin America is, after all, the only part of the world which is both Christian *and* underdeveloped. In many ways, then, the council provided a forum for the articulation of basic issues and dimensions of change in the Church. Let us turn now to consider these in detail.

Basic Issues

Much of the motive force for recent changes in the Latin American Church has come from the gradual working out of the impact of the Second Vatican Council (Vatican II) and the subsequent Second General Conference of Latin American Bishops held in Medellín, Colombia, in 1968. A fresh look at these two key conferences is particularly appropriate now, in light of the recent Third General Conference of Latin American Bishops, held in Puebla, Mexico, in early 1979. (The Puebla meeting was intended to review and evaluate the decade since Medellín while charting a course for the future. It is considered in greater detail in chapter 10, below.[28])

Vatican II marked a major attempt to rethink the nature of the Church, the world, and the proper relation between the two. Alongside the traditional model of the Church as an institution, which had stressed eternal, unchanging aspects of belief, structure, and hierarchy, the council elaborated a vision of the Church as a "Pilgrim People of God"—a living, changing community of the faithful making its way through history. Viewing the Church as a Pilgrim People of God means, in a very basic sense, accepting the

[28] For fuller discussions of Puebla see Poblete, "From Medellín to Puebla"; Berryman, "What Happened at Puebla"; Wilde, "Ten Years of Change in the Church"; and the sources they cite.

importance of temporal, historical change, both as a fact in itself and as a powerful source of changing values.[29] This acceptance of change, as opposed to more traditional insistence on transcendental stasis and permanence, has had far-reaching and (one suspects) unanticipated consequences for the Church. For if situations and institutions are historically determined, then no particular social form is fixed; all change, and no one form is necessarily right. From this new perspective, it is no longer possible to be certain about the proper relations among individuals and groups within society, or even within the Church. Moreover, attention to the historical sources of change leads quite readily to a concern for understanding how societies came to be the way they are. Once this step is taken, the Church is decisively freed (at least in potential) from its previous identification with conservative forces and existing structures. Societies change as a matter of course, and moreover they can be changed by human will, and need not simply be endured in hopes of a better life to come.

Viewing the Church as a Pilgrim People of God also had a profound impact on the structure and meaning of authority in the Church—the kinds of authority, activity, and obedience seen as necessary and legitimate. As we shall see (chapter 5, below), this new model, by laying such great stress on the historical experience of change, helped move the Church away from its predominant concern with roles, rank, and juridically defined hierarchy, and toward testimony and witness (in the biblical sense of solidarity through shared experience) as sources of authority and models for action. This new emphasis is of central importance; for, if au-

[29] For a fuller account of the Second Vatican Council see Hebblethwaite, *The Runaway Church*, or O'Dea, *The Catholic Crisis*. The implications of new models of the Church are discussed in detail in chapter 5, below. See also Smith and Sanks, "Liberation Ecclesiology." The emergence of new models of the Church can also be seen on a different though related dimension. Traditionally, Catholicism has taken a very broad view of its membership. As a universal Church, it was open to all who met only minimal requirements for entry. Thus, Catholicism traditionally rejected the Protestant model of sects, which look to an elite core of members who are highly motivated, aware, and knowledgeable. There is considerable evidence in Latin America now that many Catholics are moving to a view of the Church which stresses greater knowledge, more conscious commitment, and high levels of participation (all sectlike qualities), with important implications for the authority structure of the Church and for the relations of groups within it.

thority is grounded in testimony and witness, then the holders of authority (bishops for example) are moved to action and are expected to act, as a necessary expression of their religious roles.

The link of authority to action has also had a major impact on the scope and meaning of obedience within the Church. The expectation of relatively automatic obedience to superiors has increasingly been called into question by priests, nuns, and lay people who feel that leaders have a legitimate claim to authority only if they act to promote social justice. Moreover, by putting the bases of authority and obedience on a more egalitarian, community-oriented footing, the stress on action and shared experience has greatly enhanced collegiality and power sharing within the ecclesiastical institution itself.[30]

These new perspectives were amplified by the council's more general revaluation of the meaning of social action, which gave it new autonomy and status in the greater Catholic scheme of things. This general revaluation has added several new dimensions to Catholic thinking, most notably an opening to secular disciplines, particularly the social sciences, as sources of valid knowledge about the world, and, related to this, a recognition of the autonomous validity of temporal values and of the possibility of drawing valid religious lessons and meaning from the problems and experiences of daily life. Vatican II began this incorporation of secular social thinking in a mild way, with general sociological analysis and a broad concern for "development." But as we shall see, this small opening quickly expanded, above all in Latin America, to encompass new ideas about violence, "structural change," and essentially Marxist notions of economic dependency, praxis, and revolution. The possibility of drawing valid religious values from the temporal world is related, for it implies a basic reorientation of Catholic activism. Whereas earlier approaches all in some measure sought to transform the world in accord with the principles of a known body of Christian doctrine, these new perspectives lead in a different direction.

The starting point here is now social, not religious. Thus, rather

[30] See chapters 4, 5, 7, 8, and 9, below, for a consideration of these points in Venezuela and Colombia. Gilfeather has pointed to the tensions and frustrations *within* the Church experienced by sisters who come up against resistance to change on these dimensions. See her "Women Religious, the Poor, and the Institutional Church in Chile."

than form specifically or exclusively "Christian" groups, those inspired by religious faith should, in this view, join with others sharing their social goals, be they Christian or not. In Latin America, this perspective led quickly to the development of extensive and often controversial Christian-Marxist alliances—alliances whose goals were derived not from authorized expressions of Catholic social doctrine, but rather from a searching look at society, a look taken more and more frequently in the light of Marxist categories of analysis.

Of course, the council's impact did not reach so far all at once. The first fruits of these changes came rather in a flurry of interest for "development" (already anticipated by Latin American Christian Democracy) and in a series of development projects of Christian inspiration. This orientation peaked in the early years of Christian Democratic rule in Chile, when it seemed as if that party might indeed make development a success within this framework. But by the time of Medellín, this optimism had all but disappeared, and the appeal of Christian Democracy had soured after a rash of divisions, conflicts, and disappointments. At Medellín, the bishops took quite a new tack, and their conclusions mark a milestone in the recent development of Latin American Catholicism.[31]

Like Vatican II, Medellín turned to a broad reconsideration of all aspects of religious life, locating them specifically within the context of contemporary social transformation in Latin America. For our purposes, Medellín is particularly important for its treatment of the key issues of force and violence, and the related question of social division and class conflict.

The matter of violence was put in perspective at Medellín by

[31] In treating development, Medellín differs sharply from the Second Vatican Council and from the early encyclicals of Popes John XXIII and Paul VI. The council viewed development largely in terms of the rich nations helping the poor, whereas at Medellín development was seen explicitly from the perspective of the poor and conceived in terms which are much less church centered. Gutierrez notes that "Vatican II talks about a Church in the world and describes the relationship in a way which tends to neutralize the conflicts; Medellín demonstrates that the world in which the Latin American Church ought to be present is in full revolution. Vatican II sketches a general outline for Church renewal: Medellín provides guidelines for a transformation of the Church in terms of its presence in a continent of misery and injustice" (*A Theology of Liberation*, p. 134).

Pope Paul's comments, during his visit to Colombia, condemning violence as antievangelical and unchristian.[32] While supporting efforts at social change, the pope thus ruled out violence as a legitimate tool of social transformation. The bishops differed. Basically, they argued that many kinds of violence exist: violence cannot be considered only as individual or even collective acts of aggression, but must be recognized as well in the day-to-day operations of unequal, unjust, and oppressive social structures. This was defined as "institutionalized violence." The distinction of such institutionalized violence from more overt forms of aggression was a major step, for it opened the way to justifying counterviolence—violent acts intended to undo the inherent, institutionalized violence of the established order, replacing the old order with a more just society.

This social analysis was placed in a broader context of religious belief by the bishops' discussion of sin. Conventionally considered to refer to personal situations and individual morality, sin was extended at Medellín to characterize entire social systems whose injustice, oppression, and institutionalized violence were sinful because they imposed social conditions making a fully moral and decent life impossible. Once this kind of connection is made, it is clearly a short and relatively easy step to argue that if oppressive social, economic, and political structures are sinful, and hence prevent the full realization of human potential, then religious grace, which involves freedom from sin, is in some measure tied to change in these structures, by revolution if necessary.

Finally, the Church's attention was focused once again, at Vatican II and at Medellín, on the poor, and more generally on the sources and meaning of poverty.[33] Of course, the Catholic Church has long paid considerable attention to the poor. But in social terms, most of this concern was expressed in welfare programs—aid to the poor within the bounds of existing social, economic, and political arrangements. Moreover, poverty was seen, for the most part, as a result of individual failings; hence, charity

[32] On the pope's visit to Colombia, his speeches, and the surrounding controversies, see Vekemans, ¿Agonía o resurgimiento?

[33] Victor Turner suggests that a concern for the meaning of poverty is typical of periods of intense cultural crisis and reorientation, which he calls "liminal periods." His analysis fits the current Latin American scene well. Cf. *Dramas, Fields, and Metaphors*, pp. 265-67.

and job training were stressed. With the new orientations just described, however, poverty can be seen in a new light, as a structural (not an individual) problem. From this perspective, the misery of poverty and the injustice which causes it can never be resolved through individual charity alone. Rather, the structures which cause poverty must be changed—and this is a matter of power and political action.

More is at stake here than the simple reorientation of policies and programs: a large part of the post-Medellín debates in the Latin American Church has involved attempts to reinterpret the symbolic meaning of poverty as well. For proponents of change, poverty need no longer be simply endured, in hopes of greater rewards in Heaven. Action and change are necessary and legitimate. Indeed, the phrase "the poor shall inherit the earth" is now taken, more and more often, in a direct and literal sense. Moreover, the "poor" of the Gospels have often been transformed, among radical Catholics, into the working class or the proletariat; and action to promote the coming of the Kingdom of God has been identified, for all practical purposes, with revolutionary struggle.

This renewed and transformed concern with poverty has also been expressed in a growing movement, among priests and especially among women religious, to share the life and experience of the poor—to live with them, work with them, and join them in the frustrations and rewards of daily life. This experience has often had profound intellectual and emotional effects. By bringing religious activists into direct contact with misery and injustice, it has made them more aware of the need for change and has in this way contributed to the organization for social and political change by priests and sisters in several countries.[34]

This brief sketch of the impact of Vatican II and Medellín indicates the depth and extent of change within the Church. A predominant concern with stasis was replaced by an emphasis on change, social conflict and division were openly recognized, and a beginning was made toward a full and open commitment to the poor. And finally, at least tentative steps were taken toward the

[34] On this point see Gilfeather, "Women Religious," and Dodson, "The Christian Left in Latin American Politics." The impact of experience is discussed more fully in chapters 4 and 10, below.

legitimation of violence. How have these ideas and initiatives been expressed in Latin America? No single, unified response is visible. Instead, several attempts at synthesis stand out, and the next section examines these in detail, through a look at some cases.[35]

Cases: Left, Right, and Center

The case of Camilo Torres is a good place to begin, for in many ways Torres was a precursor who exemplified in his own brief career all of the elements of change just discussed.[36] Torres entered the priesthood under the influence of French social Catholicism as espoused by Dominican priests then in Colombia. His vocation was thus strongly influenced by a particular dedication to social reform through Christian action. This orientation was reinforced by his advanced clerical education, which took him to Louvain University in Belgium. In the mid-1950s, Louvain was a center for reform-minded Latin American Catholics and a source of much Christian Democratic thinking. Thus, when he returned to Colombia in late 1958, Torres came inspired by ideas of development through Christian action.

But he soon grew frustrated with strategies geared to the persuasion of elites, reformist methods, and with the very assumption that some uniquely Christian solution to social problems existed. His career evolved rapidly, and in 1965 he founded a movement, the United Front, intended to bring together all progressive forces in the pursuit of political change. These activities led to conflict with the ecclesiastical hierarchy, which ended with Torres' voluntary "reduction" to lay status in order to devote himself full time to politics. Events moved swiftly: the United Front was formed in May 1965, Torres left the priesthood in June, entered a guerrilla front in October, and was killed in early 1966 in a skirmish with an army patrol.

This brief but spectacular career raises at least three issues for Latin American Catholicism, all of which were taken up and treated more systematically in later years: first, the relation of religious faith to action in the world; second, the status of power,

[35] The continued attempt at synthesis of religion and politics by Latin American Catholics of many different ideological persuasions is of great importance. The general point is explored further in chapter 10, below.

[36] On Camilo Torres see particularly Broderick, *Camilo Torres*.

force, and violence; and third, the proper relation between Catholics and other (specifically Marxist) groups in the promotion of change.

Camilo Torres believed that authentic religious faith requires action to transform an unjust world. Religion for him was not simply "spiritual," a disembodied faith brought out only on Sundays. Rather, it was an integral part of life. Hence, genuine faith can only achieve full expression in a just and equitable society. In his words, "When circumstances impede men from devoting themselves to Christ, the priest's proper duty is to combat these circumstances . . . the revolutionary struggle is a christian and priestly struggle."[37]

It is important to be clear about the issue. Torres did not oppose politics to religion, or somehow put politics before religion. Rather, he saw the two as intimately and necessarily joined, and looked for the way religious commitments require action to make them effective. In his view, a true Christian is obliged to be political, for only in this way can love of one's neighbor, the key Christian precept, be made effective. Individual acts of kindness and charity are negated by unjust structures of society. And since these structures are founded on power, only power (not appeals to conscience or good will alone) can change them. His rapid turn to politics and guerrilla action flowed directly from these understandings. In Torres' view, once one recognizes the fact of social division, and becomes aware of the full implications of phrases like "love thy neighbor," then the use of power and even violence as means to a more just society is legitimate.

Further, Torres anticipated the extraordinary development of Marxist-Christian dialogue and cooperation. For as he moved away from Christian (and Christian Democratic) reformism, with its concern for building Church-related programs, he came logically to value alliances with any and all groups dedicated to the cause of revolution.

The career of Camilo Torres is important; for it was not a fluke or a chance aberration, but rather a response to many pressures for change that were increasing worldwide, in Church and society alike. In Latin America, the new social perspectives have been developed most systematically in what has come to be known as

[37] Torres, *Father Camilo Torres, Revolutionary Writings*, pp. 264-65.

Liberation Theology.[38] A brief look at Liberation Theology will round out our view of the left's response to contemporary changes in Church and society.

As the name itself implies, Liberation Theology is concerned with the meaning of religion for social and political liberation, and vice versa. It has evolved in recent years as a distinctively and self-consciously Latin American approach to the relation of religion and politics. The Latin American focus is significant in itself, for it reflects a deliberate attempt to root an understanding of religious faith in the particular experience of contemporary Latin America. Theology is placed in the context of real social experiences, and this discipline, once cloistered and abstract, is transformed into a reflection on concrete historical struggles and situations.[39] Liberation Theology thus begins with a look at concrete social problems, drawing themes and imperatives for action from this analysis. The central problem for religion is then no longer atheism, indifference, or even hostility to religion per se, but rather social and political transformation. Gustavo Gutierrez states the issue sharply:

> Much contemporary theology seems to start from the challenge of the *non-believer*. He questions our *religious world* and faces it with a demand for profound purification and renewal. . . . This challenge in a continent like Latin America does not come primarily from the man who does not believe, but from the *man who is not a man*, who is not recognized as such by the existing social order: he is in the ranks of the poor, the exploited; he is the man who is systematically and legally despoiled of his being as a man, who scarcely knows that he *is* a man. His challenge is not aimed first at our religious world, but at our *economic, social, political, and cultural world*; therefore it is an appeal for the revolutionary transformation of the very bases of

---

[38] The literature on Liberation Theology is enormous and still growing; yet one very useful review remains Berryman, "Latin American Liberation Theology." Other important sources include Gutierrez, *A Theology of Liberation*; Dussel, *History and the Theology of Liberation*; Geffré and Gutierrez, *The Mystical and Political Dimensions of the Christian Faith*; Assmann, *Opresión-liberación desafío a los cristianos*; and Segundo, *The Liberation of Theology*.

[39] As Dussel puts it (*History and the Theology of Liberation*, p. 145), the text for theological reflection is not a set of abstract categories, but rather a social situation.

a dehumanizing society. The question is not therefore how to speak of God in an adult world, but how to proclaim him as a Father in a world that is not human.[40]

Liberation Theology faces the issues of power, force, and violence quite directly; it builds them into an analysis of the nature of authentic religious commitment. Like Camilo Torres, Gutierrez argues that Christians must look at society realistically, giving full weight to the struggle and conflict so visible everywhere. Traditional Catholic positions, which oppose class struggle in the name of an ideal Christian love for one's enemies, are rejected. Real Christian love, Gutierrez argues, is founded on commitment to a more just society and on action to bring it about.[41]

The influence of contemporary social science, and particularly of Marxist thought, is notable in the adoption of a perspective of continuous change, in the identification of the working class as the motor of this change, and in a deep concern with the fusion of theory and action in an authentic revolutionary praxis.[42] These elements can only be briefly discussed here.

The recognition of change is central to Liberation Theology and fits well with a view of the Church as Pilgrim People of God. From this perspective, many writers have illuminated the kinds of problems faced by religious people seeking social and political change.[43] Above all, they want to avoid any rigid identification of the Church with the present, and thus keep Catholic thought and action open

[40] Gutierrez, "Liberation, Theology, and Proclamation," p. 69.

[41] Gutierrez, *A Theology of Liberation*, p. 278.

[42] The great attraction of Marxist thought for Latin American Catholic radicals has been criticized sharply by the North American Jesuit John Coleman: "As a social scientist, I have often been puzzled, if not irritated, by the almost religious importance given to the writings and analysis of Karl Marx. At times, Marxist thought (albeit with a revisionary attempt to extrapolate a 'scientific' Marx from Marx the materialist, atheistic philosopher) is identified *tout court* with social scientific analysis. Such an approach does not accord with the antidogmatic stance of a social science" ("Civil Religion and Liberation Theology in North America," p. 133).

[43] In addition to the works cited in note 38 above, see Galilea, *¿A los pobres se les anuncia el evangelio?* and his "Liberation as an Encounter with Politics and Contemplation." Segundo's five-volume theological study, *A Theology for Artisans of a New Humanity*, also warrants special mention: cf. *The Community Called Church*, vol. 1; *Grace and the Human Condition*, vol. 2; *Our Idea of God*, vol. 3; *The Sacraments Today*, vol. 4; and *Evolution and Guilt*, vol. 5.

to change. As Hugo Assmann has written, "The transcendent quality of God rests on the fact that he is always before us, on the frontiers of the future. God is pro-vocative; that is, he calls us ahead, and can only be met as one who moves forward with his people in a continuous dismantling of structures."[44]

In Liberation Theology, change is permanent, and it is rooted in social conflict. As noted above, this point of view stems in large measure from a disillusionment with "development" as practiced in Latin America. Development was originally seen as a nonrevolutionary path to progress through economic growth and industrialization in a capitalist framework. But for radical Catholics, such development has masked and in some cases actually increased poverty, misery, and inequality. Rejecting such development, these writers have absorbed the theories of "dependency" which have emerged in Latin America in recent years.[45]

From dependency theory, Liberation Theology acquired an explanation of Latin American poverty, and thereby acquired as well a set of categories which strengthened and gave focus to its social and economic concerns. Even a cursory glance at the vast body of writing on dependency suggests the reasons for its attractiveness to radical Catholics. In dependency theory, the inequality and misery associated with capitalist development in Latin America are not accidental, but rather are a necessary consequence of the subordination of Latin American societies and economies to the interests of the dominant world capitalist powers, whose continued development depends on the exploitation of Latin America and other "underdeveloped" regions. Moreover, their policies and programs are implemented by local allies who control social, cultural, economic, and political institutions. The solution, in dependency theory and Liberation Theology alike, lies not in more of the same (i.e., more "development") but rather in the construction of a new kind of social order.

What finally is this liberation? Basically, liberation involves freedom from bondage of all kinds—the bondage of ignorance,

[44] Assmann, *Opresión-liberación*, p. 21.

[45] The literature on dependency theory is enormous. Kahl provides a good introduction to the issues and a useful account of their development in Latin America in his *Modernization, Exploitation, and Dependency in Latin America*. See also O'Donnell, *Modernization and Bureaucratic Authoritarianism*, for a very clear account of the bases of this perspective.

alienation, poverty, and oppression, and the bondage of sin.[46] Such liberation is neither wholly spiritual nor wholly material. Rather, the fusion of the two gives this perspective its unique and compelling force. Religious and political liberation go together: "purely religious" actions, limited to the institutional Church, are rejected as stemming from a false consciousness; yet "pure politics" lacks meaning in the cosmic scheme of things. In this view, the key role of religious action is in joining the two planes, but in a way that removes the traditional religious legitimation of the existing social order by channeling religious energies and motivations toward its transformation.

Religion is linked to politics through the emphasis on praxis which runs through these writings. Praxis refers to a kind of action so theoretically informed and so self-aware that the activity itself expresses the insights which logical study and reflection provide. Liberation Theology stresses both individual and collective praxis, making action a necessary consequence of authentic faith—a kind of validation of the reality of that faith. A concern for praxis thus looks toward greater self-awareness and the expression of authentic faith through action. This position carries an implicit commitment to the creation of new forms of organization, as self-aware action leads people to develop new ways of living and working together.[47] (This point is developed in detail in chapters 5, 7, and 9, below.)

[46] A statement which highlights the way in which politics, economic change, cultural transformation, and spiritual orientations are combined in Liberation Theology comes from the bishop of Riobamba, Ecuador, Msgr. Leonidas Proaño: "It concerns: (a) liberation from social domination and economic exploitation (abuses of the fundamental rights of the weak by the powerful or the less weak); (b) liberation from ignorance, which prevents understanding, dominating, and transforming the natural world, recognition of self as a person, location in and participation in social affairs, and knowledge of the true God; (c) liberation from misery and insecurity. From physical misery; that is, from hunger, sickness, and other sufferings. From psychological misery; that is, from anxieties, frustrations, and vices. Liberation from insecurity through the possession and use of the goods that are indispensable, through the creative work of the family" (cited in Roncagliolo and Reyes Matta, *Iglesia, prensa, y militares*, p. 127).

[47] On the bases of the idea of praxis in Marx's thought, see Avineri, *The Social and Political Thought of Karl Marx*, especially chapter 5. Avineri shows that, for Marx, praxis was both a particular kind of action and also a means to the development of greater self-consciousness in individuals and social classes.

The emphasis on praxis has given Liberation Theology a notable tendency to stress the primacy of politics as a form of and arena for authentic religious action. Indeed, arguments over the primacy of politics have become extremely important in the Latin American Church. Many bishops and Church leaders reject such views (and hence reject Liberation Theology as a whole) because they fear that making politics and political commitment primary leads to downgrading the transcendental and eschatological dimensions of religious faith. In large measure, then, the issue of the primacy of politics is joined with views of the nature of religion and religious faith.

Attitudes about the primacy of politics also depend on the way society itself is seen. Radical Catholics do not necessarily see political activity as always and necessarily a source of deep satisfaction. Rather, they argue that political activity is necessary when other spheres of life are limited, distorted by inequalities in the structure of power. Such structures of power can only be changed by the creation and use of power. Only for this reason do politics and political action gain primacy: when they are necessary to the creation of a better society, one in which a fully satisfying life will be possible. But in the current situation, poverty, misery, and oppression are built into restrictive social, economic, and political structures, making a fully human life impossible. In a fundamental sense, then, such structures are "dehumanizing." This is the core of the radical Catholic position in Latin America: it is not a simple commitment to politics first, foremost, and always, but a commitment which builds on a vision of the possibilities of human life and of the "fulfilled" person, possibilities not limited to what currently exists.

This concern for praxis, and for conscious, self-aware action in general, has received two notable expressions in recent years: first, in the work of Paulo Freire, the Brazilian educator; and second, in programs for cooperation and joint action with Marxists. Paulo Freire has had an enormous influence on Latin American Catholicism.[48] In his studies of education, Freire argues that education must do more than impart skills. In addition, each student must play an active role in creating his own awareness of the surrounding world. This process (*concientización* in Spanish) is intended to develop in each person a critical awareness of society as a hu-

---

[48] Freire's most influential work is *Pedagogy of the Oppressed*.

man product, and therefore changeable. To Freire, the first and most basic step toward change is to liberate people from the oppressors they have internalized. He argues that the dominated absorb the dominators' vision of them: the poor believe themselves to be lazy and stupid. Only when the social order is demythologized, through the development of critical consciousness, can people proceed to liberate themselves. In this process, the transformation of religious concepts plays a major role. For if religious symbols can also be demythologized, and freed of their ties to the existing social order, then a major step toward psychological and cultural liberation will have been taken.

A more directly political path has been followed by Catholic radicals pursuing dialogue, cooperation, and open political alliances with Marxists. These initiatives have popped up all over Latin America since Medellín, and evolved furthest in Chile during the Allende regime. The evolution of Christians for Socialism in Chile is important, for it put to a practical test most of the issues under consideration here.[49] Questions of activism, power, the meaning of politics for religious action, and the proper role for Christians (particularly priests and religious) in politics all came to the surface in a sharp and controversial form. Shortly before the overthrow of Allende, the movement was condemned by Chile's bishops, who feared that Christianity's central religious message was being swamped by an overwhelming political commitment. To the bishops, Christians for Socialism made bad policy and poor theology as well: bad policy by aggravating political divisions within the Church and committing its survival to the fortunes of the socialist regime; and poor theology by reducing the Church's dynamic to an exclusively political plane. If the Church were to become political, the mission of salvation might be lost.

> The Church is meant to be the salt of the earth. "And if salt becomes tasteless, how is its saltiness to be restored?" (Mt. 5:15). If the Church is turned into a political or temporal faction, who will save us?[50]

Since the fall of socialism in Chile, many in the Church have drawn back from full political commitment. The reaction of

[49] For a full account see the documents collected in Eagleson, *Christians and Socialism*.
[50] Cited in ibid., p. 224.

Chile's bishops has echoed throughout the region. But in dealing with the issues of politics and political commitment so sharply joined by Liberation Theology and Christians for Socialism, leaders of the Latin American Church are in a difficult situation, for they face concerted and often bitter opposition from all sides.

Considerable attention has been devoted so far to the evolution of what is generally called the Christian left. It is important to realize, however, that other, equally vigorous positions exist. Indeed, as radical Catholics moved to more open political commitments, their activism has been matched, if not exceeded, on the right, most notably by the Societies for the Defense of Tradition, Family, and Property (TFP) which have emerged in many countries.[51] Moreover, the weight of these groups on the right has been reinforced by the development, in several Latin American military establishments, of attitudes deeply hostile to the Church, rooted in the armed forces' views on "national security."

Both TFP and the military reject the postconciliar and especially the post-Medellín changes in the Church as a betrayal of the religion they were brought up to honor, revere, and defend. The basic TFP world view combines a preference for very traditional forms of Catholic religious practice with a strong commitment to reactionary social, economic, and political positions. TFP members see themselves as part of a general counterrevolutionary offensive, and they explicitly attribute most of the ills of the modern world to the aftereffects of the French Revolution.[52] The most notable aspect of their social doctrine is a belief in the absolute sanctity of private property combined with an appreciation of the healthy virtues of social inequality.[53] Naturally enough, they reject any dialogue with non-Catholic groups as the opening wedge of communist infiltration—as a clever tactic for weakening the defenses of Western, Christian civilization.[54]

The reaction of the military is less specifically religious in tone

[51] The first TFP nuclei were founded in Brazil in the years preceding the military coup of 1964. TFP militants played a major role in organizing public opposition to the Goulart regime. Later, in Chile, TFP was active in the opposition to Allende, often forming the core of right-wing groups such as Patria y Libertad.

[52] Corrêa de Oliveira, *Revolución y contra-revolución*.

[53] De Castro Mayer, de Proença Sigaud, Corrêa de Oliveira, and Mendonça de Freitas, *Reforma agraria*.

[54] Corrêa de Oliveira, *Trasbordo ideológico inadvertido y diálogo*.

and inspiration, but also reveals a deep hostility toward the contemporary Latin American Church. The military's views are grounded in their doctrine of "national security," according to which there is no real distinction between war and peace.[55] Because the nature of war and conflict has changed, all times are now times of war. As a result, national security itself can no longer be confined to the external defense of secure frontiers, but now requires internal unity and discipline to counter the social conflict and subversion which impede national progress. Since unity must be enforced and subversion combated at every turn, the role of the state and especially of its security apparatus is greatly enhanced, while traditional civil liberties and representative institutions are severely curtailed.

The military see their struggle as part of the general defense of Western, Christian civilization against communism. Hence, no contradiction is perceived between their position and "Christian principles," and extensive use is made of Christian images, symbols, and alliances wherever possible. But given the developments in the Church already described, and the ambiguities of "pastoral action" which have been noted here, the generals are continuously faced with "Christian actions" which in their eyes amount to simple subversion. Moreover, the problem is not limited to Christian radicals, for in many cases the bishops, the very leaders of the Church, instead of supporting the military's defense of "Christian values," have gradually moved into opposition over issues of human rights, social justice, and in simple attempts to defend priests, nuns, and lay people engaged in pastoral action who are arrested as subversives. The result has been a growing tension between the Church and the military regimes which now hold power in many countries.[56]

The central institutions of the Church, led by the bishops, are caught in the middle. Since the late 1950s, their general goal has been to withdraw from partisan politics and concentrate their energies on internal renewal and pastoral action. But as we have

[55] On the doctrine of national security, see (among others) Calvo, "The Church and the Doctrine of National Security"; Comblin, *The Church and the National Security State*; Stepan, *The Military in Politics*, chap. 8; and Methol Ferré, "Sobre la actual ideología de la seguridad nacional." A useful bibliography is Roberto Jiménez, *Seguridad nacional y temas conexos*.

[56] Cf. Brian Smith, "Churches and Human Rights."

seen, this position is full of ambiguities. And quite apart from its inherent difficulties, it is also under attack from many sides. The left rejects it as hypocritical and unrealistic, while the right calls the bishops to decisive action against communism. Caught in the center, the bishops are trying to pull the Church and the Catholic community together in the face of enormous divisive pressures, while yet retaining a maximum possible autonomy from governments and political groups alike.[57]

In many cases, this central position has been reached after a series of ups and downs concerning politics and political action. The enthusiasm in the late 1960s for development, social action, and internal Church reform was quickly tempered by reaction to what a number of bishops saw as the excesses of Liberation Theology and Christian-Marxist alliances. But in the shadow of the growing wave of authoritarian, national-security regimes (most notably in Brazil, Argentina, Chile, and Uruguay), many Church leaders have been forced to take a new look at the issues as politics, this time in the form of the military, intrudes once again on the life of the Church.

The evolving position of the Chilean bishops is a good example of this process; for, although Chile is an extreme case, it nevertheless encapsulates and concentrates many of the issues seen in fragmented form elsewhere. The Chilean bishops condemned Christians for Socialism because they feared a relativization of the Christian message and its subordination to political goals, and that the Church might thereby break apart as different groups claimed the mantle of its authority for their positions. Thus they argued that it is not true that everything is ultimately political, and that politics need not be a primary form of commitment; limits and distinctions are required. The Gospel does not depend on political action for its effectiveness, and the Church in any case takes no particular political model as its own (transcending all). And finally, Church action is basically different in *kind* from political action, because force and power (so central to politics) are set aside.[58]

[57] An example of the dilemmas this produces is the complex situation of the Chilean bishops since the overthrow of Allende. See Sanders and Smith, *The Chilean Church*.

[58] The bishops' statement is reproduced in full in Eagleson, *Christians and Socialism*, pp. 179-228.

But by 1977 the tables had been turned: the Allende regime was no more. But gone with it were not only the activists on the left (in Church and society alike), but also the entire apparatus of Chile's civil society and its juridical, republican traditions. In 1973, a number of bishops were willing to help legitimize the military regime, seeing its ascendancy at the least as a respite from turmoil and constant conflict. But by 1977 the conflict had not gone away. Rather, the "internal" war continued, with the Church itself now coming under attack.[59] The Church's response has taken many forms. In 1977 the bishops published a collective pastoral letter entitled *Our Life As A Nation*, which explicitly took issue with the doctrine of national security and reaffirmed the values of democracy, pluralism, and openness. They rejected the regime's attempt to cast itself as the defender of Christian values, noting that

> we do well to recall the teaching of the Church. She strongly upholds legitimate pluralism in the realm of ideas and socio-political groups, while also pointing out the need for national unity and the proper way to obtain it. . . .
>
> The road to peace and unity cannot be reached through imposition. Unity, like truth (including religious truth) cannot be imposed by force. It must be proposed to people so that it can be accepted on the basis of inner conviction and a personal decision.[60]

In Chile, as elsewhere in Latin America, the bishops are groping for ways to preserve the unity and autonomy of the Church, and yet maintain its ability to contribute creatively to the welfare of the community through social and pastoral action.[61] I will con-

---

[59] Note the very rough treatment accorded to several Chilean bishops at the Santiago airport of Pudahuel on their return from the Riobamba conference in Ecuador. Like the other foreign bishops involved, they had been expelled from Ecuador and were met at the Santiago airport by a shoving crowd largely organized by, and composed of, Chilean secret service agents. On this incident see Roncagliolo and Reyes Matta, *Iglesia, prensa, y militares*, pp. 131-52, and Sanders and Smith, *The Chilean Church*.

[60] Chilean Episcopal Conference, "Our Life As A Nation," reproduced in LADOC 7:6 (July-Aug., 1977), pp. 8-9.

[61] They hope to maintain the unity of the Catholic community around the Church's central ecclesiastical institutions. Hence they reject those who argue, like Camilo Torres or many Liberation Theology writers, that the Church's unity requires the construction of a new social order.

sider the dynamics of this central position in greater detail in the concluding chapter, but one point warrants further attention here. As Brian Smith has shown, the organizational flexibility of the Church has been one of its greatest assets.[62] While it cannot change authoritarian regimes on its own, nevertheless the Church has managed to organize and finance institutions to help the victims of oppression while keeping alive the hope for a different kind of future. In many cases, Church organizations (particularly at the local level) have in effect become surrogates for the social and political interchange no longer permitted in society at large. This potential for serving as an institutional shield, a shelter for activities prohibited by the government, makes the hierarchy's deep concern for preserving the institutional unity of the Church all the more understandable. The full impact of these developments on the life of the Church is still unclear, but it seems inevitable that this growing, direct involvement with the poor and weak, against the power of the State, will find the Church itself becoming a victim of the State.

FACING THE FUTURE: ISSUES AND PROBLEMS

Throughout the course of events reviewed in this chapter, the ecclesiastical hierarchy has generally resisted attempts to push it along explicitly political tracks.[63] In this regard, it is important to bear in mind that both the Christians for Socialism, on the left, and the TFP-military position, on the right, emphasize political action as legitimate and necessary for the Church. Each wants to harness the moral authority of Catholicism to its own image of the good social and political order. Each defends a different image of the Church, and calls it to combat in a different cause. The bishops, in the middle, resist "politics" as such, but politics clearly lies at the core of all these disputes.

In Latin America today, then, religion is a problem for politics, and politics no less a problem for religion. Institutions in each sphere grope for new understandings of themselves and of their relation to the others. To discern the future relation of religion

[62] Brian Smith, "Churches and Human Rights."

[63] The bureaucratic politics of this process are yet to be studied in full. One major point here has been the struggle to control and orient CELAM. See Berryman, "What Happened at Puebla," and the sources he cites.

and politics in Latin America, and to clarify the subsequent argument of this book, it will be useful to distinguish here between issues and problems. By "issues" I mean the points of explicit public controversy which emerge and hold public attention from time to time. By "problems," on the other hand, I refer to the more fundamental dilemmas and oppositions from which the issues themselves arise. Issues are effects, manifestations; problems are causes—superstructure and base, if you will.

Many issues currently exercise Latin American Catholics and from time to time engage the attention of the bishops. Some, like birth control, are perhaps notable by their absence from this discussion. Birth control is surely a visible issue, but it is marginal to the concerns of this book because as an issue it poses no basic redefinition of the relation between religion and "the world," no evolution in the terms and meaning of conflict. The issues which I believe are now of central importance (and likely to remain so in the future) include social conflict and division; force and violence; relations with Marxism and with the "national security" state; and the organization and containment of conflict between "left" and "right" within the Church.

In looking at these and other issues, it is important to go beyond the description of particular incidents to get at the more general problems from which they arise. Two fundamental problems are at work which, taken together, will generate an unending series of disputes, confrontations, and controversies, each adapted to the particular historical circumstances in which events are played out. The master problem, in my view, is the perception of the religious institution itself, and of the nature of religious commitments, held by Catholic leaders and activists. This is a "master" problem; for, as subsequent chapters will show, the self-images of religious leaders determine the direction, intensity, and style of action that members undertake. It is the stuff of which commitments and martyrs are made.

The second, lesser problem is the impact on the Church of changes in social and political context—the challenges and opportunities available in surrounding society. The way Church leaders see social problems, and the typical way in which they are linked to society (e.g., through ties of organization, subsidies, schools, and the like), play a major role in shaping action. But while social context is important, I place this aspect of the problem in a lesser position because I believe that, for religious people, political responses are mediated through a set of self-images and role definitions which shape what they think they ought to do, as members of a transcendent Church, regardless of what the temporal challenges or problems are seen to be. Actions do not always (or even very often) flow directly from perceptions; and, as subsequent chapters will show, many bishops draw a sharp distinction between the analysis of social problems and the role they, as Church leaders, ought to take.

Clearly the problem of religion and politics (and of politics and religion as well) is complex and multifaceted. In analysis it is difficult to avoid reductionism of some kind; but I believe that a combination of analytical perspectives bringing concepts of religion and politics directly together, and grounding their relationship firmly in national history and institutional traditions, offers the most promising strategy for understanding the question as a whole. The next chapter continues with a closer look at Venezuela and Colombia.

3

Settings for Change: Venezuela and Colombia

THE Roman Catholic Church is both universal and particular. Spread over the entire world, it maintains considerable unity in doctrine and practices while nonetheless adapting to the contours of each particular society. The "secret" of this organizational success lies in a combination of strong institutional loyalties founded on the centrality of Rome with an extreme de facto decentralization. This high level of heterogeneity and decentralization raises the question of how change in the Church is related to social context: Is change primarily a process of internal transformation, or is it better understood in terms of a response to developments in society at large? If change arises from a combination of internal and social factors, what is the nature of the mix? And finally, exactly what is meant by the phrase "society at large"? Is the relevant "society" found at the level of the neighborhood, the parish, the diocese, or the region, or rather on the larger stage provided by the nation-state?

The answers to these questions are by no means cut and dried; much depends on the goals of the inquiry. Traditionally, the central administrative and sacramental unit of the Catholic Church has been the diocese—each governed independently by a bishop subject only to the relatively loose authority of the pope. Each bishop is technically a successor to the Apostles, and his authority is described in Church documents as "ordinary," that is, of independent validity and not delegated by some higher power. Historically, the theological and juridical independence of the diocese was reinforced by formidable barriers of topography and transportation in Latin America, which made action on a national scale impossible.

Thus, until recently, it is fair to say that the nation did not exist in the organizational schemes of the Church. But as we have seen, in recent years the nation-state has become a focal level for Church life. In many countries, bishops now meet regularly in national conferences, serve together on national commissions, and increasingly conceive of Church actions on a national scale. In addition, national organizations of laymen and "independent" Catholic groups of many kinds have enhanced organizational growth on the national level.

This development of national structures and orientations within the Church reflects the growing significance of the "nation" in other fields as well: transportation has been extended and integrated; communication systems of all kinds bridge hitherto massive gaps between regions; comprehensive programs of education, public health, and social assistance have been created; and finally, the structures of national government have expanded dramatically in recent decades. In all these ways, the nation has become increasingly important.

For working purposes, then, much of the argument of this book is pitched at the national level. It is important to note that more is involved at this level than the reordering of ecclesiastical institutions to permit greater efficiency, for members and leaders of the Church are also members and leaders of the nation. They share in national history, deal with all kinds of national institutions every day, and carry with them the memory of those traditions, issues, and conflicts which have shaped national experience. As we shall see, these experiences and memories condition subsequent perception and action in powerful and often striking ways.

This chapter explores the national setting of change in the Church through a general consideration of the evolution of Venezuela and Colombia as modern nations. A brief sketch of national developments is followed by an exposition of the historical and structural evolution of the Church in each country, with particular attention to the evolving public stance of the bishops as reflected in pastoral letters and other documents issued over the last several decades.

Venezuela and Colombia: A Brief Historical Sketch

A comprehensive history of these two nations is beyond the scope and purpose of this book. Such histories exist in abundance, and it is not necessary to repeat their arguments here.[1] Rather, my goal in this section is to isolate a few persistent themes of national history and style.

The differences so visible today between Venezuela and Colombia have, in many ways, grown sharper and more pronounced with the passage of time. Colombia was a much more important economic, political, and ecclesiastical center in the colonial era than was Venezuela, and it managed to retain its more powerful and well-rooted institutions into and through the nineteenth century. Conservative victory in the civil wars of the nineteenth century ensured that the power of such institutions—most notably a strong central state, a unified economic and social elite, and a powerful Church—would be carried over into the twentieth century, bringing as well the styles of action and the axes of conflict characteristic of earlier times. The heavy weight of well-established practices, procedures, and traditions is everywhere apparent in Colombia.

This slower pace of change has both structural and symbolic sides. In structural terms one finds, for example, relatively slow economic change; the Colombian economy remains basically tied to agriculture. Moreover, the nation, which has long had a larger population than Venezuela, urbanized much more slowly. The stability of the population contributed mightily to the persistence of traditional social ties and loyalties, and helps explain the tenacious survival of the old party and interest-group structure. Thus the traditional political parties in Colombia, Liberal and Conservative, retain the structural forms of nineteenth-century politics: they are still rather loosely organized electoral alliances, run at the top by competing elite lineages and drawing support in different regions on a basis of enduring local and seigneurial loyalties.[2] In

[1] The relevant literature is vast, and I cite only a selection here. On recent Colombian social and political history, two useful works remain Dix, *Colombia*, and Fals-Borda, *Subversion and Social Change in Colombia*. See also Payne, *Patterns of Conflict in Colombia*. For Venezuela see Levine, *Conflict*; Martz, *Acción Democrática*; and, on the all-important question of petroleum, Tugwell, *The Politics of Oil in Venezuela*.

[2] Useful reviews of nineteenth-century thought in Colombia include Molina, *Las ideas liberales en Colombia—1849-1914*, and Jaramillo Uribe, *El pensamiento colombiano en el siglo XIX*. On urbanization see Camacho de Pinto, *Colombia*, and Cardona, *Las migraciones internas*. Changes in

symbolic terms, the survival of traditional ideologies and legitimations of power and privilege is particularly notable in the political party system and in the continued prominent role of the Catholic Church.

The Venezuelan pattern is extremely different. Its civil wars of the nineteenth century lasted longer, and destroyed the unity of the traditional social and economic elite. Moreover, the seemingly endless series of conflicts were won at each turn by Liberals, who used their victories to strip the Church of what little of its property, social functions, and influence had survived from the general poverty of colonial life. Thus, in contrast to Colombia, from the late nineteenth century Venezuela was marked by an aggressive secularism and official indifference to religion.

Despite these political and religious differences, however, the social histories of the two nations were quite similar until just after World War I. Both had agricultural economies, and few cities of note. Education was limited, illiteracy widespread, debt peonage common, and mass participation in national affairs practically unknown. But just after 1920 Venezuela took a turn toward becoming a fundamentally different *kind* of society from Colombia. I refer to the impact of oil.

Elsewhere I have suggested that the discovery and large-scale exploitation of petroleum had at least three major effects on Venezuelan society and politics: on the role of the national state and the evolution of political groups and patterns of action; on the structure of the economy; and on the distribution of the population. A review of these effects highlights the dimensions of the transformations in Venezuela stemming from oil.[3]

Revenues from oil strengthened the national state enormously. Oil money paid for an effective national bureaucracy, an infrastructure of transportation to link the nation together, and a permanent standing army which consolidated the power of national institutions. Regional militarism was wiped out, and the expanding strength of the central state further reinforced earlier trends toward

---

family structure are reviewed in Pineda, *Estructura, función, y cambio de la familia en Colombia*. A very useful study of the Colombian party system remains Garces, "La continuidad del sistema a través del cambio."

[3] Cf. Levine, *Conflict*, especially chapters 2 and 3, and Tugwell, *Politics of Oil*.

official control of what little was accomplished in the way of social welfare, education, health, and the like. The Church and other private groups were relegated to a minor role.

The impact of petroleum on the structure of the economy and on emerging demographic patterns is closely related. The oil boom led to a complete restructuring of Venezuela's economy around petroleum. In a largely agricultural nation, agricultural exports actually declined after 1920, in both relative and absolute terms. Moreover, an accompanying depression in agriculture led to a wave of foreclosures and a notable concentration of rural landholdings. These developments, together with the attractiveness of the oil boom, stimulated such an immense migratory process all across the nation that a country almost two-thirds rural in the census of 1936 counted itself as almost 80% urban only thirty-five years later. Table 3.1 compares the tremendous pace of urbanization in Venezuela to that in Colombia.

In Venezuela, the combination of a strong state, an economy undergoing an externally stimulated boom, and massive internal migration had notable long-term consequences for social and political structures. The strong state eliminated the political groups and loyalties of the nineteenth century; and rapid social, economic, and demographic changes transformed the lives of many Venezuelans, putting them on the move. Thus, a mobile, "available" mass was created, which later formed the basis for the popular, mass-based political parties which have dominated political life in Venezuela since the 1940s.[4] Thus, by 1935, when the aged dictator Juan Vicente Gómez died, Venezuela was ready for profound change; the old order was gone, and the new was yet to be created. As Ramón J. Velásquez puts it, "In 1935, younger generations doubted that inter-party struggle had ever existed in Venezuela in any period of its history. . . . The regime founded by Cipriano Castro in 1899 and consolidated by Juan Vicente Gómez in his 27 years of absolute power had cut down the centuries-old trees of the political parties and not even the memory of that political scene remained. Venezuela was like a plowed field, awaiting the seed."[5]

In all these dimensions, then, change was swifter, more sudden, and much more widespread and complete in Venezuela. Social

[4] Levine, *Conflict*, chaps. 2 and 3.
[5] Valásquez, *La caída del liberalismo amarillo*, pp. xix-xx.

TABLE 3.1
POPULATION AND URBANIZATION IN VENEZUELA AND COLOMBIA

	Venezuela	Colombia
Population (in thousands)		
1920	2,408	6,089
1950	4,902	11,334
1960	7,349	15,397
1970	10,399	21,156
Population Classified as Urban (%)		
1936	35.0	—
1938	—	29.1
1941	39.0	—
1950	49.8	—
1951	—	36.3
1961	67.5	—
1964	—	52.4
1971	78.4	—
Population Living in Cities of over 20,000 (%)		
1936	17.0	—
1938	—	13.2
1941	18.7	—
1950	32.7	—
1951	—	23.0
1961	47.3	—
1964	—	36.6

SOURCE: Adapted from data in Ruddle and Hamour, eds., *Statistical Abstract of Latin America*; República de Venezuela, *X censo de población y vivienda*, vol. 1; and República de Colombia, Departamento Administrativo Nacional de Estadística, *XIII censo nacional de población resúmen general (15 de julio de 1964)*.

and political mobilization, as expressed primarily in mass-based popular political parties, has been much more thorough. The whole structure and tone of national life are different: the central social, economic, cultural, and political institutions of Venezuela are all relatively new. In Colombia, on the other hand, the structures and forms of action of the past continue to dominate national life. These broad differences in social and political evolution are important to the present analysis, for they make different kinds of problems central in each case. In Colombia, the basic problem for elites has been to *preserve* existing structures and retain old loyalties. In Venezuela, the problem has been to *create* new institutions, to reach and engage the loyalties of a mobile population in new and fast-changing circumstances.[6]

To round out this sketch of the social and political evolution of Venezuela and Colombia, one further theme warrants separate attention here—the role of violence. The preceding chapter showed that violence is a central issue for the Latin American Church; in both Venezuela and Colombia modern political life has also been marked by several kinds of violence. Consideration of the nature of violence in the two countries throws considerable light on the meaning of politics and its implications for the Church in each.

Violence and the Church

In Colombia, political violence has been endemic since the civil wars of the nineteenth and early twentieth centuries. Massive violence broke out again in 1930 and in 1946, on the transfer of national power from one party to another. In each case, violence was sharp and widespread as the new "ins" pushed their enemies out of public jobs and power. This trail of bloody incidents, however, was but a tame prelude for what Colombians refer to simply as The Violence (*La Violencia*)—a massive and savage explosion of killing and civil warfare which claimed hundreds of thousands of lives in the decade after 1948.[7] The Violence is significant for our purposes in its impact on the political parties and on other social institutions, most notably the Church.

In directly political terms, The Violence almost destroyed the old system. Interparty and intergroup strife became so intense that at several points mutual extermination seemed likely. Violence was initially touched off by the assassination, in 1948, of Jorge Eliécer Gaitán, a popular Liberal leader. It quickly expanded into an orgy of anti-Conservative, anticlerical, and antigovernment acts. The initial wave of incidents was followed by gradually intensifying Liberal-Conservative conflict, in which Conservatives (then in

---

[6] Thus in Venezuela many institutions—political, social, economic, and cultural—are relatively new. For a fuller discussion of this point see Levine, *Conflict*, chaps. 2 and 3.

[7] On The Violence see Wienert, "Violence in Pre-Modern Societies"; Guzmán Campos, *La violencia en Colombia*; and Levine and Wilde, "Church, 'Politics,' and Violence."

control of national government) used the police, army, and informal vigilante groups while Liberals responded in kind. Traditional political structures broke down completely.

The Liberals boycotted the next elections, which were "won" by Laureano Gómez, leader of the most reactionary and traditionally Catholic wing of the Conservative party. Violence intensified under Gómez, who set out to "purify" the nation. He was finally removed from office in 1953 by a military coup, and violence then died down briefly, only to surge again in the late 1950s, transforming itself over the next decades into something more akin to the guerrilla movements in other Latin American nations.

The political solution to The Violence in Colombia took form in an explicit pact between Liberals and Conservatives, written into the national Constitution, and known as the National Front. Beginning in 1958, the National Front sought to end interparty violence by removing the fear of mutual extermination. The Constitution was amended to guarantee regular alternation in power (and proportional sharing of legislative and bureaucratic positions at all levels) between Liberals and Conservatives *regardless of the outcome of elections.* In this way, elites in both parties joined forces to preserve the system by eliminating the very violence which had threatened to sweep them all away. This comfortable agreement for sharing power is the kind of political system which greeted Camilo Torres on his return from Louvain in 1958.

Massive violence also had a powerful impact on Colombian social structure. The Violence spurred extensive migration to the cities, as individuals and sometimes whole communities fled rural terror. These demographic shifts helped undermine the bases of many traditional institutions, including the old political parties, as previous networks of loyalty and identification lost their compelling force in new urban settings.

The Violence also had a major impact on the Church. From 1887 to 1930 the Church prospered under Conservative rule and regularly supported that party's candidates and positions. This comfortable situation was disrupted by the Liberal governments that held power from 1930 to 1946. Old conflicts over ecclesiastical privileges were reopened, and a visible threat was posed to the status and image of the Church as a central institution of national life. Thus, when The Violence, with its anticlerical overtones, erupted on a large scale after 1948, the most immediate visible response within the Church was to identify the cause of religion wholly with the Conservative party and to condemn the Liberals as atheists and communists.

Those within the Church who espoused this view saw The Violence as a Liberal strategy of revolution aimed, among other things, at destroying the Church. Prelates thus intervened directly and forcefully in electioneering, with an apocalyptic sense of what was at stake. An extreme but not wholly unrepresentative example is the Lenten message of Msgr. Miguel Angel Builes, bishop of Santa Rosa de Osos, delivered on the eve of the 1949 elections. He called all Catholics to a struggle "against all the powers of Hell aligned to destroy" the Church.

> In the manner of generals of armies that give speeches to enlighten and fire their soldiers with passion, I who by the will of God am now before a portion of the soldiers of the Church militant, direct my call to you for the next electoral battle, which is the battle for the Church in our country. . . . The ideal of Catholics is to sustain on high the ensign of the Cross that fluttered at Calvary, on the top of our temples and over the tombs of our dead. Our ideal is to defend Christ and his sacrosanct rights."[8]

Bishops such as Msgr. Builes thus condoned and even encouraged the direct partisan involvement of parish priests during the worst years of The Violence: they mobilized their flocks against the Liberals, swore out "safe conduct" passes for certified Conservatives, handed out Conservative party ballots in parish offices, and the like.[9]

Other forces within the Church in the late 1940s (initially a distinct minority) opposed taking sides in the political battle. They were led by the archbishop of Bogotá, Msgr. Ismael Perdomo, and included Msgr. Luis Concha Córdoba, later to become archbishop of Bogotá under the National Front. Msgr. Perdomo forbade clerical support of one party over another, or even mention of party in sermons. "The immense majority of Conservatives and Liberals," he wrote in his pastoral of April 1949, "defends

---

[8] Cited in Nieto Rojas, *La batalla contra el comunismo en Colombia*, p. 285.

[9] A Colombian novel which gives the full flavor of this period in rural towns is Caballero Calderon, *El Cristo de espaldas*.

the same creed, is educated under identical moral norms, and feels equal veneration for the spiritual jurisdiction of the Catholic religion."[10] He rebuked militant partisans, pointing out that "while we boast of our so-called 'Christian civilization,' we profess and at the same time practice hatred, and are very far from practicing the fundamental Christian doctrine: love."[11]

Such a division over the role of the Church in partisan politics has a long history in Colombia. In times of crisis, violence, and civil war, many in the Church have been ready and willing to cast their lot with the Conservative party. This tradition has been matched by one opposing partisan commitment. Led by the archbishops of Bogotá, this group of prelates strove to avoid identifying the interests of the Church with those of any particular secular group. In their view, such identification would destroy the unity of the Church, because priests and bishops might see their primary commitments as lying with their secular allies, rather than with the Church per se. Moreover, the Church held a special role as "the religion of the nation" (in the words of the Constitution). Given the strength of political identifications in Colombia, overt partisanship by the bishops would thus necessarily alienate the Church from half the national population.

The breakdown of the old political system after 1948, the imposition of military rule in 1953, and above all the devastation of The Violence itself helped resolve this debate in favor of the less interventionist position. A clear consensus developed in the hierarchy that the Church ought to stay out of "politics," defined as partisan political activity. The bishops also came to believe that The Violence was not the product of one party alone, but rather the result of "hereditary hatreds" between groups in the nation, hatreds which Church involvement could only reinforce. If there was to be peace in Colombia, the two main parties had to coexist, and the Church thus enthusiastically blessed the formation of the National Front. Since the Liberals agreed at the same time to lay the "religious question" to rest, the Church found a rationale for final withdrawal from "politics." From frequent partisanship, the ecclesiastical institution thus moved to a neutral position between the groups, and active support for the National Front.

The Violence also had other, more subtle effects on the political

[10] Cited in Martz, *Colombia*, pp. 83-84.
[11] Cited in Zapata Isaza, *¿Patricios o asesinos?* p. 263.

views of the bishops. Many remember the savagery of those years with profound horror and have come implicitly to identify *any* kind of political involvement with renewed violence on a large scale. The implications of this point will be developed further in chapter 6, below. For the moment it is sufficient to realize the link between The Violence, a general rejection of "politics," and concentration by the bishops on the rejuvenation of Church organizations and structures.

The Violence showed the bishops that Colombians were not, as the prelates had complacently assumed for so long, *un pueblo culto y cristiano* (a civilized and Christian people). Taking a fresh look at its own society, the hierarchy now saw it as mission territory. Thus, having renounced the strategy of partisan political action, the Church turned instead to strengthening its own institutions. New dioceses and parishes were created on a large scale, particularly in the growing urban areas, in order to make more effective use of clerical personnel. On the national level, new bureaucracies were created to staff the Bishops' Conference, and new centers were established to study both the Church and society at large. Social and pastoral outreach were broadened through a variety of initiatives (which will be examined more closely in subsequent chapters on organizational change). In building a more effective presence in Colombian society, the Church came to feel more self-reliant, less linked to particular secular interests, and less dependent upon them.

Venezuelan politics in the modern period are not usually thought of in terms of violence, but violence is nonetheless a persistent theme in national life; it has had a major impact on groups, institutions, and patterns of behavior. Indeed, until 1958 Venezuela was the Latin American country of military coups and repressive governments par excellence. Authoritarian regimes built on oil revenues ruled from 1903 to 1935, under the leadership of Juan Vicente Gómez, and then, with minor modifications, under his heirs until 1945. A brief three-year experiment in democracy then intervened. It was brought to a close by the military coup of 1948, which ushered in a decade of savage and bloody repression.

Of course, violence in Venezuela has never been limited to military coups and the acts of security forces alone. Political groups on all sides have regularly employed individual terrorism, organized violence, and guerrilla warfare in pursuit of their goals. In any case, violence is never limited to overt acts. The very emergence of popular mass-based political movements, which ultimately transformed Venezuelan society and politics, carried with it the implicit *threat* of violence, the threat to use force, if necessary, against established social groups. Many years and much delicate political maneuvering were required before sectors in the Church, the military, foreign business concerns, and agricultural elites accepted the legitimacy of the policies, programs, and power of reforming groups like the Democratic Action party (Acción Democrática), the dominant political party.[12]

After the restoration of democracy in 1958, Venezuelan political leaders generally agreed that the democratic experiment of 1945 to 1948 had failed because interparty conflict had been so bitter and extreme that many groups felt threatened, and hence were willing to support military intervention. To avoid a repetition of such situations, the leaders of most major parties made conscious decisions, after 1958, to limit and control the scope and intensity of partisan conflict. This determination to contain conflict and its potential for violence was matched by a widespread revulsion against the excesses of military rule, so visible in the bloody and corrupt regime of General Marcos Pérez Jiménez, which held power from 1948 to 1958. The particularly unsavory character of this regime gave the new democratic political arrangements a considerable breathing space after 1958, with enough time and good will to give the institutions a chance to work.

There are parallels in the Venezuelan and Colombian Churches' reaction to violence. I noted earlier that The Violence had a deep impact on the Colombian Church, spurring it to internal renewal and withdrawal from partisan politics. Once a fervent supporter of the Conservative party, the Church transformed itself into a partisan of the system as a whole, a position most bishops clearly saw as nonpolitical. The Venezuelan pattern is similar, though less extreme. Among the traditional groups threatened by the rise of mass politics and social reform in the Venezuela of the 1940s, the Catholic Church stands out for the depth and bitterness of its

[12] On this process see (among others) Levine, *Conflict*, and Powell, *Political Mobilization of the Venezuelan Peasant*. The Democratic Action party's relations with the military are discussed in Lieuwin, *Generals vs. Presidents*, pp. 86-91; Alexander, *The Venezuelan Democratic Revolution*, pp. 105-17; and Taylor, *The Venezuelan Golpe de Estado of 1958*, pp. 68-71.

alienation. The Church rejected the very principles of democracy and majority rule, which had brought the Democratic Action party to power, because it saw those policies and programs as the opening wedge of a general attempt to destroy Catholic life in the nation. Self-defense was thus the watchword of Church leaders.[13]

For these reasons, many Church leaders joined other forces greeting the military coup of 1948 as a salvation from persecution.[14] But the regime so widely greeted in 1948 eventually turned sour. By the mid-1950s, repression began to touch the Church itself; even priests were arrested and jailed for "subversive activities." Moreover, by this time the Church in Venezuela (like its Colombian counterpart) was coming under the influence of postwar expressions of Catholic social doctrine; so the concerns of the hierarchy gradually began moving away from an exclusive stress on self-defense and anticommunism, and toward a greater concern with social justice.

These developments pushed Church leaders to denounce the dictatorship. The first major step came in a pastoral letter from the archbishop of Caracas in May 1957, in which he attacked the regime for its lack of concern for social justice and human welfare. This public stance marked the beginning of a change in the Church's attitude to politics in general. The traditional reliance on allies among key economic, social, and military elites was gradually replaced by a greater sympathy for democracy, and for the values of pluralism and equality it represents.[15]

Violence again shifted focus and direction in Venezuela with the emergence of a strong Marxist guerrilla movement in the 1960s.[16] The Church responded with a shift toward the center of the political spectrum. Alienated now from the traditional violence of the

[13] Cf. Levine, *Conflict*, chap. 4, and Levine, "Democracy and the Church in Venezuela."

[14] Cf. Levine, "Democracy and the Church," and Colmenares Díaz, *La espada y el incensario*.

[15] This stimulus to opposition to the dictatorship of Pérez Jiménez was a major factor in smoothing the way to better relations between the Church and Acción Democrática. On the Church's side, the new appreciation of democracy and the search for new social bases to which it led are explored in detail in Levine, *Conflict*, chap. 5.

[16] For a moving record of personal experiences in the guerrilla movement see Zago, *Aquí no ha pasado nada*. Gott, *Guerrillas in Latin America*, offers a useful general account.

right (as embodied in the military), and fearful of revolutionary violence from the left, the Church moved firmly away from partisan political involvement of any kind, toward "neutrality" and support of the democratic system as a whole.[17] Moreover, as in Colombia, the Church in Venezuela devoted considerable energies after 1958 to building an effective net of vigorous Church-related organizations in many fields, institutions capable of presenting a Catholic "presence" in areas hitherto left to secular forces.[18]

Thus in both countries violence moved the Church to withdraw from partisan politics while accommodating itself to the political system as a whole. In Colombia, as we have seen, this position was challenged by Camilo Torres, who sought to replace such "neutrality" with vigorous promotion of mass political action in the context of a Catholic faith redefined to make support of revolution an integral expression of Christian charity. In Venezuela, however, challenges of this type were delayed and muted. They took longer to emerge because the Church was not as strong, articulate, or influential as in Colombia, and hence was less likely to throw up a Venezuelan Camilo Torres. Further, they were muted because Venezuelan politics were *already* based on open, mass participation. Whereas in Colombia Torres posed a challenge both to traditional politics and to the position of the Church, in Venezuela a full-scale challenge from the revolutionary left had already been defeated. Thus, as we shall see, later leftist initiatives by Venezuelan Catholics did not take an explicitly political form at all, and no guerrilla priests emerged to follow the path laid out by Camilo Torres. Instead, an emphasis on community action and on politics in the broad sense of a concern with power, distribution, and human welfare became prominent among radical clergy as the nation entered the 1970s.

The discussion to this point has provided a general portrait of Venezuela and Colombia, with particular attention to politics,

---

[17] This move was deliberately stimulated by the Democratic Action party, which represented itself to Church, business, and military elites as the only alternative to Marxist revolution. Political leaders argued that right-wing military rule would only magnify the influence of the extreme left over the underground opposition and that revolutionary victory would clearly destroy all established institutions. In this way the party, once seen as a radical and fiercely anticlerical, came to be perceived as a bulwark of stability.

[18] Levine, *Conflict*, chap. 5, and Levine, "Democracy and the Church."

violence, and the Church's response to them. But what of the Venezuelan and Colombian Churches themselves, as institutions? In societies which are so different, what paths have they followed to the present day? The next section explores this question in detail.

The Church in Venezuela and Colombia: General Patterns

The Colombian Church has always been more powerful than its Venezuelan counterpart, which remains poor and weak. As we have seen, the Church in Colombia carried over a dense network of organizations and a great tradition of leadership from colonial times, whereas the postcolonial Church in Venezuela (weak to begin with) was devastated; for all practical purposes it ceased to function in many regions. In drawing a more complete and formal comparison of the two Churches, I will first examine their legal status, structure, and resources, and then take a look at the evolving public stance of Church leaders, with particular reference to their images of the Church and of national society as a whole.

The legal status of the two Churches is a useful indicator of their place in the institutional order, of the role others expect them to play in social and political affairs, and of their overall impact in national life. Here again, the Colombian Church stands out as unusually favored. Until 1973, a Concordat (originally signed in 1887) defined the Church's legal status and role. This agreement is a model of the traditional ideal of Christendom—complete Church-State integration. The Church is described as an "essential element of the social order" and is given a major role in many aspects of social life. For example, education at all levels was to be maintained "in conformity with the dogma of the Catholic religion" (art. 12), and religious instruction was obligatory. The Church also received the predominant role in registering births, with parish records having preference over civil records. In addition, the management of death was placed in Church hands, as cemeteries were turned over to the ecclesiastical authorities.

Marriage, another major step in the life cycle, was also placed firmly under Church control. Civil divorce did not exist, and civil marriage for baptized Catholics was made contingent on a public declaration of abandonment of the faith. These statements were to be made before a judge, posted publicly, and communicated to the local bishop. It is difficult to imagine a more effective mechanism of ostracism, or a more telling example of the fusion of civil and religious powers than these arrangements.[19] Finally, the Church wields broad civil powers in the more than 60% of Colombia's area designated as "mission territories." There, an agreement made in 1953 gave the missionary orders extensive control over education as well as broad civil authority.[20]

The Concordat and additional accords clearly left many areas of Colombian life to Church control and management. Although the agreement was renegotiated in 1973, the only changes immediately visible were in the *possibility* of civil divorce and in the elimination of publc apostasy as a prerequisite for the civil marriage of baptized Catholics. In some instances, the power of the Church actually increased. For example, its missionary role was extended, with provision made for development of a "special canonical regime" for mission territories *and* "marginal zones" (largely urban slum areas).[21]

This predominant role is unimaginable in Venezuela. At each stage of life in which the Colombian Church plays a major role (registry, education, marriage, and death), secular, governmental control is the rule in Venezuela. The Church is strictly a junior partner. Indeed, until 1964 state control was remarkably extensive. Under the Law of Ecclesiastical Patronage of 1824, the Church had no legal personality; it could hold no property and enter no contracts. Bishops were in theory elected by the Congress, and local prefects were charged with preventing "innovation" in ecclesiastical matters. A modus vivendi signed in 1964 replaced this old statute and freed the Church of many onerous aspects of state control, while providing some concrete benefits such as a legal personality and relaxed conditions for the immigration of clergy. But the conditions of the agreement are modest, and the Church's

[19] These arrangements were known as the "Ley Concha" (the Concha Law), after the man who negotiated them with the Vatican for Colombia. Jaramillo Salazar, *Epítome de la Ley Concha*, provides a full account.

[20] Most of this territory is sparsely populated, largely by tribal Indians. In recent years the missions have come under sharp attack. A well-known critique is Bonilla, *Servants of God or Masters of Men*.

[21] The new concordat was extensively discussed in the Colombian press. My account draws heavily on *El Tiempo* (Bogotá) in July 1973 and on articles in ANALI-CIAS, a Jesuit monthly, in August and September 1973.

role in Venezuela remains sharply limited, especially when compared to its role in Colombia.[22]

Legal status is also an indirect indicator of the resources available to each Church, and a closer look at resources bears out the striking contrasts already noted. Consider, for example, administrative structure. Although both Churches have expanded notably since 1900, the pace of growth has been much higher in Colombia, where many more new dioceses have been created. A greater number of dioceses reflects a more articulated organization, one more attuned to local and national needs. The greatest gap in resources, however, comes in clergy. Throughout the modern period, Colombia has had many more priests than Venezuela. Moreover, in Venezuela over three-fourths of the priests have been foreign, while in Colombia the vast majority have been native. In any given year, up to ten times as many priests are ordained in Colombia as in Venezuela. Since 1950 the lowest number of priests ordained in Venezuela was 4 (in 1957), and the high point was reached with only 20 ordinations, in 1963. The corresponding figures for Colombia, in contrast, are a low of 49 in 1950 and a high of 146 in 1966. Table 3.2 shows the overall contrast.

TABLE 3.2
ORDINATION OF PRIESTS IN VENEZUELA AND COLOMBIA

	Venezuela	*Colombia*
1950	11	49
1955	7	61
1960	12	90
1965	15	135
1969	13	92
Totals (1949-69)	267	1,881

SOURCE: CELAM, *Seminarios*, pp. 83, 100.

Colombia's advantage in dioceses and clergy is partly attributable to its greater size; but, even in comparing ratios of clergy to population, the Church in Colombia appears much stronger. Each

[22] A comprehensive account of the *modus vivendi* is Rodríguez Iturbe, *Iglesia y estado en Venezuela, 1824-1964*. See also Kennedy, "The Legal Status of the Church in Latin America," for a useful comparative overview.

Colombian priest serves considerably fewer people than his Venezuelan counterpart, and the ratio of diocesan priests to population is particularly favorable in Colombia. Diocesan priests (i.e., those under the direct authority of the local bishop rather than members of religious orders) staff most parishes. Given the dense network of Church schools in Colombia (largely staffed by religious orders), one might have expected a drop in the ratio of diocesan priests to total population, with the drain of clerical personnel to the schools. But the overall Colombian advantage is maintained (see table 3.3).

TABLE 3.3
SELECTED DATA ON THE CHURCH IN VENEZUELA AND COLOMBIA

Year	Number of Dioceses[a]	Diocesan Priests	Persons per Diocesan Priest	Total Priests	Total Persons per Priest
Venezuela					
1944	—	357	12,000	630	6,900
1950	14	399	13,300	786	6,900
1960	16	536	12,400	1,218	5,500
1970	24	836	12,004	1,976	5,079
Colombia					
1945	—	1,549	6,224	2,557	3,970
1950	33	1,750	6,465	3,003	3,774
1960	48	2,339	6,146	4,094	3,765
1970	56	2,980	7,114	4,864	4,358

SOURCES: Venezuelan data on number of dioceses from CISOR, *Iglesia y sociedad*, p. 24; other data for 1944, 1950, and 1960 from Alonso et al., *La iglesia en Venezuela y Ecuador*, p. 155; and for 1970 from CISOR, *Iglesia y sociedad*, p. 24. Colombian data on number of dioceses from Zuluaga, *Estructuras eclesiasticas de Colombia*, p. 10; other data from pp. 14, 35.

[a] In 1900 there were 6 dioceses in Venezuela; 7 in Colombia.

These data reveal the greater social presence of the Church in Colombia, as more dioceses, parishes, and clergy make for more points of contact with the people. In addition, the Colombian Church is much more highly organized at the national level. The National Bishops' Conference of Colombia has been meeting regularly since 1903, and by 1972 the conference had developed a large permanent, professional secretariat, operating out of its own new six-story building in Bogotá. Moreover, beginning in the 1940s the Church hierarchy sponsored the creation of an extensive network of Catholic Action groups, trade unions, adult education programs, and community organization projects. In Venezuela there is little of this. Only in 1972 was an effective, permanent secretariat of the Venezuelan Bishops' Conference (founded explicitly on the Colombian model) even established. Furthermore, as we shall see in chapter 7, the attempts by the Venezuelan hierarchy to stimulate Catholic Action organizations have been limited by lack of resources and public apathy. On the whole, Catholic groups in Venezuela are but a faint echo of their Colombian counterparts.

Despite these sharp differences, in each nation it is possible to see a developing attempt, within the Church, to fashion tools for dealing effectively with the modern world. The tools, of course, differ according to the circumstances of each case, and according to the way each Church's leaders have articulated the problems and necessities they face. I have suggested some of the relevant dimensions here, and subsequent chapters will provide greater detail. To complete this initial portrait, I must now consider the evolving public position of Church elites in each nation, as they have responded to change both in their own institutions and in society as a whole.

THE PUBLIC CONCERNS OF THE BISHOPS

Most of the subsequent analysis of this book is based on interviews—conversations with bishops, priests, leaders and members of lay organizations, and informed observers. These data are enormously rich and varied, and provide unique insights into the mentality and operating style of Catholic elites. But at the very least, such information must be set in the context of the "official," public positions the bishops take.[23] After all, the bishops are the most visible leaders of a highly salient national institution.

[23] As we shall see, public and private views often diverge, not from any calculated insincerity on the part of the bishops, but rather because the process of drafting Church documents is one of bargaining and compromise. As public statements are put together, individual bishops often sacrifice their personal positions in order to ensure a unified public stance for the Church as a whole.

Political and social leaders, as well as the average believer, take their statements as the "position of the Church" and act accordingly.

For these reasons, a clear understanding of the evolution of the hierarchy's public statements is central to any complete analysis. Moreover, with the growing institutionalization of each national hierarchy as an effective working unit, such pronouncements are more common and more completely worked out—often with the aid of professional staff. One Colombian bishop suggests that a sure sign of recent change in the Church is precisely the decline of individual pastoral letters and a growing emphasis on forging a unified, collective position.

> I believe that one of the most important phenomena—I don't know if anyone has pointed this out to you—which the teaching authority of the Church (through the bishops) presents is that today very few *diocesan* pastoral letters are written. Rather, we try to order and unify criteria on a collegial level, without this being an obstacle to anyone who wants to provide particular orientations to his diocese. He is free to do so.
>
> To achieve this unity, it is also no obstacle that there are some bishops who appear as "advanced," and who the public likes to see as leaders in social questions. They draw back a little because they want to respect the atmosphere of unity among the bishops. And we are very jealous of this unity. Fortunately, no great frictions have ever occurred.[24]

The analysis which follows runs from the 1940s to the mid-1970s and focuses on the bishops' views as expressed in collective pastoral letters. Two central areas are explored: first, changing views of social and political problems; and second, evolving visions of the Church itself. Although the two dimensions are quite difficult to disentangle empirically, for analytical purposes they will be treated separately here.

In Venezuela, for the first forty years of this century, the combination of a solid and stable dictatorship with a weak, pliable, and complacent Church meant that the Church could hardly take (or even imagine) any differentiated, critical position in social

[24] Interview 80123, 1 May 1972.

affairs. The social concerns of the hierarchy were generally limited to occasional local charity, while most of the Church's talent and resources went into the construction of a vigorous system of elite Catholic schools.

Beginning in the 1940s this satisfied, unreflective conservatism was disturbed by the new social and political forces building in Venezuela. From this time until the reemergence and consolidation of democratic politics after 1958, it is fair to say that the social and political concerns of the Venezuelan hierarchy revolved around the question of democracy—the question of its emergence in Venezuela (as embodied in the Democratic Action party), its meaning for the Church, and its gradual expansion from a simple matter of majority rule in politics to a more full-fledged analysis of social justice and economic equality. Four milestones mark the way in this process: first, the intense conflict from 1946 to 1948 between the Church and the "revolutionary government" of the Democratic Action party over educational policy; second, the Church's evolving stance toward the military regime of Pérez Jiménez; third, the hierarchy's vital support for pluralism and democracy after 1958; and fourth, the emergence in the 1970s of a minority radical critique within the Venezuelan Church.

The conflict over the regulation of examinations and over educational policy in general, which dominated the Church's political stance in the late 1940s, has been extensively documented elsewhere; only a brief sketch is necessary here.[25] Basically, the expansion of public education and the attempt to set general standards for school examinations was taken by Church leaders and Catholic activists as part of a general attack on religion by the atheist, socialist, and secularizing regime. The Church took a defensive posture, reacting to perceived threats to its school system; in this reaction, the hierarchy displayed a profound distrust of political pluralism and democracy.

Taken together, these considerations explain much of the bishops' general political stance. As noted earlier, most of the resources created in the Venezuelan Church after 1900 went into education. Left relatively alone under military rule, the Church had managed to rebuild itself substantially from its poverty of the nineteenth century. But in 1945 the sudden rise to power of the

[25] Levine, *Conflict*, chaps. 3 and 4.

Democratic Action party caught the Church by surprise, confronting it all at once with the currents and forces of the modern world, which hitherto had seemed safely far away. The bishops' reaction was to hang onto all they could, hoping to return to their secure (if minor) position of earlier years.

In this way, disputes over rather technical questions, such as the regulation of school examinations, quickly took on the dimensions of a holy war. In a collective pastoral written in late 1947, the bishops spoke directly to Catholic educators.

> Beloved children, priests, religious, and laymen who collaborate in education in all its phases, you are the organs of the Church's education. Hence it is natural that she defend, shelter, and bless you with special care. It matters not that they slander you. That only signifies that you really participate in the spirit of our Lord Jesus Christ, who prophesied: "In the world you will suffer combats; if they persecuted me, so will they persecute you." Rejoice that, for this reason, your names are written in the Kingdom of Heaven.[26]

To the bishops, Venezuela was a Catholic nation by definition. Hence no government could legitimately pursue policies counter to the interests of the Catholic "majority," as defined by the hierarchy. The new democracy, resting on the "majority of the voters," nevertheless took this path; it was therefore rejected as suspect and dangerous. Preferring a stable, authoritarian regime, the hierarchy greeted the 1948 coup with open enthusiasm. But as we have seen, by 1957 the Church had become a major voice in opposition to continued military rule; the public statements of the hierarchy helped stimulate and legitimate broad opposition to the regime, particularly among dissident elements in the military, and in business and economic elites in general. Why this turnabout?

Like many changes which appear sudden in retrospect, the reorientation of the Venezuelan Church did not occur overnight, but rather had been brewing for some time. A greater concern for social justice lay at the root of these changes. Open conflict with the regime arose over the issues of human rights and the "social problem" in general. The May Day, 1957, pastoral letter mentioned

[26] Conferencia Episcopal Venezolana, *Carta pastoral colectiva sobre los problemas planteados a la educación católica en el país*, p. 18.

earlier argued that, despite the regime's claim to represent progress, prosperity, and a "New National Ideal," there was widespread poverty, social injustice, and a brutal disregard of human life. Respect for human rights was stressed, and, as part of this call for reform, a free labor movement was demanded. This letter was followed by a series of critical articles in the Church's daily newspaper, *La Religión*, to which the regime replied with heavy-handed repression and violence. Throughout the 1950s some few clergy and bishops had protested the abuses of the regime's notorious security forces. But the new experience of being a main target of repression made the military regime all the more intolerable to the hierarchy. This feeling, added to the growing conviction that social conditions were unjust and intolerable, led the Church to greet the restoration of democracy in 1958 with considerable public joy.

Although private fears remained great, in public the Church went a long way toward praising democracy, thus giving it added legitimacy in the eyes of many who had bitterly opposed democratic governments in earlier years. A collective pastoral published a month after the fall of Pérez Jiménez urged Catholics to give the new political system a chance. The bishops affirmed that "democracy is perfectly adapted to the spiritual functions of the Church, and does not create problems of any kind for her. The fact that peoples choose their legislative, executive, and judicial authority; that they take an active part in the problems of the nation; that they live them, resolve them, and feel responsible for the course of events, is best adapted to human nature itself."[27]

While helping to legitimate democracy and political pluralism, the Church was also making an effort, as an institution, to move out of partisan politics.[28] The Church's relation to Christian Democracy in Venezuela is especially important here. Although the Christian Democratic party (COPEI) has never been a confes-

[27] Conferencia Episcopal Venezolana, *Carta pastoral colectiva que el episcopado de Venezuela dirige a su muy venerable clero y amadísimos fieles* . . . , pp. 5-6.

[28] The Church's relation to democracy in Venezuela has been complex and dialectical. On the one hand, since 1958 the Church has accommodated itself to democracy, through acceptance of the Democratic Action party and general adjustment to the idea and practice of open, mass politics. On the other hand, the Church has profited from the policies of democratic regimes, which have provided a favorable environment for action, with ample resources, subsidies, and opportunities to innovate.

sional party, the presence of committed Catholics in government, first in a coalition with the Democratic Action party (1958-63) and then in power alone (1968-1973), was nevertheless a source of reassurance to the hierarchy, an implicit shield against the dangers of renewed official anticlericalism.[29] A 1973 pastoral summed up this attitude: "The Episcopacy, respectful of the plurality of political options possible within the framework of the same faith, and bearing in mind the concrete conditions of national life, has avoided any kind of manifestation which might be interpreted as an unwarranted intervention in this field."[30] The bishops' support for pluralism and democracy is genuine and strong, and continues to provide an aura of moral authority to the democratic system. But this overall stance is combined with a social orientation which is conservative at best. Thus, in their public statements, the bishops stress the need for social justice, but place this commitment in the context of an emphasis on individual moral improvement. For example, while calling (in 1974) for a national struggle against poverty, the bishops located the origins of poverty not in the structural factors they themselves cited, such as income distribution or unemployment, but rather in the moral decomposition of the nation. "Serene reflection in the light of the principles of the faith leads to the conclusion that many problems have their deepest roots in vices and the lack of a fear of God. The cold egoism which dominates powerful and humble alike leads them to act out again the drama of Cain and Abel."[31]

As we shall see in later chapters, this public combination of openness, that is, a willingness to tolerate and interact with groups

[29] I deal with the Church's relation to COPEI extensively in *Conflict*, chapters 3 and 5, and also in "Democracy and the Church." For present purposes, the existence of COPEI as a Christian Democratic party and its relations with the Church are simply not very important. This is not because COPEI is unimportant in Venezuela, but because the topic of Christian Democracy, both in general and in the specific case of COPEI, simply does not come up in interviews and discussions with the bishops. Their political concerns are focused more generally on issues of poverty, activism, and the like; and relations with COPEI are simply not salient. Moreover, recent research indicates that the relation between Catholic religiosity and preference for COPEI is quite weak. This reflects the extensive separation of religious from partisan issues and choices in contemporary Venezuela. See Martz and Baloyra, *Political Attitudes in Venezuela*, pp. 103ff.

[30] Conferencia Episcopal Venezolana, *Iglesia y política*, p. 3.

[31] Conferencia Episcopal Venezolana, *Ante la situación social*, p. 6.

THE PROBLEM AND THE CONTEXTS

of all kinds, with a conservative stance on social questions is reflected in the bishops' personal attitudes as well. Politics and the social order are recognized as major problems, and the bishops would indeed like to help solve them; but neither the problems nor the solutions are taken as central to the Church's mission. The "radical" position outlined earlier, which rejects "neutrality" of this kind as little better than an alliance with the established order, finds little echo in the Venezuelan Church. Nevertheless, by the early 1970s the debates sweeping Latin American Catholicism finally came to Venezuela. Activist clergy challenged what they saw as the hierarchy's overly comfortable accommodation with the political system: they sought to convert the Church from a reliable supporter and sanctifier of the current system into a permanently critical element, always ready to defend the poor and downtrodden, to denounce injustice and work for change.

This challenge brings little public reaction from the bishops. My interviews suggest that many bishops have thought about the problem at some length (see chapter 6, below); but public comments are rare, and almost always framed in such a way as to preserve the hierarchy's public stance of neutrality. Msgr. Ovidio Pérez Morales, often considered one of Venezuela's most "advanced" prelates, articulates this position in a way that speaks clearly of the hierarchy's fears and cautions. After acknowledging that "political action" is an essential part of a priest's role in the community, he warns:

> Sensitive to the values of justice, the pastor must, nevertheless, be cautious about any intrusion of disguised clericalisms. He must remember that efforts in the struggle for power can compromise the genuineness of his "witness," which, although it might seem less effective politically, may nevertheless be more in accord with the attitude of service and poverty of the Gospel. ... Insofar as possible, the doors of his house should be open to all, and his arms spread in understanding and goodness; he is the minister of reconciliation and not of judgement, and may not advance, through his own impatience or personal opinion, the eschatological judgement of God.[32]

These reservations about political action are widely shared by Venezuelan and Colombian bishops, and they provide a valuable

[32] Pérez Morales, *Liberación-Iglesia-Marxismo*, pp. 57-58.

link to the concept of the Church itself, which guides their thought and action. Many observers have noted that the Catholic Church, as a church (as distinct from the sects which lie at the roots of Protestantism), typically poses only minimal requirements for membership. Thus a broad, even if less informed, group of faithful is preferred to the highly selective, informed, and motivated minorities characteristic of religions organized as "sects." Obviously, however, a broad definition of the Church clashes with any call to define "authentic" faith" in terms of particular social or political goals. The threshold is too high; it necessarily divides the Catholic community.

Since Venezuela's bishops begin from a weak position, they are especially eager to avoid alienating potential members on political grounds. Therefore, they are committed to respecting the values of the mass of Venezuelan Catholics, who, while they defer to the Church in general terms, are largely ignorant of the finer points of Catholic orthodoxy. The Venezuelan bishops want to open the Church to masses, not limit it to elites. One influential Venezuelan bishop put it this way, in his address to the 1968 Medellín meetings:

> Stated another way, the Church must continue to be a Church of the masses, or else it is condemned to becoming a select sect. She must continue to be a Church whose institutions give a Christian sense of belonging to the great numbers, and not be a confessional church, a "diaspora church," of fervent groups lost among the countless areligious masses. . . .
>
> Here it is necessary to recall the distinction between a sect and a Church. The sect does not have a universal character, but is a group of elect who have had and live a more or less homogeneous religious experience. Often it is a closed and aggressive group. The Church, on the contrary, is not a closed group, and tends toward the universal communication of her program, ever seeking to become incarnate in the world and its culture and accepting many of its values.[33]

This concern for serving the entire culture-community is matched by a strong desire to keep Catholic activities within the institutional structures of the Church, a concern which the presentation just cited goes on to stress. Otherwise, the groups might become mere

[33] Henríquez, "Pastoral Care of the Masses and the Elites," pp. 185, 187-88.

"friendship circles, operating on human bonds arising from mutual sympathy, rather than . . . truly ecclesial nuclei. And at worst, if they are formed at the margin of the ecclesiastical institution, there is a risk of their becoming sectarian groups."[34]

In their public comments on the Church itself, Venezuela's bishops stress the need for priests to continue holding their separate status: priests must remain clearly differentiated, set apart from the bulk of the faithful by their mystical authority and their role as special ministers of God. The bishops spend a great deal of time reiterating the importance of priestly celibacy.[35] When they turn to the social role of the clergy, they add little to the considerations already noted. Thus the activities proper for priests, which include service to others, are sharply distinguished from those appropriate for lay people, which include direct social and political action.

It is difficult to get a firm grip on the Venezuelan hierarchy's image of the Church through examination of its public statements precisely because these images are so largely taken for granted. The great value the bishops place on unity and identification with Rome makes for a public stance of unreflective conservatism, of preoccupation with technical questions such as the form in which communion should be received (kneeling or standing). But, as we shall see, in private the bishops reveal a view of the Church that varies considerably from what is visible in public. The difference lies less in formal definitions than in a sense of style and operative norms, which comes through in personal interviews and in action. With rare exceptions, the Venezuelan Church is not an intellectual Church; its articulated public positions are conventional at best. But it is a Church with strong pastoral inclinations, which make its operating style more flexible and easygoing than a reading of documents alone would indicate. Thus, whereas in public the Venezuelan bishops stress the need to keep priests in a separate, set-apart category, and regularly issue strong denunciations of Marxism, as we shall see in interviews and in the routines of daily life they freely acknowledge and welcome changes in the authority structure of the Church, and display great openness to dialogue and cooperation with Marxists. These points are de-

[34] Ibid., p. 218.

[35] For example, see Conferencia Episcopal Venezolana, *Carta del episcopado venezolano a sus sacerdotes.*

veloped further in the next three chapters, but first we must consider the public positions of the Colombian hierarchy.

In Colombia, the public record is much more richly documented, over a longer period of time, than in Venezuela. In general, the evolution of social and political views is similar in both countries. From the 1930s on, the Colombian hierarchy has been gradually but definitely moving away from a predominant concern with defense against liberalism and socialism, and toward a growing acceptance of democracy and of all major groups acting within the framework of its institutions. A growing sensitivity to questions of social and economic reform is also visible, going hand in hand with a major transformation in the hierarchy's public image of the Church itself, and particularly of its relation to the Colombian nation.

Four broad "eras" are visible in the development of the social and political views of Colombia's bishops: before 1930, from 1930 to the mid-1950s, from the mid-1950s to 1969, and from 1969 to the present. Over the whole period, the year 1930 stands out, for it marked the end of almost a half century of uninterrupted Conservative rule. With the Liberal party's rise to power, the ecclesiastical hierarchy's latent preoccupation with self-defense, partisan political action, and anti-Liberal, anti-Protestant measures came into the open.

These concerns had long been present. The importance of political questions, for example, is revealed, as in a mirror, by the hierarchy's warning, as early as 1913, against an overzealous anti-Liberalism in the pulpit, which obscured other, equally important concerns.

> While it is a duty to instruct the faithful in these matters, be very careful not to make speaking against liberalism a constant theme of preaching, for there are other points of which the people are ignorant, and which, if they understood them, would contribute not a little to clarify their intelligence and improve their habits, and in this way they would be kept more easily from error and defend themselves from the seductions of the unpious.[36]

[36] Conferencia Episcopal de Colombia, *Conferencias episcopales de Colombia*, 1:139.

Although they cherished peace and political concord, the bishops took care to draw their limits in such a way as to exclude individuals or principles contrary to received Catholic law or doctrine. The controlling image was Christendom—a state and social order informed and guided at every step by Catholic norms. The bishops felt secure in this ideal. It had been powerfully reinforced under the decades of Conservative rule, which enhanced the legal and institutional status of the Church.

In such a context, social doctrine consisted, above all, in providing charity where necessary, but always with praise for the poor and simple life. Thus, a 1930 pastoral letter identifies the major problems of Colombia as liberalism and the anticlerical press ("El mayor enemigo de Cristo Rey: la prensa anticristiana"),[37] praises the spiritual treasures of poverty, and urges peasants to remain in the countryside and listen to their priests. In this way, a stable and traditional "Catholic social order" could be maintained.[38]

The Liberal party's rise to power in 1930 naturally disturbed this comfortable situation; over the next twenty years and beyond, one can see a rising curve of explicitly antiliberal, anticommunist, and anti-Protestant denunciations. These reached a high point in the crisis of 1948 and the subsequent massive violence. This stance is well reflected in two collective pastorals: the first was issued on May 6, 1948, less than a month after The Violence was touched off in Bogotá and quickly spread through the nation; the second, issued in late June of the same year, was dedicated to a detailed denunciation of the errors of liberalism and Marxism, and a defense of Catholic social doctrine.

In the aftermath of Gaitán's murder, the archbishop's palace in Bogotá was burned to the ground, and churches were attacked throughout the nation. In the May 6 pastoral the bishops, taking their position as representatives of a "civilized and Christian people,"[39] condemned in the strongest possible terms all recent attacks on the Church and its representatives. Blame for violence was laid squarely on anti-Catholic propaganda, moral disintegration, and the inflamed passions of those who sought to undermine the social order, of which the Church was an integral part. Thus, while they recognized social and economic problems, the bishops

[37] Ibid., 1:380.   [38] Ibid., 1:381.   [39] Ibid., 1:465.

limited their solutions to urging the rich to help the poor and to recalling the poor to their duties, which went along with their rights. The poor were also reminded that "they should ennoble their lives with the dignity of honest and productive toil, with the nobility of pure habits, with the welfare and propriety of a life lived in virtue, and not cheapened by the degradations of vice."[40] To the bishops, in 1948, poverty was less a product of the social structure (a matter of the general distribution of resources and opportunities) than a result of the faulty habits of the poor. In this vein, the pastoral of June 29 advised the workers:

> The workers should strive to save all they can, not to waste the fruit of their work in things which are useless and even harmful for their bodily and spiritual health; they should strive to improve their conditions of life in food, clothing, home hygiene, and in the upbringing and education of their children. In this way, while raising their own level of living they will also stimulate the generosity of the employers, who will give them better pay for their work when they see that an increase in wages and salaries really leads to greater welfare for their workers, and not, as unfortunately often occurs, to an increase in drunkenness, gambling, and other vices.[41]

These exhortations were grounded in a view of Catholic social doctrine that stressed the sanctity of private property and glorified the status and virtues of the small farmer. Given this moralistic and conservative social orientation, combined with an overwhelming concern for institutional self-defense, the hierarchy initially saw The Violence as a war of legitimate self-defense in a Liberal campaign against religion. But, as we have seen, the extraordinary scope and savagery of The Violence gradually led many bishops to reconsider. Most importantly, they began to question the assumption that Colombia was uniformly and adequately Christian ("a civilized and Christian people"). Thus, in a pastoral issued in 1953 the bishops argued as follows:

> We recognize as a well-known gift of God the fact that Colombia is a unanimously Catholic country. But we believe that anyone who reflects carefully on recent events will be persuaded

[40] Ibid., 1:460.   [41] Ibid., 1:485.

that they show visible evidence that the conduct of a large number of Colombians has not always been in accord with their status as Catholics, nor with the principles which a profession of Catholic faith presupposes. In a word, we must admit that in many cases, unfortunately, Catholicism is on the lips, but not in the depths of heart and spirit.[42]

This reconsideration of how "Catholic" Colombia actually was, and hence of the meaning of political struggle for the Church, marks a second watershed for the hierarchy. Starting in the mid-1950s, the bishops gradually withdrew from partisan involvement and began emphasizing national unity and the need for an end to violence. Yet their social views hardly changed. Although the postwar period did see the emergence of a powerful Catholic trade-union movement, as well as the beginnings of a new set of Church-related rural literacy and social promotion programs,[43] by 1958 the hierarchy was still stressing the need for harmony among social classes, speaking of the mutual duties of owners and workers, and concentrating on moral obstacles to social progress, such as alcoholism. Social problems were rooted in moral decay.

> Many times in our country, winds have been sown, and logically we are now reaping storms; moral consciousness was often weakened, occasionally on purpose, and now we are suffering the resulting disorder in the economic and social field; many times favor was given to immorality and the commercial exploitation of vice, and today we face overstimulated passions which are difficult to check; error was given a place, and even defended many times, and now we are feeling its sinister consequences; the duties of justice, especially social justice, were often not fulfilled, and now as a result problems of considerable scope and difficult solution are being posed.[44]

Reading between the lines of the bishops' statements on social issues, it is clear that they saw the Church as basically identical with the Colombian nation. The controlling image is Christendom, a view of society in which everyone is bound together in a common

---

[42] Ibid., 1:502-3.

[43] See chapter 7, below, for a full account.

[44] Conferencia Episcopal de Colombia, *Conferencias episcopales de Colombia*, 2:204.

religious faith and guided by its norms and doctrine. This ideal of Christendom is so deeply rooted that one suspects that even a radical shift in social views (should it occur) is not likely to displace the Church, as an institution, from the center of any proposed solutions to social problems. Thus, for example, it is easy to imagine the Colombian Church favoring more equal income distribution, agrarian reform, and the like; but it is considerably harder to envision its leaders willingly turning over to others (in government, political parties, or some other secular institution) the moral authority to develop norms in these areas without reference to the Church.

Religious unity, as expressed in the structures of the Catholic Church, has long been taken as a necessary basis for national unity. One 1944 pastoral letter puts it clearly, rejecting notions of the separation of Church and State.

> For us in Colombia, the Catholic Church has a special significance, for it is intimately tied to the very heart of our nationality. The Catholic Church was present at our birth as a nation, and it has been the Catholic Church which has accompanied all our steps. Our culture, our spirit are deeply suffused with the teachings of the Catholic Church, and it would surely be an omen of a genuine and terrifying cataclysm, the separation of the Church which we, more than anyone, should call our Mother. For this reason all who try to subvert this religious unity, which is built on the adherence of all Colombians to the Catholic Church, not only steal our most precious possession, which is superior to all others, and one for which we must unhesitatingly sacrifice even life itself, but also undermine the foundations of our country, our progress, our welfare.[45]

Such unity was not seen merely as a vague sentiment of religious solidarity, but rather as expressly mediated through the structures of the Church. This stress on the Church as a symbol for and an agent of unity helps us understand the vast scope of authority the bishops claimed in national life. For Colombia's hierarchy, therefore, the maintenance of strict distinctions between clergy and laity within a hierarchical structure of authority was all-important. A 1954 "Pastoral Instruction" dealing with the nature of the

[45] Ibid., 1:458-59.

bishops' authority summarizes the hierarchy's position in extremely broad terms. Given the importance of authority to the subsequent analysis of this book, I quote at length.

> There is a substantial difference between the Church and democratically constituted nations. While citizens of these nations may intervene in public affairs according to particular circumstances and laws, in the Church those who pretend to exercise functions which the will of Jesus Christ reserved for the pastors of his flock, the pope, and the bishops, are guilty of a real usurpation, reckless and unjustified, and undermine the very foundations of the society established by the Son of God.
>
> The faithful give obedience to their pastors, not only in those matters strictly related to faith, but also in all things which are the object of episcopal authority. The bishops are teachers of the truth, but they are also guides and leaders of the Christian people, who owe them the singular reverence and obedience due the supreme authority with which they are invested. No human authority, no matter how high, has the right to judge the acts of the bishops; such judgement is exclusively reserved to the Holy See.[46]

During the 1960, this-long-standing self-image was shaken by a series of events: the reforms of Vatican II, which opened up views of the Church stressing greater participation and lay autonomy; the challenge of Camilo Torres, which pointed to the need for political commitment despite, and often in opposition to, the bishops; and the Medellín Conference of 1968, which took a hard look at politics and social justice while echoing the calls of the Second Vatican Council for greater collegiality and for sharing authority in the Church. But despite these challenges, the image of the Church that guided Colombia's bishops through the decade remained largely intact. The Church was still seen primarily as an institution, one whose emphasis was on hierarchy, on legal and juridical norms, and on the differentiation of roles, statuses, and functions between bishops, clergy, and laity, with the latter in a strictly subordinate position.

The process of challenge and revaluation within the hierarchy culminated in 1969 with the publication of a collective document,

[46] Ibid., 2:32-33.

The Church Facing Change [*La iglesia ante el cambio*]. Here was a major reassessment of the Church's image of itself and of the world. This document, along with two subsequent publications—*Justice in the World* (1971) and *Christian Identity in Actions for Justice* (1976)—represents the Colombian hierarchy's response to the challenges that the 1960s presented to its understanding of society, of politics, and of the Church itself. The response follows the general Latin American pattern noted in chapter 2: an initial enthusiasm for social action and renewal of Church structures quickly declined, being replaced by a growing concern for the unity of the Church and the maintenance of its central pastoral functions.

Enthusiasm began at a high point in *The Church Facing Change*, which expressed notable concern for social problems, an acceptance of sociological analysis, and a remarkable openness to change. As time went on, however, the bishops became more concerned about the dangers of "sociologism," by which they meant a concern for social questions so strong that it obscures the transcendental and eschatalogical goals of the Church. Notes of caution are already visible in *Justice in the World*, which contains the record of the Colombian participation in the 1971 Synod of Bishops held in Rome. Five years later, reflecting on the growth of radical groups of priests and laity in Colombia (and having the example of Chile's experience with Christians for Socialism), the bishops explored the question again. In *Christian Identity in Actions for Justice* they took a long step away from social and political involvement, condemning the Catholic left in extremely harsh terms. In all three documents the articulation of social and political positions is explicitly linked to a consideration of the nature of the Church itself. Thus the analyses of these two dimensions, hitherto kept apart, will here be joined.

The Church Facing Change has three major sections: "Human Promotion," "Evangelization and Growth of the Faith," and "The Visible Church and its Structures." A close reading of the first two sections reveals the depth of change. In discussing "human promotion," for example, the bishops stress the need for structural change in the economy and in society. Their tone is far removed from that of 1958 or 1960. Responding perhaps to the strictures of Medellín, they openly discuss poverty, unemployment, dependency, and the like, in the context of a call for general political reforms to make further change possible. Negative aspects of social life in Colombia are viewed frankly and openly—a stance difficult to imagine even ten years earlier. Throughout, the bishops stress the need to look directly at social reality and to prepare the clergy to deal with the social problems of contemporary Colombia.

> In courses and in other ways as well, the clergy must be given a more precise and objective understanding of current Latin American and Colombian social and economic problems, [and] be given access to sources of information and scientific disciplines to stimulate them to become familiar with the current advances, methodology, and theory of models appropriate for developing countries. In this way they can fulfill their proper priestly ministry, moving with greater precision and seriousness in the realities of the temporal world.[47]

Openness to change and social reform went hand in hand with a decline in the strident anticommunism and triumphal self-congratulation that was characteristic of the past. The bishops now spent little time telling themselves how "civilized and Christian" Colombia was. Rather, through analysis of the meaning of religious faith as actually practiced, they sought to build new means for reaching the mass of the people. This reassessment acknowledges a state of "crisis" in the Church; resolution of the crisis requires new mentalities and a thorough reformulation of institutional relations, both within the Church and between it and the world at large. Special stress is laid on the close connections between social change, intra-Church relations, and the evolving nature of authority in the Church: "In the search for these new relations the greatest difficulties arise on issues of authority, the teaching office of the Church, the sacramental ministry, and social change: four areas closely linked in the [internal] life of the Church, and of the Church in the world."[48]

The Church Facing Change is notable above all for its remarkable openness to social analysis and to change in all areas.[49] The bishops were extremely sensitive here to the way changes in the

[47] Conferencia Episcopal de Colombia, *La iglesia ante el cambio*, par. 69, p. 39.

[48] Ibid., par. 335, pp. 128-29.

[49] As we shall see, this openness was soon replaced by a wariness and concern over the "sociologization" of Church institutions. Here, Colombia follows a trend visible in many Latin American Churches.

Church's social position affect its internal structure and orientations. But signs of caution and withdrawal began to appear almost immediately, and they took systematic form in *Justice In the World*. This document is actually a collection of several different papers prepared for the 1971 synod: a working paper on "Justice In the World" prepared for the Rome meetings; the Colombian hierarchy's analysis and criticism of that draft; the speeches of Colombia's representatives to the synod; the full text of the Colombian report, entitled "Justice in Colombia"; and finally, the definitive text of the synod's declarations on the theme of justice.

The Colombian bishops were highly critical of the initial working paper. They found its analysis to be simplistic and misleading, attributing most of the injustice in the world solely to dependency and to the exploitation of underdeveloped by already-developed nations. Moreover, since this kind of analysis often leads directly to revolutionary violence, it is well, according to the Colombians, to be cautious. More generally, the bishops were concerned by the predominance in the working paper of purely temporal issues. As the archbishop of Bogotá put it, an exclusive concern with temporal matters distorts the proper role of the priest; it confuses the people and stimulates them to distrust their government.

> The danger which is visible for priests lies in their devoting all their work and ministry to temporal liberation alone: they carry out this task in such a way that they have no other goal than that of filling the consciousness [of their people] with seditious and even violent methods, while at the same time they accuse the teaching of the bishops and of the Church itself of being alienating. . . . Christian charity must certainly struggle to defend the oppressed, while at the same time embracing, with love, even the aggressor who is being fought against. For this reason, if the cause of liberation is converted into a trench, the Christian conscience can do no less than question itself anxiously.[50]

In their exposition on "Justice in Colombia," the bishops put together perspectives which we shall see combined again and again in subsequent chapters. They analyze the Colombian situation in notably structural terms: they speak directly and often eloquently of poverty, unemployment, and social and political problems as the

[50] Conferencia Episcopal de Colombia, *La justicia en el mundo*, pp. 87, 91.

result of unjust structures of power in society itself. This analysis is accompanied by a recognition of the growing acuteness of these problems and of the spread of radical ideas among elites and masses alike. But when it comes to action, the bishops are very cautious. Above all, they want to avoid breaking the "unity" of society or of the Church, with the resulting risk of violence so familiar to Colombians. The Church must stress unity over division, love over fear and hatred.

> Perhaps in the past his [the Christian's] revulsion from violence led him to minimize injustice or resign himself to it, but today sensitivity to injustice and oppression tends to aggravate itself and run the risk of contributing to escalation of the struggle between men who should be brothers. It is sad that now no way out is seen other than the defeat of an adversary. The eschatological teachings of the Sermon on the Mount and their culmination in the nonviolence of the Cross cannot be converted directly into norms of human conduct for complex situations, but they can and must be translated into love in the midst of even the most difficult and intractable conflicts.[51]

In any case, the Gospels cannot be used as a direct guide to action. All the Church can do is to stimulate laymen to act, avoiding wherever possible the twin temptations of passivity and violence. There is no more talk of the need for clergy and bishops to join in human promotion. The predominant note is caution.

In *Christian Identity in Actions for Justice* the wheel has turned full circle. The initial drive to renovate the Church and to participate in the struggle for social change has been tempered by fear that too active a role in social and political affairs divides the Church, leading to serious distortions of the very meaning of religion and of the Church itself as an institution.

As a thorough and considered response to the pressures, challenges, and debates which marked Latin American Catholicism throughout the 1960s and 1970s, *Christian Identity in Actions for Justice* deserves careful attention. Much of the document consists of a harsh and bitter critique of the Catholic left and of Liberation Theology in particular. The bishops concentrate their attack on the conversion of basic eschatological categories of traditional Catholic faith into purely temporal notions: they reject the transformation

[51] Ibid., p. 113.

of the "poor" of the Gospels into the proletariat, the conversion of sin into social injustice, and the identification of evangelization with the promotion of social change and *concientización*. This transformation of religious concepts is seen as an attack on the very bases of the Catholic religion, removing its transcendental essence while undermining the recognized authority of the bishops—successors to the Apostles.

In contrast to these trends, the bishops reemphasize the mysteries of the Church, and they especially stress the need for unity. Such unity necessarily involves more than simply avoiding public division. Rather, it comprises the unity of all social classes within the Church, the unity of laity, bishops, and clergy, and the unity of action and meaning in this world and the next. The bishops take special pains to oppose any attempt to distinguish a Church conceived as the "People of God" from the hierarchical Church they lead. For the Catholic left, a Church conceived in this way

> would be constituted on the base of the proletariat, which would be the real "People of God." It would have its own novel ministries, its own liturgy, of which we have already seen symptoms and manifestations in some "celebrations" and even in books now circulating with special rituals; it would also have its own theology, since previous efforts are rejected as appendages of capitalist ideology; it would advance a peculiar pastoral action, centered on political "praxis." Inspired in propositions which lack any support in ecclesial tradition, and working through a national, Latin American, and worldwide network, they proceed to create groups for study and action which seek to make a revolution within the Church. If unfortunately such ideas and procedures were to gain strength, we would be facing a systematic demolition of the Church and an erroneous doctrinal position, with drastic consequences.[52]

The bishops fear that these political trends divide the Church, making any and all of its efforts more difficult. By building political division into the very heart of the Catholic community, these ideas,

> far from having helped to create sensitivity and awareness about the grave problems of our society, not only represent a discour-

[52] Conferencia Episcopal de Colombia, *Identidad cristiana en la acción por la justicia*, par. 119, p. 46.

> aging factor which even leads to harmful reaction among those who situate the meaning of their commitment within the lines set by the Church, but in addition they delay and hinder possible actions. The useless tensions they generate within the Church itself are, without a doubt, an obstacle for the intensive and coherent kind of action which is necessary in important areas of social pastoral work, illuminated by the doctrine of the Church, which must be deepened and extended, particularly at the present time, with reference to the defense of human rights, the Christian concept of property, and the authentic values of democracy.[53]

Thus, the positions espoused by the Catholic left and those identified with Liberation Theology are rejected for reasons of policy and theology alike. As policy, they are imprudent and counterproductive. Moreover, the theology on which they rest is fundamentally wrong, and it is destructive of the unity of the Church. If taken to their logical conclusion these views would, in the bishops' opinion, reduce the Church either to a small set of highly motivated militants or turn it into simply one revolutionary faction among many. For the bishops, defense of the Church as an institution is thus linked directly to rejection of the primacy of politics, a key theme of Liberation Theology. For, as we have seen, if politics indeed becomes primary, then political commitments may be made the basic standard of Christian authenticity, gutting Catholicism of its transcendental content. The ecclesiastical institution would become simply one of many social-reform groups, and its unique ability to transmit the message of salvation would be irreparably damaged.

But the bishops do not abandon the search for social reform and political change. By no means. Rather, they step back from assuming any direct leadership, preferring instead to have the Church stimulate others to action. They insist on the need for political neutrality, despite criticisms that such neutrality is little more than disguised support for the status quo.

> There are always some who will accuse the Hierarchy of using its neutrality to mask a commitment to the established order. Even at the risk of incurring this erroneous interpretation, the

[53] Ibid., par. 172, p. 65.

Church must stand aside from party conflicts. Called as she is to be a center of unity, she must preserve full liberty to proclaim the Gospel to all, to call men to conversion, and to carry out her mission of serving as a conscience (at once stimulating and critical) of the society in which she lives.[54]

The Colombian bishops maintain that social and political change is urgent, yet they reaffirm the Church's nondirective role in these secular areas. The Church is to concentrate instead on activating capable lay people, who, guided by authentic and authoritative expositions of Catholic doctrine (provided by the bishops), will transform society accordingly. The stress on unity and on rebuilding the Church's somewhat shaken authority structure is quite central; for, to the bishops, this position ensures that *whatever* action is taken, it will be guided by a unified Church in which all groups (bishops, priests, religious, and laity alike) find their proper and complementary places. Overemphasis on the "People of God" *as opposed to* the Church as an institution destroys the Church *however* it is envisioned. Thus, for the Colombian hierarchy, a reassertion of more traditional concepts and values became necessary.

By the mid-1970s, then, the Colombian and Venezuelan hierarchies have entered a paradoxical opposition. Colombians, long renowned for their conservatism, espouse a fairly radical critique of society in the context of a renewed emphasis on traditional models of the Church. Their Venezuelan colleagues, meanwhile, project a more cautious social position laced with conventional moralisms, but set in the context of an ecclesial style more open to innovation and change in the Church and in society at large. As we shall see (chapters 4, 5, 6, and 7, below), this paradox informs us about much of the impact each Church has in its own society.

So far, our attention has been centered on the changing relation between religion and politics, especially in the way concepts, symbols, and patterns of action in one sphere affect understandings and behavior in the other. Stress has been placed on the close relation between material and symbolic elements as both of them change. Thus, in considering the issues in general and also in terms of the particular evolution of Venezuela and Colombia, I have

[54] Ibid., n. 23, p. 24.

centered attention on three sets of factors: first, on the resources, structures, and general expectations predominant in the political system; second, on the structures and traditions of the ecclesiastical institution in each nation; and third, on the attitudes and values of Church leaders, with special reference to their social and political views, the images of the Church which inform their religious stance, and the interaction of the two.

The analysis to this point suggests, in a tentative way for the moment, that the bishops' social and political perceptions, on the one hand, and their images or visions of the Church, on the other, represent related but essentially independent dimensions of belief and action. The three chapters in Part II deal with the bishops in considerable detail, exploring the ways in which these different dimensions clash, converge, or bypass one another in particular circumstances. Chapter 4 is a "collective portrait" which limns the broad characteristics of the bishops as a group. Chapter 5 then explores their images of the Church, with particular attention to their views on the evolving nature of authority. Finally, chapter 6 examines the social and political views of the hierarchy—the world it sees and the role it envisions for the Church within that world.

Part II

THE BISHOPS AND
THEIR WORLDS

4

The Bishops: A Collective Portrait

MUCH of the impact of religious institutions depends on their leaders—on the problems they see, the roles they assume, their characteristic styles of action, and the constraints and imperatives they shape their action to fit. The study of elites, however, is not an end in itself. Rather, the analysis of Church elites is used here as a point of departure for analysis of the Church as a whole. My interest is not in Church elites per se, or in elite analysis in general, but rather in the relation between elite perspectives and predispositions and backgrounds, institutional structure, and social context.[1]

This chapter provides a collective portrait of the bishops of Venezuela and Colombia. I begin with an outline of salient characteristics of personal background, career, and role orientations as seen in the context of the way bishops run the Church in their own dioceses. This overview is followed by extended profiles of four bishops who illustrate some of the most notable patterns. These general and individual portraits lead to a review of several recent typologies of religious leadership in Latin America. The chapter closes with speculation on the utility and the proper form of such typologies for more general studies of religion and society.

The study of bishops is clearly of great importance. Although

[1] Here I share C. Wright Mills's view of social science as "the study of biography, of history, of the problems of their intersection within social structure" (*The Sociological Imagination*, p. 134). In general, although studies of elites devote much attention to background and career variables, they have been less successful in relating these variables to measures of attitudes. Searing and Edinger point out that background variables are often "brought to the research from the outside and not themselves evaluated within the context of the research project. Moreover, not only does the relevance of the social background variables as a set remain unquestioned, but the relative strength of one background variable vis-à-vis another is rarely determined" ("Social Background in Elite Analysis," p. 431). Their discussion of the use of nationality is also of great interest. See also Putnam, *The Beliefs of Politicians*, especially chapters 1 and 2.

they are not the only elite group within the Catholic Church, bishops nonetheless play a uniquely central role in the Church's organization and in its sacramental life.[2] As an independent and relatively autonomous successor to the Apostles, each bishop wields vast authority in his diocese. In Ivan Vallier's words, the bishop is, "in the broadest sense of the term, a local religious king."[3] What are these men like?

PERSONAL CHARACTERISTICS

Who are the bishops? What are they like? At first glance, their most striking characteristic is homogeneity. If one were to draw a profile of the "typical" bishop in either country, it would look more or less like this: he has held the rank of bishop for about ten years; he is of middle or lower middle-class origins, in his fifties, and moderately well educated. There is some regional concentration: bishops come disproportionately from the more traditionally Catholic areas of each nation (the Andean States of Táchira and Mérida in Venezuela, and the Departments of Antioquia and Caldas in Colombia). In race, the bishops are mostly white, with occasional mestizo features. I met no black or Indian bishops in either country.

This overview masks notable national differences. Venezuelan and Colombian bishops differ most strongly in patterns of age, education, and career (see table 4.1). Colombians are somewhat younger than Venezuelans, but no strong generational differences are visible: older and younger bishops are more or less alike in social background, rural-urban origins, region of birth, and the like. Variation is more notable in career patterns. Colombians are much more likely to have followed the classic path to promotion in the Church, which is through positions in education (primarily as professor or rector in a seminary, training future clergy) and through the *curia*, or Church bureaucracy (e.g., as private secretary to a bishop, as vicar general of a diocese, or more recently as

[2] Other elite groups include officials of large religious orders (such as Jesuits or Salesians) and leaders of educational and welfare institutions nominally affiliated with the Church but financially and organizationally independent of the hierarchy.

[3] Vallier, *Catholicism*, p. 86.

A COLLECTIVE PORTRAIT

officer of some department in the bureaucracy of the National Bishops' Conference). Venezuelans, on the other hand, are much more likely to have worked as parish priests than are their Colombian colleagues. Indeed, many Venezuelan bishops were promoted to the rank of bishop directly from their parish work. Venezuelan bishops are also much less educated as a group than are the Colombian bishops: fewer than half the Venezuelans have pursued studies beyond the seminary.

TABLE 4.1
PERSONAL AND SOCIAL CHARACTERISTICS OF THE BISHOPS

	Venezuela (N=22) N	%	Colombia (N=38) N	%
Position				
Auxiliary bishop	3	14	6	16
Bishop	14	64	25	66
Archbishop	5	23	8	18
Years as a bishop				
Less than five	6	27	13	34
Five to fifteen	10	45	13	34
Over fifteen	6	27	12	32
Age				
Over 55	14	64	17	45
Under 55	8	36	21	55
Education				
Seminary only	13	59	12	32
Advanced	9	41	26	68
Studies in Rome	9	41	12	32
Career (posts mentioned)[a]				
Education	8	36	27	71
Curia	10	45	21	55
Parish work	15	68	12	32
Adviser to movements	2	9	5	13
Journalist	1	5	1	3
Father's occupation				
Professional-civil servant	8	36	13	34
Business-commerce	7	32	15	40
Small landowner	4	18	5	13
Peasant-worker	1	5	3	8
Large cattle rancher	1	5	—	—
Military	—	—	1	3
Not ascertained	1	5	1	3

TABLE 4.1 (*cont.*)

	Venezuela (N = 22)		Colombia (N = 38)	
	N	%	N	%
Origins				
Urban area—large city	5	23	12	32
Small city	3	14	6	16
Small town	14	64	19	50
Countryside	—	—	1	3
Region of birth[b]				
Andes	6	27		
Central	7	32		
Plains	1	5		
East	5	22		
West	3	13		
Antioquia & Caldas			18	47
South (Nariño, Cauca)			2	5
Center (Tolima, Huila, Valle)			7	18
Cundinamarca-Boyacá-Santander			11	29

[a] Up to two mentions of a career position prior to promotion to bishop were coded for each individual. Hence, the results cannot be directly summed.

[b] In Venezuela, the regions refer to the following states: Andes (Táchira, Mérida, Trujillo); Central (Carabobo, Aragua, Federal District, Miranda); Plains (Barinas, Apure, Guárico); East (Anzoátegui, Monagas, Bolívar, Sucre, and Nueva Esparta); and West (Zulia, Falcón, Lara, Yaracuy). In Colombia, Caldas refers to the old state of Caldas, which comprises the present departments of Caldas, Quindío, and Risaralda.

Education and career are closely related, and they deserve special attention here as key factors in the formation of each bishop's contemporary perspectives. Although it is difficult to disentangle the influences of education and career empirically, for purposes of analysis I will treat them separately, beginning with education.

Clerical education is traditionally quite limited, with a heavy emphasis on abstract learning (primarily philosophy and theology) that is largely divorced from the concerns of day-to-day life. This abstract orientation was reinforced by the structure of the traditional seminary. Run as boarding schools, traditional seminaries were kept rigidly isolated from the community. Thus, future members of the clergy lived in a sheltered and artificial environment, "removed from the world and taught that it was to be approached only with extreme caution."[4]

Of the 60 bishops I interviewed, only 4 (3 Venezuelans and 1 Colombian) entered the seminary as "adult vocations" (after high school or from a university). The rest began their clerical careers at the age of eleven or twelve, in minor seminaries.[5] Advanced education has typically been more of the same in terms of scope and setting. Most advanced study takes place in Church institutions that are concentrated in Rome. Thus, of the 35 bishops with advanced education, 21 studied in Rome. Their studies were also quite limited in content, with a preponderance of canon law and theology. Training in "modern" areas like education or psychology is rare.

Advanced education is clearly on the rise in these two Churches. Only half the bishops over fifty-five years of age have taken advanced studies, as opposed to two-thirds of those under fifty-five. But national patterns differ strikingly. Almost two-thirds of the entire group with advanced training is under fifty-five (the approximate median age). But younger Venezuelans are substantially less educated than their elders, whereas 80% of the Colombian bishops under fifty-five have advanced education (see table 4.2). Not only is advanced education less common in Venezuela (and concentrated in different age groups), it is also considerably more limited in scope. All Venezuelans with advanced education studied in Rome, and all were trained in traditional fields. Meanwhile, in Colombia less than half the more educated bishops studied in Rome; and "modern" fields of study, though rare, are at least represented.

The importance of having been educated in Rome warrants separate attention. As T. Howard Sanks shows, the education offered in the Gregorian University (the institution attended by most of those who studied in Rome) encouraged rigid and juridical ways of thinking, based on a view of the Church which magnified the importance of authority, hierarchy, and certainty. In this view,

[4] Bruneau, *The Political Transformation*, p. 133. This is gradually changing, with the development of programs of seminary reform intended to reduce the isolation of seminary students from the surrounding community.

[5] These minor seminaries are in notable decline throughout Venezuela and Colombia. Many have been closed.

TABLE 4.2
AGE AND EDUCATION OF THE BISHOPS (%)

	Education		
Age	Advanced	Seminary	Totals
	Both Countries		
Over 55	48	52	52
Under 55	69	31	48
Totals	58	42	
	Venezuela (N = 22)		
Over 55	43	57	64
Under 55	37	63	36
Totals	41	59	
	Colombia (N = 38)		
Over 55	53	47	45
Under 55	81	19	55
Totals	68	32	

"Order means subordination of lower to higher; each thing in proper hierarchical arrangement. This must be clear and certain and unchanging. Then we have stability. There is no place in this paradigm for change, uncertainty, probability, or open-endedness. That would mean disorder and instability, and these are definitely negative values."[6]

Moreover, the orientation of what Sanks refers to as the "Roman School" helped magnify the importance of ecclesiastical questions and minimize all others. In this way, the isolation and confinement of early clerical education was reinforced, extended, and glorified. The atmosphere of *Romanitas,* according to Sanks, "is difficult to describe to those without experience of it. The net effect is to elevate ecclesiastical and theological concerns way above their significance for the rest of the world. It is a very closed, self-sufficient world centered around the papal court."[7]

The pattern of educational differences is matched by variations in career. I noted earlier that Venezuelans have more pastoral experience than Colombians, who instead tend to have risen through the Church's educational system and internal bureaucracy. These

[6] Sanks, *Authority in the Church,* p. 112.
[7] Ibid., p. 125.

dimensions are important, for it is often argued that bishops, living far from the day-to-day problems of average people, lack experience of the real world. With such limited experience, the argument runs, bishops simply fail to understand such problems; they deal with them in rather rigid theological or administrative categories. By contrast, more pastoral experience might lead to a greater concern with personal relations and to a more notable emphasis on community and cooperation, as opposed to stress on hierarchical authority and the maintenance of theologically "correct" positions.

To gauge the nature of career patterns more carefully, separate indices were built to assess the degree to which each bishop had been exposed to pastoral and to bureaucratic-educational roles. Exposure to each role was rated as exclusive, as none at all, or as mixed, including at least some exposure to both roles. These exposure levels are coded respectively as high, low, and medium. Over 23% of Venezuelans, as opposed to only 3% of the Colombians, scored high on pastoral experience, while over two-thirds of the Venezuelans mentioned at least *some* parish work, as opposed to less than one-third of the Colombians. The pattern is reversed for bureaucratic and educational careers. Here, over twice as large a proportion of Colombians are at the high level, while only 3% report no such experience. In contrast, a third of the Venezuelans lack any exposure to such roles.

Level of education is associated with particular career patterns. Table 4.3 shows that Venezuelans with no training beyond the seminary are almost three times as likely to score high on pastoral experience than their more educated colleagues. Over three-fourths of this group mention pastoral experience at least once, as opposed to only 55% of the more educated. At the same time, more-educated bishops are much more likely to mention bureaucratic-educational roles. In Colombia, on the other hand, education has less impact. The more abundant opportunities for experience in bureaucratic-educational roles available in the more developed institutional setting of the Colombian Church means that almost all Colombian bishops have some such experience. But even there, the more educated are somewhat less likely to have had pastoral experience of any kind.

These data provide a first glimpse of a pattern which will appear repeatedly in subsequent analysis. Advanced education is associated with strong differences in Venezuela, but with few or none in

TABLE 4.3
CAREER PATTERNS OF THE BISHOPS (%)

	Venezuela (N = 22)			Colombia (N = 38)		
Career Experience	Seminary Education	Advanced Education	Totals	Seminary Education	Advanced Education	Totals
Pastoral Careers						
Low	23	44	32	58	73	68
Med	46	44	46	33	27	29
High	31	11	23	8	—	3
Totals	59	41		32	68	
Bureaucratic-Educational Careers						
Low	46	11	32	8	—	3
Med	31	67	45	50	42	45
High	23	22	23	42	58	53
Totals	59	41		32	68	

Colombia. Moreover, the direction of differences in the two nations is often opposed. Why? The reason lies in the nature of the education that is most characteristic of Venezuela's bishops. Recall that all the Venezuelans with advanced training studied in Rome and that, moreover, older bishops are the most highly educated. In Rome they doubtless absorbed grand visions of the Church. Surely, from a Roman perspective, the status and role of the Church appear greater than when seen from the eye-level view of a poor, weak, and isolated parish, diocese, or national Church. In addition to the Roman attitudes (of which more later), those who studied in Rome acquired a certain status and the necessary cachet qualifying them to occupy the limited number of prestigious positions available in the Venezuelan Church. In Colombia, by contrast, both opportunities and educational qualifications are more widespread. Hence their impact is bound to be less.

RUNNING THE LOCAL CHURCH

A second part of this collective portrait concerns the daily and routine activities of the bishops. We now know who the bishops are, but what do they *do*, day in and day out?

Most of a bishop's time and energies are spent in his diocese, taking care of the daily business of the Church. This means a great deal of time spent sitting in offices, doing paper work and receiving visitors—clergy, lay people, and even wandering interviewers. When I asked one Venezuelan how he spent most of his time, he responded,

> Unfortunately just as you see me now, here in the office. Listening to those who come, some to complain, and to others, to the parish priests—to the people who come. In the afternoons we do not receive visits, but rather I work with the vicar general, studying the problems of the diocese, answering the correspondence which comes in, etc.[8]

When we think of a bishop's office or home (the two are often combined) it is easy to be misled by an outdated terminology that persists in referring to the bishop's house as a "palace." Most bishops I visited live quite modestly, and with the exception of major archdioceses in large cities, or of areas with particularly rich Catholic traditions, they run their offices with minimal staff and almost no secretarial assistance. Thus, it is not rare to find the bishops answering the telephone, typing letters, greeting people at the door, and so on. Here is one Venezuelan's typical day (I quote at length to give the full flavor of his routine):

> Let us take a regular, normal day. The bishop prays, meditates, celebrates mass. I celebrate it sometimes in the morning, sometimes in the afternoon—here in the chapel of the house. In the morning, I receive people who come to visit me, to discuss any kind of problem—be they priests, religious, or lay people. They can be the most diverse sorts of problems, from a case where they want to begin a marriage case [in ecclesiastical tribunals] through a problem of a married couple, of an engaged couple, of a child, a father, or an employee. In the field, let us say, of the lay people who want to talk with me. Running through all this, through a person who comes to ask for a contribution to go to San Fernando de Apure, or who is here but needs to go to San Cristobal or to Maracaibo—all these things, even professional questions. Or, for example, sports associations who want one to give them some help, or educational questions. In the area which is not properly, directly within my specifically spiritual

---

[8] Interview 60126, 9 July 1971. A number of the questions analyzed in this and subsequent chapters were first used by Thomas Sanders. See *The Chilean Episcopate*.

mission, all these things fall. Then the priests, the religious, delegations which come from parishes. In one parish they may be very happy with the priest; or they may come from another because they are unhappy. This all runs until one-thirty or two o'clock in the afternoon. Then I have lunch, usually with some priest or with several who have come; I rest, and then in the afternoon, although in principle I should be visiting some town, parish, or something like that, or writing some letters—nevertheless people often come in the afternoon as well. You cannot say no to them. And in the evening, if I am here, if I have no other commitment, such as meetings in which I have to participate, with the City Council or some other institution . . . then if possible I use the time to read or write something. I usually go to bed very late. Because in the evening and at night is precisely when I have the feeling that no one is going to call on the telephone, or ask me for this or that. Around two in the morning, for example, I try to read, to use this time. It is the only way.[9]

Being the all-purpose reference point for the entire community is not easy; as one might imagine, many bishops reach the end of the day utterly exhausted, unable to find the time or breathing space for thought, study, or relaxation. As one Colombian told me, "Today has been a quiet day here, but you cannot imagine some days, so filled with tasks, and me alone taking care of all of them. So I arrive at the end of the day so tired that I have no time for study, and what is worse, I lack the tranquillity necessary for study."[10]

Much of the bishops' time is spent receiving people. This activity has its ceremonial side, as many visit the bishop as a sign of respect or deference; but in many areas the bishop also serves as a kind of personal, local welfare agency. In small communities the bishop is a notable, a man of recognized status and position to whom respect and deference are due and from whom favors can be asked. As notables, bishops serve both as leaders of their own institution and as general go-betweens, helping individuals and communities to deal with the large, complex institutions of the society. Thus, when I asked one Venezuelan why people came to see him in his office, he replied,

To beg. To beg and to ask for recommendations for public jobs.

[9] Interview 60120, 2 June 1971.   [10] Interview 80149, 27 Apr. 1972.

This in spite of the sign I put outside ["The Bishop Does Not Give Recommendations for Public Jobs: Please Don't Make Him Waste His Time"]. They trick the secretary, and once they get in here, ask me for them.[11]

The kinds of daily activities mentioned in these passages clearly influenced the bishops' responses to a question dealing with their contacts with local or regional government. Although a substantial proportion limited themselves to commenting prudently that such relations are "good," by far the largest single activity referred to is that of intermediary—smoothing the way for individuals and communities and helping them acquire needed goods and services. The areas of contact mentioned by bishops are also revealing. Social welfare is mentioned most often (90% of the responses in Venezuela), followed by references to matters of morals or censorship, and then by references to activities intended to bring groups and social classes closer together (see table 4.4).

TABLE 4.4
CONTACTS WITH GOVERNMENT (%)

	Venezuela	Colombia
Nature of Contact[a]		
Relations "good"	18	28
Service[b]	12	17
Intermediary	71	42
Unifier	—	11
Other	—	3
Areas of Contact Mentioned[c]		
Welfare	90	68
Morals	—	16
Unifier	—	11
Education	—	5
Other	10	—

[a] N = 17 for Venezuela, 36 for Colombia.
[b] Service refers to acting as member of boards of various official and semi-official agencies.
[c] N = 10 for Venezuela, 19 for Colombia.

Of course, the daily activities of the bishops are not limited to "fixing" things for others. Much time and energy is spent running

[11] Interview 60126, 9 July 1971.

the administrative affairs of the Church. How are these activities carried out? Are there different *styles* of administrating? I have suggested that Venezuelans are less educated, are more "pastoral" in their career experiences, and are located in a less institutionally developed Church. It stands to reason, then, that their style of action at the local level should also be more personal, and less structured, than in Colombia. This aspect of the life of the local Church comes out clearly in the bishops' responses to several questions I posed concerning the general area of local-level planning and participation, particularly their relations with clergy.

Relations with the clergy are an acid test of the operating style of each bishop, and of the degree to which general pronouncements about change in the Church are translated into new forms of behavior. The general issue of clerical (and lay) participation in running the Church is quite salient to bishops in both countries. I gauged experiences and orientations with this question:

> Of course the bishop wants to understand the opinions of his clergy and maintain close contact with them. How do you manage this?

The responses confirm the general impression already noted: the Venezuelan Church is more paternal and less institutionalized. Thus personal contact (either with priests visiting the bishop or, more importantly, the bishop traveling to the parishes) is central in Venezuela. Although such contact is also important in Colombia, formal structures such as regional vicariates or diocesan priests' councils have greater weight there. The relative absence of well-established structures in the Venezuelan Church is further revealed in the bishops' comments on planning. When I asked, "In general, how does the process of pastoral planning function in the diocese?" almost half replied that no such process existed in their diocese, or that all attempts to establish one had failed. In contrast, only a quarter of the Colombians paint so dismal a picture. Pastoral Councils (composed of clergy, lay people, and institutional representatives) were encouraged both by Vatican II and Medellín as a means of increasing participation in the life of the Church, and they are mentioned by approximately equal numbers of bishops in each country. Decentralized planning structures like zones or vicariates are twice as prevalent in Colombia, reflecting once again the greater density of Colombia's ecclesiastical structures (see table 4.5).

TABLE 4.5
RELATIONS IN THE LOCAL CHURCH (%)

	Venezuela (N = 21)	Colombia (N = 38)
Contact with Clergy		
Personal	71	53
Organizational	19	34
Priest Councils	10	11
Other	—	3
Status of Pastoral Planning in the Diocese		
Failure, none exists	43	27
Pastoral Council	29	24
Decentralized structures	10	22
Hopes for future	19	22
Other	—	5

Running the local Church in a more direct and personalized fashion has mixed consequences. On the one hand, it undoubtedly encourages what one might call orthodoxy by intimacy. In Venezuela, it is quite clear that bishops like their clergy to visit, chat, and pass the time of day—not simply to report, but also to renew and maintain a spirit of friendship. Personal ties are highly valued. Affective ties and orthodoxy go together in that much of Venezuela's clergy is foreign, often coming from countries with highly developed ecclesiastical institutions and bureaucracies. But the priests find it difficult to adapt to the local system; in turn, the Venezuelan bishops, unable to penetrate the minds of these priests, almost universally distrust and misunderstand the foreign clergy on whom they depend. The result is that the reliance on personal contacts leads to countless incidents and blowups and creates a generally difficult atmosphere.

On the other hand, such personalized relations within the circle of intimacy, though they have sometimes intensified frictions, have also contributed to reducing other sources of tension within the local Church. In this way the personal ties respond to the new vision the Second Vatican Council proposed, a vision of a Church where bishops, clergy, and laity could interact freely and without reservation. As one Colombian bishop explained,

> I am going to give you some facts that seem significant to me. Purely and simply I would say that I was a priest for nineteen

years—seven years as an assistant and twelve as a parish priest with six months as rector of a seminary. In these nineteen years, aside from the absolutely necessary, I did not have more than five personal interviews with the bishop. And apart from official correspondence, I did not have more than four or five letters from the bishop. In my eleven years of seminary, I never met with the bishop—not even once. In contrast, I feel the need to be in permanent dialogue with the priests. And if they do not come to me, I seek them out.[12]

This same bishop went on to note the changed style of operation in his diocese, pointing out that

now there are not so many decrees in the diocese, but rather actions and pastoral activities more than writing, than desk-bound activities. These are decisions taken together. And I understand that this is not renouncing authority, but rather sharing it. So that this is the major change, the relations of the bishop with clergy, with a tendency to complementary action, to collaboration, all of which are conciliar terms, found in all the documents—and all point to the same realities."[13]

A major theme of this book is that such visions of the Church, and the accompanying styles of running the local ecclesiastical institution, spill over to shape the general way in which bishops (and others in the Church) deal with the secular world around them. Consider the way bishops treat their official visits to the parishes. Each bishop is required to visit his parishes on a periodic basis, to perform certain sacraments, resolve local problems, and so on. Traditionally, such "pastoral visits" have been the occasion for considerable ceremony, with processions, receptions, and the like. But for some, this has changed.

Before, pastoral visits were made in the urban core, spending seven or eight days in the town dealing with various groups. For the last two years, however, I have been arranging pastoral visits through key rural zones (*veredas centrales*)—zones around which four or five others cluster. For three days a team of priests and sisters works to prepare the visit in this zone. Then I arrive and spend two or three days there dealing with various

[12] Interview 80123, 1 May 1972.   [13] Ibid.

groups and organizations. . . . All in all I spend eight days in the parish visiting central rural zones.

In August and September of last year I visited seventy zones in this way. Now, how did I arrive at the conclusion that this was necessary? In some missions we held in this area in 1968 (in twenty-eight centers), I stayed a few nights in the *veredas*. And in one house they told me this is how we like it, that you come to our house, because if you go to the town, there the mayor, the teachers, etc. all grab you, and we barely see you at Mass.[14]

In this particular man, as in others like him, one senses a pattern whereby a curious reversal of expectations occurs—I am speaking, of course, of the social scientist's expectations. As we shall see, advanced education and experience in prestigious Church roles are both strongly associated with so-called progressive or advanced positions on social and political issues. Such individuals are more likely to use a *structural* language in speaking of social problems; in many cases they draw close to a radical critique of social, economic, and political conditions. But such concerns are more often reflected in abstract formulations than in concrete commitments to action. When members of this group move from the abstract and general to the specific and concrete, we often find less willingness to be committed to action.[15]

This pattern of course cuts across nations; but, taking national groups as units, it is clearly more characteristic of Colombians, who, after all, are more educated and more enmeshed in the bureaucratic roles of the Church. The Venezuelan pattern is quite different. Here, cautious and careful statements of position on the general level are often paired with a much more relaxed and open stance, with more willingness to act in specific circumstances. As one priest put it,

> The Venezuelan episcopate is 110% in favor of traditional principles. For this reason, I always say that it is better not to seek definitions, because definitions imply principles and norms, and the hierarchy is rock-solid when it comes to principles. But when it comes to action and to practical questions, they work with common sense. And so that is the way we work—de facto and trying to stay on the practical level of common sense."[16]

[14] Ibid.
[15] This phenomenon is explored more fully in chapter 6, below.
[16] Interview 60306, 17 June 1971.

THE BISHOPS AND THEIR WORLDS

A final insight into the activities of the bishops and their views of the needs and priorities of the local Church is provided by their responses to two general questions: (1) "Taking everything into account, if you were given $10,000 what would you do with it in the diocese?"; and (2) "In general, how do you see the major problems facing the Venezuelan [Colombian] Church nowadays? Which seem to you to be its most important necessities or priorities?"

The hypothetical availability of $10,000 to spend in the diocese clearly surprised and enticed a number of bishops. Some obviously felt that *I* might somehow have the money to give, and almost all, as it turned out, already had applications in, for that amount or more, to some foreign agency, most often to the two West German bishops' funds, Adveniat and Miserior. The most commonly mentioned uses for the $10,000 were one or another form of education, ranging from active programs of catechism in outlying areas to the formation and maintenance of artisanal schools or cooperatives. These suggestions were followed, in order, by more traditional needs such as hiring personnel, building churches, and the like. These two categories (education and "traditional needs") exhaust the alternatives mentioned in Venezuela, but a fifth of the Colombians, reflecting the more extensive institutional structure of their Church, also cited the maintenance of existing charity and welfare programs, referred to in table 4.6 as "works."

TABLE 4.6
USES OF $10,000 IN THE DIOCESE (%)

	Venezuela (N = 21)	Colombia (N = 38)
Traditional	33	24
Education-pastoral	67	55
Charity-works	—	18
Other	—	3

The bishops' analysis of Church problems on a national level is somewhat more complex, but the results are in line with our observations so far. Thus, the most commonly mentioned problems in Venezuela were lack of personnel and of money. Colombian bishops pointed to insufficient knowledge of the faith among the population at large, social injustice, and the general lack of authentic faith—that is, the presence of many nominal Christians who failed to live out their beliefs. To analyze these responses more carefully, I have grouped them into three broad categories: internal problems, moral problems of the nation, and social problems of the nation. For each bishop, up to three responses were coded, and separate indices were built to gauge the extent to which any given kind of problem was mentioned exclusively or predominantly (high), mentioned at least once, along with others of different kinds (medium), or not mentioned at all (low). Considerably different patterns emerge in the two countries (see table 4.7). As might be expected, Venezuelans concentrate on internal problems, which really *are* pressing for them. Their focus on such issues is in contrast to the Colombians, who are much more likely to stress (or at least to mention) the moral and social problems of the nation.

TABLE 4.7
MAJOR PROBLEMS OF THE CHURCH (%)

	Internal Problems			Moral Problems of the Nation			Social Problems of the Nation		
	Low	Med	High	Low	Med	High	Low	Med	High
Venezuela (N = 22)	14	18	68	50	36	14	86	9	5
Colombia (N = 36)	33	36	31	42	28	31	64	22	14
Totals	26	29	45	45	31	24	72	17	10

Recall that for many years the Church was closely identified with the nation in Colombia. This orientation clearly remains vital to Colombia's bishops, who still, to a considerable degree, identify the problems of the Church with those of the nation. Their resulting sensitivity to social problems is doubtless praiseworthy, but a few drawbacks may be noted. In the Colombian context, such identification leads to an implicit (and often quite open) arrogation to the Church of the right and capacity to formulate solutions to these problems—not so much in a technical sense, as in the sense of passing judgement on their moral validity. Thus, in Colombia it is hard for the Church to relinquish the guiding roles handed down from the past and accept a more circumscribed position in national life. In contrast, the more meager traditions and straitened circumstances of the Venezuelan Church make accommodation to secular groups, cooperation with them, and a general live-and-let-live attitude much more likely. Although their formal positions on issues may be less "advanced," in concrete terms Venezuelans are more likely to be open to many practical forms of dialogue and change.

To round out this portion of the analysis, we shall glance at the effects of advanced education on these attitudes toward Church problems. Recall that Venezuelans are both less educated and more pastoral in career experience. Does level of education also affect views of the problems of the Church in general? As table 4.8 shows, once again, controlling for education has a much more notable effect in shifting our measured relationships in Venezuela than in Colombia. The less educated Venezuelans are even more

TABLE 4.8
MAJOR PROBLEMS OF THE CHURCH, BY COUNTRY AND EDUCATION (%)

	Internal Problems			Moral Problems of the Nation			Social Problems of the Nation		
Education	Low	Med	High	Low	Med	High	Low	Med	High
Venezuela (N = 22)									
Seminary (59%)	8	8	85	77	8	15	100	—	—
Advanced (41%)	22	33	44	11	78	11	67	22	11
Totals	14	18	68	50	36	14	86	9	5
Colombia (N = 36)									
Seminary (31%)	46	9	46	46	18	36	73	18	9
Advanced (69%)	28	48	24	40	32	28	60	24	16
Totals	33	36	31	41	28	31	64	22	14

likely to mention and stress internal problems, and much less prone to cite moral or social problems at all, than are less educated Colombian bishops.

To this point, I have presented considerable data on the personal backgrounds, daily routines, and selected attitudes of the bishops. At the same time, I have begun to sketch out the rudiments of a classification, pointing in broad terms to two types of bishops, pastoral and administrative, and noting the relation of each type to education, experience, and selected attitudes. I have also suggested a link between experience and styles of action—a link not necessarily expressed in social or political attitudes. I will elaborate this typology shortly, after outlining several profiles of individual bishops who exemplify, in one form or another, the combinations and patterns suggested so far. With these profiles in hand, the distinctions and types laid out here can be developed more fully, with a greater sense of their individual, human implications. The selections which follow are not intended as a representative sample of the bishops, but rather as illustrations. They give voice to the numbers, add color and life to the narrative, and provide a foretaste of the broader range of questions to be dealt with in later chapters.

Four Matched Profiles

The individual portraits offered in this section are matched in at least two senses: by country, with two Venezuelans and two Colombians; and by the degree to which they conform to what are conventionally thought of as "traditional" and "progressive" (or "renovating") types within the Church. Traditionals here are Msgr. Baltasar Alvarez Restrepo, bishop of Pereira (Colombia), and Msgr. Angel Pérez Cisneros, archbishop of Mérida (Venezuela). The progressives (or renovators) are Msgr. Tomás Enrique Márquez Gómez, bishop of San Felipe (Venezuela), and Msgr. Felix María Torres Parra, bishop of Sincelejo (Colombia).

Msgr. Alvarez was born on June 29, 1901, in Sonsón, a small city in the heart of one of Colombia's most traditionally Catholic regions—Antioquia, source of many priests and bishops. He comes from rather comfortable circumstances (his father was an architect), and he pursued studies in both Colombia and Europe, acquiring a licentiate in canon law in Rome. Msgr. Alvarez is a good example of the classic career pattern of Colombia's bishops. His entire career prior to his being named a bishop was spent in education, and all in the city of Manizales, capital of the Department of Caldas and a central focus of *antioqueño* culture. He taught in the seminary and later served for seventeen years as rector of a school before being named auxiliary bishop of Manizales, in 1949. In 1952 he became first bishop of Pereira, a rapidly growing city on the southeastern fringe of the *antioqueño* cultural area.[17] His entire career has thus been spent within the educational and bureaucratic structures of the Church. Moreover, all his active life has been passed in the heart of Catholic *antioqueño* culture.

As one might expect from a man with this kind of background, Msgr. Alvarez spends much time in office work, dedicating himself particularly to the promotion of schools and other educational activities. The diocese is well structured and organized; so his contact with the clergy is carried out both through visits and regular monthly meetings in each of the several zones into which the diocese is divided. This good organization depends on an abundance of clergy. As noted, Pereira lies in a traditionally Catholic area, and indeed Msgr. Alvarez is one of the handful of bishops I interviewed who saw no scarcity of clergy in his diocese, now or in the future.

The question of clergy is important, for this bishop clearly works with a vision of the Church which is powerfully hierarchical, and he finds no particular problems with the traditional model. I have suggested that models of the Church and images of oneself and one's roles spill over into social relations in general, creating distinctive styles of action. In this case, the operating style of the bishops emphasizes centralized clerical control. He takes a hand in all the operations of the diocese, and also of the various Catholic organizations, working in each case through priests he appoints as "advisers" to lay movements. When I asked if there were any problems specific to the diocese, derived from its social or economic character, the bishop replied by emphasizing the loyalty of Pereira's Catholics, and the complete availability of clergy to guide them at every turn. "In the area of religious administration, I can tell you that here there is not a single parish which does not have a priest leading it. I can also say that on the several different fronts of the apostolate, such as workers, young workers, or peasants—all of these have one or more priests to guide them."

This orientation responds both to a vision of the Church cen-

[17] Pereira is the capital of the Department of Risaralda, one of three carved out of the old Department of Caldas.

tered on bishops and clergy and to a view of local and national society in which social problems appear primarily in terms of moral decay and social welfare, to be dealt with by exhortation and charity. Ten thousand dollars would be used here to finance an old-age home. When I asked Msgr. Alvarez what he considered to be the most important activities of the lay apostolate in the diocese, he ignored the question, repeating that in each group there were always priests "directing" things. From this point of view, social problems are visible; but the role of the Church lies not in direct action, but rather in fostering unity among the social classes while working, through charity, to improve the lot of the poor. This is the traditional Catholic view of the "social question":

> ... undoubtedly the most important apostolate we have among the lay people is in the social area. And here we are trying intensely to create an atmosphere of union between the social classes, and help to the workers and the poor.

Msgr. Alvarez sees the problems of the Church at the national level as one with the moral and social problems of the people. Thus, after noting the great lack of education in the masses, he laid stress on one peril in particular:

> And in the moral field, unfortunately I have the impression that people drink a lot. They drink a lot of liquor, and this has as a result the decay of morals in the town. This is one of the greatest problems we have here in Colombia—to struggle against the vices of alcohol and the disintegration of habits and customs.

Correspondingly, recent changes coming from the Second Vatican Council, or those visible in the Colombian Church as a whole, are mostly seen in sacramental or technical terms. Thus the reworking of the schedule of religious services and the presentation of the Mass in Spanish were stressed, with considerable attention also given to various juridical and organizational changes, among them the development of a social insurance program for the clergy.

This is what might be called a comfortable position. It is not reactionary, for Msgr. Alvarez does not reject the changes derived from Vatican II, but neither is it change-oriented. Change is absorbed, but most things go on largely as they always have. This general stance is perhaps best exemplified in the bishop's response to a question about the future: ". . . How do you believe the Church in Colombia will be different twenty years from now?" The bishop answered:

> In my view, it cannot be denied that we are passing through a grave religious crisis. But I have the hope that this crisis will pass, and that the Colombian Church will return to organize itself and follow in the same paths as always. Of course it cannot be denied that some changes will occur, but really substantial changes, no.
>
> Yes we are passing through an acute crisis, but when one reviews the history of the Church, one sees this in other times as well, and this passes. It is the same with vocations to the priesthood. We are in a crisis of vocations, but it will pass.

All in all, Msgr. Alvarez is quite open to dialogue and cooperation with Marxists, but only, as he put it, because "we are obliged to cooperate, as the pope says, for human promotion, for the drawing together of social classes, and for help to the poor. But without class hatred." This is cooperation of quite a limited sort, rather difficult to envisage within an ecclesiastical structure built so closely around the directing and orienting role of the clergy.

The bishop of Pereira, then, is a faithful representative of a traditional type of Church leader; the archbishop of Mérida provides an interesting parallel—a man of similar traits and orientations who is, nonetheless, much different in personal background and operating style, and who is constrained, like most Venezuelan bishops, by a serious lack of resources and personnel. A closer look reveals the source of these similarities and differences.

Msgr. Angel Pérez Cisneros was born in the small town of Turmero, in the eastern part of the Archdiocese of Caracas, on September 30, 1911. He comes from a lower-middle to lower-class environment: his father was an artisan in construction. After completing seminary studies in Caracas, he took no advanced education. Instead, after ordination in 1937 he worked exclusively as a parish priest until 1960, when he was named bishop of Barcelona, a port city in eastern Venezuela. In 1969 he was named to head the prestigious Archdiocese of Mérida.

A COLLECTIVE PORTRAIT

Within Venezuela, Mérida is something special; its unique status deserves separate attention here, if only to place Msgr. Pérez's comments in perspective. Mérida, capital of the state of the same name, is a small city in the Andes and has long been a cultural, political, and ecclesiastical center for the entire Andean region. It is one of the oldest dioceses in Venezuela, and for many years the Church, along with the university (also one of Venezuela's oldest), has dominated the city's cultural life. The region as a whole is generally considered to be one of the most traditionally religious areas of Venezuela.[18] Thus the archbishop of Mérida (anyone who fills this role) necessarily faces a series of expectations which might not apply in other regions.

Although Msgr. Pérez, like many bishops, is forced to spend a great deal of time in office work and receiving visitors, he stresses personal contact of a warm, paternal kind. Much time is spent visiting the scattered parishes of his jurisdiction, and his relations with the clergy are characterized by intense personal contact.

> Now the audiences which I give are not official in kind, but rather paternal. I want to put emphasis on the paternal aspect. For example, the priest, the son-priest, comes with some problem of his work, of his parish. After we finish with official problems, I always ask them to stay a few minutes, a few hours, so that we can talk as father and son, son to father, friend to friend. I do this and I always stress it so that the priest can have the kind of bishop the Second Vatican Council delineated—that is, to have a relation of father and son, son to father, and friend to friend, and not a relation with a boss who gives orders and nothing more.

The result is unity in the clergy: "the unity one sees is due, I believe, to the intensity of the visits I have tried to make; so that I have no 'rebel clergy' here. We are all friends." This highly paternal and personalized style fits well into Msgr. Pérez's overall vision of the Church. In discussing recent changes (both those derived from Vatican II and those most visible in the Venezuelan Church in recent years) he gives striking and decisive emphasis to

---

[18] A Church-sponsored study of popular religiosity in Venezuela took Mérida as an example of an area of high traditional religiosity. See CISOR, *Religiosidad popular en Venezuela*.

the development of new ways of thinking about the Church and its relation with the world. The two are clearly linked in his mind, for a view of the Church which stresses more open and equal relations between bishop and priests, priests and laity, and bishops and laity leads to new forms of action almost inadvertently, through subtle alterations in the framework of meaning and action. Here is Msgr. Pérez on the main dimensions of change in the Church:

> In my view, the fundamental change which has been underway has been the incorporation of the activities and criteria of lay people, an integration which is constantly growing within the context of greater union between laity and episcopacy. And this really is one of the fruits of the Vatican council. With respect to the role of the bishop, or the role of the laity, these have changed a great deal. Now one no longer sees the bishop as an abstract being, removed from the problems of the people or the life of the people, but rather as an integral part of the life of the people.

Finally, like many Venezuelan bishops, Msgr. Pérez locates the major problems of the Church in the internal needs of the institution. If given $10,000, he would put it in a common fund to improve the conditions of life of the clergy, who often live in considerable poverty, particularly in the more isolated mountain parishes. Clergy, after all, are the central agents of the Church, "the means the bishop has for working in various fields are priests. They are his arms, his eyes, his hands. They are everything to him. So in order to be able to do anything, we have to strengthen what already exists, strengthen and enrich it, especially in terms of the conditions of life which allow priests to carry out a fruitful labor."

Msgr. Pérez was reluctant to engage in any extended discussion of social or economic problems either in Mérida or in the nation as a whole. He recognizes such problems, and he relates them to the general level of "intermediate development" that Venezuela now occupies. But whatever the analysis of problems, he draws a sharp line between recognizing problems and defining a role for the Church in their solution. Solutions are the task of lay people, those with special competence and training in these areas. The Church can stimulate them to action, but to

> the Church as such, as a juridical entity, to the Church as such does not fall the provision of solutions. It cannot offer solutions

with its own means. What it can do and what it has done for some time is to help people make their own solutions. Of course there are some problems of parishes, some social projects, but these are on a rather reduced scale, given the very economic problems [of the Church].

The bishop of Pereira and the archbishop of Mérida share a number of similarities, but differences in personal style and emphasis stand out. Differences are not primarily ideological, for on social questions their views are quite alike: both favor greater interclass harmony, and neither could be described as particularly "advanced" in social thinking. Rather, the variations in style are rooted in different visions of the nature of the Church itself, which lead to dispositions to openness on the one hand, and a concern for hierarchical control on the other.

Differences in style are particularly visible in the responses to questions on dialogue and cooperation with Marxists. Recall the overwhelming limitations stressed by Msgr. Alvarez. In contrast, Msgr. Pérez is wary about Marxists using Catholics to boost their own popularity, but in general he is willing to cooperate: "To that I would answer fully and completely *yes*—that *yes* one must cooperate in actions, in any type of action for the good of the community." This broad openness, which (as we shall see in chapter 6) is characteristic of the Venezuelan bishops as a whole, reflects a more open personal stance and a de facto accommodation to the realities of politics in Venezuela. This accommodation is particularly apt in Mérida, whose university attracts a large number of Marxists and left-wing activists.

In profiles of this sort, it is difficult to disentangle the effects of social and institutional context from those of personal background and belief. Clearly, the two bishops just studied both operate in the highly structured and somewhat constraining environments of areas with rich religious traditions. In my fieldwork throughout Venezuela and Colombia I often encountered the comment that bishops from more "marginal" areas are more open in social attitudes and also more tolerant of innovation and participation within the local Church. According to this point of view, greater day-to-day contact with poverty and misery, combined with increased distance from the centers of ecclesiastical power and control, leads to tolerance for innovation—not from ideological or theological conviction so much as in response to the experience and necessities of daily life. It is hard to validate this kind of impressionistic judgement in any rigorous way. But clearly there is some truth here; and, with this kernel of truth in mind, we shall look at two more bishops, each of a less traditional cast and each working in economically marginal and religiously less traditional areas of the nation. Consider first Msgr. Tomás Enrique Márquez Gómez, bishop of San Felipe.

Msgr. Márquez was born on July 15, 1915, in the tiny town of Santa Ana del Norte on the Island of Margarita (State of Nueva Esparta), in eastern Venezuela. He comes from what might be termed the respectable, small-town middle class: his father was a civil servant in several capacities, first as a teacher and later as a judge. The son's studies were all carried out at the Interdiocesan Seminary in Caracas. Although advanced studies in Rome were planned, the war intervened and the plans were dropped. From ordination in 1940 to his first episcopal post as auxiliary bishop of Ciudad Bolívar in 1963, Msgr. Márquez worked exclusively as a parish priest in the small towns and cities of eastern Venezuela. In November 1966 he was named bishop of San Felipe, a small city in the west, where I interviewed him.

The bishop of San Felipe is an exceptionally vigorous and energetic man. He uses his time carefully, spending the morning in his office and devoting each afternoon to visiting different barrios and parishes in the area. People of all kinds come to visit him, for reasons ranging from the specifically ecclesiastical (e.g., visits by priests or leaders of Catholic organizations) to the personal and spiritual. I mentioned that I had seen some signs in bishops' offices warning that "the bishop does not give recommendations for public jobs," and he replied, "I have no sign of that kind. I like people to come. It is a way of getting to know them and to understand their problems. And whatever I can do, I do it gladly."

Like many Venezuelan bishops, in discussing relations with the clergy Msgr. Márquez stresses personal contact, both through visits and regular monthly meetings. These meetings typically last half a day: "we lunch together and we pass the day together . . . and according to the theme at hand, we discuss the problems, we dialogue, and try to resolve them—their problems and my problems. There is a swimming pool, and, swimming and talking together, we get to know one another better, and we are able to help each other more in the solution of our mutual problems." Msgr.

Márquez clearly values close, personal contact and also feels strongly that the clergy (like the Church as a whole) needs to bring itself up to date and acquire the training and skills needed to deal more effectively with the problems and opportunities of the modern world. Reflecting on his own experience, he noted a lack of adequate preparation.

> I am going to tell you something. I have been a priest for thirty years now. And in our ministry, we have improvised a great deal, to the point that in our work we are experts in a bit of everything. Now, I believe that this in itself is one of the causes of the poor yield of our efforts in many fields. If we talk of specialization in the world, clearly this is needed in the Church as well.

His overall vision of the Church grows out of this viewpoint. Thus, for Msgr. Márquez the most important consequences of the Second Vatican Council lie in the new, open dialogue it encouraged between the Church and the world. Before, the Church was outdated and out of touch; but now, "we are in a better position to reach people, and we are more committed to [dealing with] the structural problems of the world." This new opening to the world leads to a greater concern for social problems and also to a revaluation of the Church's own activities, to playing down the traditional stress on massive public events and concentrating instead on the development of a greater sense of community and understanding within the Church. Msgr. Márquez stresses informed participation in the life of the Church, and he compares this new kind of Christianity with the kind he himself led as a parish priest years ago.

> That is to say, this is not the kind of Christianity we lived in the parish, which was good because there were processions, lots of rockets, and the like. I lived this; I was a good parish priest because I made an extraordinary Holy Week. But what did it consist of? I had little children dressed as angels. I had a great illuminated cross on the mountain. I stood behind a curtain, and at the moment of Christ, the curtains were drawn and there I was, preaching. Very dramatic. That is to say, a Christianity of emotions, and not a Christianity of the message, dedicated to bringing a message. And now we see this [change] in the liturgy,

that the people are no longer mere spectators, but rather they participate more.

These reflections reveal a notable shift, for this bishop, away from the traditional Catholic model of a Church open to all and imposing only minimal demands, toward a Church which may, in effect, become a minority—a minority of the better-trained, more knowledgeable, and more committed members of the population. This tendency is further reflected in views on important lay groups. For Msgr. Márquez, the crucial group has been the Cursillos de Cristiandad (Little Courses in Christianity), an organization dedicated to stimulating consciousness of religious obligations and to deepening individual spirituality. The Cursillos (described in detail in chapter 7, below) are important to Msgr. Márquez not so much as movements, but rather to the extent to which they produce a core of committed Christians, especially among elites in economy, politics, and cultural life.

This stress on a church of the committed emerges most strongly in Msgr. Márquez's response to my question on the likely shape of the Church in twenty years. He sees the future as quite promising,

> promising for these reasons: not for having more churches or more chapels, but rather for having more aware Christians, more of a base. Of course this cannot be the same for everyone. But it must be based on a conscious elite, which is an elite precisely for its awareness, and not for economic or political reasons. You cannot indoctrinate thirty thousand. But you *can* indoctrinate a thousand, and have these thousand persons as a nucleus. And this was precisely our problem before—our over concern with sacramentalizations. It was a matter of numbers—how many baptisms, how many marriages, etc. We did not ask if they developed a genuine Christianity in their lives, in their relations with their neighbors.

Talking to Msgr. Márquez, one gets an overwhelming sense of a desire for change, born out of a pervasive dissatisfaction with the way his background prepared him to deal with a changing world. The search for more adequate skills and the corresponding openness to change within the Church go along, in this case, with a complex view of social problems and of the Church's proper role in their solution. Looking at his own diocese, the bishop sees poverty and unemployment as central problems, but attributes them primarily to lack of initiative and to the absence of a habit of saving. To correct this, he sponsors cooperatives which encourage regular saving and put a greater emphasis on thrift. Paradoxically, despite this campaign for *personal* change within the diocese, Msgr. Márquez insists that the major problems on the national level lie in *structural* inequality: "I believe that the great problem of Venezuela is one of great imbalances in the social field—imbalances of a structural, not an isolated kind."

This said, the Bishop goes on to argue that structural problems of this kind can be solved if everyone pulls together. Here the Church can play a vital role by helping to promote unified criteria on the fundamental questions of development. This determination to stimulate common efforts for the general welfare is extended to any and all groups. When I asked about dialogue and cooperation with Marxists, Msgr. Marquez replied as follows:

> I have no problem in telling you, for me it is convenient. And not only with Marxists or communists, but I also extend it to other denominations and religions. Before, Catholics could not attend Protestant services. All this has changed. So that anything which is dialogue is good. And in the specific case of Marxism, I can't see why not. If it is a question of dialogue, dialogue is always good. And if it is one of cooperation, one assumes the work is good. If they work to raise the level of life in a *barrio*, how can I not also try? I am not committing myself to a doctrine, only to action.

As I suggested earlier, this attitude is common among Venezuelan bishops; it reflects a desire to find good points in others, wherever possible, and points of possible cooperation.[19] This overall stance fits well the general stress on concrete action that characterizes, I have argued, bishops like Msgr. Márquez. The fourth bishop combines many of these elements: he represents in some ways a great potential for renewal, but is isolated in a poor and marginal diocese—Msgr. Felix María Torres Parra, bishop of Sincelejo.

[19] In a similar comment one Colombian bishop, whose diocese contains large areas of concentrated Marxist organization and activity left over from The Violence, noted that he welcomes the presence of such groups since they have a great capacity for organization and solidarity, which can be turned to good account. Interview 80123, 1 May 1972.

The youngest of the four bishops being looked at here, Msgr. Torres was born on June 12, 1923, in the village of Yaquara, in the south-central Department of Hulia. His father was a small businessman in the rural towns of the area. Msgr. Torres has taken some advanced studies, which led to a licentiate in canon law; but these, like his seminary training, were all carried out in Colombia. Msgr. Torres was ordained in 1946; his career combines work as a parish priest in several towns in Huila with a *curia* position as vicar general of the Diocese of Garzón, which embraces most of the Department of Huila. He has held several episcopal positions, first as auxiliary bishop of Cartagena, then as apostolic administrator of Santa Rosa de Osos. He was named first bishop of Sincelejo in 1969.

Sincelejo, a new diocese, lacks institutional structures. Thus much of the bishop's time is spent dealing with the urgent needs of organization and responding to the extreme social and economic inequalities of the region, an area with large cattle ranches and considerable poverty, unemployment, poor health, and poor housing. There are relatively few clergy in the diocese; so contact is not difficult. In addition to occasional personal visits, Msgr. Torres reaches his clergy through regular monthly meetings and by means of the Priests' Council.

The general poverty of Sincelejo, the scarcity of resources and lack of training in the population, create a dilemma for the bishop. On the one hand, he believes that social and economic leadership is not a proper function either for him or for the priests under his direction. On the other hand, in situations as unequal and rigidly stratified as these, Church leaders often find themselves pushed into political disputes, almost by default.

> Of course, the Church, although this is not its principal function, must exercise a role of leadership. Then we find that one comes up against existing structures, which see one as an enemy because one speaks of the needs of the peasant, even saying that they have to be better paid for their work—better salaries.

The need is there, says the bishop, and the Church must take it up, "But always in a supplemental form, that is, seeing the need, he [the priest] must try to form leaders, but in the meanwhile, when there is a situation of injustice which shows no sign or hope of solution, and appears permanent, he can channel the efforts of the community in this direction."

This orientation toward serving needs defined by the community, including direct action where required, fits the vision of the Church articulated by this bishop. Considering the changes instituted by Vatican II, he stresses the emergence of a new mentality in the Church, oriented to serving rather than to receiving favors or to dominating. This mentality also includes a new sense of the Church as a community, rather than as primarily an institution with clearly defined roles, statuses, and structures. When I asked which changes seemed most notable in the Colombian Church in recent years, Msgr. Torres continued to stress the role of changing mentalities.

> Perhaps external changes are not so significant yet—that is, at the national level. In the dioceses there are changes which can be seen now (more in some), but I believe it is a question as much of the change of focus which we ourselves must undergo —a change of mentalities—because we are making changes, but sometimes the changes seem a bit external to me, because if mentalities do not change, then these changes will bear no fruit. For example, liturgical reform: without a "mentalization," as much of the faithful as of ourselves, within a given time we will be as routinized as before.

Stress on community, on participation, and on new orientations is thus combined here with a positive injunction to the agents of the ecclesiastical institution (priests and bishops alike) to serve the community. When I asked the bishop to specify the Colombian Church's major problems, he pointed directly to the need to stop tolerating social and economic injustice—to the problem of building a kind of Christianity which would no longer be compatible with injustice of any kind.

> This is the great task. For example, take our socioeconomic structures. They are full of Christian people, but nevertheless we have gotten accustomed to certain situations and socioeconomic functions which are unjust, but which do not seem unjust to us. So we are in this. You can see the problems of the Agrarian Reform—Christian people, who go to Mass and the like, but when it touches their pocketbooks, they are opposed.

These views put a considerable emphasis on social action, combined with religious education and catechism, to make people more aware of the social implications of religious faith. In this line, the Church must also reach out more vigorously to deliver its message to the people. Thus, $10,000 in Sincelejo would be spent providing teams of teachers and catechists with the technical means (film projectors, audio equipment, books, transport, etc.) to enable them to work more effectively.

Msgr. Torres's view of national problems is of a piece with what we have seen so far. While recognizing the difficult problems connected with underdevelopment, he believes that many injustices could be eliminated if only political groups would work together, instead of merely battling over the spoils of patronage. In this sort of narrowly defined political situation, the Church should use its influence and resources to form the community conscience. Moreover, the Church also acts by setting an example, and therefore it must avoid even the appearance of being compromised with unjust or unfair situations.

For Msgr. Torres, then, the problems are pressing and the Church must act. Where emergencies force it to act directly, the Church must not hesitate. Where more time and leeway exist, lay leaders should be stimulated to act instead. In either case, the Church has a major role to play. Clearly, this point of view is in keeping with the traditions of the Colombian Church, which has always assumed a major social role regardless of its ideological position. It thus makes sense that this bishop, like his presumably more "conservative" Colombian colleagues, is reluctant to engage in dialogue or to cooperate with Marxists. He rejects concrete cooperation and puts such extensive qualifications on dialogue as to make it, in effect, impossible. The problem, in his view, lies in creating conditions of equality in such a dialogue.

> I believe that dialogue at a level of equal intellectual capacities is good. Within Marxism good things can be discovered. Evidently one cannot say that all of Marxism is bad. But I also have the impression that those priests who enter into dialogue are absorbed by it—they lose their own philosophy. They say it is only a system [of action], but a system is also a philosophy and a way of life.

What do these profiles and the general data presented so far tell us about the bishops as leaders, and about the institution they direct? Clearly, no simple and direct line can be drawn from background through social and institutional context to attitudes and styles of action. First, elements of one or the other national tradition and of the local context significantly affect the impact of background factors like age, education, or career—both by making some patterns more probable in a given nation and, more importantly, by giving different meanings to the particular variables. Moreover, at a deeper level it is apparent that more than one dimension of attitudes and action is at issue here; so the very idea of simple, direct relationships is probably flawed from the start. At the very least, two dimensions have emerged: sociopolitical perceptions, and visions of the Church. I have already noted, in a limited way, the degree to which visions of the Church and of religious faith itself spill over into more general styles of action. But such orientations are not necessarily identified with any particular, explicit position on social or political issues. Rather, they find expression in modes of daily action, in the *style* which marks any initiative. These notions will be developed more fully in subsequent chapters. For the moment, I simply set forward the idea of independent dimensions suggested by this collective portrait. It will be used below to evaluate possible typologies of Latin American religious elites—that is, to evaluate several offered to date and to suggest some possible modifications.

Conclusions: Typologies and Their Uses

In recent years, scholars have proposed different typologies of Catholic bishops in Latin America. Typologies are useful tools of analysis, but they should never be ends in themselves. The purpose of building types and categories must always go beyond classification alone: typologies should be subordinated to theoretical needs. Thus, in reviewing current typologies and offering my own, I devote particular attention to the theoretical bases of each classification, and to the theoretical context in which it is set. Two typologies are of particular interest here: the path-breaking classification offered by the late Ivan Vallier, and the more recent and more subtle work of Thomas Sanders.[20] Since Vallier's work

[20] For Vallier see the book and articles already cited, and see also his "Religious Elites." Sanders' work is more scattered. The majority of it is found in letters to the Institute of Current World Affairs, written in 1967 and 1968. Particularly notable are "A Typology of Catholic Elites" and "Religion and Modernization: Some Reflections." All fourteen letters have

has inspired much research on the Latin American Church, it seems proper to begin with his ideas.

In several articles, and finally in an influential book, Vallier argued that the key to understanding the Church in Latin America lies less in analysis of its religious message or political ideology than in understanding the regular and routine ways in which the structures of the Church are tied into those of the surrounding society. In his view, explanation of the Church's social role consists in clarifying the strategies Church leaders have used to maintain the Church's influence.

> I place first emphasis on the structural changes that are occuring between the Church (and its immediate institutional extensions) and the wider society. Although ideas and attitudes help to symbolize and legitimate these structural changes, they hold little importance unless new roles, new levels of interdependency, and new principles of corporate problem solving also occur and become institutionalized.... It is not so much a question of the individual's religious orientations, but the kinds of implications corporate structures of religious control hold for the functioning of the secular power structures, for the integration of social groups, and for the stability of the general ground rules that impinge on everyday exchange and role systems.[21]

From this basic notion, Vallier developed a typology of Catholic elites distinguishing four groups: politicians, papists, pastors, and pluralists. His typology is grounded on two central theoretical assumptions. First, he maintains that an institution's strategy for building influence and its organizational routines are central to its social impact, more central than religious or social ideas per se. Second, he believes that changes in these areas of the Church have enormous potential significance for Latin American development as a whole, as they may free the Church to assume a role of general moral and ethical guidance, once it is liberated from political ties and commitments. This last point was crucial to Vallier because, working with a functionalist model of society, he believed that social coherence hinges on normative unity, and he argued

---

been collected and published under the title of *Catholic Innovation in a Changing Latin America*; however, all references here are to the original letters.

[21] Vallier, *Catholicism*, pp. 157-58.

that the Church is uniquely fitted to provide such unity, which would serve as a basis for harmonious and successful development in the entire region.[22]

From Vallier's perspective, once the Church passed out of the colonial period, where it held a formal religious monopoly, "political" strategies began to dominate the orientations of Church leaders. Centered on the defense of Church interests and privileges against challenges from liberals, Protestants, and later from Marxists, such political strategies took form in short-term attempts by Catholic elites to influence other elites in economic, political, and social life. Through alliances with these elites, the Church ensured its control over different social groups and areas of life. The main point is that the Church oriented itself to outside groups for support and protection, and in turn became identified with them. The traditional relationship between the Church and the Conservative party in Colombia is a good example. To Vallier, the politicians who run the Church in this way have neglected their own base. The population is simply assumed to be Catholic, and hence for political purposes it is practically ignored.

With the erosion of the traditional societies in which such notions of Catholic universality were valid, and with the related emergence of vigorous challenging groups, new "papist" strategies came to the fore. These put a new emphasis on the unity of the worldwide Church (and thus on the pope) as part of a general drive to rejuvenate the inner structures of the institution. A key element here was the attempt to develop autonomous social bases by enclosing the faithful in a vast interlocking net of Catholic groups and programs—trade unions, youth organizations, schools, professional societies, and the like. Catholic Action programs reflect this orientation. As Vallier put it,

> Rejecting traditional sources of political involvement, the "papists" focus on building a Church that relies on its own authority and its own resources to achieve influence and visibility. Direct political involvements between the Church and political parties are eschewed, even forbidden. Thus the hierarchy, the clergy, and the laity constitute a missionary elite concerned with expanding the frontiers of Christian-Catholic values. The prin-

[22] On the assumptions underlying this perspective in the sociological analysis of Latin America, see Levine, "Issues."

ciple that underlies the laity's participation is "collaboration with the hierarchy," that is, full obedience to and full supervision by Church authorities.[23]

To Vallier, "pastors," the third type, differed from the previous types in their stress on continued reform and rejuvenation of the Church, now focused less on general structures than on the development of the local Church as a viable socioreligious community. Religious elites of this type stress the creation of religious symbols, "providing pastoral leadership, encouraging new forms of spiritual expression, and injecting new degrees of flexibility into the local Church."[24]

Finally, "pluralists" are distinguished from pastors in that they embody a cautious return to the social scene. In different ways, both papists and pastors represent strategies of building influence over the long term by withdrawing from direct involvement in social and political questions. Both types of leaders concentrated their efforts, instead, on rebuilding the Church's inner life: first, through creation of a net of centralized, hierarchically controlled organizations; and second, through development of a more vigorous local life in the Church. Pluralists, on the other hand, took these new autonomous resources and applied them to society again, but with much more modest and limited goals. No longer seeking to dominate society or manipulate elites, pluralist Catholic leaders now concentrate on what Vallier considered their most important function—providing generalized moral and ethical leadership. This, in turn, gives greater depth to the meaning of membership in the religious community.

> Their major objective is to develop policies and programs that will allow the Church to assist the institutionalization of social justice on every front that provides the opportunity. Thus the center of attention is moved away from traditional concerns with political power, from hierarchy and clericalism, and from worship and the sacraments, to grass-roots ethical action in the world.[25]

Vallier's four types are thus differentiated primarily on functional grounds. Politicians and papists are concerned with society

[23] Vallier, "Religious Elites," p. 204.
[24] Vallier, *Catholicism*, p. 115.
[25] Vallier, "Religious Elites," p. 205.

as a whole and especially with the threats it poses to a weak Church, and hence they move (in different ways) to protect and insulate the ecclesiastical institution and the Catholic community as a whole. Pastors and pluralists, on the other hand, look to renewing the Church through liturgical innovation, formation of small communities, and promotion of lay initiative. They differ in the scope of their social goals and in the way they approach society, but their styles of action are both rooted in the idea of a revitalized local Church.

Despite the differences between these types, it is worth noting that *all* are committed to working within the institutional framework of the Church as a means of somehow reconstructing or protecting a scheme of Christian values with which to integrate society. In Vallier's typology, even pluralists seek to turn the Church itself to the promotion of change, rather than to work for such change within any available framework, religious or secular. The whole typology is confined by an *ecclesiastical* vision of the Church: all four types in one way or another conceive of action largely within the Church's official structures.

Vallier's theses can be criticized on several grounds. In theoretical terms, there is no particular reason to believe either that social integration is primarily normative or that the Catholic Church is somehow uniquely fitted to provide such integration, were it necessary.[26] In more specific terms, Vallier's work suffers from confusion about the scope and meaning of politics, and about its relation to religious thought and action. Vallier's predominant concern was to find a way for the Church to extricate itself from political entanglements. In his view, such involvements lead only to dependence on others, to commitments which limit the independence and gut the inner life of the Church. Thus, he commended "socio-ethical leadership" to the religious elites as an alternative to traditional political ties.

Now there is surely an important difference between the old-style partisan politics and the new pastoral strategies that Vallier envisaged, but the entire distinction is too neat, too clear-cut. It assumes that a strict empirical separation between religious (or pastoral) action and politics is both possible and desirable; Vallier thought of pastoral action in quite narrow, "purely religious"

[26] On the problems of functionalist analysis, see Levine, "Issues," and the works cited therein.

terms, rejecting as regressive any spillover into politics. But as I suggested earlier, such a rigid distinction is false and misleading: it does not fit the categories used by actors in Latin America today, and it thus fails to grasp the dynamic relation between beliefs and social action. Pastoral action and socioethical leadership of the kind Vallier recommended are, contrary to his view, inevitably and inextricably involved in politics.

It is difficult to separate the two spheres. As the bishop of Sincelejo reminds us, the pursuit of pastoral goals often leads to political involvement, if only to defend the Church from attacks by those threatened by the very pastoral actions of the priests or bishops. Where, then, is the line to be drawn? The problem with Vallier's typology, and with the theory that undergirds it, is that it is too static, and gives too much emphasis to structures and routines. Surely we are obliged to ask *where* such structures and styles of action come from and *why* they are attractive to Catholic leaders in the first place. But once this step is taken, it becomes possible and even necessary to join the sociopolitical and religious spheres, recognizing that elite styles of action in the several areas may be related to one another.[27]

Thomas Sanders has made a considerable advance. He argues that a useful typology should combine attention to structures and functions with analysis of the mentalities of elites, in an attempt to understand *why* different orientations arise and to assess the degree to which they are rooted in more general mind-sets, which may affect behavior in a wide range of areas. He lays out four broad elite types: reactionaries, conservatives, progressives, and innovators. Let me review these in turn.

Reactionaries are militants in the defense of tradition. Their position combines quite traditional religion and extreme political conservatism, and it is well represented by the TFP groups described in chapter 2. Reactionaries reject the reforms of Vatican II; for, as Sanders notes, "All of the phenomena that the reformers

[27] Furthermore, Vallier's pervasive stress on influence is unsatisfactory. In his view the Church, as an organization, seeks to maintain influence; it shifts its programs and strategies according to the effect of any particular modality on the institution's "influence" in society. But "influence" is too abstract and sterile a term to be useful in comprehending and explaining the innovations and conflicts visible in the Latin American Church today. Influence for what? Community building to what ends? Vallier never addresses these questions.

found obnoxious—authoritarianism, clericalism, scholasticism, Latin liturgy, defensive preoccupation with heresy—are precisely what the Reactionaries glorify."[28]

Reactionaries are a small group, clearly defined and set off within the Church. Conservatives, by contrast, share many of the positions espoused by reactionaries but are much more amorphous as a group, because their conservatism is largely unreflective. Some aspects of bishops of this type have been noted earlier in this chapter, and Sanders sums up neatly:

> They obey the authority of the Church, but not fanatically. They believe in a society rooted in Christian values, but do not fight for it. They were jolted when the vernacular masses went in, but they accept them now. They do not think much about theological change or social responsibility because they do not keep up that well with what is going on in the Church. They just attend mass fairly regularly and have an uncomplex faith.[29]

Progressives and innovators may be grouped together in Sanders' typology because they represent the "modernizing elites" of the Church. Both welcome the changes which have occurred since 1960, seeing them as useful opportunities to reshape the institution and the religious life within it. They differ primarily in their view of the Church's relation to society and in the role they give "Christian values" in social and political change. Progressives stress the articulation of modern social doctrine and the reorganization of the Church (centered on small groups of committed Christians) as means for the reconversion of society. But innovators no longer seek to reconvert society or reestablish in some form the Christendom of old. Rather, they see the Church as a permanent minority in Latin America, and do not believe that Catholics have any uniquely valid norms for guiding social institutions. In political terms they, like Camilo Torres, favor socialism and firmly reject the notion of Christian political groups, as a contradiction in terms. Christian Democracy has no attraction for them, for they believe that Christians should be spread throughout all organizations, serving as a ferment within them: "Innovators have a deep sense that organizations of Christian inspiration are defensive in intent and transitory, and that the proper role of Catholics is to act merely as

[28] Sanders, "A Typology," p. 3.   [29] Ibid., p. 6.

individuals, along with conscientious non-Catholics in secular institutions."[30]

This typology is an advance over Vallier's because it incorporates elements of mentality and motivation, linking these directly to patterns of action. Yet despite its advances, Sanders' work also suffers from a curious lack of dynamism. Although the analysis of each type's religious and political commitments is excellent, the scheme as a whole is static. There is little dialectic between social and religious positions, or between substance and style on a variety of issues. Clearly, behavior does not stem solely from an individual's vision of the Church, nor does it arise exclusively from his view of the world. Rather, there is an elective affinity between the two such that one provides for the other and makes it more likely. In Sanders' analysis, one recognizes the consequences easily enough, but it is difficult to sort out the dynamic processes which produce them.

I believe that no single typology embracing both religious and sociopolitical action is possible. Rather, the perceptions, styles, and patterns of action in each dimension have different sources. While they may converge in actual behavior, the empirical combinations which arise are often not those which exclusive attention to ideology, structures, religion, or politics alone would imply. Thus, bishops of a notably "pastoral" sort may refashion the local Church, share authority, and in effect cooperate with all kinds of non-Catholic groups in social action while remaining in the conservative (or at best moderate) camp when it comes to general discussions of social issues.

For these reasons, the observer cannot assume that the several dimensions necessarily reinforce one another, or that they are related in some deductive manner. This is an empirical question. Although the problem is complex, it is not wholly intractable; for it is possible to describe and understand the positions and then explore the way they come together in any given instance. Let me outline the types I believe most useful, in both the "religious" and the "sociopolitical" spheres.

In more "religious" terms, a distinction can be drawn between "ecclesial" and "ecclesiastical" visions of the Church. This distinction, quite common in Spanish, calls to mind contrasting

[30] Ibid., p. 10.

emphases on the Church seen as a community of the faithful (*lo eclesial*) and the Church seen as a hierarchical, juridically defined institution (*lo eclesiástico*). *Ecclesiastical* images and styles of action stress distinctions of rank and obedience to hierarchically constituted authority. The roles of clergy and laity are kept strictly separate, with the clergy dominant. *Ecclesial* positions are different in both tone and substance. The term comes from the original word for Church in Greek, *ekklesia*, meaning "assembly" or "to call out." Both these root meanings speak to the character of the Church as a community of believers that is called out, brought together in shared faith and experience. Seen in these terms, the Church is no longer set apart from and protected against the world. Rather, it is part of that world; so participation and sharing are stressed. Relations of various groups within the Church are more collegial and egalitarian, with considerable emphasis on shared authority and responsibility. The next chapter explores the theoretical bases and behavioral implications of these different images. But for the purposes of this typology, a broad delineation of the types is sufficient to allow us to relate the ecclesial and the ecclesiastical to the social and political sphere.

Three broad sociopolitical orientations can be distinguished: traditional, activation, and activism. These positions refer not so much to ideology as, once again, to the style and form of action deemed appropriate for the Church—the way elites see the proper role of the Church (however they define it) in dealing with social problems. As used here, "traditional" refers to activities which center either on conventional charity and social welfare or on the provision of general moral guidelines for the whole society. "Traditional" positions accept existing social and political arrangements, and direct efforts toward the resolution of conventional moral quandaries. Holders of such "traditional" views are probably closest to Sanders' conservatives; reactionaries as he describes them are extremely rare among the bishops.

Activation and activism both look to social action. They distinguish between strategies favoring the stimulation of lay people to action (activation) and those promoting or sanctioning actions by agents or leaders of the Church itself (activism). This distinction rests on who acts, in what capacity, and with what authority. As Catholic thinkers gradually abandoned traditional models of Christendom and began to stress the autonomy of temporal values and activities, they tried to develop new doctrines to describe and legitimize the new situation. The writings of Jacques Maritain were especially influential—above all, through his distinction between "acting as a Christian" and "acting as a Christian as such," which points to a difference between Christians who act in accord with their principles and those who serve as designated, official agents of the ecclesiastical institution.[31] In practice, this distinction directs the bishops and all the official personnel of the Church to evangelize the faithful and provide inspiration to the temporal world. The construction of a just society is then left to lay people, who after all have the technical skills required for this task.

This position draws a sharp line between the roles appropriate to clergy and laity. For those who support activation, the Church cannot even pose solutions to social problems, much less undertake to implement them directly. This would be both bad theology and imprudent policy: bad theology by ignoring the proper autonomy of the temporal world, and imprudent policy by involving the ecclesiastical institution per se in the very kind of political disputes from which the bishops have been trying to escape.

Obviously, activism is a considerable step beyond activation. In activation strategies, the Church is prepared to co-opt and legitimize groups once they are formed; it rarely commits itself or its resources to their ultimate success or failure. In this view, that would be "politics." But proponents of activism call the Church to the direct and open use of its own human and material resources in the promotion of change. In this camp we find some bishops and many clergy and lay people, among them advocates of Liberation Theology and members of various Marxist-Christian groups.

What I propose, then, is not one typology but several, distinguishing religious from sociopolitical dimensions of action. Table 4.9 sums up the possibilities. The distinctions drawn in the table, and elaborated in the preceding discussion, point to basic analytical and empirical differences. Once the types are clearly delineated, the problem becomes one of tracing out the relations, both analytical and empirical, between them, seeking patterns in the way religious and sociopolitical perspectives come together. A dynamic, dialectical analysis of this kind, which is sensitive to the mutual influence between ideas and models from each sphere, makes

[31] Maritain, *True Humanism*, p. 291.

TABLE 4.9
TYPOLOGIES OF CHURCH ELITES

Vallier	Sanders	Proposed
Politicians	Reactionaries	*Religious*
Papists	Conservatives	Ecclesial
Pastors	Progressives	Ecclesiastical
Pluralists	Innovators	*Sociopolitical*
		Traditional
		Activation
		Activism

possible a more adequate response to the central issues of this book: first, how ideas take form, or crystallize in regular patterns of action; and second, the way institutions develop characteristic styles of action which spill over from within to shape the activities of their members in more general social relations. The chapters which follow develop these ideas more fully, starting with the bishops and moving down and out to organizations and local activities.

5

Visions of the Church: Authority and Its Problems

PRECEDING chapters have touched briefly on the general issue of images of the Church and their relation to the concepts of authority held by Catholic elites. It is now time for a more complete analysis of these questions. This chapter begins by exploring several models of the Church now current in Catholicism, tracing their roots to alternative notions about the meaning of authority. These concepts and definitions are then examined in the context of the bishops' responses to questions on several key dimensions, most notably: changes in the Church since the Second Vatican Council, recent changes within each national Church, identification of the major problems facing each Church on the national level, and views of the future. The implications that such alternative concepts and models have for organizational structure and for the style and substance of action will also be considered.

Throughout, it will be apparent that visions of the Church and attitudes to politics are closely related. It is important to bear in mind that in this context politics is neither limited to activities directly affecting government nor simply to electoral or partisan involvements of various sorts. Rather, politics *of any kind* concerns power, legitimate authority, and the bases of community. Thus, as the foundations and the expression of authority (and of legitimate and even necessary action) in religion are transformed, this process necessarily affects perceptions and actions in society and politics as a whole.

As we have seen, a central feature of this process is the reconceptualization of the Church's relation to the "world." This rethinking of the Church, the world, and the proper ties between the two has helped to make earlier distinctions between Church and world lose much of their presumed sharpness; spheres of belief and action hitherto held apart flow easily together, and mutual influences in both directions become more notable. Of course, such influences have always been present; for, as Clifford Geertz reminds us, religion is both a model of and a model for society.[1] As a model of society, religious values, practices, and organizations reflect dominant social patterns. As a model for society, these same values, practices, and institutions are projected into the environment as generally valid paradigms, templates for perception and action that penetrate and organize daily life in subtle and elusive ways.

In Catholicism, these transfers have occurred many times, giving the Church a certain archaeological look, with a complex and layered mix of thirteenth-century orders, medieval dress, and Counter-Reformation and nineteenth-century practices and devotions, all coexisting with new and often revolutionary ideas and practices. The dilemmas thus created for the Church have been noted by Ivan Illich.

> Traditional pastoral analogies become anomalies in the asphalt, steel, and concrete context of city life. Urban renewal and new expressions of community call for another look at older terminology. Kings, crowns, and staffs have lost their meaning. Men are not subjects of sovereigns, and they impatiently question how they can be sheep led by a shepherd.[2]

Given the traditionally prominent position of religion in Latin America, its model-giving function is especially important. Indeed, as we have seen, much of the recent conflict and controversy which has swirled around the Church centers precisely on a struggle to control the content of religious symbols and thus to influence the more general social and political thrust of the religious institution. In this struggle, changing understandings of authority in the Church play a major role. Ideas about authority are central to institutional change because the concept of authority is the glue that holds groups and institutions together in a given form. Further, recognition of legitimate authority provides a focal point for continuity in the midst of change. Finally, changing definitions of the source and scope of legitimate authority open up new spheres of action as appropriate and necessary for the institution and the faithful. In this way, the Church's social projection grows from its evolving sense of self.

---

[1] For a full discussion see Geertz, "Religion as a Cultural System."
[2] Illich, "The Vanishing Clergyman," p. 84.

Authority and Ecclesiology

Not all authority is the same. Its bases and modes of exercise are not necessarily "authoritarian"; many forms are possible. Writing on democracy when the idea was still new and shocking, Alexis de Tocqueville recognized this point. He argued that authority is not absent in democratic societies, but rather takes new forms: "Its place is variable, but a place it necessarily has. The independence of individual minds may be greater or it may be less: unbounded it cannot be. Thus the question is, not to know whether any intellectual authority exists in the ages of democracy, but simply where it resides and by what standard it is to be judged."[3] De Tocqueville's point has special relevance for students of the Church today. Given the change and turmoil which has followed Vatican II and Medellín, it must seem to many Catholics as if all authority has come under attack; but the issue is more complex, for it involves not a simple rejection of authority, but rather a search for new foundations for religious authority. In the words of one Latin American priest, "Elimination of authority in the Church? What is at issue is rather the de-ideologization of the notion, and a search for a new form of its exercise which corresponds not to a scheme appropriate for monarchical society, but rather to a new kind of egalitarian relations between Church and community."[4]

The search for new bases and forms of authority leads quickly to fundamental questions of legitimacy. Authority, of course, is always closely tied to legitimacy; both concepts refer to the conditions under which commands and directives are accepted voluntarily, because they are seen either as correct, or as deriving from a source somehow "qualified" to command. In the Church, this qualification comes ultimately from the grace of God; it is mystical in origin. For many centuries, however, the exercise of authority in the Church has been virtually identified with ecclesiastical office and tied closely to obedience within hierarchically structured and juridically circumscribed situations.[5] The model of authority im-

---

[3] De Tocqueville, *Democracy in America*, 2:9.

[4] Cetrulo, "Conclusión crítica," p. 419.

[5] In his discussion of the "Roman School," Sanks notes that there, "authority is the very foundation of the church. . . . In this mode, unity depends on subordination. There could be no unity unless all are properly subject to some authority—the people to their bishops, the bishops to the pope. . . . The authority did not depend on the ability of the truth to con-

plicit in these practices is shot through with concepts borrowed from politics. But while societies have changed, the Church has remained frozen, still projecting the old images. As John McKenzie notes: "There has been no development in the theory of authority to correspond to the political evolution of recent centuries. Likewise, there has been no evolution of the forms of authority in the Church; the Roman and diocesan offices are still organized as the staffs of absolute monarchies."[6]

Many contemporary discussions of authority in the Catholic Church point to the general distinction, drawn ever more sharply since Vatican II, between a concept of authority that emphasizes equality, mutuality, and communitarian structures, and one that gives greater weight to hierarchical themes and juridical definitions, stressing the general subordination of laity to clergy and bishops.[7] As J. B. Metz points out, the move away from traditional, hierarchical concepts is part of a general revaluation of the paternal models and images long basic to the Church. Metz argues that for centuries the Church has confused religious authority with the authority of the patriarch. Now this is changing, with vast implications.

> "From patriarchal authority to the authority of witness"—one should not underestimate the changes this implies for the norms of the ecclesiastical exercise of authority. It decisively brings the practical understanding of church authority and church office to the church's enduring witness and to the whole of the church as a "pilgrim people of God." The recent council emphasized this new view of authority in order to define the meaning and function of church leadership as testimony.[8]

---

vince, but on the legal right of the bearers of authority to command. And so a great deal of time and energy was expended to show that these were the legal heirs who had validly and legitimately succeeded to the authority" (*Authority in the Church*, pp. 11-13). See also Congar's essay on the history of authority in the Church, "Le développement historique de l'autorité dans l'église," and McKenzie's historical study, *Authority in the Church*.

[6] McKenzie, *Authority in the Church*, p. 19.

[7] The issue of authority has been the subject of extensive debate in the Church since the Second Vatican Council. In addition to the works cited in note 5, above, see Dulles, *Models of the Church*, and Meissner, *The Assault on Authority*.

[8] Metz, "Prophetic Authority," p. 195.

Both old and new concepts of authority are grounded in different understandings of what the Church itself is. Hence, some exploration of the relevant ecclesiologies may be useful at this point. While many possible models of the Church can be suggested,[9] two are particularly salient in contemporary discussions: the Church as institution, and the Church as Pilgrim People of God.

Those who view the Church primarily as institutional tend to identify it in practice with the ecclesiastical institution. Great emphasis is placed on rank and on obedience to legally constituted authority. The roles of clergy and laity are sharply distinguished, with the latter subordinate. Finally, the entire model is conceived of as complete and ahistorical; the Church is presented as timeless and unchanging. Brian Smith and T. Howard Sanks state this perspective well: "the Church is seen as a supernatural society, complete and juridically perfect, that passes judgement on the world, whose value is received from something outside itself, where the Church is related to the world on the analogy of soul and body, the latter existing only for the good of the former."[10]

The model of the Church as Pilgrim People of God stands in direct contrast, for it sees the Church primarily as a historical community of believers. The Church is no longer depicted as a perfect society of the saved, set apart and protected from the world, but rather as a group in constant dialogue with that world. Great stress is placed on the historical experience, of change, and a concern for shared experience and mutual responsibility is prominent. For these reasons, an expanded and more autonomous role is given to the laity.

The Second Vatican Council's stress on a vision of the Church as a Pilgrim People shifts its notions of authority away from hitherto predominant concerns—obedience, rank, and hierarchy—and opens the door to an emphasis on event, witness, and testimony. and their expressions in solidarity through shared experience, as sources of authority and models for action. This shift has major consequences for the life of the Church. For if authority is grounded in testimony and witness, then believers (elites and rank and file alike) come to see action as a necessary expression of

---

[9] These are fully discussed in Dulles, *Models*, where five models are elaborated: the Church as institution, as mystical communion, as sacrament, as herald, and as servant.

[10] Smith and Sanks, "Liberation Ecclesiology," p. 11.

their religious roles. In this way, the most recent self-image of the Church provides a model for its relations with society, a model whose implications are particularly notable in three areas: a pervasive commitment to social activism, a renewed emphasis on collegiality, and a growing concern for lay participation.

Social activism is nothing new to the Church. Concern for social issues and programs has a long history, reinforced in this century by a series of well-known papal encyclicals. Nevertheless, it is fair to say that since the Second Vatican Council the emphasis on social activism has grown and also has shifted its focus. The renewed interest in social questions is related to a general rediscovery of biblical sources, models, and metaphors. Just as a definition of authority in terms of testimony and witness emphasizes shared experience, solidarity, and action, so too the use of biblical (especially Old Testament) models stresses the role of God as an active presence in the world. Belief and authentic faith are seen as most completely expressed in actions to promote social justice.[11] Moreover this activism has a different focus, because, with the pervasive stress on historical experience, it is no longer a simple matter of applying known doctrine to the case at hand. Rather, authentic action begins with social analysis, with a searching in society for the "signs of the times"—events or situations which stimulate religious reflection. As Roger Vekemans complains,

> Now one does not move from a well-established doctrine toward a situation to be influenced or even transformed in accordance with this doctrine, but rather returns from a lived situation toward that which can give it meaning. Coming from the world, one directs a question to Christian faith, but also, in given historical circumstances, a direction, a request, a call.[12]

The renewed interest in collegiality is more organizational and structural, although here, too, changes begun within the ecclesiastical institution spill over to affect social relations in general.

---

[11] This point is made in Míguez Bonino, *Christians and Marxists*, and in Miranda, *Marx and the Bible*.

[12] Vekemans, "La iglesia en el proceso de liberación," p. 82. Vekemans speaks further of changes in the Latin American Church in terms of *mundanización, politización*, and *praxeologización* (i.e., overwhelming concern for the world, strong drive for political action, and emphasis on action, or praxis, as the ultimate source of validity).

This is because "collegiality" refers not only to the delegation of decision-making power, or to its broader distribution among the bishops,[13] but also to the idea that authority arises from varied sources within the Church, not from a single source that is mediated through Church offices.[14] Thus collegiality is related to the issue of action; for, although in the words of the council, "the Church has always had the duty of scrutinizing the signs of the times,"[15] in practice, differences increasingly turn on the issue of *who* is to select and read the signs. The recognition of multiple sources of authority thus means that collegiality between pope and bishops and among bishops themselves may be paralleled by more "collegial" relations between bishops and priests, priests and laity, and among lay people themselves in parishes and Catholic organizations.

Notions of collegiality and shared responsibility thus spread down and outward within the Church. Simultaneously, such ideas are often brought in at the base by lay groups pressing claims for their own autonomous values and authority. The question of collegiality thus contains within it the more general issue of the status and role of the laity, and hence of the proper scope and form of lay participation. Are the laity essentially children to be protected, shielded, blessed, and directed—a flock to be guided by its shepherds? Or, rather, do they incorporate and represent autonomous values? These considerations form part of a more general revaluation of "the world" by Catholic thinkers: no longer is the world simply a stage on which eternal, unchanging, and abstract moral principles are played out; now it is a potential *source* of religious values for Catholics.

These issues are joined in many forms and areas, and they hold

[13] As we shall see, many bishops clearly limit collegiality in precisely this way, taking it as a warrant for greater authority among the bishops vis-à-vis Rome while denying its extension to more collegial practices within their own spheres of authority.

[14] In his analysis of New Testament concepts of authority, McKenzie highlights two themes: first, authority is not central to biblical discussions at all; and second, in the final instance, authority derives from the Holy Spirit and is given to the whole Church, not to its leaders alone. *Authority in the Church*, p. 58. See also Meissner, *The Assault on Authority*, pp. 174ff., for a discussion of multiple sources of authority in the Church.

[15] "Pastoral Constitution on the Church in the Modern World" (Gaudium et Spes), in Abbott, *The Documents of Vatican II*, par. 4, p. 201.

notable consequences for the inner life of the Church and for the form and the substantive concerns of Catholic organizations. Within the ecclesiastical institution, greater attention to collegiality and lay participation reflects a heightened sense of the Church as a community, and of the need to reduce social distances within it. Many bishops I interviewed spoke of the need for greater simplicity in the lives of bishops and clergy, eliminating elevated titles and abandoning any hint of ostentation or luxury. Two Colombians put it this way:

> I believe it is this, that these differences have been greatly reduced. The priest no longer is a person removed from the community in which he lives, but rather works with the people and is committed along with them. This is what the people sense. Of course, intellectually, one sees more changes, but for the people this is what is easiest to grasp . . . the people see that the clergy is closer to them, shares with them—this is what the people want.[16]
>
> I believe that one very notable change is that we have realized that here we were separated from the people by a series of obstacles, barriers: the very fact of calling one "Most Excellent Bishop," the image the people had (which was correct) that the bishop was a different kind of being, the bishop with a different cassock, of special colors, and with a beautiful pectoral cross; and it is the same with calling the bishop's house an "episcopal palace."[17]

This preference for simplicity reflects the bishops' desire to draw closer to the average member of the Church, to take a step, however small, toward greater integration with the daily life of the community.

Concepts of authority also have many consequences for the structure and the substantive concerns of Catholic organizations. These will be explored in great detail in chapters 7 and 8, below. Here, I shall simply point out the degree to which traditional models of authority and of the Church are associated with particular styles of organization. The powerful network of groups developed in this century under the rubric of "Catholic Action" is a good example. Catholic Action groups share several structural

---

[16] Interview 80114, 13 June 1972.   [17] Interview 80111, 30 Oct. 1972.

characteristics. First, close links to the hierarchy are stressed, often through the person of a "spiritual" or "moral" adviser appointed to each group by the bishop. Second, great stress is placed on centralized control over the selection and training of lay leaders. And finally, goals are in large measure set by the bishops, and subordinated to their vision of the Church's broader goals.[18]

Combining the new perspectives on authority, collegiality, and lay participation described here leads to organizational consequences which are less clear-cut. Such models lend themselves less to fixed, permanent organizations; they favor instead loose, shifting coalitions of laity and clergy who come together for particular ends and then dissolve, re-forming later for other purposes. In general, these are relatively homogeneous groups that emphasize common experience and reflection as guides to action.[19]

Two central theses have been advanced so far in this chapter. The first is that concepts of authority, the Church, and the like affect the substance of action by determining the source of values to be implemented. In this vein, we have seen how institutional and hierarchical concepts draw their goals and orientations from a store of presumably timeless and unchanging moral and doctrinal precepts, whereas more communitarian concepts derive their values from surrounding society, seeking the "signs of the times" which the faith illuminates. Action in the latter case is then oriented toward the continuing transformation of that society, not toward its preservation and defense. The second major thesis is related; it concerns the impact of such concepts on styles of organization and action, most notably in terms of the structure and goals of Catholic associations. One Colombian priest, a specialist in working with youth, puts these relationships in the perspective of his own area.

Work with young people has changed much as the faith has

[18] See, for example, the excellent study by Poggi, *Catholic Action in Italy*.
[19] One organizational expression of these models is in the "base communities," which have developed vigorously in Latin America in recent years. Some of the issues raised by these communities are discussed further in chapters 7 and 9, below. In addition, see Bruneau, "Basic Christian Communities in Latin America"; Pro Mundi Vita, *Basic Communities in the Church*; and United States Catholic Conference, *Basic Christian Communities*.

changed. Before, faith was above all a question of sacraments. Later, it became a question of groups of social assistance. Thus catechism groups in and out of schools had a welfare orientation. Now we are coming to form groups with a political commitment. . . . These orientations vary according to the concept of man and God: man as a being already made, once and for all; man as a dependent being; or man as a being in action. . . . The first concept corresponds to a static and obscure God, and produces groups like the Legion of Mary, who come together to say the rosary, with no relation to reality, since they see reality as something already made, complete. The second corresponds to a God who requires or asks those who have more to give to those who have less, who speaks of a paternalistic charity. This is a paternalist God. In this view, a pyramid exists. God has everything: those who are close to Him have more and are obliged to give to those who have less, until one gets to the bottom, to the man who has nothing and no one below him. And the third vision is of God as the future of man: a God who makes history and proclaims the realization of man in all his human aspects—of social justice. A God who reveals himself in history. This is the meaning of the "People of God."[20]

The detailed exposition of changing concepts of authority, Church, and the like is necessary but not sufficient for our purpose. Church leaders, activists, and average members do not operate in a void, but instead take their guiding concepts and fit them to action within specific contexts and issues. The next section explores these questions further, through analysis of the bishops' attitudes on several key dimensions of change in the Church.

THE VIEWS OF THE BISHOPS

To gauge the bishops' views more accurately, I posed a series of questions dealing with change in the Church at different levels, taken from varying points of view. I shall begin analysis here with a look at responses to two central questions: (1) "Among the changes instituted by the Second Vatican Council, which seem to you to be the most important?" and (2) "What do you see as the

[20] Interview 80506, 17 Feb. 1972. For a discussion of the Legion of Mary and similar groups see chapter 7, below.

most important changes in the Colombian (Venezuelan) Church in recent years?"

Speaking of the most important changes since the council, both Venezuelans and Colombians most often single out new patterns of authority. These are followed in frequency by mention of the Church's renewed commitment to social progress and by discussions of juridical-organizational changes within Church structures. Many bishops simply point to the greater dynamism that pervades the entire Church. One Colombian bishop described changing patterns of authority in this way:

> In my view, in terms of priority, the principal change is the change in the form of the relations between hierarchy and clergy, religious, and the faithful as a whole. That is to say, to the degree to which pope and bishops, and their collaborating agencies, understand that our function in the Church, more than of command, is a function of service, we will then try to find every possible means to make this service into a reality.[21]

A Venezuelan made this point in a similar way, arguing that the core of change "lies in this very exercise of authority in the Church, in this sense of communion, of the importance of dialogue between the bishop and the priests, and with the laity."[22] These changes in notions of authority and in the sense of the Church are often expressed in what may seem unimportant and incidental changes: the way bishops and priests dress, the kinds of houses they live in, the use of formal titles, and so on. But such changes are important. Thus, one Venezuelan archbishop, whom I interviewed during a day-long ride by jeep to a remote ranch in his diocese, stressed the importance of simplicity and of the need for bishops to go out into the world.

> Here things are simple, as you can see. Here I am, in a jeep, talking to you, talking with others, going out to see them. This, all this, could not even be conceived of twenty years ago. Twenty years ago, when I arrived at [his former diocese] and drove a truck, the whole city was scandalized. I told this to the pope, I told him that I did not go there to stay in the sacristy, to genuflect and nothing more, but rather to go where the problems

[21] Interview 80123, 1 May 1972.   [22] Interview 60115, 19 Aug. 1971.

are ... and moreover to emphasize human problems. Not just take the man and put him in a church. If he is hungry, what good is it to put him in a church? This doesn't help him at all. His human problem must be resolved.[23]

A Colombian bishop carried this kind of change further, by stressing the growth of a sense of community in the Church. "We cannot speak of institutional changes. I believe there is a spirit more important than institutional changes, which is the spirit of conversion of the Church into a community—of what might be called the de-institutionalization, the dismantling of the institution. So far this has only been seen a little, one might say almost in incidentals; but the spirit exists, and this spirit will make us a more evangelical, more dynamic, and more integrated Church, which at the same time will be better able to respond to the needs of the modern world and serve it better as a salt and ferment."[24]

Although not all bishops view these changes in a wholly favorable light, most welcome them as a necessary step toward rejuvenating the inner life of the Church by encouraging greater simplicity, dialogue, and informed participation.[25] These concerns stand out in the bishops' views of major changes in each national Church. Thus, in Colombia, changed authority relations and an expanded role for the laity were the most common responses, followed at some distance by mention of the Church's greater commitment to social progress and the consolidation of Church organizations. The Venezuelan pattern is generally similar. Authority relations are by far the most notable area of change, followed by mention of social progress and juridical-organizational changes. One influential Colombian bishop argued that the entire process is rooted in the Church's developing sense of self-criticism, which facilitates discussion and change. "At this time, the most important change which the Church has seen is that the Church has become critical

---

[23] Interview 60107, 6 July 1971.   [24] Interview 80121, 22 Mar. 1972.

[25] Several bishops felt that lay participation in the Church could be overdone. For example, one Venezuelan noted that "in the promotion of the lay apostolate, although good in general, at times we have fallen into danger. Thus, many lay people, without preparation, consider themselves in a position to direct the Church—since now we are all the Church, and the People of God, and so forth—and they begin to encroach on the field of the priestly ministry proper" (Interview 60112, 9 Aug. 1971).

of itself. From being an institution which bordered on the magical, a Church which was perfect, which could not be wrong, now, in contrast, this new vision has united us in reflection."[26]

This openness to internal dialogue and self-critical reflection is further expressed in real changes in Church governance, most notably in the relations of bishops to clergy. Whereas the bishop was once the unquestioned and unchallenged local authority, now dialogue and consultation are common. Altered relations between bishops and clergy are also reflected in changes (or attempts to effect changes) in relations with lay people and lay organizations. Change has proved more difficult here, for while many bishops talk of the need to end clerical dominance of lay groups, old patterns are hard to root out. One Colombian bishop with extensive experience in lay groups put the problem this way:

> We have not been able to discover a formula by which lay people can act independently of the hierarchy, because all these were hierarchical movements, very closely tied to the hierarchy, with the laity in an infantile position. And on the other hand we, the hierarchy and the clergy, have not known how to handle this new, postconciliar laity, so that all in all it is a strange situation. I do not consider it positive.[27]

Underlying many of these new perceptions, patterns of action, and the problems they occasionally bring is a basic revaluation of the world. Many bishops express a sense of the autonomy and independent validity of temporal values that is new to them. As one influential Colombian pointed out, "Before, we were very suspicious of them. But through *Gaudium et Spes* we have learned a greater, more objective appreciation for the values of the world, and for the need to collaborate in the progress of the world."[28]

As these remarks indicate, the bishops do not limit their concerns only to authority and to the nature of the institutional Church. Indeed, many see changes in the Church primarily in terms of a greater commitment to social progress. For several Colombians, the Church's growing interest in social reform is closely linked to the elimination of its previously close ties with the Conservative party. The Church is now free to act:

[26] Interview 80139, 10 June 1972. [27] Interview 80110, 11 July 1972.
[28] Interview 80122, 25 Apr. 1972.

Cutting the ties of the Church, as an institution, with purely partisan conflicts; rapprochement with one group from which she had been officially distant since the last century [the Liberal party], growing identification with the interests of the people in its poorest sector, as well as the clarity with which her mission is being developed in the sense that she serves not only souls, as was thought earlier, but also exists "for man and for the whole man."[29]

In the analysis of these questions about change in the Church, up to three responses were coded for each bishop. Separate indices were then constructed to gauge the degree to which change in any given area was emphasized: lows indicate the percentage of bishops who made no reference to a particular category; highs, of those who mentioned it exclusively or predominantly; and medium refers to those who mentioned a given kind of change at least once. Recall my earlier suggestion that differences between Venezuelans and Colombians would grow sharper as they moved from general perceptions to consider the concrete circumstances of each national Church. Table 5.1 shows that, in general, Venezuelans concentrate much more on questions of authority. Moreover, when they turn to consider their own Church, Venezuelans stress questions of social progress less, and authority more, than their Colombian counterparts.

Clearly, a move from generalities to particulars leads to different directions of change in the two countries—a result which fits well within the pattern of national differences already discussed. But the question of authority is sufficiently important to the argument of this book that analysis must go beyond simply noting the national patterns. To understand the full meaning of change in the Church for the bishops, responses must be examined more closely —first, to assess the impact of education; and second, to see how views of change on different levels (after Vatican II and in each national Church) are related to one another.

Consider education first. Given my earlier discussion of the meaning of education in the Church, one might expect that bishops with advanced education would be, at the very least, more *aware* of general currents of change. But controlling for education makes for relatively little variation in their views of change in the Church

[29] Interview 80142, 21 Aug. 1972.

TABLE 5.1
DIMENSIONS OF CHANGE IN THE CHURCH (%)

	Authority Relations			Social Progress			Juridical Organizational			Dynamism Openness		
	Low	Med	Hi	Low	Med	Hi	Low	Med	Hi	Low	Med	Hi

Most Important Changes in the Church Since the Council

Venezuela (36%)	23	33	43	52	43	5	62	33	5	71	19	10
Colombia (64%)	32	35	32	68	32	—	54	35	11	60	30	11
Totals (N = 58)	29	35	36	62	36	2	57	35	9	64	26	10

Most Important Changes in the Venezuelan (Colombian) Church

Venezuela (36%)	24	29	48	67	19	14	62	38	—	71	19	10
Colombia (64%)	46	24	30	49	32	19	68	22	11	84	8	8
Totals (N = 58)	38	26	36	55	28	17	66	28	7	79	12	9

as a whole (see table 5.2). The strongest visible differences come in perceptions of the juridical aspects of change, which are mentioned much more often by the less educated bishops, who also are *less* likely to mention the dynamism of the postconciliar Church.

The impact of education is more pronounced within nations. Tables 5.2 and 5.3 show that as the bishops move from the general to the particular, leaving Vatican II and concentrating on change in their own Church, the more educated among them turn away from the transformation of the Church as a community, focusing instead on the transformation of society ("social progress"). While level of education makes little difference to the pattern of responses within each country on changes since the council, sharp differences emerge within each nation when the bishops consider changes in their own national Church. In both countries, the less educated are much more likely to stress changes in authority relations, while those with advanced training mention authority less, concentrating instead on dimensions like "social progress."

TABLE 5.2
DIMENSIONS OF CHANGE IN THE CHURCH, BY EDUCATION (%)

Education	Authority Relations			Social Progress			Juridical Organizational			Dynamism Openness		
	Low	Med	Hi	Low	Med	Hi	Low	Med	Hi	Low	Med	Hi
Most Important Changes in the Church Since the Council												
Seminary (40%)	26	35	29	57	39	4	39	52	9	78	17	4
Advanced (60%)	31	34	34	66	34	—	69	23	9	54	31	14
Totals (N = 58)	29	35	36	62	36	2	57	35	9	64	26	10
Most Important Changes in the Venezuelan (Colombian) Church												
Seminary (43%)	20	24	56	64	20	16	68	28	4	88	12	—
Advanced (57%)	52	27	21	49	33	18	64	27	9	73	12	15
Totals (N = 58)	38	26	36	55	28	17	66	28	7	79	12	9

TABLE 5.3
MOST IMPORTANT CHANGES IN THE VENEZUELAN (COLOMBIAN) CHURCH (%)

Education	Venezuela (N = 21)						Colombia (N = 37)					
	Authority Relations			Social Progress			Authority Relations			Social Progress		
	Low	Med	Hi	Low	Med	Hi	Low	Med	Hi	Low	Med	Hi
Seminary[a]	15	23	62	77	8	15	25	25	50	50	33	17
Advanced[b]	37.5	37.5	25	50	37.5	12.5	56	24	20	48	32	20
Totals	24	29	48	67	19	14	46	24	30	49	32	19

[a] In Venezuela, 62% have a seminary education; in Colombia, 32%.
[b] In Venezuela, 38% have an advanced education; in Colombia, 68%.

The roots of this pattern can be found in the combination of national context, education, and career outlined in the previous chapter. The lingering effects of the "Roman school" on the mentalities of the bishops dispose them to be cautious about implementing change in their own backyards, despite a general acceptance of the impact of Vatican II. Moreover, as we have seen, lower levels of education (particularly in Venezuela) go along with more pastoral career patterns, whose humanizing effects presumably encourage a greater concern for the quality of relations within the Church, while leading to greater tolerance of actual innovations in this area.

To this point, I have assumed that perceptions of change on different levels in the Church, particularly in terms of authority, are mutually dependent. But the results so far cast some doubt on this assumption. How, really, are views of authority on different levels of the Church related? Looking at the data in general, only a slight relation emerges between perceptions of authority in Vatican II and within each national Church. But national patterns are strong, and they are different. Colombians, for example, display a consistent relation between scores on both indices: lows on the Vatican level are likely to be low on the national level, and the same holds for those scoring high. In Venezuela, however, those scoring high on authority as a most important dimension of change in the Venezuelan Church are equally likely to score either low or high on emphasizing authority as an aspect of change in the Church as a whole since the council. Moreover, those scoring low on authority since Vatican II are much more likely to score high on emphasizing changes in authority at home than are those high on this Vatican-level measure (see table 5.4).

Clearly, while questions of authority are important to the perceptions and views of the bishops, their impact is not uniform throughout the Church. Bishops do not live in a void, but work their general views out in the concrete circumstances of national and local life. Thus it is not surprising that social context plays a major role in setting the scope, direction, and interrelation of the bishops' views of the Church. For Venezuelans, a concern with changes in authority relations in the national church is not especially dependent on perceptions of authority in the Church as a whole. Colombians, on the other hand, are much more consistent in logically and philosophically relating the two levels. Why? For Colombians, the general traditions of the Church are surely *reinforced* by the power and established status of the ecclesiastical institution and by the general religious orientation of Colombian society. But this is not the case in Venezuela, where social patterns are neither built nor justified in terms of an ideal "Christian" society, but rather reflect the complex and often contradictory patterns of a secular society.

TABLE 5.4
INDICES OF AUTHORITY COMPARED (%)

Authority Relations in the National Church	Authority Relations Since the Council			
	Low	Med	High	Totals
Both Countries (N = 56)				
Low	38	33	29	38
Med	20	40	40	27
High	32	32	43	36
Total	27	34	38	
Venezuela (N = 20)				
Low	20	20	60	25
Med	—	67	33	30
High	44	11	44	45
Total	25	30	45	
Colombia (N = 36)				
Low	44	38	19	44
Med	33	22	44	25
High	9	39	42	31
Totals	31	36	33	

These considerations prompt further exploration of the bishops' views of their own Church. (The reader will recall my earlier discussion of the major problems of each national Church.) The bishops' views of their own Church's central problems may also tell us a lot about their image of the Church itself—let us listen a moment.

For most Venezuelans, the Church's overwhelming problems are its lack of money and personnel. These problems make it hard for many dioceses to maintain even a skeletal staff in the field, and they effectively choke off innovation. For some, the lack of money forces the Church into a repugnant position of asking fees for services, which alienates the people. Discussing his economic problems, one Venezuelan bishop held his hand to his throat as if he were being choked, saying:

> This is the way we live all the time. We lack the means to support the parish priests. Our great goal is the elimination of ec-

clesiastical fees—charges for baptisms, for burials, and the like. Here [in his diocese] we do not charge for confirmations. Marriage is another matter. But with burials it is shocking, with burials and funerals—for 50 it is like this, better for 100. Shocking. We have managed to make confirmations free: since it is me alone, I make the sacrifice. But we are in a blind alley because the priests live from this; many times they have no other income. We have no other sources of income.[30]

In Colombia such dilemmas are less pressing, and greater emphasis is given to the social and moral problems of the nation. Pointing to the vast range of difficulties associated with development, one Colombian bishop argued that these are the problems of the Church itself. "Of course in general the Church takes part in the world. Therefore, necessarily we have the same problems the world has: these are reflected in the Church, and therefore in *our* Church as well."[31] Several Colombians further pointed to the Church's need to find a way to talk about injustice in contemporary society—to discuss structures of injustice in a creative way. In this vein, one bishop drew an explicit link between social and political reform and the Church's own capacity to reform itself. A reformed Church would legitimate new social ideas while releasing energies long pent up in rigid ecclesiastical structures.

> I would say that the Church has to face up, with great spirit, to change in the socioeconomic and sociopolitical structures of the country. In this she has a prophetic role, in shaping consciousness through formation of the national community, and also a role of service, through her own example, which implies a continuous need for reform in her own structures.
>
> Even though ecclesiastical structures are doubtless the fruit of every culture and epoch, there is no doubt that the rigidity of our structures has nevertheless contributed to maintaining the structures of dependency and oppression of civil society.[32]

Of course most Colombian bishops are well aware of the strength of their own Church, but many are concerned about whether the *kind* of strength and power derived from the past will equip it to face the future. "I would also add this. We also need a

[30] Interview 60126, 9 July 1971. Only bishops do confirmations.
[31] Interview 80146, 9 June 1972.   [32] Interview 80121, 22 Mar. 1972.

more grown-up Christianity, which is not, let us say, which does not feel itself strong only because of the traditional concessions, aids, and privileges it has received from the civil authorities, but instead the Christian, on the day these privileges disappear (be they renounced or taken away)—Christianity remains alive."[33]

While Venezuelans understandably concentrate on simply building an institution that is solvent, Colombians reach out more effectively into society to strengthen the delivery of the gospel message. A young Colombian bishop argued that a new style of evangelization is required. In his view, priests serve several different functions: they provide sacraments, offer moral and prophetic judgements, and guide or even rule the community. These three types of priests and lines of action, in his view, correspond to three visions of Christ: as priest, prophet, and king. The bishop then put the argument in more down-to-earth ("folkloric") terms, writing his own typology of priests as follows:

1. Christ the Priest, magician or sorcerer.
2. Christ the Prophet, traveling salesman.
3. Christ the King, *cacique* or boss of the town.

The first priest, he of the ritual, is the sorcerer, the magician. Of course I am not saying he *is* a sorcerer, but he might seem so in these terms. Don't go and say that a Colombian bishop said that the priest is a sorcerer. The other is a boss, like a political boss. Then, what we need is one who knows how to sell an idea. There is a kind of traveling salesman, a man who goes from town to town selling lotions, ointments, cures, and things of that kind.[34]

These different types of priests are present in every community. The old-style priest wanted to be the general leader of the town, "But what the people care about is ritual, and the old type of priest wants to be a guide, a leader or boss. And I believe that what we really, definitively need is the prophet, evangelization, pastoral action."[35]

With all the changes the bishops see in the Church, how do they view the future? I put the question in this way: "Looking towards the future, how do you think the Church in Venezuela [Colombia]

[33] Interview 80102, 13 July 1972. [34] Interview 80152, 23 May 1972.
[35] Ibid.

will be different twenty years from now?" There is little difference between Venezuelans and Colombians on this question. Most bishops in each country see further evolution on the lines already outlined, particularly in terms of authority relations and the development of more authentic faith. Many note a trend to greater lay participation, and most welcome it. A small number (one Venezuelan and five Colombians) see the Church of the future as a minority—a select group with greater awareness, training, and understanding of the faith. Despite their small number, these latter bishops' responses are worth a closer look; for, as I suggested earlier, they run counter to traditional concepts of the Church as embracing all who accept its sacraments. The idea of a minority Church, consisting largely of the highly prepared and motivated, is attractive to these men precisely because it responds to the concerns for more effective evangelization outlined here. As one young Colombian put it, "We will have a more committed laity, and a greater apathetic mass which is removed in sentiment from the Church. Now we have more people tied by sentiment to the Church, but in the future they will be more apathetic. Thus it will be a more defined Church. I would like to be part of that Church."[36]

The future is a challenge, for it calls the Church to new and potentially different kinds of actions. One bishop noted that this worries the clergy, for they will be asked "to provide things they themselves have never received."[37] Most bishops are quite open to change and see the Church also evolving in response to social transformations. The core will remain intact, but externalities will change according to circumstances. As one Colombian noted,

> I believe that the Church is eternal and will remain identical until the end of time. The different modalities of course may change. What these modalities will be, what the future will be, well, let us leave it to the prophets to speak of the future, and we will content ourselves with fulfilling our obligations and duties in the time which falls to us, which is the present, no?[38]

Not all bishops are so reticent, however. One Venezuelan reflected on the future at some length, and his remarks (quoted here in full) give the richness and interconnection of the changes that he and others like him foresee.

[36] Ibid.
[37] Interview 80153, 20 Nov. 1972.
[38] Interview 80134, 22 Nov. 1972.

There will be changes, and I see certain orientations from which these changes will arise. In the area of greater lay participation within the Church, this will intensify notably, in a greater and more intense service to the human community, with a spirit of greater evangelical simplicity. Things will change a lot in this sense. That is not to say that the Venezuelan Church has ever been very powerful—we have had a somewhat different history. But nevertheless this orientation to service, simplicity, and real, true testimony will become much more intense.

In the area of ministry, we will enjoy a greater variety of types and forms of ministry. . . . There will be, shall we say, a more institutionalized dialogue and greater co-responsibility in the direction of the Church itself—at the level of bishops, bishops-priests, priests-laity, and including the religious orders. Well, in sum the situation of the Church, and many of its changes, will of course depend on the type of society we have twenty years from now. Certainly, certainly it will be very different from the kind of society we have now . . . more egalitarian, with more participation, and, we hope, much more just than the society we have now. This society will impose a particular style on the Church.[39]

In addition to noting the mention of specific processes or types of change, I also looked for the kind of context in which a bishop set his discussions of the future. Did he confine himself to the institutional Church, or did he consider, more broadly, its relations with society? Or did he range more widely still, to consider the development of more authentic faith and understanding among the people, or the emergence of a greater sense of community, belonging, and purpose in the Church? Venezuelans and Colombians are quite similar here, with one notable exception. As table 5.5 shows, almost half the Colombians discussed the future of the Church in terms of more authentic faith, morality, and understanding among average Catholics. But, in Venezuela, far fewer bishops stress this area, and over a quarter of them look for the growth of a sense of community and belonging in the Church.

This pattern of national views fits the image of the two Churches developed in these pages. On the one hand, we have the Colombian Church—well structured, adequately staffed, and powerful—which

[39] Interview 60130, 27-28 May 1971.

TABLE 5.5
CONTEXT OF DISCUSSIONS OF FUTURE OF THE CHURCH (%)

	Venezuela (N = 17)	Colombia (N = 34)
Institutional church	12	12
Church-society ties	35	29
Faith, morality, and understanding	24	50
Sense of community	29	6
Sociopolitical change	—	3

is aware of new trends in the Church, but constrained by its own traditions and past successes from translating them easily into new patterns of behavior. On the other hand, the Venezuelan Church is poorly organized, weak, and lacks money and clergy; Venezuelans have had less exposure to the currents of change in the Church at large. Nevertheless, the realities of daily life in a plural, secular society lead the Venezuelans, in practice, to *greater* concern for the kind of openness and community espoused at the international level by the Second Vatican Council. A summary of the pattern of differences that have emerged so far between the bishops and Churches of the two countries is provided in table 5.6.

In both Churches, the bishops are concerned about changes in authority and are open, in varying degrees, to transformations both in the inner life of the Church and in the kind of projection into society which flows from these altered self-images. Clearly, if attitudes and dispositions were all there is to social reality, we would be assured that the Church in each country is well on the way to dramatic changes in the areas discussed so far. But of course things are never so simple. Attitudes are always tempered by intervening factors, so that the link from general positions to particular actions is never direct. The backgrounds and personal experiences of the bishops and the institutional traditions and routines of each national Church combine with predominant images of the Church to filter and shape the impact of general currents of change on particular stances and actions in Church and society alike. Figure 5.1 portrays the process of change laid out to this point.

As I noted earlier, the difficulties generated by changing concepts and practices in the Church most often arise in the context

TABLE 5.6
ECCLESIAL DIMENSIONS OF CHANGE

	Venezuela	Colombia
1. Institutional context	Weak & building	Strong & defending
2. Elite careers favored	Pastoral	Bureaucratic-educational
3. Changes emphasized since the council	Authority/ social progress	Authority/ juridical
4. Changes emphasized in national Church	Authority/ juridical	Authority/ social progress
5. Change in emphasis on authority, from council to national	Increase	Decrease
6. Problems of national Church	Internal	Moral and social problems of the nation
7. Style of action	Paternal/ open	Institutional/ more guarded

NOTE: This analytical table is carried forward in table 6.13, with the addition of social and political dimensions.

of organizational structures and ongoing practices; the ideas the bishops praise in general terms come back to haunt them in the form of pressures for greater independence and responsibility from lay organizations and clergy. Fuller consideration of these factors intervening between ideas of authority and its actual exercise brings us to the subtitle of this chapter, "authority and its problems."

PROBLEMS OF AUTHORITY: CLERGY AND LAYMEN

To this point, I have shown that many bishops are quite open to changed authority relations within the Church, although the degree to which they emphasize these as opposed to other dimensions of change varies with the concrete circumstances in which they live. Despite this general receptivity to change, many bishops clearly retain a *clerical* view of the Church. While they recognize that "the Church" is more than the ecclesiastical institution alone, when it comes to daily practice they think almost automatically of clergy.

FIGURE 5.1
Pocesses of Change in the Church

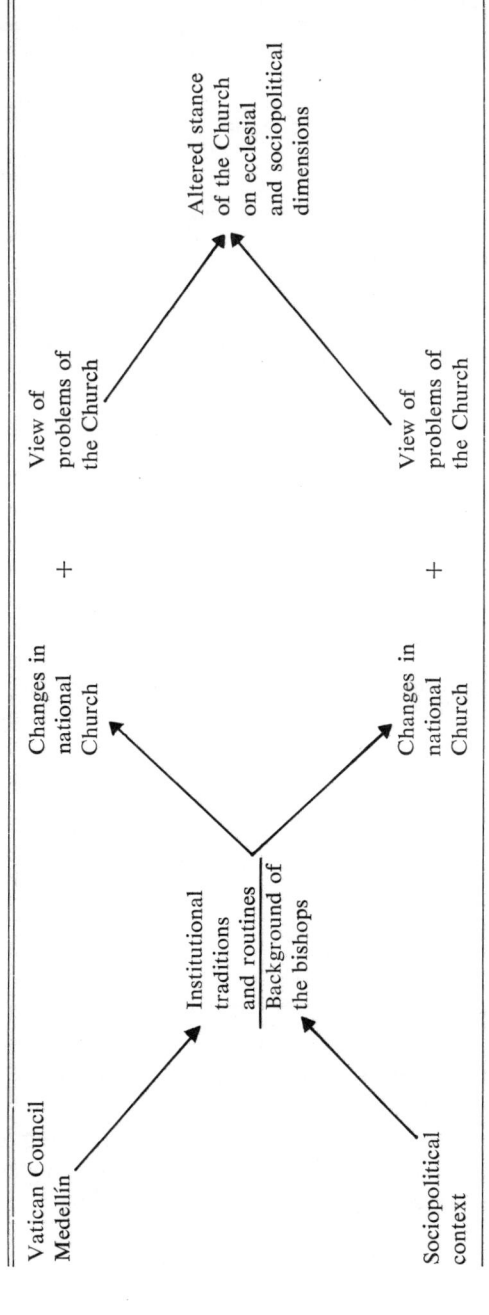

```
Vatican Council          Changes in              View of
Medellín      ───▶      national        +       problems of
                         Church                  the Church
                            ▲                        ╲
                            │                         ╲
                    Institutional                      ▶  Altered stance
                    traditions                            of the Church
                    and routines                          on ecclesial
                    ─────────────                         and sociopolitical
                    Background of                         dimensions
                    the bishops                        ▶
                            │                         ╱
                            ▼                        ╱
                         Changes in             View of
                         national        +       problems of
                         Church                  the Church
Sociopolitical  ───▶
context
```

Thus most administrative, teaching, and pastoral tasks are routinely assigned to the clergy.

The implications of such a predisposition to think in clerical terms are visible in the bishops' reactions to the scarcity of clergy. Native clergy have long been rare in Venezuela, and even Colombia shows signs of future scarcity. But although most of the bishops recognize the problem, the "solutions" they propose depend heavily, in both countries, on vocational campaigns intended to attract more students to the empty seminaries—more of the same, in other words. Only a handful (2 of 22 Venezuelans and 4 of 38 Colombians) propose the development of new forms of ministry that would incorporate the laity, such as married clergy, or permanent deacons.

In addition, although the bishops pay lip service to the institutional changes called for by the Second Vatican Council, such as Priests' Councils or Pastoral Councils, their relation to the clergy remains, in practice, personal and "paternal." Fully 40% of the bishops said that Priests' Councils do not function at all in their dioceses, and barely a quarter said they operated effectively. As we have seen, personalized relations have both advantages and disadvantages. On the plus side, they combine flexibility and openness with a more humane and caring mode of interpersonal relations, giving a new tone to life within the Church. Disadvantages, particularly from the point of view of subordinates (clergy and laity alike), are also notable. Most prominent are unpredictability and the absence of anything like due process in the Church. When relations are fully personalized, they obviously vary with the personalities involved. Moreover, a considerable basis of mutual trust and common understandings is required. But the large numbers of foreign clergy (particularly in Venezuela) find themselves at a distinct disadvantage in such arrangements: they are outsiders, unable to interact in a properly down-home style.

I noted earlier in this chapter that the new ideas and concepts articulated at top levels in the Church often double back on the bishops, appearing the second time in a threatening light. Once reform and change get underway, the concepts inspiring changes, which begin in a limited and controlled context, may be picked up and pushed harder and faster by organized lay groups than is comfortable for the bishops.[40]

[40] Moreover, laymen often resist being "set free" by the bishops. Long

The redistribution of authority is quite complex, for while the bishops see the need for withdrawal from some fields of action and for concentration on others more central to their mission, in any field they have trouble accepting the *institutionalization* of new, more collegial patterns of authority and action. Among many bishops, the reluctance to put changes into practice throughout the Church stems from a view of collegiality which really amounts to a warrant for oligarchy. These bishops do not accept a quasi-populist plurality of sources of authority in the Church. Instead, they mix biblical and juridical affirmations about the functions of the college of Apostles and the college of bishops, as sharing by right in the government of the Church. From this perspective, a bishop may affirm collegiality vis-à-vis Rome, yet remain strongly opposed to any extension of collegial practices in his own diocese. The bishop's gut reaction is to see his own position as threatened, and to pull back.

To assess the full meaning of such orientations, their implications must be traced through the context of the day-to-day life of the Church, particularly in areas where bishops, clergy, and laity regularly come together, such as in Catholic associations, or on the more intimate stage provided by the diocese. This chapter's general analysis of concepts and their expression in the minds of Church leaders provides a base line for assessing the dynamics and implications of organizational and local-level change in a systematic way. That analysis, which will be carried forward in Part III, rests on the central notion advanced here: divergent ecclesiologies and concepts of authority run deep in the Church, and have so comprehensive an influence that ideas about religion and the Church spill over from the limited arena of the ecclesiastical institution to shape the structure and substantive direction of Catholic actions when dealing with the world.

Conclusions

In reflecting on the process of change in the Church, it is important to realize the degree to which the recent upheavals in Latin

---

accustomed to working under the guidance, protection, and control of bishops and "clerical advisers," they often bitterly resent the Church's withdrawal from active direction of their affairs. See chapter 7, below, for a full discussion.

American Catholicism have resonated with broader changes in Latin American societies. As noted earlier, the convergence of a dominant Church in the midst of change with societies caught in the process of evolving new self-images (ranging from dependency to national security) makes for a setting uniquely geared to innovation, conflict, and self-questioning. Moreover, issues of political action, and profound debates over the meaning of politics and the Church's proper relation to it, have taken center stage. Why is politics so important to this process? Why are political issues so central to the current debates? If my analysis is correct, it could hardly be otherwise. For the redefinitions of authority and of legitimate action, which undergird the changes examined in this chapter, affect religion and politics alike. Of particular importance is the trend toward action, participation, testimony, and witness as bases for authority, and the related development of a framework of mutual responsibility as their expression. Such concepts are crucial, for they spur those who hold them to see increased involvement in social action (and hence, inevitably, in politics) as a necessary expression of religious faith. In this way, authority concepts in religion are closely tied to politics. They define the scope of legitimate action and the proper forms for its exercise—two dimensions which together account for much of the Church's projection into society.

Throughout this book, I have argued that ecclesial and sociopolitical dimensions should be kept separate, at least for analytical purposes. Such separation is based on my desire to avoid placing incorrect and inappropriate political labels on actions which arise primarily in response to religious, not political, concepts and motivations. But this is not to say that politics plays no role, nor is it to exempt these actions from political consequences.

I explicitly reject the notion that the bishops, because of their more central religious role, are not "really interested" in politics. This chapter and the next make it very clear that the issues and dilemmas of politics are extremely salient to most bishops today. Their problem is not political awareness or its absence, but rather uncertainty over *how* to act, *what* to do. Confronted by the rapid and often bewildering changes of the last twenty years, many bishops are simply unsure—unsure of the best way to understand social change, unsure of themselves, and, finally, unsure of their proper role in society.

Sorting these elements out is a slow and painful process. Like everyone, bishops respond to the issues and problems of the day within the limits set by their resources, training, and experience; but the positions assumed and the styles of action employed also grow out of the special way bishops see their evangelical and pastoral responsibilities. These, in turn, depend on their view of what the Church is in the first place. In any case, whether or not an individual bishop is "interested" in politics, the actions of the Church as an institution have clear political consequences. The Church necessarily affects politics by providing models of appropriate behavior and areas of legitimate concern. The nature of these concerns, and their relation to concrete political issues in Venezuela and Colombia, are the subjects of the next chapter.

6

The Church and the World: Perception and Action

This chapter explores the political role of the Church. It begins with an analysis of the bishops' views of social and political problems, and also of the kinds of actions they see as both possible and proper for the Church. The central issues of activism and violence, and their meaning for the Church, are considered separately. These social and political perspectives are then directly related to the dimensions of authority and ecclesiology discussed earlier. Finally, the implications of this volatile mixture of new styles of politics and religious life are examined in the context of evolving issues in the Church, in Venezuela and Colombia, and in Latin America as a whole.

As we have seen, a key element in the changing significance of politics for the Church has been the struggle to transform religious symbols. As part of this process, the very notion of "pastoral," surely a central category of religious action, has been reworked and expanded to include a series of activities which easily slide into what is commonly thought of as "politics." This is the kind of pastoral action—mute solidarity with the poor and oppressed by sharing their suffering, active *concientización* and prophetic denunciation of injustice, and mobilization of the poor for social and political conflict—about which politicians and governments have complained in recent years.[1] They see the new pastoralism as simply a new form of clericalism: the old politics with a new name. As we have seen, more than a few bishops share this view.

In considering these phenomena more carefully, it is important to bear in mind that this overlap, or behavioral convergence, of religion and politics works in both directions. For while authority, Church, and pastoral action have all grown in scope and changed in meaning, politics itself has undergone considerable transforma-

[1] Cf. Brian Smith, "Churches and Human Rights," or Dodson, "The Christian Left."

tion. At the very least, two different concepts of politics are at issue here. In the first, more narrow concept, "politics" refers to the activity of governing and more generally to the mobilization of individuals and groups to influence government. Politics thus understood is associated, above all, with the activities of interest groups and political parties, either within or directed toward government. This kind of politics inherently involves partisanship, power, and conflict.

Since the Second Vatican Council, the Church has deliberately moved away from this kind of political involvement. In addition, the past few decades have seen a great withdrawal from partisan entanglements on the part of the institutional Church in both Venezuela and Colombia. But as Church elites have moved away from this kind of politics, they have been hit by demands for a new kind of political involvement. To radical Catholics, the Church remains "political" and involved in "politics" despite its leaders' pretense of "neutrality."

This radical critique is rooted in another, broader concept of politics, according to which "politics" involves much more than parties, groups, or the official acts of government. Rather, "politics" is seen in terms of the structures of power, authority, legitimacy, and distribution which favor some interests at the expense of others. In this view, politics pervades all social relations, since all are suffused with power. Thus, if all actions are inherently and necessarily political, it follows that the Church has not withdrawn from politics, cannot withdraw from politics, and should not even attempt to withdraw from politics. To refrain from overt partisanship and then claim that this is the same as abstention from politics is seen as both hypocritical and unrealistic. Such abstention implies support for existing social and political arrangements by, in effect, allowing the weight of Church influence to fall on the side of those who already hold power in and benefit from the existing order. When it espouses a narrow concept of politics and derives norms of proper behavior from it, the Church (according to these critics) simply disguises its own deep involvement with structures of power, and hence with injustice. Since the Church is inevitably political, it must consciously *choose* to be political in the cause of human liberation: in practical terms this means it ought to act for social and political change. Several different dimensions of belief are involved in this debate, and the next section examines them in detail.

DIMENSIONS OF BELIEF

The lengthy and often bitter debates within the Latin American Church since Medellín make it clear that the relation of the Church to the world involves several dimensions of belief that are not necessarily related to one another in any causal or temporal way. At the very least, the disputed areas include: the terms of reference the Church provides for understanding and evaluating the world; the guidelines to be set for action by the Church as an institution and by the faithful; and the relations deemed appropriate with secular and non-Catholic groups in general. These issues are addressed here by analyzing the bishops' attitudes on three dimensions: structuralism, Church role, and dialogue.

Analysis of structuralism is based on the bishops' responses to this question: "In general, what do you think are the major problems facing the nation?" I distinguish broadly between "structural" and "moral" kinds of answers. Structural responses see national problems primarily in terms of social, economic, and political structures—artificial, human, and therefore changeable sets of social arrangements. Moral responses, on the other hand, emphasize problems of individual culture and self-discipline, or crises of belief and personal orientation. Individual virtue and private conversion are stressed. But from a structural point of view, a fully moral and authentically religious life cannot be ensured by moral indoctrination or cultic acts alone. Rather, social conditions must be transformed to provide adequate income, education, health, housing, and the like, which all equip people to lead a fuller religious life.

In general, structural responses predominate in each country, although more strongly in Colombia, where 79% of all answers fall into this group, as opposed to 56% in Venezuela. Among Colombians, the most commonly mentioned structural problems were social justice and underdevelopment, followed closely by references to unequal income distribution, unemployment, and the need to reform education. Venezuelans, on the other hand, mentioned problems of political organization most frequently, followed by income inequality and social injustice. As one Venezuelan bishop put it, "There is a problem which is to implement a more effective equality and social participation, which will eliminate the gap between groups within the country. We are a rich country, but also a country (although rich as a whole) with grave deficiencies among large social groups in education, housing, and things of this kind. Thus, there are enormous and unacceptable differences."[2]

As to moral responses, Venezuelans stressed problems of youth and the family, whereas Colombians complained most often about the lack of "Christian formation" in the population, the spread of communism, and problems in the family. Personal conversion and private virtue are emphasized in these responses. For example, two bishops—the first Venezuelan, the next Colombian—argue that

> in terms of problems there is the problem of youth, which is growing up with an orientation which may lead to distortions. Also the problem of the family, which is getting worse with divorce.[3]

> We are faced with somewhat intensive Protestant propaganda and, on the other hand, the conditions of underdevelopment—with Marxism and socialism—and some want to give all this a certain flavor of Christian socialism. In my opinion [they] are doing harm, because the poor and humble classes come to believe that their redemption will come through a socialist regime. ... In my opinion, there is a lot of demagogic talk about "underdevelopment," and this is harming the constitution of the country. Marxism is atheistic and thus affects the religious life of our country.[4]

Up to three responses were coded for each bishop. Then an index of structuralism was built to gauge the extent to which each bishop viewed national problems as wholly or predominantly structural (high), as moral (low), or mixed about equally (medium). While structural responses predominate in both countries, Colombians are much more structural in their views of their nation's problems (see table 6.1).

[2] Interview 60130, 27-28 May 1971.
[3] Interview 60117, 18 Aug. 1971.   [4] Interview 80128, 5 June 1972.

TABLE 6.1
STRUCTURALISM INDEX (%)

	Structuralism			
	Low	Med	High	Totals
Venezuela	38	19	43	37.5
Colombia	11	17	71	62.5
Totals (N = 56)	21	18	61	

Structuralism has vast implications for Catholic thought; some have already been noted. Viewing problems in structural terms opens the bishops (and the institution they lead) to a new approach to social affairs: religious thought and action, once isolated from the world, can now reach into daily life, drawing problems and model solutions from it. Rather than begin with moral principles and then proceed to social action, one may now start with social questions, seeking the meaning of Christian commitment in actual social circumstances. In the words of one Jesuit commentator,

> Colombia cannot be considered a Christian country. It is not a country inspired in the gospel message: to prove this, it is enough to open your eyes and look around. A country cannot be Christian where there exist, are tolerated, and grow ever greater such absolutely enormous social gaps between the few who have a lot and the many who have nothing. This is a defect in the structuring of Colombia. . . . A country of this kind is Christian in name only—though the statistics say what they will, though the Constitution may be openly confessional, though every year the chief of state dedicates the nation to the Sacred Heart of Jesus.[5]

This perspective implies a new thrust for Catholic social action. Although Catholics have always been urged to alleviate misery through the provision of charity, these views go far beyond simple charity, pointing instead to the need for basic social, economic, and political transformations to change the social structures which make charity necessary in the first place. To understand the full

[5] Castillo Bernal, "Teófilo escribano de frente."

meaning of this heavy stress on structuralism, such general views must be directly tied to action. For it may well be that the spread of structural perspectives is simply a reflection of international fashions in the Church, a kind of intellectual fad. Indeed, since Vatican II and Medellín, a more sociological and structural language has become common coin in the Church. In documents, speeches, pastoral letters, and interviews, Church leaders use structural terms to such an extent that Segundo Galilea, a Chilean theologian, writes of "a race of advanced ideas in a closed circle."[6] He notes, however, that while ideas abound, "The tremendous ambiguity of the post-Medellín Latin American Church lies in possessing abundant principles and working hypotheses without having generated sufficient pastoral or social imperatives. This is a source of frustration for many."[7]

This inflation of language raises serious questions about the kinds of commitments to action carried in the new styles of thought and speech. Will new ways of describing the world lead to new forms of action? If so, for whom? Certainly these are open questions, for in the Church, as in most organizations, actions rarely flow directly from attitudes and perceptions. Many factors intervene, such as resources, opportunities, and the way that elites define the most appropriate kinds of action for their institution. So, to assess the bishops' commitments to action, the question on national problems was always immediately followed by this one: "In your view, what can the Church contribute to solving them?"

As I have suggested already, a number of bishops distinguish the analysis of problems from specification of the Church's own role, arguing that direct social and political actions are outside the Church's sphere of competence. In this view, the Church lacks both the expertise and the authority to solve social problems. So many variables affect the evaluation of temporal solutions that the Church cannot justifiably give religious sanction to any particular choice; many are compatible with Christian values. Moreover, the Church's essential concern, it is argued, is with salvation and eternal life. While they acknowledge the presence of injustice and the need to promote human liberation, for many bishops the problem remains essentially one of personal conversion, not structural change. As one influential Venezuelan noted, "Real liberation be-

---

[6] Galilea, ¿A los pobres? p. 29.   [7] Ibid., p. 25.

gins with one's own self. Changing structures is not so easy. But that each of us manages to liberate himself from his egoism, his envy, his immorality—this is possible, and must be done."[8]

In contrast, others argue that life must be taken as a whole: spiritual and temporal dimensions of existence cannot be neatly separated; the whole person must be considered. In the words of one Colombian bishop, "Of course the Church was not sent to preach in the temporal field before the spiritual, but the fact is that you cannot separate the two, you cannot separate man. Thus, I have always felt that my mission as bishop has not been to save souls, but to save persons. Of course eternal life comes later, but it begins here below."[9]

These considerations reveal the great complexities of the Church's political position. In the analysis which follows, three roles are distinguished for the Church: traditional, activation, and activism. As these have already been described in general terms (chapter 4, under typologies), only a brief review of their main characteristics is needed here. Traditional and activation responses predominate; so let me begin with them. Traditional roles for the Church (mentioned in 39% of Venezuelan and 41% of Colombian answers) stress charity and the provision of general moral guidelines to society. These were the most popular traditional responses in both countries, along with mention of the Church's role in promoting Christian unity as a counter to class conflict. Some representative views follow—two Colombians first, then a Venezuelan:

> The Church's role? To illuminate, above all. If we believe that the goal is the common good, then the Church has a role. It already possesses, in the great encyclicals, in the Council, a position on these questions, and tries to enlighten people according to these perspectives—all the more so since here everyone wants the Church to make declarations.[10]

> Now what can the Church do? Well, provide norms in this process, and of course foresee and correct errors which may arise.[11]

> The Church should be like Christ crucified—with its arms open

[8] Interview 60115, 19 Aug. 1971.   [9] Interview 80135, 12 July 1972.
[10] Interview 80109, 15 Mar. 1972.   [11] Interview 80141, 29 July 1972.

to all people. With each arm open to a different part of the people. In other words, it should be a point of unification for all people, a point where all can collaborate.[12]

Traditional positions take existing social and political arrangements as given, and they direct Church efforts to the resolution of conventional moral dilemmas, or to the provision of charity and social assistance. Roles more attuned to social action take several forms. In chapter 4, I drew a basic distinction between the *activation* of others (especially lay people) and the promotion of *activism* among the leaders and agents of the Church itself. This distinction rests on who acts, in what capacity, and with what authority. As roles for the Church, both activism and activation are directly related to the different ecclesiologies reviewed earlier in these pages. The reader will recall that the more institutional models of the Church laid great stress on dissociating the activities of lay people from those of the Church per se, which in effect was identified with its hierarchy and clergy. In this view, the proper role of the hierarchy and clergy was strictly pastoral—centered on teaching and guiding lay people, who then participate as secular individuals in those political activities from which the Church as an institution abstains. Political neutrality is seen here as an essential condition of pastoral effectiveness. For without the shield of neutrality, the Church can be too easily identified with the success or failure of particular temporal movements, losing its transcendental qualities and exposing itself to possible institutional destruction, should it wind up on the losing side.

Those who view politics in the broader sense employ another model of the Church, however—one emphasizing mutuality and sharing, identifying it with the "People of God." They see the Church more as a historical community than as a set of structures; and although respecting the role of the hierarchy, they do not take the hierarchical distinction of roles and offices as essential to Church life. Partly for this reason, they deny that a proper distinction can be made between the kinds of social action appropriate to clergy and laity. A priest is first and foremost a Christian, and his primary charge, that he love his neighbor, may lead to political involvement through testimony and the bearing of witness.[13]

[12] Interview 60110, 4 June 1971.
[13] This is the position taken by Camilo Torres, for example.

Among the bishops, activation is far more popular than activism. Indeed, activation is the dominant type of response in both countries (42% of all mentions in each). The most popular single answer defines the Church's role as stimulating others to act. Direct intervention would mean the reconstruction of a discarded clericalism, a return to the very partisanship only recently abandoned. Instead, emphasis is placed on the training and "formation" of lay activists: economic, social, and cultural elites, trade union and peasant leaders, politicians, and the like.[14] A recent collective pastoral letter by the Colombian Bishops' Conference put the case for activation in these terms:

> While it is necessary to affirm clearly that the mission of the Catholic layman is to order temporal affairs correctly in the light of the gospel, the office and duty of pastors does not consist in resolving economic and social questions, but rather in teaching, sanctifying, and ruling in the area of faith, communicating to the faithful those renovating energies of grace which they will later project into public life, on their own account and risk, with the liberty and responsibility which corresponds to them as laymen.... To proceed in any other way would be to abdicate our role as pastors of a Church which cannot identify itself with any civilization, culture, regime, or ideology, and convert it instead into simply one more worldly force.[15]

The bishops are thus reluctant to be drawn into the partisan political arena, by either clergy or laity. Indeed, one Colombian bishop told me that the very stress on lay participation, so notable since Vatican II has often proved to be a source of new problems, by producing an "area which is very delicate and [which] refers to reaching an equilibrium between the actions of the hierarchical Church and those of laymen in the temporal and political field."[16] But exactly what sort of equilibrium does most of the hierarchy espouse?

In general, the role the bishops see for the Church calls for it to tread carefully the fine line between providing general legitimation and sponsorship for action in the world, on the one hand, and

---

[14] Even such programs as these have become controversial in recent years. See chapter 7, below.
[15] Conferencia Episcopal de Colombia, *Identidad cristiana*, p. 23.
[16] Interview 80123, 1 May 1972.

sanctioning, on the other hand, direct participation by hierarchy, clergy, and pastoral leaders in these activities. They urge others to act, but this action must be independent. Laymen are on their own. First a Venezuelan, then a Colombian comment.

> I believe that the Church's contribution, the contribution she can and must give, is through creating consciousness among laity, so that they will solve their own problems. That is, the Church must serve as stimulator and mentalizer of solutions. The Church per se, as a juridical entity, cannot create solutions.[17]

> The most important thing is to spread ideas. I do not give out money for food, for houses, or for welfare projects. Because if I can provide ideas to the rich, I create in them awareness of the need to create sources of employment. Thus I get more out of giving ideas to the rich. No, no, no, not a single piece of bread. Man does not live by bread alone (laughter).[18]

Activism goes much further. In addition to urging others to act, its proponents call the institutional Church and its personnel to a direct and open involvement in the promotion of change. Less than a fifth of all responses fall in this category (19% in Venezuela and 17% in Colombia). The suggested concrete actions range from "bearing witness" by sharing the lives of the poor and oppressed, to vigorously denouncing injustice in all fields, to, at the extreme, organizing, leading, and acting as members of groups promoting change. Such suggestions for action often overlap. Thus, in a speech to the Superior War College, one Colombian bishop noted that if the established social order is based on injustice, then its destruction is legitimate. The Church is obliged to "go beyond the clear exposition of principles regulating economic and sociopolitical relations to the frank and brave denunciation of situations which violate the ethical order, even if this puts the mere established order in danger."[19] Several Venezuelans go further.

> The problem is how to orient the actions of the Church. I believe that the actions of the Church must be directed toward service. Not pacifist in the bad sense of the term—to avoid conflict, that there be no frictions—but rather in the sense of achiev-

[17] Interview 60118, 14 June 1971.   [18] Interview 80110, 11 July 1972.
[19] Castrillón, "Política y pastoral," p. 90.

ing a better-structured society, much more just and solidary. All of which implies that the Church has to side with the weak, the weakest ... and the goal is not simply, as I said, a rather fictitious peace, but rather the establishment of a different order.[20]

I believe that the priest must place himself at the head of the people in the solution of its problems, of all its problems, with the goal of arriving at a complete liberation of man."[21]

For each bishop, up to two responses on the role of the Church were coded, and separate indices were constructed for each of the three positions just discussed. Leaving more detailed analysis for a further section, I shall simply point out here that despite the greater structuralism of Colombian bishops, relatively little difference in the role they define for the Church appears between the two national groups (see table 6.2).

TABLE 6.2
CHURCH ROLE INDICES (%)

	Church Role									Totals
	Traditional			Activation			Activism			
	Low	Med	Hi	Low	Med	Hi	Low	Med	Hi	
Venezuela	45	32	23	32	45	23	73	23	5	37
Colombia	47	29	24	34	37	29	74	24	2	63
Totals (N = 60)	47	30	23	33	40	27	73	23	3	

The bishops' rejection of activism is strong, but not surprising. Their position stems from several convictions, most notably the association of activism with conflict and violence, and the association of activism with division, both within the institutional Church and in the Christian community as a whole. Both sorts of association are seen as potentially very harmful to the Church, however "Church" is defined. The bishops correctly see that activism requires direct involvement in social and political conflicts. This is rejected as "politics." Social conflict, moreover, has at best an ambiguous status in Catholic thought, which, as we have seen, has generally tended to stress intergroup harmony. As Arthur Utz

[20] Interview 60130, 27-28 May 1971.
[21] Interview 60126, 9 July 1971.

points out, even the council's renewed stress on pluralism and change has failed to alter this basic orientation to harmony: "With all this, nevertheless, there is no acceptance of sociological theory according to which society is governed by the perpetual confrontation of interests (conflict theory). Throughout the evolution of the positions taken by the Church, a common unifying thread is visible, the idea of the common good as a genuine value of integration."[22]

Furthermore, activism leads to division. In my interviews, many bishops (above all in Colombia) recalled instances where political positions had bitterly divided the hierarchy and alienated the institutional Church from substantial portions of the population. As we have seen, most bishops hold the traditional view of the Church as open to all, not merely to a select and militant minority. Thus they fear that the more the institution becomes identified with any partisan political position, the more religious faith and practice will be forced to pass the test of political ideology and praxis before it is acknowledged as authentic. This would destroy the Church as they know it. In the words of Msgr. Alfonso López Trujillo, now archbishop of Medellín and president of CELAM,

> Recognizing the essential nobility of political action, which according to the papal expression can be an eminent form of charity, the Church wants the priest, whose fundamental mission is one of service to the profound unity of the Church through the ministry of the Word and of the Eucharist, to make this difficult sacrifice [of political action] in order to teach more profound values: so that all Christians (with no distinctions of any kind) can come to him without problems or reservations which spring from tensions or differences with respect to systems, models, or political programs. This is the way to avoid, regardless of risk or trouble, having the word of the Gospel chained to or dependent upon discrimination between social classes.[23]

To this point, the political role of the Church has been considered in quite general terms. But to assess the relation of beliefs to action in a full and accurate way, concrete alternatives must be considered. The relation of Catholics to Marxism and to Marxist groups is, as we have seen, a major issue in Latin America today, and

[22] Utz, "Ojeada Sobre la Evolución de la Doctrina Social de la Iglesia," p. 17.
[23] López Trujillo, "El Compromiso Político del Sacerdote," p. 51.

openness to dialogue and cooperation with Marxists provides a useful and convenient guide to the action-implications of general views on the role of the Church. I asked the bishops this question:

> Nowadays, one finds among many people a desire to dialogue, cooperate, and even participate with people of a Marxist orientation in common organizations and actions. Do you believe this constitutes a problem, or can it be a legitimate expression of Catholic social action?

Responses fall into three broad categories: acceptance, qualified acceptance, and complete rejection. As used here, acceptance refers either to full approval of both dialogue and cooperation or to acceptance of concrete cooperation alone. The assumption behind this classification is that common initiatives are a more valid indicator of the strength of dispositions to action than is dialogue alone, which can easily turn into a stylized exercise, devoid of real significance. One Colombian stressed the need for common action in this way: "With respect to the Marxists, I would almost say, if their intentions are good, that there is more that unites us than divides us. Thus, there will be areas in which we can work together without our trying to convince them that they are in error or their trying to convert us into Marxists, each instead respecting the mentality and philosophy of the other."[24]

Many hedge their bets by approving dialogue and cooperation only with numerous qualifications, such as limiting participation to the highly trained and educated for fear that less sophisticated Catholics would be lost to Marxist wiles. One bishop argued that exposing such persons to Marxist ideas "would be equivalent to setting them to think along Marxist lines, and the next step is to act according to Marxist methods."[25] Several expressed fear of being used by Marxist politicians for their own political ends.

> Now this lack of honesty on the part of the Communist party would be reinforced in its impact, because our people would never understand the Church's walking arm in arm with Marxism. Acting in this way we would create a confusion as great as that we already have in so many ideas.[26]

[24] Interview 80116, 19 May 1972.   [25] Interview 80125, 10 July 1972.
[26] Interview 60114, 1 Aug. 1971.

In addition, some bishops draw a distinction between general social cooperation and cooperation of an explicitly political sort. Whereas the former is acceptable, the latter is rejected outright, for fear of identifying the Church with specific political programs. Here is one Venezuelan's view:

> Now political cooperation, in this atmosphere—here one has to move with great care in each case, because the Church, first of all, cannot absolutize any particular historical or political moment. We transcend that. We cannot give ourselves completely to *this* solution, here, because we—this will be transcended, history does not end here. The Church has a historical trajectory of twenty centuries which transcends this. Yes, to give support to the common good, but not to tie oneself totally to a Marxist or socialist movement which could mortgage us historically. In this, one must move with the greatest care, to anticipate the consequences before jumping into a political kind of cooperation.[27]

Finally, a substantial group rejects dialogue and cooperation outright. One bishop noted that they *could* get together to pray an *Our Father*, while others simply reiterated the Church's traditional opposition to Marxism. One Colombian said that "I know that in Chile recently fifty priests visited Fidel Castro and declared themselves identified with his Marxist ideas. I judge this to be a very grave error and a contradictory position. Marxism is atheist and materialist, and the Church is a spiritual leader. Thus it is absolutely scandalous to manifest sympathies for the grave errors the Church has always condemned . . . this is unacceptable, unacceptable."[28] A Venezuelan bishop compared Marxism to a disease, noting that "I do not believe that their desire to dialogue is in good faith . . . moreover, I need not catch a disease in order to know about it. For example, take tuberculosis: if I want to know about tuberculosis, I can go to a medical book where they will tell me the symptoms, but I need not catch it to know about it."[29]

Table 6.3 shows that a strikingly large percentage of bishops in each country is willing to accept *some* kind of dialogue and/or cooperation with Marxism. This is surprising given the Church's traditional condemnations of Marxism and the generally conservative reputation of Venezuelan and Colombian bishops within the

---

[27] Interview 60104, 11 June 1971.   [28] Interview 80128, 5 June 1972.
[29] Interview 60108, 12 July 1971.

TABLE 6.3
DIALOGUE AND COOPERATION WITH MARXISTS (%)

	Dialogue			
	Accept	Qualified	Reject	Totals
Venezuela	48	29	24	36
Colombia	24	38	38	64
Totals (N = 58)	33	34	33	

Church as a whole. A survey of the reputedly more progressive Chilean hierarchy in 1968 revealed considerable openness to Christian cooperation with Marxists in projects promoting the common good.[30] The disposition of the supposedly more conservative Venezuelan and Colombian bishops to similar views indicates that this kind of orientation is perhaps more prevalent in Latin American episcopal thinking than has previously been supposed. It is difficult to be precise about the sources of this new openness to Marxism. Undoubtedly there are a variety of factors, ranging from the influence of recent papal documents to delayed impact of the Vatican's *Ostpolitik*.[31] Furthermore, as we shall see, national differences play a significant role, particularly in determining which kinds of bishops are favorably disposed to dialogue and cooperation with Marxism, and also in determining how attitudes on this dimension are related to the other dimensions analyzed here.

So far, the three dimensions—structuralism, Church role, and dialogue—have been examined in general terms, and a first step has been taken in delineating national differences. How are these dimensions related to one another? A common assumption is that structural perspectives are associated with greater dispositions to action and with greater receptivity to dialogue and cooperation with Marxists. This hypothesis rests on the belief that those who see their nation's problems in structural terms will want to participate in changing the very social factors they themselves consider crucial. Instead of simply reiterating moral doctrine, or getting lay people to act, they will become involved in community organization and social action. By the same logic, seeing problems in structural terms ought to make bishops more open to coopera-

[30] Cf. Sanders, *The Chilean Episcopate*.
[31] Hebblethwaite, *The Runaway Church*, pp. 149-79.

tion with others concerned with the same concrete problems, regardless of ideology.

But no such direct progression from perceptions to role definitions to actions is visible. Why? First, as noted earlier, language may change faster than action; and, in any case, general perceptions of social problems may be independent of role definitions. Moreover, the pattern of response is different in each nation, and national differences help shape the relation of perceptions and action. How can these national differences be explained? The historical and structural evolution of the two Churches has been considered in some detail. The reader will also recall that, on other indices, advanced education is associated with notable differences within and between nations. How is level of education related to these social and political attitudes?

Controlling for education makes relatively little difference to the results on structuralism, or to the several indices of the role of the Church. In each country, the more educated are slightly more structural, and also more likely to score low on traditional roles and medium or high on activation. But the variations are not very great. The most striking differences come in connection with Marxism. Here, education is associated with notably different patterns of response in each country (see table 6.4). Colombians with ad-

TABLE 6.4
DIALOGUE AND COOPERATION WITH MARXISTS, BY EDUCATION (%)

| Dialogue | Venezuela (N = 21) ||| Colombia (N = 37) |||
	Advanced Education	Seminary Education	Totals	Advanced Education	Seminary Education	Totals
Accept	12	69	48	28	17	24
Qualified	38	23	29	40	33	38
Reject	50	8	24	32	50	38
Totals	38	62		68	32	

vanced education are generally more open to dialogue and cooperation and more likely to qualify their answers, moving away from outright rejection. But in Venezuela, advanced education reverses the overall national pattern of openness noted earlier. Moreover, the magnitude of change attributable to education is greater in Venezuela.

Similar patterns are visible in terms of career. So far, we have found that more pastoral experience can be seen as leading to greater flexibility and openness in day-to-day social contacts, whereas a concentration on bureaucratic and educational roles can reinforce a tendency to rigidity and isolation. The data in table 6.5 confirm there notions only in part, for they show that, in Venezuela, those with greater pastoral experience are much more accepting of dialogue and cooperation with Marxists, whereas among Colombians the reverse is true. Clearly the impact of pas-

TABLE 6.5
DIALOGUE AND COOPERATION WITH MARXISTS, BY CAREER (%)

	Pastoral Career			Bureaucratic-Educational Career			
Dialogue	Low	Med	High	Low	Med	High	Totals
Venezuela							
Accept	29	44	80	71	33	40	48
Qualified	29	33	20	14	33	40	29
Reject	43	22	—	14	33	20	24
Totals (N = 21)	33	43	24	33	43	24	
Colombia							
Accept	32	9	—	—	18	32	24
Qualified	40	36	—	—	41	37	38
Reject	28	55	100	100	41	32	38
Totals (N = 37)	68	30	3	3	46	51	

toral experience depends not only on such experience alone, but also on the milieu in which it is located. "Pastors" in Colombia are notably more isolated within the institutional Church, and they make their way in a much less secular and plural society. Hence the relative impact of career is different from that in Venezuela. National context thus makes a consistent and rather independent difference to the orientations, and especially to the dispositions to action, of the bishops.

When structuralism, Church role, and dialogue are directly related to one another, it becomes clear that, contrary to much popular wisdom on the subject, structural perspectives are neither uniquely nor even especially associated with activation or activism. Rather, *all* views of the role of the Church share, to a great extent, the language of structuralism. Indeed, striking by its absence is any substantial number of bishops who fit conventional stereotypes—that is, who combine moralistic views with traditional ideas about the Church's proper social role. In fact, of those scoring high on traditional roles, almost 80% also score high on structural perceptions of problems.

Controlling for nation and education thus yields little or no variation in the distribution of responses, with one exception. National differences follow the overall pattern of greater Colombian structuralism already noted, while level of education makes little difference to the general pattern of relation between structuralism and dispositions to action. Only when we consider the link between Church role and attitudes to dialogue and cooperation with Marxists do notable patterns emerge, confirming the trends already described. Although Venezuelans and Colombians specify broadly comparable roles for the Church, among Venezuelans almost every category of role definition is more favorably disposed to dialogue and cooperation than is its Colombian counterpart. The results on activation are especially striking. As one moves from low to high on this index, the percentage accepting dialogue and cooperation almost doubles in Venezuela, while it drops even more sharply among Colombians than it rises among Venezuelans. Finally, although almost three-fourths of the bishops in both countries score low on activism, almost twice as large a percentage of the Venezuelans in this group favor dialogue (see table 6.6).

What do these results mean? What do they reveal about likely patterns of action? Answers to these questions require attention to at least three distinct but related issues: first, the nature of national differences; second, the relation in the bishops' minds between activism, politics, and violence; and third, the broader implications of the different role definitions the bishops espouse. Consideration of this last point will bring us back, finally, to a more detailed look at the relation between the sociopolitical dimensions examined in this chapter and the various images of the Church and concepts of authority discussed earlier. Let us consider these in turn, beginning with another look at the national differences so prominent in this analysis.

TABLE 6.6
Dialogue and Cooperation with Marxists, by Church Role Indices (%)

	Church Role									
Dialogue	Traditional			Activation			Activism			Totals
	Low	Med	Hi	Low	Med	Hi	Low	Med	Hi	
Venezuela										
Accept	67	29	40	43	40	75	40	80	—	48
Qualified	11	43	40	43	30	—	33	—	100	29
Reject	22	29	20	14	30	25	27	20	—	23
Totals										
(N = 21)	43	33	24	33	48	19	71	24	5	
Colombia										
Accept	17	18	50	42	21	9	22	33	—	24
Qualified	44	27	37.5	42	36	36	33	44	100	38
Reject	39	55	12.5	17	43	55	44	22	—	38
Totals										
(N = 37)	49	30	22	32	38	30	73	24	3	

National Patterns Reconsidered

A broad overview of Venezuelan and Colombian bishops' attitudes on the dimensions considered here yields a paradox. Venezuelan bishops appear much less structural in their views of the world, but much more willing to accept dialogue and cooperation with Marxists—an activity directed in fact to the transformation of that world. The issue of Marxism is important, for relations between Christians and Marxists are often taken as an acid test of the Church's real willingness to pursue social change. Moreover, as noted earlier, the question of Marxism is a point of growing controversy within many national Churches.[32] Yet acceptance of dialogue and cooperation with Marxists seems to be a step required neither by structural perspectives nor by less traditional definitions of the role of the Church. Instead, national context appears particularly important. Why is the Venezuelan pattern so striking, and so different from the Colombian?

The greater willingness of the Venezuelan hierarchy to accept dialogue and common effort with Marxists may simply reflect a realistic acceptance of the nature of their society, and of the

[32] Cf. Eagleson, *Christians and Socialism*.

Church's actual status in it. The Venezuelan Church is weak. As one group among many in a pluralist society, it has perforce learned to coexist with powerful and articulate parties on the left, ranging from the mild democratic socialism of the Democratic Action party to more radical Marxist parties. Accommodation is thus well suited to the actual political context of the Venezuelan Church. Moreover, many Venezuelan bishops have had long experience as parish priests. In the parishes, they had to deal with many different groups and situations—an experience which surely helps move them away from the rigidly held positions inculcated by a predominantly abstract education and reinforced by a bureaucratic career.

In Colombia, on the other hand, the church has long held a dominant social position: it has been seen by others, and has seen itself, as a central source of national culture and values. Given this historical role, a commitment by the Colombian hierarchy to national change is likely to be seen as something uniquely *theirs* to legitimize and set in motion. In addition, the greater resources of the Colombian Church make such pretensions a real option. In any case, there are no strong Marxist parties in Colombia, and those which do exist are almost all committed to violent revolutionary strategies. Hence, dialogue and cooperation with Marxists is likely to be seen as superflous or worse—a Pandora's box best left closed, particularly when a central role in society is at issue. Marxist parties are stronger in Venezuela, although even there they remain relatively minor. But in Venezuela the entire political spectrum is further to the left than in Colombia, and the whole political system is permeated by the semisocialist legacy of the Democratic Action party's long periods in power.

These differences in national context are further evident in the reasons offered by bishops who are cautious or fearful about interaction with Marxists. Political context and direct personal experience both seem to play major roles here. Almost 30% of the Colombians fear losing unsophisticated Catholics to Marxist influence, and 23% reject dialogue and cooperation on the grounds that Marxists are simply evil and cannot be trusted. At the same time, among the Venezuelans (who, after all, have more occasion to deal with potentially effective leftist parties), 27% fear being used by Marxist groups, while only 8% of the Colombians cite this possibility.

In this light, the great impact of advanced education on bishops' attitudes in Venezuela begins to make sense. Recall that the Venezuelans with advanced education all studied in Rome. In Rome they took on grand views of the Church and also the powerful anticommunism of the period. But younger Venezuelan bishops, who are less educated, reflect the political evolution of recent years, and the general accommodation between groups in Venezuelan society.

The bishops' attention to politics is not exhausted by questions of activation, activism, or even relations with Marxism. "Politics" is a double-edged concept for the bishops, referring both to narrow dealings with government and public officials and also to broad movements of social conflict and violence. Indeed, when many bishops think of "politics," especially as presented to them by radical Catholics, they conjure up images of disorder, fighting, and violence above all. The enormous significance of violence to both Church and society in Colombia, and its notable if less prominent role in Venezuela, thus warrants special attention. The next section looks specifically at violence and its relation to activism and "politics" for the Church, setting consideration of attitudes aside for the moment to look more closely at the bishops' reactions to concrete historical cases and circumstances.

POLITICS, ACTIVISM, AND VIOLENCE: A SPECIAL PROBLEM

Many Colombian bishops have vivid memories of The Violence and fear that renewed clerical activism in politics (indeed, almost any large scale activism) will lead to massive bloodshed again. Over and over, in my interviews with Colombian bishops, the theme of violence and its relation to political activism was spontaneously raised. One prelate recalled arriving to establish his new diocese at the height of The Violence and finding it torn apart by strife: "Violent action is never appropriate for us. It is very grave, just as the example we provide is definitive. One only realizes that after confronting it, as occurred with me, finding the diocese at that time full of violence. Violence is frightening, it is terrible. Here people were being killed all the time—one looked each day to see how many had been killed."[33] When pressed as to whether current agitation for political activism among radical Catholics is neces-

[33] Interview 80117, 12 June 1972.

sarily violent, this same bishop went on to insist that political activism inevitably leads to violence.

> It ends there, it ends up in that. That is the problem of violence—it is uncontainable. Once at a luncheon I met a man who they say is one of the architects of The Violence. We began to talk, and he said: "I tell you, Monsignor, do something to stop The Violence. We politicians played with violence to frighten and menace one another, and it got out of hand. We did not want this." And this is the problem with violence: they begin it and don't know where it stops, because passions continue to rise.[34]

While many Catholic radicals now consider violence a legitimate and potentially effective means of revolutionary social transformation, those with some experience of Colombian society and politics are understandably skeptical. Few other nations can offer so stark an example of so much violence and bloodshed producing so little social transformation and revolutionary change. While many bishops indeed acknowledge that "any priest worthy of the name" feels compassion for the circumstances of the poor and wants to help, they see violence as counterproductive, harming mainly the poor and weak, who serve as permanent shock troops for competing upper-class cliques. An elderly bishop speaks to this point:

> Now, when we come to a point where the only means is violence, where it is said that only through violence can anything be achieved, then really . . . what changes is not the sense of compassion, but rather the system for improving the situation. [But] this is, after all, an illusion of sorts, because it will not help at all. Violence does not resolve anything, nor is it evangelical. One always knows, when violence occurs, who will fall: the selfsame peasants—the poor soldier who is a peasant, the policeman who is a peasant. The people who die are all peasants. In these struggles, the great and weighty people will not fall, they will not fall. So it is clear that violence is stupid, because it goes against the very same peasants who are those who, for a wage, sacrifice themselves and have to fire on other peasants, and the others also shoot against peasants. *And the struggle is between themselves.* . . . It is an injustice that the poor man should be the victim and the community just remain the same.

[34] Ibid.

Things are not going to change that way. That strategy is anti-evangelical and irrational to boot.[35]

Thus, when the bishops in Colombia reject "politics," they are turning away from both politics of the narrow partisan kind and politics conceived as broad involvement in radical movements for change. In their view both are inextricably linked to the potential for massive violence—violence which is rejected for both theological and practical reasons. In theological terms, the bishops follow the Gospels and also the continual injunctions of Pope Paul VI to avoid violence. Moreover, given Colombia's recent history, their analysis has a strong practical appeal, for political involvement by the Church has in fact been associated with intense conflict, destruction, and grave threats to the Church's very existence.

Part of the danger to the Church is seen to lie in the way politics brings division, limiting the Church's unity and effectiveness as an institution.[36] The sense of corporate identity and desire for unity is very strong among Colombian bishops, who see their Church as unified and who value that unity highly.[37] The drive for unity in the Church is thus a major component of the bishops' retreat from "politics." But politics of course keeps creeping in, despite the bishops' best efforts. Its notable persistence is due in large measure to the very flexibility of the concept. Consider, once again, the various meanings of "politics."

At the beginning of this chapter, I outlined two concepts of politics commonly used and confused in current debates about (and within) the Church. Each describes a range of possible "political" functions for the Church and at the same time provides a guide to permissible political actions. But each has notable deficiencies,

[35] Interview 80134, 22 Nov. 1972.

[36] Many noted the disastrous effects on bishops, clergy, and faithful of earlier divisions within the hierarchy over the selection of the Conservative party's presidential candidates.

[37] Almost 90% of the bishops say there is now sufficient unity within the Colombian Church, with another 8% noting that unity was strong among the bishops but less than ideal at other levels. Contemporary unity is attributed to many factors, most notably to growing ideological agreement; greater institutional discipline (common devotion to Rome is often mentioned); the recent development of strong national bureaucratic structures (which encourage unity by facilitating contact and consultation); and withdrawal from the partisan commitments of the past, which had often divided bishops into opposing groups.

both as descriptive concepts and as guides to action. The narrow view is too formalistic: it identifies politics and power too exclusively with government, and it ignores concentrations of private and corporate power which shape society and government. The broad view, on the other hand, runs the risk of making politics so diffuse and unfocused that the term serves no useful purpose—if politics is everywhere and in everything, it is nowhere in particular.

These two concepts of politics are based on the views and arguments put forward by different groups. A more analytical concept may help clarify matters. In general, it is clear that politics concerns not only influencing *how* government acts, but also *whether* it acts at all. Politics is thus deeply involved in setting agendas. Not all social "problems" become political "issues," for only a limited number of concerns and controversies reach the public agenda. The ability to influence the writing of that agenda, the issues taken up and the alternatives perceived, is an important part of the political process. The definition of the political situation faced by decisionmakers goes a long way toward determining their decisions.[38]

Here the transformation of "pastoral action" noted earlier becomes especially important, for when the Church speaks of bearing "witness" and setting "guidelines for action" it clearly intends to legitimate certain concerns for the political agenda. It hopes to influence the definition of the political situation through its pastoral action. This becomes particularly evident when social problems are viewed in sociological or "structural" terms, rather than, say, in terms of individual moral failings. The Colombian bishops will find it increasingly difficult to disavow the way "pastoral" action becomes "political" in this sense, despite their broad commitment to keeping the Church out of politics. Their dilemma is ever more acute, for the "formation of Christian consciences" and the "prophetic" denunciation of injustice are clearly intended to influence whether government acts; yet these are pastoral actions embraced even by many moderate and cautious bishops.

The guide to action provided by this third concept of politics is more complex and indirect than in the previous two cases, and it takes full advantage of the multiplicity of levels in the Church.

---

[38] Cf. Schattschneider, *The Semi-Sovereign People*, chaps. 1-4; Bachrach and Baratz, "Decisions and Non-Decisions," and their earlier "Two Faces of Power"; and Cobb, Ross, and Ross, "Agenda Building as a Comparative Political Process."

The fact that the Church has many levels and sites for action (parish, diocese, movement, order, nation, etc.) makes it possible for action on one level to affect and manipulate responses and action on others. An emphasis made in the hierarchy, say, on preserving (or perhaps on challenging) the status quo alters the agenda of society in general and thus motivates many isolated acts by individual priests and religious at the local level. Or, cases of clerical solidarity with peasant invasions of land, for example, confront bishops with a choice of supporting either their priests or the local authorities. The case of Jesuit Father Jaime Santander in 1972 (one of many political confrontations involving priests that year) is instructive. After being arrested by the civil authorities in the town of Manatí, Father Santander received full support both from his religious order and from the entire Episcopal Commission on Social Action. The Jesuit superiors of Colombia asserted:

> We feel ourselves as one with the priests, religious, and lay people who, following the norms of the hierarchy, and with a truly evangelical spirit, have committed themselves to the defense of the weak and given voice to those who had none. For this reason, we are profoundly troubled that forces exist in Colombia which attempt to gag evangelical freedom with tactics ranging from the subtle labeling as "subversive" or "rebel" of every priest committed to a social apostolate, all the way to having them put in jail.[39]

The important point here is that this kind of "political" involvement is practically unavoidable, even for those rejecting "politics" and holding an institutional conception of the Church. For, to the bishops, becoming "political" in this way does not depend in the first instance on their own commitment to social action or to clerical involvement in politics. Indeed, to the extent to which the bishops think of an initiative as "political" they are likely to reject it. But such actions are not seen as political, but rather as pastoral. Although strong traditions impel the bishops to stay out of "politics," equally powerful traditions impel them to exercise and defend "pastoral" actions and, even more important, to preserve unity within their institution and defend it from external attack. Thus, while rejecting "politics" in principle, the bishops are increasingly drawn into "political" actions. Naturally, they try to restrain grass-

[39] *El Tiempo* (Bogotá), 10 Aug. 1972.

roots initiatives of this kind, but they also must adapt to pressures from below. Widespread arrests of clergy (which have occurred with increasing frequency in Colombia) are likely to call the bishops' strong sense of corporate identity into full play, moving the bulk of the Church into more direct conflict with public authorities.

The process outlined here for Colombia does not hold everywhere. As I have suggested, the fact that both Venezuela and Colombia are relatively open and free means that the Church is much less likely to be backed against a wall in defense of its pastoral actions there than in the more repressive and authoritarian circumstances of Chile, Brazil, or El Salvador. In Venezuela, specifically, the constraints on activism differ from those in Colombia. By tradition, the Venezuelan hierarchy is less willing to act at all. Moreover, it is easier in practice for the bishops to sacrifice a troublesome priest, because most of them are foreign. The recent case of Father Francis Wuytack, who was deported from Venezuela for being a "foreigner meddling in politics," is a good example.

Father Wuytack was a Belgian priest working in La Vega, one of the poorest slums of Caracas. His work was marked by an attitude of testimony, witness, and direct action; he sought to share the living conditions of his parishioners, identify with them, and join all their struggles. A series of public demonstrations at the gates of the national Congress, in which he and his people protested poor living conditions and widespread unemployment, led to his deportation. In Venezuela, a permit is required for all public demonstrations. But no permit was obtained, and several days later (on June 20, 1970), Father Wuytack was expelled from the country. His expulsion was carried out in secret, but once it became known a storm of protest broke over the Church.

The hierarchy asserted that it had taken no part in the expulsion, but said that the measure was legal, and criticized Wuytack for being involved in politics. But on the next day eighty-eight priests from the Archdiocese of Caracas delivered an open letter to the bishops, following this two days later with a demonstration in front of the Interior Ministry and the archbishop's offices.[40] The

[40] Such a demonstration was unprecedented. In addition, the expulsion touched off an extensive debate in the national press, centered on the anomaly of a Christian Democratic government, with the acquiescence of

THE CHURCH AND THE WORLD

points raised in the open letter of June 22 were further developed in a note delivered to the bishops of Caracas three days later by this new group of protesters. They directly asked, What are the consequences for religious faith of the kinds of secular action engaged in by Father Wuytack?

> Francis struggled against the institutional violence of our society. The people of La Vega, today separated from him, continue to suffer each day the violence of hunger, poor housing, lack of schools, unemployment, inadequate medical care, etc. The people call out to Heaven, as in ancient times the Chosen People did. Doesn't it seem to you that the Venezuelan Church must be the interpreter—in words and deeds—of the answer God wants to give His people's cries? How can we, you and us, fulfill this mission? For the people, the pretty words of Medellín and Paul VI are not enough. Francis is gone and the situation remains the same, as does our responsibility. What line of action can we take? What backing can we count on, given the risks, and our right to make mistakes in the search for action?[41]

The signers of the letter flatly rejected the hierarchy's claim that it had no part in the expulsion, arguing that "not taking a position means already having a position, and approving without reservation the decision taken by the civil authorities. Silence and passivity are complicity."[42] Debate on the expulsion focused on the meaning of "neutrality" in politics. Those who saw Father Wuytack as a prophet leading his people viewed the bishops as comfortable ecclesiastical bureaucrats, committed to the system and out of touch with the day-to-day realities of average peoples' lives. These perspectives were summed up in a homily read the following Sunday in churches served by those priests who had joined the protests.

> God's call and the impulse of His grace led Father Francis to live his Christian faith not only in prayer masses, but first of all as concrete service to the needs of his brothers. . . . This is the important, profound, and really biblical content of the lesson

---

the hierarchy, expelling a priest whose major offense seemed to be solidarity with his parishioners.

[41] Segura, *Wuytack*, p. 60.   [42] Ibid., p. 59.

we have learned from Father Francis Wuytack. This is the really priestly part of his work. . . . It was the people which suffered and cried out in demonstrations, accompanied by its friend and priest. And so it passed that, faced with a people aware of their rights, and faced with a priest not of the traditional kind, who stood united with his people, the powerful felt their tranquility threatened. And so came the beatings, the arrests, the threats, and finally the expulsion. They accuse him of disturbing the public order, as if disorder were not really caused by the injustices and miseries the people suffer.[43]

The Wuytack case is a good example of the potentially volatile political implications of actions rooted in new visions of the Church; it illustrates the political imperatives of such religious action. Wuytack's experience follows the general pattern sketched out here, but the differences with Colombia are as important as the similarities. There was little direct, explicitly partisan political linkage or result to Wuytack's actions. Moreover, mass action is a legitimate political resource in Venezuela; hence mobilization per se is less of a threat than in Colombia, where Camilo Torres posed a deep challenge both to the Church and to the political establishment. On the other hand, Father Wuytack was clearly expendable. Venezuela's bishops are not anxious to lead the defense of foreign clergy (whom they often mistrust) and not willing in general to take on the government in any cause. Thus, Father Wuytack was unceremoniously hustled out of town and not defended, like Father Santander.

In concluding this section on politics, activism, and violence it is important to link attitudes to violence to specific options for violent acts. The linkage is complex and often confused. Although the general position of the Church has clearly favored nonviolence, elaborate doctrines of the just war and of legitimate rebellion against tyranny have been developed over the centuries. Why, then, is violence so hard to condone and accept as necessary in present-day Latin America? What distinguishes these cases from more obvious examples of tyranny and just war?[44]

One basic difference lies in the extremely diffuse notion of

[43] Ibid., pp. 66-67.
[44] A useful account of the Catholic position which addresses these questions is Davies, *Christians, Politics, and Violent Revolution.*

power contained in the "broad" view of politics espoused by Catholic radicals, and the concomitantly generalized and diffuse nature of their challenge to established authority. The radical position does not simply argue against a corrupt or unjust government, or denounce a particularly predatory landowner or employer. An accusing finger may indeed be pointed at individuals, but the challenge is far more basic and general. The call is to change entire *structures* that are seen as unjust, structures whose operations and maintenance go far beyond the acts of any single individual, no matter how powerful. Because individual responsibility cannot easily be fixed, the problem of justifying violent corrective action becomes enormously complicated. Thus, in a speech to the Superior War College cited earlier, Msgr. Castrillón went on to argue that:

> If the injustices of the present order could be located with precision in a determinate group of persons, [then] even though violence is not Christian, it would be Christian to use it against the violent oppressors in order to become free of them, if this were not possible through reasoned and peaceful means. But the complex organization of society and the modern techniques of State security impede the accurate fixing of responsibilities, make necessary innumerable sacrifices of innocent persons, and throw into question the justice and welfare to be implanted [by violent attempts at change].[45]

Much of the problem in accepting the "broad" view of politics lies in the difficulty of locating targets—that is, specific structures and individuals against whom rebellion and violent actions may be justified. Historically, doctrines of legitimate rebellion and just war have often been tied to defense of the Church against external attack. But such attacks are not at issue in Colombia or Venezuela today. Rather, political authorities in most cases strive mightily to retain the good will of the Church. Nevertheless, the general process described here—whereby bishops and other Church leaders are drawn into political conflicts through defense of individual priests, religious, and lay leaders who find themselves under attack—is beginning to emerge in Colombia, albeit in a limited way; and it is less pronounced in Venezuela. Although it is hard to define any

[45] Castrillón, "Política y pastoral," p. 93.

precise threshold, it seems clear that if there is a gradual accumulation of incidents and attacks on individual clergy, the institutional Church will be able at some point to identify the concrete locus of authority and responsibility essential to legitimizing acts of opposition, which may include violence. Neither the Colombian nor the Venezuelan hierarchy is on the verge of any such step, but their situations remain relatively comfortable. Were the context to turn more repressive, it is easy to see how the Church could feel its institutional integrity threatened by restrictions on pastoral action and thus be drawn increasingly into confrontations with political authorities. There are many precedents.[46]

In any case, the Church's changing concept of its pastoral tasks will doubtless continue to involve it in the politics of agenda setting. The nature of this involvement, and particularly of the Church's effectiveness in translating political issues into outcomes, will vary from nation to nation. But in all cases it is pastoral action which takes religious motivations into the political arena, and in turn brings politics, activism, and violence to a central position in debates within the Church. The bishops draw back from concrete commitments, fearing the loss of the Church's transcendental goals in the stress on short-term political alliances and programs that is typical of those who put activism first. But perhaps the religious origin of activism, which flows not from political motives per se, but rather from a broad view of the Church's own religious and pastoral imperatives, offers a means of avoiding the loss of transcendental values; for these, and not political goals, remain the driving force and purpose of "pastoral action," whatever the implications others may draw.

As this analysis makes clear, the relation of religion and politics becomes extremely complex, particularly as one gets down to action. The many nuances in the link between religion and politics, between spirituality and political commitment, are only beginning to be explored in depth.[47] For the bishops, the problem is perhaps

[46] This process has been amply documented throughout Latin America. A good example is the evolving relations of the hierarchy to the military government in Brazil. Cf. Bruneau, *The Political Transformation*, chaps. 9 and 10.

[47] In this regard see, above all, Galilea, "Liberation as an Encounter," and other essays in Geffré and Gutierrez, *Mystical and Political Dimensions*.

even more difficult. With them, the issue goes well beyond individual beliefs and personal preferences. As bishops these men carry an important institutional responsibility: they feel deeply the need to maintain the Church as a unified, open set of structures through which a changing faith can continue to find expression under many circumstances. In a real sense, bishops must be all things to all people—a requirement which clearly rules out many activist commitments. The next section fills out and completes our examination of their role.

VISIONS OF THE CHURCH AND PATTERNS OF ACTION:
THE ROLE OF THE BISHOP

The findings presented so far throw some light on the dynamic relation between beliefs and action for the leaders of the Catholic Church. But much remains in shadow. Looking at social and political views alone, the results are ambiguous, for no simple one-to-one relation can be found between such views and strategies for action. Rather, a structural perspective seems to pervade many different definitions of the role of the Church. Moreover, when concrete alternatives for action are put forward (such as dialogue or cooperation with Marxists), national differences become especially prominent. These findings suggest a need to go beyond social and political attitudes alone, and to complete the analysis begun in previous chapters, by bringing ecclesial and sociopolitical dimensions together. By comparing visions of religion and of the Church directly with visions of society, we move toward a clearer and more complete understanding of the role the bishop sees for the Church itself, and for himself as its most visible public leader.

The relation between structuralism and particular forms of action is weak. But perhaps this is only to be expected, as bishops often draw a clear and firm distinction between analysis of society (for which "sociological" categories are considered quite appropriate) and specification of the Church's proper role in it. To understand action, social views are perhaps less important than the bishops' vision of the nature of religious commitment and of the Church itself. How are the two related?

Consider the question of authority, which, I have argued, is central to views of the Church. If we consider the relation between measures of stress on authority as the most important change in the

Church, on the one hand, and indices of structuralism or Church role in general, on the other, no strong or consistent patterns emerge. But insight begins with a look at career, for different kinds of bishops favor activation in each country. In Venezuela, those high on pastoral experience favor activation, while among Colombians this position is dominated by those with more bureaucratic (or educational) career experience (see table 6.7). To

TABLE 6.7
ACTIVATION AND CAREER (%)

Activation	Pastoral Career			Bureaucratic-Educational Career			Totals
	Low	Med	High	Low	Med	High	
Venezuela							
Low	57	20	20	29	20	60	32
Med	29	60	40	43	50	40	45
High	14	20	40	29	30	—	23
Totals (N = 22)	32	46	23	32	45	23	
Colombia							
Low	35	27	100	100	35	30	34
Med	31	55	—	—	53	25	37
High	35	18	—	—	12	45	29
Totals (N = 38)	68	29	3	3	45	53	

a certain extent, these results reflect the greater institutional structuring of lay groups in Colombia, where organized opportunities on a large scale really exist. But in Venezuela each bishop is left to generate his own opportunities on the local level. The national infrastructure simply is not there. The preference for activation by men of such different backgrounds in each country also tells us something about openness to dialogue and cooperation on the local level in Venezuela, where getting others to act means, perforce, working with what little exists in the community (usually partisan political groups) rather than operating in the secure confines of ecclesiastically controlled organizations.

Turning to Marxism, striking national differences emerge immediately. In Venezuela, a high stress on changing authority relations (both since the council and also in the national Church) is most likely to be associated with acceptance of dialogue and cooperation with Marxists; but the reverse is true in Colombia (see tables 6.8 and 6.9). As we have seen, a concern for changing authority relations is associated in some measure with greater openness and willingness to draw models and ideas from secular, non-Catholic groups. This openness fits the Venezuelan context well: a weak Church in a pluralist society must be open to borrowing and cooperation. But in Colombia, the Church is not weak, and any dealings with Marxism are likely to occur only within a highly

TABLE 6.8
DIALOGUE AND COOPERATION WITH MARXISTS, BY CHANGED AUTHORITY RELATIONS SINCE THE COUNCIL (%)

	Venezuela (N = 20)				Colombia (N = 36)			
	Authority Relations Since Council			Totals	Authority Relations Since Council			Totals
Dialogue	Low	Med	Hi		Low	Med	Hi	
Accept	22	22	56	45	56	33	11	25
Qualified	17	67	17	30	21	43	36	39
Reject	40	20	40	25	23	31	46	36
Totals	24	33	43		31	36	33	

TABLE 6.9
DIALOGUE AND COOPERATION WITH MARXISTS, BY CHANGES IN AUTHORITY RELATIONS IN THE NATIONAL CHURCH (%)

	Venezuela (N = 20)				Colombia (N = 36)			
	Authority Relations in National Church			Totals	Authority Relations in National Church			Totals
Dialogue	Low	Med	Hi		Low	Med	Hi	
Accept	20	10	70	50	56	22	22	25
Qualified	20	60	20	25	46	15	39	36
Reject	40	40	20	25	36	36	29	39
Totals	25	30	45		44	25	31	

structured and controlled situation of "officially" sponsored dialogue, of which there have been several cases to date. Hence, among Colombian bishops, the ones most tolerant of dialogue, paradoxically enough, are the ones most closely wedded to a vision of the Church still heavily under the control of the hierarchy —the very bishops who score low on changing authority relations. In a hierarchical Church, initiatives like dialogue and cooperation with Marxists can be guided in a prudent and highly circumscribed manner.

Looking at the question of the Church's commitment to social progress, little relation appears between perceived change in this area in general (since Vatican II) and attitudes to dialogue and cooperation with Marxists (see table 6.10). But considering change

TABLE 6.10
DIALOGUE AND COOPERATION WITH MARXISTS, BY SOCIAL PROGRESS IN THE CHURCH SINCE THE COUNCIL (%)

	Venezuela (N = 20)				*Colombia (N = 36)*			
	Social Progress Since Council				Social Progress Since Council			
Dialogue				Totals				Totals
	Low	Med	Hi		Low	Med	Hi	
Accept	56	33	11	45	67	33	—	25
Qualified	33	67	—	30	79	21	—	39
Reject	60	40	—	25	62	39	—	36
Totals	50	45	5		69	31	—	

within each national Church, a pattern emerges which once again runs counter to much of the popular wisdom on the subject. In each country, those accepting dialogue and cooperation are more likely to score low on seeing social progress as a major aspect of recent change in their own Church (see table 6.11). Apparently, a commitment to promoting social progress by the Church remains tied to a desire to keep the Church in a guiding and controlling role, a role which necessarily excludes or downplays free, open, and equal dealings with Marxists.

TABLE 6.11
DIALOGUE AND COOPERATION WITH MARXISTS, BY SOCIAL PROGRESS IN THE NATIONAL CHURCH (%)

| | Venezuela (N = 20) |||| Colombia (N = 36) ||||
| | Social Progress in National Church ||| | Social Progress in National Church ||| |
Dialogue	Low	Med	Hi	Totals	Low	Med	Hi	Totals
Accept	80	—	20	50	67	22	11	25
Qualified	40	40	20	25	69	23	8	36
Reject	60	40	—	25	21	50	29	39
Totals	65	20	15		50	33	17	

The pattern is remarkably clear and consistent throughout: as one draws closer to concrete questions of action, national differences play a greater role in shaping the way the bishops' beliefs and actions go together. Why, for example, should an emphasis on change in authority relations be associated with opposite stances on Marxism in Venezuela and Colombia? The answer lies in a contextual view of the men and the institutions they lead.

Colombian bishops rise in an institution which is well organized and staffed, tied into elite groups at all levels, and generally expected to take a central social role. Thus, while greater emphasis on structural problems in society may well dispose them to promote social reform, such initiatives emerge and take shape within well-established traditions of clerical domination. The point becomes particularly clear with reference to authority as a dimension of change in the national Church. Colombians are less concerned with this issue than are Venezuelans, but those who do concentrate on it *also* reject dialogue and cooperation. Their concern lies with rebuilding the Church's structures and rejuvenating its operations, not with spreading the net of "the Church" more widely. The actions favored by Colombian bishops thus fit the traditions of a proud and triumphal Church, a Church constrained by the successes of the past—by the structures, organizations, and symbols which carry over to the present day. Renewed concern for social progress and reform leads Colombian bishops away from dialogue and cooperation with Marxists, not toward it. Indeed, whatever the direction of Church action in Colombia, for the bishops it will be of a piece with the past, in its tendency to give the Church a dominant role in providing norms and values.

But in Venezuela the heritage of the Church is much more modest, and the relevant social world more thoroughly pluralized. Thus Venezuelans, while at best "moderate" in their social views and their vision of the Church's role, are quite willing to interact with Marxists, to draw models and values as necessary from surrounding society. Their overwhelming concern is to develop links with society; and, in a poor-man's game where none exist, almost any will do. Thus, for the Venezuelan bishops, a concern with the Church's authority relations extends beyond the confines of the institutional Church, spreading into the very concept of community they use in day-to-day affairs.

An interesting confirmation of this analysis comes when we look at the context in which bishops view the future. Recall that the two national groups were quite similar; but, whereas Colombians stressed the growth of more authentic faith, morality, and understanding, Venezuelans mentioned this less and added a category largely overlooked in Colombia: the development of a greater sense of belonging, purpose, and community in the Church.

These differences reveal a Colombian hierarchy intent on the re-Christianization of society, in contrast to a Venezuelan hierarchy in the process of building—not reconquering—a community. Relating such views of the future to the issue of Marxism yields a striking result: in *both* Venezuela and Colombia, those looking at the future in terms of faith, morality, and understanding are the most likely of all to reject dialogue and cooperation outright (see table 6.12). Thus, the drive to re-Christianize society, which itself rests on a particular vision of the Church (linked to notions of Christendom) in some measure cuts across national differences.

These considerations, added to what we already know about the impact of education and career on the perceptions and action orientations of the bishops, completes the portrait which has been developed since chapter 3. The Venezuelan Church is weak, and its very weakness frees it from many of the commitments of the past, while reinforcing a general disposition to tolerance and cooperation with others. But tolerance, adaptiveness, and accommodation are not simply a function of weakness. They also grow out of a genuine

TABLE 6.12

DIALOGUE AND COOPERATION WITH MARXISTS, BY THE CONTEXT OF DISCUSSIONS OF THE FUTURE OF THE CHURCH (%)

	Context of Discussions					
Dialogue	Institutional Church	Church-Society	Faith, Morality, Understanding	Sense of Community	Sociopolitical Change	Totals
Venezuela (N = 17)						
Accept	100	50	25	40	—	47
Qualified	—	12.5	25	40	—	24
Reject	—	37.5	50	20	—	29
Totals	12	35	24	29	—	
Colombia (N = 34)						
Accept	50	11	6	100	100	21
Qualified	25	56	41	—	—	38
Reject	25	44	53	—	—	41
Totals	12	29	50	6	3	

concern for pastoral, humane relationships and an appreciation of their impact on the Church, both in general and especially within Venezuela. Of course, evangelical and pastoral concerns are important to the bishops of both nations; but in Colombia they are expressed through a much more highly structured and politically involved set of organizational routines, whereas in Venezuela they are looser and more open to interchange at the local level. Table 6.13 summarizes the kinds of differences identified so far on both ecclesial and sociopolitical dimensions of change.

CONCLUSIONS

Throughout this book, I have stressed the need to keep ecclesial and sociopolitical dimensions separate in *analytical* terms. But for complete understanding, these analytical dimensions must be brought together in a way which responds closely to the *empirical* dynamics and constraints of any given social and institutional context. This process—moving from ideas and social context to action, and back again in an endless dialectic—is outlined in figure 6.1. Although all such attempts at linear portrayal are overly

TABLE 6.13
ECCLESIAL AND SOCIOPOLITICAL DIMENSIONS OF CHANGE
(CONTINUED FROM TABLE 5.6)

	Venezuela	Colombia
1. Institutional context	Weak & building	Strong & defending
2. Elite careers favored	Pastoral	Bureaucratic-educational
3. Changes emphasized since the council	Authority/ social progress	Authority/ juridical
4. Changes emphasized in national Church	Authority/ juridical	Authority/ social progress
5. Change in emphasis on authority, from council to national	Increase	Decrease
6. Problems of national Church	Internal	Moral and social problems of the nation
7. Style of action	Paternal/ open	Institutional/ more guarded
8. Structuralism	Lesser	Greater
9. Church role	Limited activation (weak structures)	Activation (strong structures)
10. Dialogue and cooperation with Marxists	Yes	No
11. Activism and violence	No	No
12. Goal of "re-Christianizing" society	No	Yes

schematic, they help bring out the central role of the Church itself as a matrix through which the bishops' other attitudes, values, and resource capabilities must pass to become effective in action.

In this way, the Church, taken as a set of structures and as a core of identities and conceptual archetypes, conditions action in the larger society by providing evaluations and motivations for action. Clearly, no single pattern can describe the relation between religious and sociopolitical categories. General statements do not grasp these differences adequately, for it is only in the particularities of action that they find full expression. Thus, analysis cannot remain at the level of categories such as activation (which itself is shared by bishops espousing both ecclesial and ecclesiastical visions of the Church), but must instead look closely at the nature

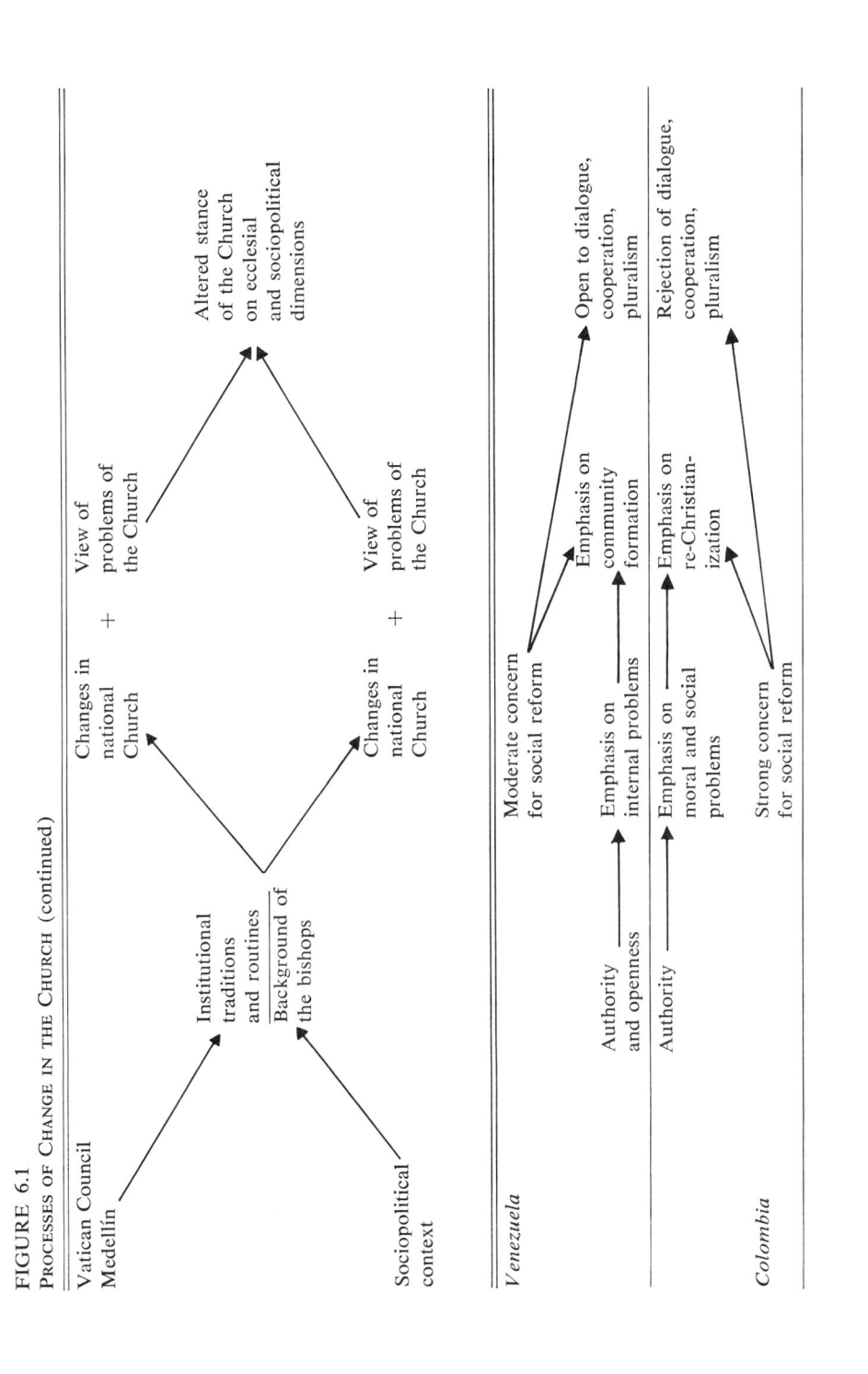

FIGURE 6.1
Processes of Change in the Church (continued)

Vatican Council Medellín

Vatican Council Medellín → Institutional traditions and routines / Background of the bishops → Changes in national Church + View of problems of the Church → Altered stance of the Church on ecclesial and sociopolitical dimensions

Sociopolitical context → Background of the bishops → Changes in national Church + View of problems of the Church → Altered stance of the Church on ecclesial and sociopolitical dimensions

Venezuela

Moderate concern for social reform → Emphasis on community formation → Open to dialogue, cooperation, pluralism

Authority and openness → Emphasis on internal problems → Emphasis on community formation

Colombia

Authority → Emphasis on moral and social problems → Emphasis on re-Christianization → Rejection of dialogue, cooperation, pluralism

Strong concern for social reform → Emphasis on re-Christianization

of the activity within each category. This task will be undertaken in detail in later chapters. The point to bear in mind here is that moving from generalities to specifics, taking concrete activities under consideration, regularly leads to more sharply differentiated and defined results.

Pure types are always hard to find in the real world, and the world of the Church is no exception. The patterns traced out here are abstractions. Like all such abstractions, they gloss over and obscure substantial variation. The next three chapters draw out the potential for intra- and international differences in the conditions of action in Catholic organizations and selected dioceses, and they also develop the consequences, for the Church, of the mix between ecclesial and sociopolitical attitudes, on the one hand, with variations in social and institutional context, on the other. I have argued all along that significant differences within the Church come out most strongly in the particularities of action. Let us turn, then, to consider such actions more closely.

Part III

CASE STUDIES IN STRUCTURE AND STYLE

7

Structure and Style: National Organizations

WHEN looking at the Catholic Church, one must go beyond the bounds of the ecclesiastical institution and its clerical personnel to include the broad community of believers which makes up the Church's base and clientele. Although all baptized Catholics are technically members of the Church, an important distinction can be drawn between this minimal membership (and the community it delineates) and more active forms of involvement through participation in specifically Catholic or Church-related organizations. This chapter explores the changing structure and style of this organized community of the Church, taking the evolution of key Catholic groups and the issues which concern them as further indicators of the dynamic and changing relations between Church and world.

For group members and for the hierarchy as well, the organized Catholic community (and especially its changing relations to the ecclesiastical institution) holds special significance as an expression of lay participation and as a means of motivating and channeling the impact of Catholics in social life. Different models have inspired Catholic organizational activity over the years. Within the Church, Catholic organizations have traditionally been seen as extensions of the will and activities of the ecclesiastical institution, specifically of the bishop. This view took on particular force with the appearance and evolution of Catholic Action movements in Europe and Latin America after World War I. Responding to perceived threats of expanding secularization and leftist influence, the hierarchy sought to "penetrate" society through a network of safe, reliable, and yet vigorous organizations among workers, peasants, students, professionals, and other key groups. These organizations were conceived within a model of the Church as institution, with considerable emphasis placed on a combination of loyalty, doctrinal orthodoxy, and structural subordination, traits which go together both in analytical terms and in fact.[1]

Given their close ideological and structural ties to the hierarchy, organizations of this kind have often been seen as available resources for the bishops—bridges extending ecclesiastical structures and activities into the surrounding world. In support of this view, as we have seen, an elaborate doctrine was developed within the Church of the need for a "distinction of levels," with different and complementary roles for clergy and laity.[2] Such a doctrine reinforces the idea that lay organizations are resources for the institutional Church, that *they* are the proper vehicles of Church action in the world, and that their members are called specifically to kinds of action from which clergy are barred.

The relation between lay organizations and the hierarchy thus has several basic components when seen from the perspective of the bishops. The groups are subordinate to the hierarchy, conceived as resources within a broad scheme of loyalty and obedience. The requirements of loyalty and structural subordination are reflected in a series of organizational linkages and in a concern, by the bishops, for doctrinal orthodoxy. This subordinate status is itself framed within an overall desire for the groups to have valid and vigorous roots in the "world"—to have a real social base. The ambiguities here are immediately visible, for groups with firm and flourishing *temporal* roots and concerns may of course follow paths and be moved by interests quite different from those which the bishops see as primary.

With one foot in the "Church" and another in the "world," lay Catholic groups often express a series of contradictory commitments and understandings in their own views of necessary and proper action. Moreover, the analysis of authority and politics in preceding chapters casts considerable doubt on any view which reduces Catholic organizations to mere clay in the hands of the hierarchy. There are several key areas in which concepts of au-

[1] Cf. Poggi, *Catholic Action in Italy*, pp. 51-54, for a useful discussion of Italian Catholic Action in these terms.

[2] A critical view of the "distinction of levels" notion is offered by Gutierrez, who argues that this distinction was never clear in practice: "The greater part of the Church remained untouched by this Church-world distinction, for it was contradicted by the strong bonds which consciously or unconsciously tied the Church to the existing social order" (*A Theology of Liberation*, p. 58).

thority and visions of the Church affect the structure and substantive interests of Catholic organizations. First, the greater appreciation of temporal values implied in models stressing historical experience and change leads to a search, in the situations of daily life, for problems, motivations, and categories of analysis to guide action. Action begins with experience, not with deductions from abstract doctrine. Second, these changes go along with a new stress on authority as service, which finds expression in calls for shared responsibility at all levels and in efforts to reduce external signs of status and rank. These conceptual changes make for notable transformations in the life of Catholic organizations and in their relation to the ecclesiastical hierarchy.

Throughout this book, I have argued that there is an elective affinity between certain kinds of structure (whose form expresses implicit models of the Church) and certain patterns of interest and styles of action. Before moving into detailed analysis of the groups themselves, it may be well to define "structure" and "style" in more specific terms. As used here, "structure" refers above all to the way groups are linked to the hierarchy. The bishops' long-standing concern for reliability and control takes structural form in the appointment of priests as "moral advisers" to the groups. Through these men, and the general conformity in doctrine and orientation they try to ensure, the hierarchy seeks to maintain leverage within the groups. But in recent years, the role of clerical advisers has entered into crisis, especially in Colombia, where it has been most highly developed. The changing status and role of clerical advisers to lay groups thus constitutes a basic indicator of structure—an implicit measure of the kind of relation which exists between lay groups and the bishops. Other related measures include leadership selection (from within the group or imposed from without) and criteria for leadership (technical and group-oriented or ecclesiastical and related to loyalty).

"Style" and "content," as used here, refer to predominant concerns and patterns of action. Content can be reduced to the basic alternatives of pietism (stress on personal spirituality, inner conversion, and proselytism) as opposed to commitments to technical, social, and political action. "Style" is harder to pin down in precise terms, but as used here it refers above all to the nature of relations *within* the group itself and to the way group members approach the world: as something to be controlled, limited, and (re)-conquered for the Church, or as an environment posing valid and independent problems and challenges to the members' own faith and commitments.

Taking "structure" and "style" together, a broad distinction can be drawn between groups whose rigid structure and close ties to the hierarchy express a cautious, careful, and paternalistic mode of action, and those with looser, more open internal linkages that reflect and reinforce a social concern springing from the base and expressing itself in more group-oriented terms. As I pointed out in chapter 4, the key distinction here is one of style and orientation. Differences of style are fundamental, in my view, for they speak to the way in which *any* group participates in the organizations linking it to the Church: as passive clients or recipients of charity, or rather as active subjects whose knowledge and experiences provide valid guides to understanding and action.[3]

In light of these considerations, it is not surprising that Catholic organizations have faced more and more problems in recent years that center on the nature of their ties to the hierarchy, and on the implications of those ties for the content and style of group action. An important source of this growing friction, particularly in Colombia, has been the bishops' drive for greater centralization, strengthening and extending group ties with the hierarchy. Here it is important to be very clear about what is at stake, for the relation of bishops to groups is often more complex than a simple concern with obedience would indicate. At least two threads are visible, reflecting in some measure the independence of ecclesial and sociopolitical dimensions stressed in earlier chapters. In the first place, in accord with recent calls for greater recognition of the autonomy of lay values and experiences, there is a growing disposition by the hierarchy to withdraw from direct involvement in, and day-to-day management of, social and political questions. But in the second place, while the bishops pull back from direct action, they nonetheless continue to assert a general desire to regulate, or at least to influence, the moral values and life styles of group leaders and members.[4] This is expressed in the drive for greater centralization.

---

[3] This distinction is powerfully developed in Freire, *Pedagogy of the Oppressed*, especially chapters 1 and 2.

[4] Cf. Poggi, *Catholic Action in Italy*, pp. 79ff., on the theme of "safety first."

In combining withdrawal from direct action with centralization of control in other areas, the bishops seem to be following the advice of Ivan Vallier: abjure direct political involvements and concentrate instead on developing autonomous resources and generalized socioethical leadership.[5] But, as one might expect, this strategy runs into considerable difficulties, because it comes into conflict with changes within the groups themselves, changes which are often expressed in ever closer ties between pastoral commitments and sociopolitical activism.

The problem for the bishops is that the process of change cuts two ways. While new models and concepts trickle down from the top, many organizational leaders and activists have begun to expand their own definitions of the Church and of their proper role within it. Thus the idea of increased lay autonomy, growing out of a more communitarian or *ecclesial* concept of authority, often leads to group activities which threaten *ecclesiastical* authority as traditionally understood. There is irony here, for many Catholic organizations, originally founded to counter a perceived threat (most notably from communism) themselves become threatening to the hierarchy as they develop new ideas of autonomy and expand their political involvements.

As for the groups, they face a particularly difficult and double-edged crisis of authority. If they hold closely to the bishops' line, they avoid "trouble," but often at the price of growing irrelevance to society and the loss of members and organizational vitality. This has been the fate of many Catholic organizations in Latin America, most notably among youth and students. On the other hand, if group leaders originally raised in a pietistic orientation "discover the world" and move toward direct action in it, they may tread on sensitive "political" grounds, and they risk censure and abandonment by the hierarchy. In a rough form, one might argue that the stronger the group, the more it runs the risk of conflict with the bishops by insisting on independence. Weaker organizations, by contrast, are likely to resist the hierarchy's withdrawal from direct involvement, seeing this as a betrayal of old commitments.

With these considerations well in hand, let us now examine the evolution of major Catholic lay organizations in Venezuela and Colombia.

---

[5] Vallier, *Catholicism*, especially pp. 69-71, 79-81, and 83-87.

STRUCTURE AND STYLE

THE EVOLUTION OF ORGANIZATIONAL STRUCTURES

As we have seen, despite their interest in and concern for change within the Church, bishops are often reluctant to accept the *institutionalization* of new patterns of authority and group relations, favoring instead either traditional clerical and hierarchical structures or informal, personalized arrangements, both of which stress considerable deference to episcopal status and values of loyalty and obedience. This pattern is visible in the *kinds* of lay organizations the bishops favor. Given the inherent difficulties just noted in work with groups more oriented to independent social action, it is not surprising that, when asked to identify key lay organizations, bishops in both countries stress groups of a notably pietistic and explicitly "religious" orientation. I asked the bishops this question:

In general, among the activities of the lay apostolate the diocese has, which do you consider to be the most important?

Responses here provide a useful contemporary base line for the analysis of Catholic groups.[6] Up to four mentions were coded for each bishop, and tables 7.1 and 7.2 show the groups named as well as the areas of lay activity specified as important in each country (up to three areas were coded per bishop). The bishops' responses show a striking preference for traditional pietistic organizations with very close structural ties to the hierarchy. Thus, groups like the Little Courses in Christianity (Cursillos de Cristiandad), the Legion of Mary, the Christian Family Movement, and various national and local Catholic Action groups head the list in both countries. All these groups share an overwhelming concern for individual spirituality and obedience to the hierarchy. Organizations less tied to the bishops, more open internally, and more socially and politically active are only sparsely represented.

The groups named are appropriate for the areas of action the bishops cite as central to lay activity in their dioceses. Work in the general field of "catechism and family" dominates responses in both nations. Although catechism can become a controversial sub-

[6] The question as phrased may skew responses somewhat; for, in thinking about organizations of the "lay apostolate," some bishops may have set social action to one side and concentrated instead on groups of a more spiritual character, which are those encompassed by more conventional definitions of "apostolic" work.

TABLE 7.1
MOST IMPORTANT LAY ORGANIZATIONS
(up to 4 mentions coded)

Venezuela			Colombia		
Group	N	%	Group	N	%
Cursillos de Cristiandad	16	29	Christian Family Movement	19	20
Catholic Action (various)	12	21	Community religious groups[a]	15	16
Christian Family Movement	11	20	Cursillos de Cristiandad	13	13.5
Legion of Mary	10	18	Catholic Action (various)	12	12.5
Youth (various)	4	7	Legion of Mary	8	8
Catechism groups	2	4	Community organization (adult education)	8	8
Cooperatives	1	2	Unions (workers, peasants)	7	7
			Youth	6	6
			Education	6	6
			Missions	2	2
Totals	56	100	Totals	96	100

[a] Parish Councils, base communities, family assemblies.

TABLE 7.2
MOST IMPORTANT AREAS OF LAY ACTIVITY
(up to 3 mentions coded)

Venezuela			Colombia		
Area	N	%	Area	N	%
Catechism and family	20	42	Catechism and family	40	49
Youth	12	25	Adult education	19	24
Adult education	8	17	Social action-community organization	11	14
Social action-community organization	6	13	Charity	6	7
Work with nuns	1	2	Youth	5	6
Totals	48	100	Totals	85	100

ject (see chapter 8, below), what most bishops have in mind is not controversial at all, but rather a traditional form of religious education stressing individual piety and rote learning of theological maxims. In addition, "youth" and "adult education," which are also mentioned frequently in both countries, are also heavily laced with devotional themes. Social action and community organization receive only scant attention. The bishops' notable predilection for pietistic, devotional activities and traditional organizations suggests the utility of a closer look at the nature and history of such groups in each country.

To discuss the evolution of Catholic organizational structures in Venezuela and Colombia, it is important to distinguish fields of activity. At the very least, five areas can be distinguished on the national level: first, the central bureaucratic structures of the Church; second, social action groups like industrial or rural trade unions; third, apostolic groups like the Cursillos de Cristiandad or the Legion of Mary; fourth, youth and student organizations; and fifth, "independent" organizations, which are notable for their combination of Christian orientation with great structural independence from the hierarchy. This last category holds a number of groups in the educational field that were founded in both countries by the individual initiative of priests.[7]

Given the enormous differences between Venezuela and Colombia, it would be difficult and quite misleading to compare groups in the two countries in the same categories. The resources, opportunities, and alternatives to Church-affiliated organizations are so different in each case as to make such direct comparison inappropriate. But comparison is still possible; it is pursued here in major cases *within* each country, through examination of the evolution of group interests and linkages with the hierarchy. By focusing attention in this way on the spheres of action most important within each nation, it is possible to get a clearer notion of the degree to which form and content respond to the kind of threat and challenge perceived in each case.

In Colombia, a powerful and well-established Church saw growing threats from liberalism and from leftist organizations after 1930. The challenge for the Church was to defend and retain its mass base, and the organizational response was a centralized net of social action groups which emerged along with a series of "independent" initiatives later adopted and blessed by the Church. In Venezuela, a secularized nation largely indifferent to the Church, the problem was less preservation and defense than creation of a base. Thus the initial organizational response was not to build groups to

[7] The most important of these, Colombia's Acción Cultural Popular, is discussed below in this chapter. Several such organizations are visible in Venezuela. For details see Levine, *Conflict*, chap. 5.

hold the mass (some attempts were made, but these failed owing to competition from the political parties), but rather to penetrate Venezuelan elites, to build support and loyalty *within* institutions— a support Colombians could afford to take for granted.

I have already described the steady growth of the Church's central bureaucratic structures in each country, in response to the bishops' persistent attempts at greater central coordination and control. This push for central control has been most visible in recent years in Colombia, where the growing national bureaucracy of the Church (the Permanent Secretariat of the Colombian Episcopate, or *SPEC*) has absorbed many functions previously left to others. Two good examples are the recent controversy over IDES (Instituto de Desarrollo Económico y Social) and the concentration of social action organizations in the National Secretariat for Social Pastoral, a new department of SPEC. Both activities had previously been entrusted to the Jesuits, and the bishops' attempt at centralization under their direct control reflected their desire for greater doctrinal "safety" and organizational reliability.

IDES was formed by the bishops in 1967 as a vehicle for training lay leaders and creating "agents" for the Church in the social field. Leadership training was carried out through a series of courses on theology, doctrine, and social questions. In 1972 the contract for IDES was taken away from the Jesuits, and IDES was integrated into a department of SPEC. This change reflected the bishops' growing concern with the "sociologization" and secular orientation of Church institutions. The dispute centered over who should be educated by IDES, what should be taught, and with what goals. For the bishops, the primary goal of IDES was to educate Church personnel (priests and religious) and those lay leaders closely linked to ecclesiastical structures. As one officer of the new IDES told me, "There was a more or less serious problem. I don't know to what extent you could call it ideological. The problem is, Why train people? If it is to train them and launch them into the world, to social action, or rather to train them and link them to the Church. This was the basic difference."[8]

Under the Jesuits, courses at IDES included considerable attention to the social sciences as a basis for understanding the Latin American situation. Rather than stress traditional expositions of Catholic social doctrine, the Jesuits running IDES focused on "de-

[8] Interview 80206, 22 Feb. 1972.

velopment," with attention to secular ideas and groups. With the change in leadership, IDES concentrated more on theology and on the Church's social encyclicals as the Catholic answer to social problems. In this way, IDES and the groups it dealt with moved away from being a decentralized structure drawing inspiration from secular milieux, and toward becoming a more inward-looking, defensive structure secured by tight organizational linkages to the bishops.[9]

In the second field of Catholic organization, social action groups have a long history in Colombia. As early as 1913 the National Bishops' Conference was issuing norms for such groups. But the main push of nationally organized, nonterritorial structures for social action came after 1930, with a series of groups modeled on European Catholic Action movements. The most important of these were Catholic trade unions.[10]

Colombia is one of the few countries in Latin America where the Church has managed to build a major national labor movement.[11] The earliest group was the Young Catholic Workers (Juventud Obrera Católica, or JOC), first organized on a national scale in 1932. The JOC became a seedbed of leaders for all subsequent Catholic labor groups in Colombia. About a decade later, under the leadership and inspiration of a group of Jesuits, two more labor organizations were established. First was a semisecret group for the selection and training of Catholic labor leaders, intended to give them the essence of the Church's social doctrine.[12] This was SETRAC (Selection of Catholic Workers), founded in 1941. The second brought together a number of open trade unions

---

[9] The Jesuits let IDES go without much of a struggle. They felt that it was more vital to keep their operations free of hierarchical control than to retain the contract and its financial advantages. As one Jesuit official put it, CIAS (the Jesuit studies center that ran IDES) "must be free to give the results of scientific investigation. It must be free and they were muzzling us. . . . CIAS has to be independent. It cannot be gagged. And it is better this way, because no one is committed by what we say. We also have to be independent, because we want to make mistakes; and we know that we will make mistakes. But the bishops have the idea that they can never be in error" (Interview 80619, 23 Aug. 1972).

[10] Urrutia, *The Development of the Colombian Labor Movement*, pt. 4.

[11] Floridi and Stiefbold, *The Uncertain Alliance*, passim.

[12] This combination of semisecret leadership groups with open mass labor organization is not unique to Colombia. For example, see the data on Catholic labor in Mexico in Mabry, *Mexico's Acción Nacional*, chap. 2.

in the Union of Colombian Workers (UTC). The formation of these groups responded to a rising tide of social agitation and communist action, especially in regions such as the banana zones of the Caribbean coast.[13] In the words of one Jesuit involved in the formation of these groups,

> So you see that social and political matters were coming together in an explosive mixture. The Church was removed from all this and considered trade unionism as a communist creation. There were some Church initiatives which dated years back . . . but by this time they no longer functioned. So I proposed to the Bishops' Conference a plan which had to go by stages. Since we couldn't talk about unions (this was taboo) we spoke of the formation of workers' action circles. The word "circle" was in fashion then. We saw these circles as a first step in the unification of Christian forces. We had already begun, in 1941, the group now known as SETRAC, which earlier was called Movement of Union Action, and even earlier, Workers' Union.[14]

These labor organizations fit a classic Catholic Action mold. Great emphasis was placed on hierarchy and unity, both being ensured by the presence of "moral advisers" (priests) named by the bishops. Decision making and organizational control were centralized at the national level, with the Jesuit-run National Coordination for Social Action serving as "manager" for the hierarchy.[15] The social orientation stressed class collaboration and Christian harmony, an outlook very much attuned to the prevalent ideas of the 1940s. One internal document described the National Coordination's central functions as follows:

> a. To serve as organ of information in the social field for the bishops and their representatives in each diocese. To act as executor of the determinations of the bishops and the secretariat of social pastoral.
>
> b. To maintain permanent contact with government and with

---

[13] This was made famous in García Márquez's fictional account in *One Hundred Years of Solitude*; the banana strike was based on actual events in Santa Marta.

[14] Interview 80505, 16 Feb. 1972.

[15] The Coordinación Nacional brought together a variety of groups ranging from trade unions and cooperatives to study centers and professional associations.

members of Congress to make the principles of Catholic social doctrine felt. To assure good relations between the government and the movements advised by the Church.

c. To influence the mentality of employers and directors of economic life, both to make them respect Christian principles and to obtain their economic help and their collaboration in the solution of social problems.

d. To assure continuous contact with the workers' movements, be they of Catholic affiliation or not, seeking through every available means to give them orientation and advice.

e. To promote knowledge and diffusion of Catholic social doctrine through social weeks, courses for priests and leaders, the Institute of Union Development, publications, propaganda, etc., seeking collaboration from the Catholic universities, from Acción Cultural Popular, and from other specialized groups.[16]

This coherent package of tight organizational control and strict doctrinal orthodoxy of course responded well to the kind of threats the groups were formed to meet in the first place; hierarchy, clergy, and lay leaders united against leftist influence. One long-time leader of FANAL, the Catholic peasant union, remembers that the clergy was most active and involved in times of greatest struggle,

> in the most difficult times, in the times when communism had a strong influence in the countryside and in the cities, from 1930 to 1948, that period—because communism began its penetration in the twenties. From 1930 to 1948 was the strongest period for communism here. And we founded FANAL precisely in 1946. But we had already been working for some time, because the movement started in 1940, fighting communism through the JOC. If you ask the leaders with twenty or thirty years' experience in the union movement, in the UTC, FANAL, etc., you will see that they all come from this JOC group. The Church trained them through the JOC, which was the Church's only social movement which was not purely religious but rather oriented to struggle for the claims of the workers. Very different from going to Mass and marching in processions! At this time communism was very strong, and on many occasions priests had

[16] "La Coordinación Nacional de Acción Social Católica," document in possession of the author, n.d.

to risk everything to defend the spiritual heritage of the people. And many workers were also dupes of the communists, as the communists were the only ones who stood up for them. So when we began in 1940, we started to form the first recruits, to build an army for the struggle. Then in 1945-46 we entered into the fight, into battle, and ever since we have been in the thick of it.[17]

Catholic labor groups (above all the urban and industrial unions of the UTC) have grown and prospered in Colombia in recent years. However, they have been hit with an internal dispute centering on the nature of relations with the hierarchy and on the proper role of "moral advisers" within each group. Current Jesuit leaders, following the concepts laid out at the Second Vatican Council, have tried to reduce their direct involvement in day-to-day organizational activities. By setting the groups more on their own, they hope to make them stronger. But this strategy looks different from the layman's perspective. Many group leaders complain bitterly that Jesuit withdrawal from active involvement is simple abandonment. One SETRAC official put it this way:

> I don't know. Frankly I think there is less attention now. The thesis of the council that we laymen must take responsibility has been put into effect very rapidly here—too rapidly. The problem is that there is no adequate education among us, especially among the workers, where education has been difficult. We believe that in the National Secretariat of Social Pastoral they have not managed to understand the movements of lay apostolate. Either they miss it completely or they are in effect compromised with the capitalist system. Yes, especially in union questions I also believe the council created confusion here. There are some who feel that the moral adviser should not have a large role. We do not agree.[18]

In the same vein, a high officer of FANAL lamented the clergy's reluctance to get involved in conflicts. Things were better in the past, when FANAL could count on the support of a Church which was, in his words, "holy, apostolic, and warlike."

> Earlier, there was more involvement, because the national coordinator, Father Andrade, whenever there was a land in-

[17] Interview 80510, 11 Mar. 1972. [18] Interview 80509, 9 Mar. 1972.

vasion, went to talk to the invaders. When some were imprisoned, he visited them and tried to help. He participated more in the life of the organization. But now this is less so, because they say that this is not their role. It is the same with the parish priests—they no longer enter the conflicts. This is the key, they do not enter the conflicts.

"And before?"

Before, yes. We always said that whenever there was a land invasion, a priest would go at the head. But now there is little interest.[19]

This longing for the "good old days" of greater clerical sponsorship and involvement is not universal within Catholic labor. Indeed, an inverse relation is visible between the strength of the organization and the degree of closeness it seeks to maintain with the Church. Those who want close relations, like SETRAC or FANAL, are weak; they want protection when facing the world. But organizations like the UTC are well adapted to society, have a large clientele, and respond to principles of action drawn from society and its conflicts, not from Church directives. Thus, UTC officials welcome the diminishing role of clerical advisers.

The first signs of crisis came in SETRAC before they arose in the UTC. Why? Because SETRAC was anchored in the past, with a very low level of education. They did not realize that now we have a rising group of leaders, but instead continued with a very elemental program of training, and within this the advisers of SETRAC tried to dominate the leaders. And we rebelled against this and said that we would not return until the structures of SETRAC were reformed.[20]

The history of Catholic Action groups in Colombian labor thus reveals a trend common to much of Latin America—the evolution of a carefully structured model of groups organized on the national level and linked closely to the wishes and desires of the hierarchy, and then the model's decline *as such*. Individual components (such as the UTC) may prosper and expand, but their relations with the institutional Church have fundamentally changed. The fate of Catholic labor in Colombia is matched

[19] Interview 80510, 11 Mar. 1972.   [20] Interview 80512, 24 Mar. 1972.

by that of national youth groups. Until the mid-1960s, there existed an impressive collection of youth organizations that were coordinated on the national level by a Youth Central (Central de Juventudes), which was established in 1953 as a clearing house for such activities. But these groups fell apart in the late 1960s in a conflict over political orientations and activities. Thus, in Colombia, traditional Catholic youth groups have practically disappeared. Almost nothing "officially" Catholic has emerged on the national level to replace them;[21] the new youth groups operate on a much more modest and less rigidly structured model. This looser organizational form responds in part to the crisis of earlier groups and also to the resulting wariness (on the part of youth leaders and bishops alike) to get involved in potentially explosive linkages. The linkages are explosive precisely because such groups have turned away from pietistic and welfare-oriented actions and toward a deeper, more active political commitment. As one contemporary Colombian youth "adviser" put it,

> We are moving to groups with a political commitment. Thus, we are asking ourselves how far the group must go to change structures—personal as well as social and political structures. The great difference with the traditional Catholic Action groups is that now they meet not only to discuss the Gospels, but also to discuss reality, and to see where the Gospel leads us in the face of this reality.[22]

Older youth organizations may continue to exist on paper, and bishops may still refer to them as "our groups in this field," but for all practical purposes they have no control over such groups —or, more precisely, there is little to control in the first place.

This organizational dilemma, with groups caught between the bishops' demands for reliability and orthodoxy and the members' concern for activism and "relevance," is particularly notable in "independent" groups, those founded through the independent

[21] The only Catholic youth organization of any national significance at the time of research was the Young Colombian Workers, a successor to the JOC of earlier days. But even here differences are notable. Unlike the JOC, the Young Colombian Workers is not overtly Catholic, although it has a "moral adviser" who helps run the organization and indeed maintains within it a group of specially selected and trained Catholic youth leaders (much like SETRAC).

[22] Interview 80506, 17 Feb. 1972.

initiative of individual priests or groups of clergy apart from the institutional structure of the Church itself. Once the groups prove successful in their fields, the bishops have tended to bless them and call them their own. But in reality they have invested little effort and few resources in their development. This positive attitude falls in with the strategy of activation described earlier, whereby the bishops encourage others to act, but limit their own commitments. As one Venezuelan observer puts it,

> On a national level, there is nothing to which the bishops are really committed, no organization or group except perhaps the newspaper, *La Religion*. Instead, they let things be done, be created, and bless them, accept them, but there is no real commitment. . . . If the work dies, there is no bishop to say anything, to raise a voice. Partly for this reason, they like certain kinds of movements and groups, like the Legion of Mary, the Cursillos, etc., because these, above all, *respect* the bishop and defer to him.[23]

The most notable example of successful "independent" organizations in either country is Colombia's Acción Cultural Popular (ACPO, Popular Cultural Action), more generally known as Radio Sutatenza. ACPO began in 1948 as the pastoral effort of one parish priest, who used the radio to reach isolated members of his parish. By 1973 this organization had expanded into a net of institutions including the nation's largest chain of radio transmitters, its third largest newspaper, a major independent printing and publishing business, and a group of present and past pupils and trained leaders numbering in the hundreds of thousands.[24]

ACPO is dedicated to rural adult education through the use

---

[23] Interview 60603, 9 July 1973. *La Religión* is the daily newspaper of the Archdiocese of Caracas.

[24] For example, in 1966 the weekly newspaper *El Campesino* (The Peasant) had a weekly run of 52,753, with an annual run of 2,690,452. In the same year ACPO was running radio schools in 909 municipalities, with over 200,000 pupils being reached by 22,129 separate "schools." Data are from Musto, *Los medios de comunicación social al servicio de desarrollo rural*, p. 100 and p. 94. The source is a report on ACPO conducted by the German Institute of Development, which is highly critical of many aspects of the institution's operations. A vigorous reply is contained in Bernal Alarcón, *Educación fundamental integral y medios de comunicación social*.

of radio, and it is linked to the Church in three fundamental ways. First, the identity of its founder and long-time director general, Msgr. José Joaquín Salcedo, provides an obvious tie. Second, its formal statutes give ultimate control to a Governing Council in which the bishops have a majority. This council theoretically has the power to set general policies and to name the director general and members of the Board of Directors. But the council's power is in fact quite limited, since it meets only once or twice a year. ACPO is really run by a permanent professional staff, and, as we shall see shortly, the composition of this staff and its relation to the hierarchy reveals major changes since the early 1960s. Finally, on the local level, ACPO is linked to the Church through its regular system of adult education, which relies on the parish priests to stimulate the local study and cooperative action groups that make up the base of the organization.

Despite these multiple ties and identities, members of the ecclesiastical hierarchy and officials of the bishops' Permanent Secretariat often complain about ACPO's excessive independence. They argue that it works only on its own, that it does not lend its facilities to the Church's programs of religious instruction and proselytism. Why this friction? What is the real nature of the ties between ACPO and the bishops?

To understand ACPO fully, it is important to realize that its basic goal has never been to serve as a system of religious instruction, but rather to provide what is referred to as "fundamental integral education"—that is, general preparation of rural adults to improve their personal, material, and spiritual lives. To this end, the educational programs of ACPO combine training in literacy and basic mathematics with emphasis on health, agricultural innovation, and community formation. The goal is integral preparation for development, of the person and the community, in a long-term process of change.[25]

Within this general framework, ACPO's relations with the hierarchy have changed notably. In the early years, many of the institution's key administrative posts were filled by priests. As the organization expanded, special diocesan directors were named to run the institution in each ecclesiastical jurisdiction;

---

[25] This kind of long-term focus means that ACPO comes in for criticism from conservatives and radicals alike: the former see it as undermining the social order, while the latter accuse it of not doing enough in that line.

these were normally priests suggested by the local bishop. As one high ACPO official put it, the organization's early activities had a great impact on the dioceses and on the very image of the parish priests themselves.

> The figure of this priest changed. He started out to be an apostle to the peasants, but as the work [ACPO] began to grow, two things happened. The first phenomenon was a power takeover—they wanted to become not only diocesan directors of the institution, but also national directors, forming a kind of General Assembly with the power to fire the director general and to manage all the resources of the institution. This brought a first confrontation between the central office and the regional directives. And a second phenomenon was one of bureaucratization. These men, who began as apostles, changed into bureaucrats with a salary and a jeep . . . they turned into functionaries. This brought a series of problems, for example, with the cars. First, they used the cars for everything but the radio schools: to transport families, to attend to the hospitals, to carry packages for CARITAS, etc. Moreover, since they were getting a salary, the bishops saw this as a good way to finance them. So they named them as diocesan directors of ACPO and then gave them fifteen other jobs, which they then used to justify not taking care of ACPO.[26]

This problem grew as ACPO expanded, until in 1965 a decision was taken to reorganize the institution to avoid its de facto absorption by the Church, while further ensuring the application of primarily *technical* criteria for promotion and power within ACPO. Thus, priests were removed from key roles in the dioceses in 1965, and jeeps, salaries, and the like were reserved for individuals trained in ACPO's own Peasant Institutes. Meanwhile, on the national level, priests in top administrative posts were gradually replaced by lay personnel of demonstrated technical capacity. The long-term goal of these changes is to make it possible for ACPO to survive and continue with its mission once its powerful founder and director general passes from the scene. "When Salcedo dies, ACPO can find itself in two situations:

---

[26] Interview 80622, 29 Sept. 1972. CARITAS is the Church's social assistance organization.

NATIONAL ORGANIZATIONS

first, where there are no trained executives and a priest is put in charge, with priests in charge of all the management divisions as well; or second, to put better trained executives in every position, so that there is such a high technical level that it will be difficult to replace the lay executives—to build and strengthen the institution."[27] This point of view ensures a constant tension between ACPO's goal of integral rural education and pressures from the hierarchy to emphasize catechism and proselytism, and, to this end, to bring the organization more firmly under ecclesiastical control. For the leaders of ACPO, however,

> It is not within our philosophy to convert ACPO into a proselytizing organ of the Catholic Church, to defend the Church. If the Catholic Church wants to use the communications media, it can use all the media, and not necessarily its own media.
>
> If we start putting out a proselytizing effort, we can no longer say that ACPO is an agency of basic education, but rather is a work of catechism. Let's be frank: the Bishops' Conference does not understand this.[28]

ACPO's drive for greater autonomy has been reinforced by its growing financial independence and by careful attention to political neutrality. Financial pressure from the Church has been countered by support from international lending agencies, and many of the institution's divisions (for example, its printing and publishing business) have been made to turn a profit. The push for greater professional competence among the institution's permanent staff has been very valuable financially. In political terms, the fact that ACPO has always defined its goal as the long-range transformation of the rural population has helped blunt the fears of political leaders who saw it as a potential threat, and it has blocked efforts to turn ACPO's resources to partisan advantage.[29]

Taken together, the cases of IDES, Catholic labor, and ACPO provide considerable insight into the dynamics of the linkage

---

[27] Ibid.   [28] Ibid.

[29] In this regard, ACPO sees itself as fundamentally different from the Movement of Base Education in Brazil, whose adult literacy program was conceived in a quite radical vein; the Brazilian movement ran into grave problems with the military government after the 1964 coup. Cf. De Kadt, *Catholic Radicals in Brazil*, for a full account.

231

between the central ecclesiastical institution and the Catholic organizations that project a message into Colombian society. The difficulties noted here center on the sources of values which inspire a group, and, as a consequence, on the relative role and status of structural ties between the groups and the hierarchy. As groups gain experience, they develop a deeper commitment to their clientele and to the problems and opportunities which arise in the "world"; and so they inevitably come into conflict with the bishops. For although the bishops recognize (in abstract terms) the need to revalue temporal affairs, and to give them greater autonomy in the Catholic scheme of things, they often remain wedded to an organizational model that stresses tight, centrally managed links to the hierarchy.

For these reasons, the changing role of clerical advisers is a useful index of the status of the groups. Here, a dual process is visible. On the one hand, the bishops want to withdraw from direct action; but, on the other, they seek to maintain centralized ties and a general orienting role. Strong and weak groups alike find this unacceptable. Strong groups resent the interference, whereas their weaker counterparts fear the loss of guidance and control. All in all, the result is that the Church in Colombia finds itself "in control" of a series of increasingly empty structures. To a degree, it is the very stress on defending authority per se which leads to this dilemma. The bishops end up with what is, in effect, a policy of laissez-faire: they take strong public positions and expect a generalized deference to the hierarchy, yet accept the fact that individuals and groups will usually do as they please.

There is considerable irony here, for it is the very strengthening of the Church's central bureaucracy which stimulates and sharpens the crisis. As I pointed out in chapter 3, the efforts of Catholic Action in the 1940s and 1950s were supplemented in the 1960s by a series of new ideas, culminating in the document *The Church Facing Change*, which seemed to legitimize new and more open organizational ventures. But almost immediately the hierarchy began to draw back. It tried to limit the activities of Catholic groups to more specifically "pastoral" and less "political" fields; the groups were to be controlled through the creation of national coordinating structures in the Permanent Secretariat of the Bishops' Conference. But this centralization has had a Pyrrhic quality. One high official of the Jesuit order in Colombia put it this way:

> It is true that they are trying to centralize. For me this is very clear. But, on the other hand, the phenomena occurring on different levels are harder to control. For this reason, since they began centralizing, we have been moving toward other structures. I think that what is happening is that they are consolidating their structures, but they always remain within the *ecclesiastical* structures. We, on the other hand, are moving toward structures active in change—toward popular groups, for they are the locus of change, and we are having to get involved in politics. . . . In effect, the problem here is that the bishops are losing touch with the base. At the present time there is a general breakdown of apostolic organizations in the Church, above all of those organizations through which the hierarchy has been accustomed to act—traditional Catholic Action, for example.

"Why this breakdown?"

> There is a sort of disorientation. For example, take the case of Catholic Action. These are organizations formed in earlier times, with clear-cut lines of command within a hierarchical and authoritarian tradition. Now with the restructuring of ecclesiastical organizations they have changed their position within the ecclesiastical scheme of things, and the organizations don't fit in—for example, in the restructuring of ecclesiastical organizations in a more collegial form. With their more vertical and authoritarian tradition they see that they don't fit in today's Church, and they ask, What good are we? So they are disoriented and this leaves the Church with fewer action organizations. The bishops do feel these problems, but they do not see any solutions.[30]

Given this series of problems with more socially oriented groups, it is small wonder that the bishops express so strong a preference for more pietistic and deferential organizations like the Cursillos de Cristiandad or the Legion of Mary. In relative terms, these groups are more important in Venezuela than in Colombia. Hence, I will consider them primarily in the Vene-

[30] Interview 80604, 10 Feb. 1972.

zuelan context. But before starting a detailed exposition it may be useful to lay out the general pattern of development of Catholic organizations in Venezuela.

In Venezuela in the 1940s, although the Church enjoyed considerable respect and although popular religious devotion was strong in some areas, essentially there was no net of national organizations and little institutional support in society at large. The Church's organizational efforts responded to these deficiencies in two notable ways: first, in a great stress on education, with the development of a net of elite schools and some youth groups; and second, through emphasis on apostolic and pietistic organizations dedicated to securing "converts," particularly among social, cultural, economic, and political elites.[31] Venezuelan bishops repeatedly told me that a major change from the past is that now, for the first time, the Church can count on the support of key elite groups. In this process, as we shall see, the Cursillos de Cristiandad have played an important role.

To the Church, part of the importance of Catholic education in Venezuela lies in the organizational consequences of its growth. Briefly, these were three: first, a group of elite primary and secondary schools, along with a university founded in 1953; second, a powerful set of parents' associations able to act as pressure groups in support of Church positions; and third, by the mid-1960s, the beginnings of attempts to go beyond elite schooling in the development of programs of popular and artisanal education. Not surprisingly, the "democratization" of Catholic education, penetrating and working with popular groups in the cities, was carried out by organizations formally independent of the hierarchy, although encouraged and blessed by it.[32]

In other "social" fields, such as trade-union organization, the Venezuelan Church has never been able to accomplish much. Modest attempts were made in the 1940s and 1950s to sponsor

[31] For more details on the Venezuelan Church's efforts in the educational field see Levine, *Conflict*, chaps. 4 and 5. See also Levine "Democracy and the Church," for data on the evolving organizational concerns of the Venezuelan Church, as revealed in the central focus of religious orders founded in this century.

[32] Cf. Levine, *Conflict*, chap. 5. These groups, most notably Fe y Alegría (a program of *barrio*, or slum-area, schools) and APEP (an artisanal training program), bring together money and personnel from Church, private, and official sources to run their operations. Both have been quite successful.

study circles, training groups, and a core of Catholic labor leaders; but these bore little fruit. A "Christian" labor federation, CODESA, has existed for some time, but it is completely overshadowed by the general union movement controlled by the political parties. Among labor, as with youth groups, efforts at "Catholic" organization have been largely absorbed by the christian democratic party, COPEI.

The predominance of political parties, and particularly the role of COPEI in absorbing "Christian" energies in the social action field, magnified the Church's concern with education and elite-oriented apostolic groups; Venezuelan bishops give particular stress to groups like the Cursillos de Cristiandad in changing the atmosphere of Venezuelan Catholicism. What are these groups like? How do they see their own structure and goals, and, through these, the proper relation of lay people to the hierarchy?

The Cursillos were founded in Spain in the early 1950s as a means of personal conversion and individual spiritual enrichment through intense discussion and self-criticism. The first *cursillo* in Venezuela was held in 1959, and the movement spread rapidly. On each organizational level (national, diocesan, and local) the *cursillos* are run by a directorate of priests and lay people, with priests taking a clear leadership role. The movement as a whole places great stress on obedience to the hierarchy, which is ensured through the appointment of priests as advisers at all levels.[33] The bishops seek a control which is quite general. Indeed, the only provision they added to a text of "norms" submitted to them in 1970 by the Cursillo movement was an article giving the bishops *greater* power to select and control leaders of individual *cursillos*. This extreme concern for clerical direction of course responds to a model in which lay people are to be taught and guided in the framework of norms, problems, and questions provided by the hierarchy and its agents. One diocesan *cursillo* director rejected charges of excessive clericalism

---

[33] In 1970 the bishops issued "norms" for the movement, noting that "The Cursillos de Cristiandad, as a movement of Christian renovation, depend in all respects on the prelate of the diocese working through a diocesan adviser for *cursillos*." The powers of this adviser are defined in exceptionally broad terms. Cf. Conferencia Episcopal Venezolana, *Normas para el movimiento de Cursillos de Cristiandad en Venezuela*, p. 38.

in these terms: "They want the layman to have more initiative in the Church. But if he has no training in the Church, he is in danger of slipping easily into deviations, above all in matters of dogma. Training is needed. Furthermore, those laymen who work in the Church must be subordinate to the hierarchy, just as I am."[34]

The Cursillos' orientation to an elite audience is central to its purpose. As an instrument of Christian motivation, it works "not through direct and global action on the whole mass of Christians," but rather on a select group. Who should be selected? The "Manual" for Cursillo leaders written by Bishop Juan Hervas, founder of the movement, argues that

> those selected must be men of well-known human capabilities, strong and well-balanced personalities who are influential in their own fields, for whatever reason (civil authorities, doctors, pharmacists, lawyers, teachers, presidents of associations of the faithful, of brotherhoods, civil entities, etc.). Among manual workers, employees, and office personnel, selection will be made of those who naturally exercise a certain leadership or influence over the others, and possess what are often called leadership qualities.[35]

The priests who direct the *cursillos* are sensitive to the charge that their organization is limited to upper-class individuals, but they defend this as a practical necessity, pointing out that *cursillos* are a different kind of experience from traditional religious instruction, like the catechism given to children.

> To participate in a *cursillo* they are already adult, and the kind of human material we prefer has been the young couple which will be influential in the future, in their family and social circle, and of a certain cultural level—middle and above.
>
> From this comes one of the false charges made against the *cursillos*, that the *cursillos* are only for the rich. But this really is a question of suitable human material. . . . The *cursillos* are of a mental intensity which not everyone can handle; they are very intensive courses, and a person who has no experience in studying, taking notes, and the like may find

---

[34] Interview 60319, 14 July 1973.
[35] Hervas, *Manual de Dirigentes*, pp. 229, 231.

it difficult. Now if a truck driver, a teamster, comes to me, I will not tell him that he has no chance, that he may not continue. [But] the most apt person for this is someone who has been to [a] university, who knows how to take notes and knows how to discuss and talk, because at times the dialogue is very intense. In any case, a man who has not risen in life, in a country where anyone can move upward—this shows a lack of capacity to rise in life.[36]

The Cursillos de Cristiandad thus offers a case in which centralized ties to the bishops are combined with doctrinal orthodoxy and reliability. The two are bound together in a general stress on individual piety. Groups like the Legion of Mary, which also receives considerable mention in each country, are similar, though less exclusively middle and upper class in social composition. The Legion of Mary was founded originally in Ireland, in 1921, to encourage piety through special devotion to the Virgin Mary. It began operating in Venezuela in 1950, and by 1969 it claimed over 14,000 active members with another 37,000 auxiliary members. A special report prepared in 1969 reviewed the status of the Legion in Venezuela, noting that "We lay people form the major part of the Christian community. United and committed with the Hierarchy, we carry out the Lord's work. The Legion of Mary in Venezuela works this way. Its goal is to lead its members to a greater holiness through prayer and apostolic efforts on behalf of others. It is characterized by a firm and unshakable loyalty to the Church, an evangelical submission to the hierarchy, and a spirit and mystique of its own, that of the Holy Virgin—humble, sincere, authentic, and full of faith."[37]

The Cursillos and the Legion are grouped together not only by the bishops, but also by themselves. Thus, the report just cited goes on to point to the influence of the Cursillos in helping the Legion grow.

Among the external factors, above all the Cursillos de Cristiandad have been especially helpful to the Legion. In towns where there was nothing, now thanks to the *cursillistas* who became legionnaires we now have an organization . . . and finally, the progress of the Legion is the progress of the whole

[36] Interview 60319, 14 July 1973.
[37] Legión de María, *Informe especial*, p. 2.

Christian community. It is beautiful to think that every day, despite many difficulties, the Church continues to grow. We have more Christians committed as apostles in the service of Christ and his Holy Mother. All the big cities of Venezuela have active groups of the Legion. We can affirm that the moral welfare of a Catholic population depends on its having a good number of apostles. The foundation of any apostolate is a lively interest for the Church and her mission on earth. But since this interest can only spring from the conviction that one is collaborating positively with the Church, it is clear that an apostolic organization, serving as it does to form apostles, cannot put itself in any hands other than those of the priest, who, more than anyone else, participates in the mission of the Church and in effect shows himself a true pastor to the degree to which he ably manages that organization. Here lies the success of the Legion or of any other organization.[38]

This remarkable passage highlights both the strong linkages to the Church hierarchy and the very concept of "Church," centered around the ecclesiastical institution and its official agents, which makes that kind of tight linkage an imperative for the organization. In this light, the significance of the bishops' preference for groups of this kind becomes quite clear. In both Venezuela and Colombia the stress on close linkages and orthodoxy is associated with a pattern of group activity largely confined to short courses, talks, and spiritual guidance—what is often referred to in Spanish as the *cursillo y charla* (short course and lecture) syndrome. The bishops seem to want groups which will meet to *receive* orientation in this way, not those which bring ideas and orientations from their own experience.

Strong differences in institutional context and organizational density between the Churches of Venezuela and Colombia help structure each national situation differently; but, nevertheless, growing organizational fragmentation is visible in each, as the closely integrated groups of the past (especially in the social action field) turn into hollow shells. Their place has been taken by groups which either have broken free of hierarchical control or which have simply welled up spontaneously from below.

[38] Ibid., pp. 4-5.

The nub of the problem lies in the concept of laity implicit in the organizational ties examined here. This concept provides the crucial link between organizational structure and content. Despite the hierarchy's stated openness to "lay participation," for many bishops the laity remains a separate and basically subordinate category within the Church. Thus, as I suggested earlier, trends to lay participation, co-responsibility, and the like often are expressed, for the bishops, in a kind of collegiality restricted to top levels *within* the ecclesiastical structures themselves—that is, in oligarchy, not democracy. Genuine lay autonomy is resisted.

To illustrate further the scope and content of these changes, the next chapter selects two cases for more detailed consideration: the controversy over religious education and new "liberation" catechisms in Colombia, and the evolution and recent problems of youth groups in Venezuela. In each case, a close relationship can be seen between changing organizational forms, a search for Christian values through study of and involvement in social and political affairs, and a series of problems and conflicts between individuals involved in these programs and the institutional Church itself.

8

Structure and Style: Two Case Studies

In preceding chapters I have insisted that visions of the Church, and their associated concepts of authority, are the primary sources of action and commitment in day-to-day affairs. An in-depth examination of liberation catechisms in Colombia and of youth groups in Venezuela throws considerable light on the way these differences affect action. Much of the operational difference between the concepts and models considered in these pages rests on their different sources of values—the opposite starting points they take in building an orientation in the world. The basic attitudinal (or, more precisely, epistemological) difference at issue here rests on a vision of religious life and truth as alternatively *essential* or *existential*.

An *essential* position requires that action and understanding proceed from a body of fully formed, known, and certain truths and then work through a set of stable and authoritative procedures. In contrast, an *existential* position sees religious life and truth as necessarily adapting to altered historical circumstances. From this perspective, procedures can never be set once and for all. Rather, they must change with the changing needs and conditions of each historical period and social context. Although neither essential nor existential approaches exist in pure form, they can both be found in the general orientations that help to structure the stance of Catholic groups, programs, and individuals in social affairs. In the context of these two approaches to religious life, the areas of catechism and youth take on new significance.

In itself, the importance of catechism to the Church and to the bishops is not surprising. After all, a concern for the form and content of education in the faith is bound to be central to Church leaders, who want to ensure the transmission of religious values from one generation to the next. But as with many things in the Catholic Church today, the meaning of catechism and the proper scope, form, and content of religious instruction in general is no longer cut and dried.

The emergence of new forms of catechism in the late 1960s and early 1970s (in Colombia and elsewhere) responded to widespread dissatisfaction with the adequacy of Church schools and of traditional religious instruction as vehicles for the inculcation of religious values. In the attempt to build more "relevant" programs of religious education in Colombia, Catholic educators raised a series of new *political* issues, which aroused fierce opposition from the conservative sectors traditionally identified with the Church.

Politics is central to the ensuing debates, but the meaning of politics shifts dramatically. The old politics of religious education, centered on the struggle between "Church and State" over subsidies, control, and the like, yields center stage to a new politics raising fundamental questions about the legitimacy of national institutions, and taking the critical analysis of socioeconomic and political structures as the starting point for religious reflection. Before going into details of this controversy, it may be useful to indicate briefly the kinds of concerns which stimulated the formation of these new educational programs in the first place.

Church interests have been so dominant in Colombia that religious instruction has long been a required academic subject in all schools, private or public, secular or Catholic. But a recent study of students in Catholic schools, sponsored by the Inter-American Confederation of Catholic Education, revealed that Catholic education in traditional settings (like Church-run schools) makes little or no independent contribution to religious values or understanding. The system is class-bound (because of the high tuitions charged), it is ineffective, and it further distorts the distribution of resources in the institutional Church by concentrating personnel in the schools, most of which are located in larger towns and cities.[1] Thus, this study concluded that in Colombia Church-run schools do not serve as a differentiated source of religious values, but simply as extensions of other social structures, most notably class and family. In sum:

[1] Rodríguez, *Educación católica y secularización en Colombia*, passim, and especially p. 249.

The traditional role played by religion in Colombia depends in great measure on sociocultural factors in the sense that it is considered as a system of legitimation for certain social behaviors, as much on the individual as on the collective level.[2]

In response to this dissatisfaction with Catholic schools and with religious education conceived of as an abstract academic subject, attempts have been made to develop new catechism programs more relevant to the experiences of students and less rigidly tied to existing school programs.[3] Three initiatives warrant special attention here: first, the development of new "official" guidelines for catechism in the secondary schools (prepared by the Department of Catechism of the Bishops' Conference); second, the publication of a controversial catechism text intended for fourth-year secondary-school students, entitled *Liberation*;[4] and third, the emergence of independent catechism programs, such as *Denuncia*.

The documents presenting new "official" guidelines argue that catechism as such must go beyond the mere rote learning of definitions and theological formulae to incorporate the life experiences of each group, interpreting them in the light of the faith. Faith and life must be brought together.

> In the great majority of youth today we can see a profound separation between the faith they have learned and their daily life. For some, the Bible, the history of salvation, Christ, or any other dogma are theoretical things, a series of truths learned since the early years; they are religious realities of which they have, perhaps, not had any personal experience. To others they have nothing to say, they leave them totally indifferent. Or they consider religion as something from the *past* (sacred history, life of Christ) or of the *future* (eternal life, salvation of the soul). But in the *present*, the only thing they have in hand, they identify religion with Mass, First Communion, or with a few sporadic acts. To correct this dichotomy between faith and life, evangelization must change its forms of action.

---

[2] Ibid., p. 275.

[3] The men Sanders describes as "innovators" respond to these problems in a different way, by favoring the *elimination* of separate systems of Church schools. This view is not widely shared in Colombia.

[4] Avila, *La Liberación*.

... If the previous sketchy teaching of dogmas, truths, and theological systems yields no results today, [then] it is necessary to go directly to the young as people, to the important situations of their lives, to their interests. This requires of catechism teachers a sincere commitment, a true change of mentalities, to not continue "teaching religion," accepting beforehand the *ineffectiveness* of such teaching.[5]

As an alternative, a "situational methodology" is proposed, starting from the day-to-day problems and concerns of the community and using these as a basis for reflection in the faith. Thus, instead of enumerating the general characteristics of "Christian love" or "justice," catechism might begin with a look at social realities, asking, for example: Is Colombia, as presently organized, a "Christian society"? What must Christians do in such a reality? By seeking to make religious education more existentially involved, the writers of the new guidelines were responding to what they saw as a potentially alarming situation—great ferment among Colombian youth—to which the Church simply *had* to respond. One high-ranking member of the group which prepared the guidelines complained to me that critics were burying their heads in the sand.

The situation really is alarming. I have to travel all over the country, and everywhere one encounters this ferment which *must* be guided. You cannot simply deny that these things are of interest to youth. They must be guided and analyzed in a Christian sense. I see it as very difficult. We could arrive at a chaos in this sense.

In addition, generally those who criticize this are people who have nothing to do with youth. I defy them to see, to go before a group of young people and see if they accept an old-style class of religion, with formulae to memorize, with moral advice, etc. I defy them. On the other hand, those who are working with young people have said that they see in this a path, an orientation, a solution to this problem of how to present the message to youth.[6]

[5] Comisiones Episcopales de Educación y Catequesis de Colombia, *Programas nacionales de catequesis para secundaria*, p. 31. Italics in original.
[6] Interview 80211, 23 Mar. 1972.

At this point the reader may wonder what is so sensitive about all this. Why the (implied) fuss over systems of religious instruction? The reasons become apparent with a closer look at some of the recent texts and programs. In the first place, the new catechisms share the general tendency noted earlier in these pages to move quickly from a general concern with social issues to an overwhelming stress on critical analysis of the structures of social, economic, cultural, and political domination. The combined impact of Liberation Theology and dependency analysis is particularly notable here. Great stress is placed on the social and political side of "religious action," and all the sensitive questions of politics and political involvement noted earlier come quickly to the surface. In this way, a traditionally safe and orthodox activity like catechism, rooted in bastions of conventional Catholicism like the Church's own schools, begins to appear, in the horrified eyes of conservatives, as a leading edge of Marxist penetration of society. The author of one of the new texts put it this way:

> I believe that basically we are dealing with socioeconomic groups who, seeing that we begin with the *real* situation, and seeing that we *unite* this real situation with the faith, are worried.
>
> Here, the faith has traditionally been something set apart, in a closed and removed compartment. This attempt to unify an analysis of the real situation with the faith leaves people surprised, ambiguous, because to get involved in historical situations is to become ambiguous, and many people don't like this.[7]

These issues are especially touchy in Colombia; for, as we have seen, conservatives there have long been accustomed to identifying religion and the Church with national life and culture. Thus, when authorized agents of the Church begin associating religious doctrine with profound criticisms of the long-standing structures of national life, the reaction by established elites is bound to be shock, dismay, and a sense of betrayal. "They see themselves as defenders of orthodoxy, an orthodoxy in which religion enters through a traditional socioreligious mentality. So if the Church

[7] Interview 80611, 9 Mar. 1972.

takes this new path, they cannot continue being defenders of the Church, with all that this implies—being owners of the Church."[8]

Two examples of the new catechisms will illustrate their social implications. Consider first the case of *La Liberación*, by Rafael Avila. This text was sponsored by CONACED, the national association of private schools which is, in effect, run by the Church. By 1972, three editions had been issued: the first two bore the imprimatur of Bogotá's archbishop, but the last did not. This book provides a general review of philosophical and religious ideas about liberation, linking these, in the last chapter, to the "Liberation of Latin America." Throughout, every attempt is made, through questions and examples, to tie the religious message to social reality. In one passage, the author emphasizes that "On beginning these reflections, you should never have the feeling of having left the field of religion: *all national history is also sacred history*, and, in that measure, a preparation for the coming of Christ. God finds us in all the local histories."[9] The book takes a critical perspective on the social, economic, political, and even the religious consequences of the Spanish Conquest, tracing from these roots the present unjust structures of Colombian life. These are outlined in vivid detail, and students are urged to take seriously the need for action to change unjust or sinful structures.

> An inactive Christian or one who limits himself to observing events from behind the barricade of his own comfort and egoism is also an accomplice in injustice.... The Christian, wherever he is and however he can, must strive to exert a really liberating pressure on the structures of life. The Christian must commit himself even at the risk of failure, of being misunderstood, of being abandoned or criticized.[10]

Our second example, the *Denuncia* program, is a fairly large plan of informal catechism operating in many schools and in some nonschool settings as well. Training and orientation for educators, with courses and a journal called *Encuentro* (or *Meeting*), is combined with a program for youth, built around

[8] Interview 80613, 10 Mar. 1972, with a Jesuit heavily involved in such programs.
[9] Avila, *La Liberación*, p. 15. Italics in original.
[10] Ibid., p. 170.

the tabloid newspaper *Denuncia* (or *Denunciation*), which by 1972 had a subscription of about four thousand with an estimated readership of approximately twenty thousand. This program was intended to build an effective situational methodology, setting the requirements of religious faith in concrete historical circumstances. As one article in *Encuentro* noted, "God frees men in history, in space, in time, and frees them in a communitarian way, as a people, and with a view toward the formation of a people."[11] The search for a situational methodology moves quickly from social commentary to political criticism and action —not the narrow politics of traditional parties or official activities, but the broad politics of structural transformation.

> The faith as lived has a political dimension. The ideal goal of catechism is to lead the students to a maturity of faith which will make them able to face, in a positive and constructive way, the new problems of the city and the conflicts which each new situation engenders, while at the same time choosing their options in a Christian way, that is, *according to the Gospels*, which help us live our faith in any economic situation or type of society.[12]

The political thrust of this approach becomes quite clear as one leafs through the numbers of *Denuncia* itself. The tabloid is meant to be used in voluntary small groups which are action-oriented. It seeks to take religious instruction out of the classroom and away from the traditional apparatus of rote learning and examinations, grounding it instead in reflection on social reality. Articles, photos, and commentaries are heavily laced with the concepts of Liberation Theology and dependency analysis. A review of the focus of several issues gives an idea of the orientation: politics (numbers 8 and 25, with extensive discussions of the need for political expressions of Christian love); class struggles (number 9); dependency (number 21); cultural imperialism (number 10); a critical look at traditional family structures (numbers 18 and 19); the situation of women (number 24).

To find all this in a program of religious instruction was profoundly disturbing to conservatives in Colombia. Their reaction became public in early 1972 in a series of newspaper articles

[11] Barreiro, "Catequesis y desarrollo," p. 36.
[12] Ibid., p. 39. Italics in original.

attacking the "Marxist" catechisms of Rafael Avila and the *Denuncia* group. The most critical comments appeared in *El Siglo*, organ of the right wing of the Conservative party. The articles charged that *Denuncia* was preaching "crime and violence" and alleged that *La Liberación* was inciting students to hatred while propagating Marxism through the subversion of traditional Catholic values and structures.[13] Responding to a letter which defended the new programs as an improvement over traditional religion and which argued for the need to see the good (as well as the bad) in Marxism, the editors of *El Siglo* warmed to their task. Proudly proclaiming their traditionalism, they issued a complete denunciation of Marxism, flatly rejecting the idea that such a condemnation means a Christianity removed from social questions.

> We repeat. We have never argued for an essentially asocial character to Christianity. On the contrary, on many occasions, following the great thinkers of the Church, we have criticized the theses of Rousseau and Loisy, who argued that for humanity the real country of Christianity is not of this world, but in Heaven. We have understood Christianity, in its social and economic aspect, through the social thought of Saint Augustine and Saint Paul (as cited in the encyclicals), who are more intelligent than Father Díaz and ourselves. What we do not accept is the presentation of a false, subversive gospel that denies private property and preaches hate for anyone who has something.
>
> So that we follow the Christianity of Christ. Not of Father Camilo Torres nor of the Golconda group, nor that being expounded in the catechisms which gave rise to this polemic.[14]

A later article in the same newspaper, by Fray Antonio Alcalá (a pseudonym), carried the attack further. "We must not forget that the papacy continues insisting that communism is 'intrinsically evil,' in the words of Pius XII . . . and we must also not forget, in what concerns the preservation of the faith, that the Second Vatican Council, and this means all the bishops, have

[13] See *El Siglo* (Bogotá), 23 Feb. 1972.

[14] *El Siglo* (Bogotá), 26 Feb. 1972. The Father Díaz referred to here is the writer of the letter to which the article was responding. "Golconda" was a radical group of clergy and lay people founded in the late 1960s.

spoken of dialogue 'with non-Christian religions.' They have never stressed trading the Cross for sociology or anthropology, so that there would then be social justice, work, and dialogue. Much less have the council or the popes, including John XXIII and Paul VI, ever stopped considering that the faith and the Church, in doctrinal matters, continue to be conservative, traditional, and unyielding."[15] Finally, *La República*, another Conservative paper, summed up the attack by linking the new catechism programs specifically to subversive motives.

> A public indoctrination is underway which is absolutely hostile to national traditions and contrary to the consensus of the majority of the population concerning the proper scope of the educational system. . . .
>
> Today, in many schools, there are no books on religion, but rather one-sided political tracts, simplistic in their judgements on society, and false and deceitful in the conclusions they present concerning the historical processes of the country. . . . With the pretext of removing or avoiding the divorce between the Church and the proletarian masses, Marxist prophetism is nourished in classes which are supposed to be in religion. . . . That this should be happening in a democratic and spiritualist state, guided by rulers who practice the religious faith of the majority of the nation, can only be an aberrant contradiction.[16]

This powerful criticism is a good example of the potential explosiveness of attempts to reorient religious education in a way which responds to new models of authority, of the Church, and of its involvement in the world. Catechism is a particularly good case because, perhaps more than any other activity, its transformation speaks directly to the *form and content* of the religious faith passed from generation to generation. Form and content are related because as teachers open religious instruction to content from the world, involving students more actively in the process of education and in the selection of its themes, they also move to a new kind of form—one less focused on traditional settings like Catholic schools, and more open to experimentation and innovation. In this way, new ideas and orientations get built into struc-

[15] *El Siglo* (Bogotá), 28 Feb. 1972.
[16] *La República* (Bogotá), 29 Feb. 1972.

tures of action, bringing both structures and ideas together in a long-term, dialectical process of change.

The second case to be considered in this chapter, youth groups in Venezuela, reflects these same trends. This example throws considerable light on the dilemmas such trends create for the relations of Catholic groups with the central institutions of the Church. Historically, the organization of student and youth groups in Venezuela has been monopolized by political parties.[17] But despite this strong competition and the Church's organizational weakness, the hierarchy's efforts at organization have been consistent.

The party monopoly over youth organizations poses a dilemma for the bishops: How should they develop safe, reliable, and yet vital Church-related youth groups? Of course, many Catholic youth organizations of a traditional, pietistic kind exist in Venezuela; one occasionally comes across publications of the *Juventud Católica Venezolana* or the *Juventud Católica Feminina Venezolana* (*Venezuelan Catholic Youth* and *Venezuelan Catholic Female Youth*), and there is even a tiny nucleus of Young Catholic Workers (JOC). Moreover, at the diocesan and parish levels, there are doubtless similar groups which meet from time to time to discuss devotional themes or to plan welfare or charity work. But these groups are all small and ineffective—paper organizations at best. From the Church's point of view, the lack of contact with youth is alarming. Indeed, a 1971 report issued by the Center of Youth Pastoral of the Archdiocese of Caracas noted that where high levels of student protest activity (especially in secondary schools) could be found, the Church was always absent.[18]

Despite the hierarchy's approval of work with youth and despite its apparent concern for responding to youth's problems, at the time of my field research the one national Catholic youth group which could in fact claim a substantial and committed membership found itself in constant trouble with the bishops, who viewed it with deep suspicion. Why? Precisely for the qualities which attracted members in the first place—an open organi-

---

[17] On the evolution of youth groups and their relation to political parties in Venezuela, see Levine, *Conflict*, chaps. 2, 3, 6, and 7.

[18] Centro Arquidiocesano de Pastoral Juvenil, *La crisis en la educación media*, p. 12.

zational structure, direct involvement in socially and politically sensitive issues, and a clear drift toward organizational autonomy. This group, known as Jóvenes de Acción (Youth for Action), was originally founded in the 1960s in the classic Catholic Action mold, as a vehicle for the Church's penetration of the public high schools, whose student groups were dominated by the political left. But the Belgian priests brought in to run the group soon concluded that, to attract the students, linkages to the institutional Church had to be played down, and internal processes made more open and democratic. To do this, while avoiding open conflict with the bishops, the outer shell of the movement was left untouched; but in practice its goals and operative principles were radically transformed. The role of the clerical adviser, so central to the theory and practice of Catholic Action, was in practice severely downgraded. As one of the advisers put it,

> Our great advantage is that we have managed that the movement be of the young people, and not imposed from the top down. That it not be *the Church* which founds it, but rather that it be a movement of youth, gathered together around the problems of youth, problems which interest and concern them. . . . From the beginning, we have run the movement in a completely democratic way. No decision is taken here at any level without full discussion and consensus among the members. All our courses, all our activities, are a result of what they themselves decide. Each year they vote as to whether we, the advisers, should stay. . . . We live here in a glass house, completely open.[19]

The results are interesting, and they neatly fit the expectations derived from my earlier discussions of authority in Catholic organizations. Youth for Action became a vital and lively group, with a fierce interest in social and political issues and relatively little concern for intraecclesiastical disciplines or disputes. Thus, one of the Belgian advisers noted that a recent "occupation" of a downtown Caracas church by "radical" Catholics left Youth for Action members completely cold: "For the youngsters here (and in the Young Catholic Workers as well), nothing . . . it did not interest them, it had no impact in their world. Their

[19] Interview 60509, 1 July 1971.

interests are not so clerical. They are committed to work directly in the real world.[20]

This commitment to work in the "real world," and the continued involvement in social and political action it entails, underlies the group's problems with the hierarchy. The same priest just cited argues that

> the bishops support us in words, in theory, but never in practice. They are afraid of committing themselves, afraid of a committed youth because this brings political problems. But any youth movement with some degree of liberty begins to think and act in terms of real problems of experience. Within months any one will turn to social and political activity if the members feel free to think and work for themselves. And this is what the bishops do not want. Moreover, they do not understand it. They still see it as "measles," as a childhood disease that will pass with time. That is what the cardinal told me personally: "This is measles, this will pass." The kinds of groups the bishops want are of a more traditional sort, groups which get together to hear pious talks, no more.[21]

In their own documents and publications, group members stress the need for commitments to action, by themselves and by the institutional Church as well. This is combined with explicit calls for more open channels of participation within the ecclesiastical structures. Thus, in the "Conclusions" to a General Assembly held in Caracas in 1970, it was pointed out that young people felt little contact with or commitment to the Church.

> Many young people have never received any instruction or experience of a Christian kind. Those who did receive something as preparation for First Communion remember it little or see it as of no importance in their lives. Moreover, contact with parish priests is very limited, and only rarely does anyone speak of the real problems young people are living. Collaboration remains isolated in small and unimportant acts. . . .
>
> On the other hand, many young people like ourselves have had the opportunity, through different movements, to share the life of the Church, to work in projects of formation and development. They have more contacts with priests and bishops,

[20] Ibid. [21] Ibid.

and live more at first hand the inner life of the Church. These young people point to the almost complete absence of any channels for dialogue through which they can communicate their ideas and projects. They often come up against a manner of speaking which has an answer for everything, and which kills off initiatives by enumerating previous failures. A typical argument points to youth and immaturity. This attitude is often the result of suspicion stemming from lack of contact and from a different way of seeing things, as much as from a generational difference. The idea that the Church belongs to bishops and priests may be out of date, but its consequences are still alive among us.[22]

The many frustrations indicated here have also been reflected in a series of clashes with the hierarchy, centering above all on the proper relation of Christian commitment (as expressed in a group of this sort) to political action. A particularly notable dispute arose over the case of Father Wuytack, discussed in chapter 6. As might be expected, Youth for Action was strongly critical of the hierarchy and supportive of Father Wuytack.

To the Church

From responsible persons in the Church we demand clear positions, without fear or vacillation in the face of the institutionalized injustices of our society. They must avoid unnecessary contact with those who represent economic power, and thus avoid the possibility that the people will see them as accomplices in these situations. Even more, any contacts should reflect the Church's commitment to the poor and marginal.

To the Movements

The spontaneous and justified reaction against the expulsion must not be a momentary phenomenon. Alongside their specific goals, all individuals and movements should deepen their commitment to the poor and marginal. We should avoid a new kind of paternalism, but without being afraid to promote the conditions necessary for them to build their own future.[23]

---

[22] Jóvenes de Acción, "El Joven y la Renovación en la Iglesia, Sociedad, Educación."

[23] Jóvenes de Acción, "Reflexiones Alrededor de la Expulsión del P. Francisco Wuytack."

The ironies of organizational change noted in earlier chapters are fully visible here. Venezuelan youth groups and innovative catechisms in Colombia (like other vital Catholic associations such as ACPO or the unions of the UTC) were all founded to respond to threats from the outside world. But now the groups find themselves moving into crisis in their relations with the hierarchy, above all as they reach for greater autonomy and move more directly into independent social and political action. As they succeed, they become threatening. This process, which is visible in Catholic groups all over Latin America, points directly to the dilemma of the bishops: they want strong and vital Catholic groups and programs of religious education that really reach and motivate a clientele, but they demand that these be safe and reliable as well. These goals are increasingly difficult to reconcile.

The evolution of Catholic organizations considered here and in the preceding chapter brings out the enormous potential of changing views of authority, participation, and "the Church" for the life of Catholic organizations and the nature of their ties to the institutional Church. A shift in modal concepts of authority clearly requires, at some point, corresponding changes in operating style. The many difficulties encountered in institutionalizing such changes speak to the enormous complexity of the Church's situation and to the ambiguities inherent in treating Catholic groups as "resources" for the Church. Indeed, it seems clear that the more such organizations, especially in the social field, *are* "resources" for the institutional Church (that is, tied closely to its leaders through bonds of organization, discipline, and leadership), the more they are likely to lose organizational vitality. On the other hand, those groups which have become strong and active on their own preserve and extend their vitality by maintaining their distance (above all in organizational terms) from the hierarchy.[24]

[24] This suggests the great importance of the development of base communities in the Church, which offer an alternative form of organization stressing a new style of action within existing Church structures. The alternative form nurtures new qualities of independence and participation. Bruneau's work on such communities in Brazil suggests a close relation between participation in base communities and higher degrees of participation and political awareness in general. Cf. Bruneau, "Basic Christian Communities."

STRUCTURE AND STYLE

Organizational change of this kind is relatively easy to isolate and describe on the national level. But the very visibility of national conflicts and processes may be somewhat illusory. For while analysis of the Church often centers attention on the national level, a great deal of the institution's daily life is carried out in particular dioceses, parishes, and local settings. The next chapter explores the dimensions of internal transformation, resistance to change, and the possibilities of action in selected local contexts—three dioceses in each country.

9

Structure and Style: Six Dioceses

This chapter extends our exploration of the sources, parameters, and processes of change to the local level, in selected dioceses of Venezuela and Colombia. Analysis at this level provides a useful check on the validity of inferences drawn from interviews with bishops and from the study of national groups and documents. It is also important in itself, because dioceses are the key structural and administrative units of the Catholic Church. Finally, incorporating data from this level into the overall analysis strengthens the work as a whole, by building in elements of context and situation which closely correspond to those actually experienced by leaders, activists, and average members of the Church.

After completing most of the interviews with bishops, I selected three dioceses in each nation for in-depth study; selection was guided by the desire to obtain a broad range of socioeconomic and religious characteristics in order to set the general issues of perception, structure, and style into a variety of contexts. Thus, as carried out in this chapter, the analysis of change in the dioceses is not only a study of the difficulties facing Church leaders committed to change,[1] but an analysis of more general processes of both change and stagnation in the Church.

This chapter begins with a general description of the dioceses and a sketch of their bishops' most salient socioreligious orientations. This is followed by analysis of selected organizations, styles of action, and individual parishes in each. Combining attention to diocesan organizations with a look at parishes helps fill in the organizational picture; for relatively few Catholics come into direct contact with the kinds of groups examined here, but a much larger proportion of the faithful are affected by the religious and social orientation of the parish priest. A final sec-

[1] As in Bruneau, *The Political Transformation*, chap. 8.

STRUCTURE AND STYLE

tion sets this local-level analysis in the context of broader considerations about change in the Church.

Settings for Change: Dioceses and Parishes

Six dioceses are examined here: Manizales, Cali, and Facatativá in Colombia; and San Cristobal, Valencia, and Cumaná in Venezuela. These six dioceses provide a significant range of variation on grounds of traditional religiosity, ecclesiastical and Church-related structures, orientations of the bishops, and general socioeconomic context. Table 9.1 summarizes some of the relevant data.[2] For present purposes, it is convenient to consider the six dioceses as three matched pairs: first, a traditional city with its surrounding rural hinterland of strong traditional religiosity (Manizales and San Cristobal); second, a rapidly growing industrial city in an area of generally weak religiosity (Cali and Valencia); and finally, a poor rural diocese of mixed religiosity and few ecclesiastical resources (Facatativá and Cumaná).

Manizales and San Cristobal are the most traditional in the group. Each is centered on a mountain city lying in the heart of a traditionally religious state or department (Caldas in Colombia and Táchira in Venezuela) where the institutional Church is firmly rooted. The cities and regions are in some respects strikingly similar. Manizales straddles a spine of mountains in western Colombia. Founded in the mid-nineteenth century by migrants from Antioquia, it has long been a commercial, political, and ecclesiastical center. The city is well known throughout Colombia for the strong Catholic orientations and the solid power of its upper classes, whose fortunes are based on coffee and trade. San Cristobal, which lies in a high mountain valley in western Venezuela, is the capital of Táchira, the state whose military chieftains ruled all of Venezuela (with only a brief interlude) from 1899 to 1958. The economy of Táchira is also based on coffee and trade; and, like Manizales, its political orientation has generally

[2] The socioeconomic character of the dioceses is described in less precise terms here; for dioceses in Venezuela correspond exactly to political (and hence to census) divisions, but dioceses in Colombia do not. Therefore, socioeconomic data on the level of dioceses would not be comparable; so it seems better to offer general descriptions in the text, rather than numbers whose apparent precision would be misleading.

TABLE 9.1
SELECTED DATA ON THE CHURCH IN SIX DIOCESES

	Manizales	Cali	Facatativá	Valencia	San Cristobal	Cumaná
Surface area (km^2)	6,975	2,912	6,788	4,450	11,100	11,800
Parishes	68	68	32	56	47	33
Diocesan clergy	161	99	36	42	54	25
Regular clergy	51	132	29	75	12	22
Total clergy	212	231	65	117	66	47
Population	615,182	1,250,000	374,000	793,892	566,000	506,543
Persons per priest (total clergy)	2,901	5,411	5,754	6,785	8,576	10,778
Persons per priest (diocesan clergy)	3,821	12,626	10,388	18,902	10,481	20,261
Educational institutions	81	902	28	50	45	14
Beneficent institutions	46	44	14	8	7	1
Religious women (sisters)	925	1,172	196	201	252	69
Religious men (brothers)	107	159	50	106	16	23

SOURCE: Compiled from data in the *Annuario Pontifico per l'anno 1977*, Cittá del Vaticano: Librería Editrice Vaticana, 1977.

been conservative. Both dioceses have Churches which are strong in conventional terms: each enjoys (within its own country) the largest number of diocesan clergy and the most favorable ratio of diocesan clergy to population of any of the dioceses studied.[3]

Cali and Valencia stand in contrast to the two dioceses just described, yet display considerable similarities to one another.[4] Cali is a major commercial and industrial city in southwestern Colombia that lies at the gateway to the rich Cauca Valley. Cali has grown extraordinarily since the early 1950s and now counts well over a million inhabitants. The area is not noted for strong ecclesiastical structures or traditional religiosity. As a diocese, Cali is practically unique in Colombia and Venezuela in that its jurisdiction is essentially limited to the city alone. This wholly

---

[3] Useful studies of Manizales include Ocampo, *Dominio de clase en la ciudad colombiana*, and Drake, *Elites and Voluntary Associations*. See also Parsons, *Antioqueño Colonization in Western Colombia*. Little is available on San Cristobal, but see Hoskin, "Power Structure in a Venezuelan Town."

[4] On Valencia see Cannon, Fosler, and Witherspoon, *Urban Government for Valencia, Venezuela*; on Cali see Dent, "Oligarchy and Power Structure in Urban Colombia."

urban character gives the Archdiocese of Cali a structural unity and a facility for central coordination which is difficult for many other dioceses, whose territory embraces vast regions of difficult terrain. Cali has relatively favorable ratios of parishes and clergy to population. Moreover, as the major city of the region, Cali has also attracted an unusually large number of Catholic schools. This concentration of schools probably inflates the apparent structural strength of the Church in Cali, and it helps explain the very high numbers of religious personnel reported: most teach in the schools.

Valencia, in turn, lies in a hot tropical plain in central Venezuela. The city's recent growth has been, if anything, even more spectacular than Cali's; new investment has turned Valencia into the industrial center of the nation. The diocese is relatively weak in institutional structures, and particularly weak in diocesan clergy and priests relative to population. In both Cali and Valencia the very newness of growth is in some measure an advantage, for the relative absence of traditional organizational commitments has allowed Church leaders to innovate. As we shall see, innovation has indeed occurred in both cities, but with notably different directions and styles, reflecting the divergent orientations of the bishop in each.

Finally, Facatativá and Cumaná are relatively poor and almost wholly rural dioceses, each headed by a bishop generally thought of as "progressive." Each is poor and weak in both ecclesiastical and socioeconomic terms. Within their respective nations, both Facatativá and Cumaná have the smallest number of parishes and the largest surface area per parish of the dioceses studied. They also have the lowest numbers of diocesan clergy and total clergy, and very high numbers of persons per priest (especially per diocesan priest). Finally, each has relatively few Catholic schools or welfare institutions. As in Cali and Valencia, this structural weakness provides an open door to innovation, but here (above all in Cumaná) such innovation is hampered by an extreme lack of resources.

Facatativá itself is a small town near Bogotá, and the diocese, which is relatively new, occupies a prosperous farming area on the high Bogotá plain. Some industry, including large-scale cultivation of flowers for export, is beginning to spread; but on the whole the diocese remains rural in a fairly traditional way. Cumaná, in contrast, is one of the oldest cities in all of Latin America. It lies on the coast of the arid eastern region of Venezuela, a zone of extreme poverty and notable out-migration. Economic activities are largely limited to unproductive small farming, fishing, and some tourism. This is one of the least developed areas of Venezuela; it consistently ranks low in national statistics of literacy, health, and the like. Traditional religiosity, expressed in the veneration of local saints and in a popular cult of the dead, is strong in both these dioceses.

The orientations of the individual bishops are well suited to each of these six contexts. Heading the Archdiocese of Manizales at the time of research was Msgr. Arturo Duque Villegas, a man of traditional ideas, style, and background.[5] He comes from a relatively prosperous family of coffee planters, has no education beyond the seminary, and his views of the Church emphasize the preservation of the existing social order and the staunch defense of traditional Catholic values and practices against the encroachments of liberalism, Protestantism, and Marxism. Thus he opposes the new currents of political activism described here, and rejects dialogue and cooperation with Marxists. He stresses the importance of hierarchy and established authority in Church and society alike. His overall orientation to change in the Church is expressed well in his response to my question on the future.

> Well, I believe that with the eagerness of those new theologians who present as theses what are mere hypotheses, considerable harm is bound to be done to the religious life of the country. One can see, not only here in Colombia but also in all the Church, a perfectly notorious movement toward the Protestantization of the Catholic Church. Hence the attacks on papal infallibility, on the teaching authority of the Church, on the real presence of Christ in the Holy Eucharist, on the devotion to the Holy Virgin, on the images in our temples, on ecclesiastical celibacy. All these are Protestant theses which are now at work within the Catholic Church. What will be the result of all these activities? God knows. It is the duty of pastors and priests to defend the treasure of the faith, the Catholic faith,

---

[5] He resigned for reasons of age and health in 1975.

conserving from tradition everything of value and accepting from the new anything which can make our Catholicism more responsible and thus more pleasing to God.

These concerns with preservation and defense fit the context of a strongly established Church in a highly traditional Catholic region. The nature of that context, and the limits on action it imposes, will be considered further in the next section; but it is worth noting at this point the opinion of the young auxiliary bishop of Manizales.

I would point to one more [trait] which is peculiar to the city of Manizales as a city, and that is the effort of the Church in the social field, above all in the area of employer-worker relations. It has never been possible really to do much in this sense, because the elite of Manizales has been very opposed to unionism and has controlled it very firmly.

The situation in San Cristobal is similar. The bishop, Msgr. Alejandro Fernández Feo, also comes from an upper-class family (his father was a doctor) and pursued a traditional education and career. He sees his diocese as a small, sheltered corner of Venezuela, protected thus far from the encroachments of the modern world by its very remoteness and by the strongly traditional character of its peasants. In his view, the Church today has no clear lines of authority: "We must not forget that today we find ourselves in a period of confusion of criteria. A man writes a book, he says four absurdities, and no one knows who he is or with what authority he is speaking. And people hear him, and he —what he does is to seek public applause. And so you can see them, these priests, involved in street demonstrations." In such times, it is especially important to be careful about political initiatives, and above all to avoid implicitly lending a hand to Marxism through ingenuous cooperation or common action. Marxists will use this to boost their own cause, and people will become confused, thinking that the Church actually approves of Marxism. Marxists cannot be trusted.

You cannot have cooperation of this kind when they don't play fair. What they want is for the people to think that the Church no longer sees Marxism as something bad . . . and the proof [they will say] is that we are working together.

In Cali and Valencia, the opportunities provided by new growth, and the relative lack of established Catholic structures and traditions, are also well suited to each bishop's mentality. At the time of research, Valencia was headed by Msgr. Alí Lebrún Moratinos.[6] Msgr. Lebrún comes from a lower-middle-class background (his father was a clerk in a shipyard) and lacks advanced studies, although his seminary training was completed in Europe. His career was focused entirely on education and positions in the Church bureaucracy before he was named bishop in 1956. Msgr. Lebrún is quite open to change; he sees the key to Vatican II, and indeed to most recent changes within the Venezuelan Church as well, in the Church's redefinition of itself in more communitarian terms. The changing nature of authority is central to his views: the Church must identify more with the community, and, in so doing, grow and change along with it. From this perspective, the Church's basic problem is not defense and preservation, but rather the elaboration of new structures to meet a changing world.

> This is a world which is opening up. We have structures which are very old. What can we do with these structures to respond to today's world? So we have to move forward, seeing how our structures manage, opening to these advances of today's world, because every day one sees how the world keeps advancing. For example, here. For example, the problem of university students. We often talk about university parishes, but we don't know what university parishes are. It is something which has to be created.
>
> All this, no? And these are things which will continue to come up. Of course, there are some problems we might call traditional: the scarcity of priests, free union, etc. But what I am telling you is more basic. There are fundamental problems to face, because this is a whole new culture to which the Church must attend. It has to open up, no? It is not just that we don't have the people to do this, but rather that we often lack the very systems, the very structures in which all this can fit.

Under Msgr. Lebrún, the combination of his openness and his communitarian orientation, on the one hand, with the institu-

---

[6] He was promoted to cardinal archbishop of Caracas in 1972.

tional weakness of the Church in Valencia, on the other, led to considerable tolerance for innovation. The case of Cali is somewhat different. Here the archbishop, Msgr. Alberto Uribe Urdaneta, has taken the newness and the relatively weak character of Church institutions as an opportunity for *centrally controlled* innovation, using recently created Church structures as a base for action in other fields. Msgr. Uribe comes from a highly aristocratic background: his father was one of the leading figures of Colombian political life early in this century. Before being named bishop, Msgr. Uribe's career was centered in education, as professor and rector of seminaries. He took no advanced studies.

Within his program of centralized innovation in Cali, Msgr. Uribe has sought to incorporate lay talent and expertise. This policy is particularly visible in the massive medical assistance programs of Cali's CARITAS operations (totally run by laymen), and it is further visible in the interesting parish centers operating in several poor neighborhoods. The capacity of Church structures in Cali is thus closely tied to their growing openness to lay expertise and experience. By incorporating greater technical expertise, and by expanding social operations in general, the archbishop feels that the Church in Cali can play a creative and important role as a major point of unity in local life. In his view the Church's direct role is limited: her major function is to encourage and facilitate others. "Whenever there is some problem of a political kind, the authorities come to me for advice. But not political advice. I have managed that here in Cali they look to the Church. The voice of the bishop is taken into account and sought out. I tell you this because this is the way I planned it."

In both Facatativá and Cumaná the bishops are unusually open (for either nation) to change within the Church. Both speak freely of the great importance of transformations in the Church's authority structure and of the need for a "de-institutionalization" of the Church itself as a necessary step toward a more authentic expression of its religious mission. Take the bishop of Cumaná, Msgr. José Mariano Parra León. He comes from an upper-class background (his father was a doctor) and has some advanced studies. His career is unusual in Venezuela in that it combines bureaucratic and educational roles with broad experience in social action and even years of work as a journalist. Msgr. Parra León stresses the need for the Church to loosen its ties with government, with the rich, and with the military; for these ties carry commitments and public identifications which hinder contact and identification with the people and their needs. In pulling free of its old ties, the Church must reform and even dismantle many of its older structures. For example, he stresses the need for the Church to get rid of its school systems, which do little more than service the needs of the rich, tying the Church ever more closely to their interests.

The bishop of Facatativá, Msgr. Raúl Zambrano Camader, took a similar point of view.[7] Msgr. Zambrano was a man of middle-class background, and his career before being named bishop was centered on teaching and on the coordination of social action movements. His advanced education is somewhat unusual among bishops, for it included studies in agricultural economics along with more conventional preparation in canon law. He advocated a profound reform and purification of the Church's own structures so that it might freely promote social change. Freed of its own traditional structural rigidities, the Church could then set a genuine example of poverty and commitment.

> We cannot content ourselves with simply giving advice to others: we have to *act*. We have produced fine documents, but action and testimony has been lacking. It is not that the Church is rich—it is not. But in a world of poverty, it must adjust to these conditions of life. We are too much a settled, an established Church. Last week, during Lent, we had a retreat of the clergy, and the theme I proposed was precisely this: that despite the fact that we are working, and that we may seem advanced in relation to other dioceses, our position, our entire pastoral stance is an established one, and because it is so established, it lacks authenticity. Of course this theme did not please everyone; many were upset. But it is the truth.

All in all, in terms of social context, religiosity, ecclesiastical structure, and the orientations of the bishops, the three pairs of dioceses described here go together fairly well, presenting similar sets of opportunities as well as similar constraints on thought and action. The rural, conservative dioceses of Manizales and San

---

[7] He was killed in a plane crash some time after my interview.

Cristobal are led by bishops of traditional background and orientation. Here, traditional Catholic structures are well established. In such contexts, one might expect an organizational orientation to centralized control (in the hands of the bishop) with a paternalistic tone to activities and either a hostile or simply ineffective stance with regard to social change. In Valencia and Cali the situation is quite different, for the openness of the bishops and the lack of traditional religious structures leaves both more open to innovation. The particulars of this innovation vary. Msgr. Lebrún is more willing to *allow* innovation to take place: his stress on the Church as community leaves room for independent action. Msgr. Uribe, on the other hand, sponsors innovation while maintaining more centralized control: his view of the Church stresses strong lines of authority. Thus, while both bishops favor social reform and look at society in highly structural terms, their differing visions of the Church lead to quite dissimilar patterns of action. Finally, in both Facatativá and Cumaná, the general lack of resources (in Church and society alike) combines with each bishop's open mentality to produce considerable tolerance of innovation with a strong emphasis on grass-roots contact and community formation wherever possible.

At this stage, it is important to bear in mind that the goal of this analysis is not to isolate some general (and doubtless mythical) "disposition to innovate" in the local Church. The problem is not innovation per se, but rather the *kind* of innovation which takes place—the structure, style, and general orientation of action in each diocese and local setting. Combining the orientations of the bishops (which lead to certain perspectives and initiatives) with available resources and institutional structures (which provide both opportunities and limitations) makes possible a good understanding of the kind of innovation likely to occur in each diocese. Of course, in order to understand the dynamics of organizational change on the local level it is necessary to go beyond this general kind of analysis and "get inside" the relevant contexts. This can only be accomplished through close examination of the opportunities, problems, characteristic styles, and dilemmas of pastoral action in each context. The next section takes up this task, with a look at selected programs, groups, and parishes.

Pastoral Action: Strategies, Styles, and Dilemmas

In examining pastoral action, social action, and parish life in these dioceses, I do not propose a comprehensive review. That would be impossible. Instead, this section looks at a number of selected cases which throw further light on the distinction laid out earlier, between *ecclesial* and *ecclesiastical* structures and styles, and between their respective implications for action.

Consider Manizales first. I visited Manizales twice, in 1972 and 1973, and the period between my visits saw only a strengthening of the archbishop's power and more extensive manifestations of his particular views on Church and society. His stress on hierarchial authority and paternalistic orientations was dominant at every level. Of course, such influences stem not only from the admittedly strong character of the archbishop, but also from the kind of society and class structure characteristic of Manizales. But the two fit together well, and three brief examples should give the reader a good idea of their nature and mutual impact: first, a coordinating Catholic Action group unique to Manizales, known as the Corporation of the Holy Family; second, the orientations and operating style of the parish of Minitas; and third, the nature of the Church's own evolving institutional structure.

The Corporation of the Holy Family was founded in the early 1960s as an attempt to coordinate Catholic activities in the social field. Like many such groups, it began as an anticommunist organization, but soon moved almost wholly into work in the poor *barrios* of the city. By the time of my visits, the organization claimed to be running ten community centers in different neighborhoods in addition to a series of related programs. The corporation's explicit goal is to serve as a point of contact between poor people and the elites of the city: "We want to establish a true fraternity between the elite and the less favored classes."[8]

I visited a number of these *barrio* centers and found that, like many in Latin America, they offer a combination of charity (such as U.S. surplus food) with courses designed to train individuals to achieve better nutrition while preparing them for low-level jobs such as seamstress or hairdresser. Although such courses may have a marginal impact on individual lives, they do little to alter

[8] Document of the Corporation of the Holy Family, n.d.

(or even to raise the question of) the fundamental position of such people in the social order. And despite its proclaimed goal of eliminating paternalism, which has become a taboo word throughout Latin America, the corporation's efforts show little sign of any reduction in paternalism. Given its orientation to interclass harmony and material assistance, leaving existing structures untouched, the corporation's programs are inevitably justified in terms of numbers. As George Drake notes,

> The game of numbers (citing how many rolls were distributed, how many old clothes sold, etc.) continued to the point where one of the leaders of the CARITAS movement wrote an article for the local paper calling for the truth which can only derive from an examination of the existential problem, and to cease the misuse of numbers. Not having the ability to discuss the *problem* (nor any other way to measure goal attainment in solving it) the Corporación was reduced to actuarial reporting.[9]

Programs of this type reflect and reinforce a style of operation which makes the emergence of independent lay initiatives and values very difficult. People are to be recipients, not participants. One local CARITAS official put it this way: "In addition, a paternalistic and welfare-oriented standard still prevails here, and not a criterion of promotion, organization, *concientización*, and justice—not that! Here they still want to give out some aspirins, to give away a little milk. The classic example for me is the headache. They see social problems as a kind of headache; so you take a few aspirins, and it will go away."[10]

The implications of such an orientation can be seen in the parish of Minitas, a settlement of government-built housing on the fringes of the city. This parish was created in 1964 and now holds about nine thousand people. It is served by one priest, Father Hernán Montoya, aided by one nun. In Minitas the priest is everywhere, and his role is clearly one of leadership. Thus Father Montoya has established and continues to direct every imaginable sort of institution, from traditional catechism classes and organized home visits to services for the sick and aged, a community school, a health clinic, and the like. Like many priests today, Father Montoya says he rejects paternalism, but his per-

[9] Drake, *Elites and Voluntary Associations*, p. 205.
[10] Interview 80322, 2 Aug. 1972.

vasive directing presence casts doubt on this claim. For example, despite the stated goal of eliminating paternalism, at the time of research there was *no* institutionalized lay participation in running the affairs of the parish—no parish council or economic council.

Father Montoya's position is interesting and complex, for he sees himself as a local leader, adviser, confidant, and social intermediary. The role of intermediary is particularly noteworthy, for it makes the priest a key link between his parish and the larger society. This goes well beyond simply securing needed services or emergency help; it reaches the point of serving, in effect, as a kind of local employment office. Thus, Father Montoya helps Minitas residents get jobs and checks up on them if there is word of "trouble" at work or if complaints reach him from employers.[11] I asked why people come to see him.

> In the first place, there is a motive of confidence: we trust each other as friends. In the second place, when there are problems with work, they use the parish priest a great deal, to help them get a job. In these cases I give the person a recommendation, but I require responsibility at work, and I call on the person to see how it is going. I am also in contact with the chief of personnel, or the manager, to see if they are worried about the employee, if he is wasting his money. In this way, together we are a force.

This pattern of direct paternal control is further evident in the institutional structures of the Archdiocese of Manizales. Here as elsewhere a variety of new structures were set up in response to the Vatican Council's call for greater participation and collegiality. But in Manizales the various Priests' Councils, Pastoral Councils, Parish Councils, and the like have all been short-lived. Whenever they began to claim independent authority or influence they were cut back.

> They set up the machinery, but when these groups began to work, to try to change things, they were curbed. This can be seen in the fact that from 1967 to 1970 or 1971 there were three Priests' Councils. Each one, when it really began to work, was removed and another named. That is to say, things

[11] My fieldwork shows that this role, in which the priest acts as a local employment agent, is quite common in the parishes of both countries.

changed, but the hierarchy did not change. They have the apparatus, but it does not operate. Thus there are no clear pastoral guidelines. They [the archbishop] let you operate up to certain limits. That is to say, up to the point where one begins to work and define change—and then no more.[12]

In San Cristobal a similar orientation is visible, but with the weaker results one might expect in the Venezuelan milieu. Within Venezuela, San Cristobal is generally considered to be strongly Catholic and "well organized," but a closer look reveals that the organizations which exist are all of a particular traditional sort: a Catholic daily newspaper, a radio station (in grave financial difficulties), a very traditional seminary, and a series of Catholic schools. All were created by the bishop and remain under his direct control. At the diocesan level, active groups organizing or organized by lay people cannot be found. In effect, the stress on traditional lines of authority and control running between the bishop and Catholic institutions and between bishop and parish priests has been so strong that these very institutions make it hard to form new kinds of organizations, and thus make it extremely difficult to respond to the changes in Venezuelan society—which reach even into Táchira—and to the new groups these changes produce.[13] What made the Church strong in the past, facing a rural and largely illiterate society, leaves it hampered in responding to the challenges of the present. One local priest put the problem in a striking metaphor.

They just have never sat down to think about change, or about changing. This Church is like a ruined millionaire, always look-

[12] Interview 80325, 6 Aug. 1973, with a priest who was a member of one of these councils.

[13] One professor in the local seminary told me that a major problem in the traditional organizational pattern of the Church is the lack of unified action. "There is something characteristic of this area. The clergy is very noble, pure, and obedient, but with a massive kind of obedience. Here there will be no controversies within the Church. Here they wait for superior orders before doing anything. Each works in his parish without paying any attention to the others. They know the limits of the parish; it goes up to this street, and up to there is where the love of God reaches. There is a deep love for the parish, but it is very limited, and the others be damned" (Interview 60306, 17 June 1971).

ing at his empty coffers, remembering the glories of times gone by, but who in reality has nothing.[14]

Together, Manizales and San Cristobal illustrate the persistence of traditional forms of organization and action. The mentality of the bishop and the past and present nature of the socio-economic and institutional context reinforce one another here to produce a striking, and characteristic, structure and style of organization. Valencia and Cali, however, are more given to innovation; their expanding urban settings raise particular challenges for a Church long attuned to static, rural images of the social order.

Consider Valencia first. As I mentioned earlier, the city's expansion has been explosive, and the Church, although relatively weak in organizational terms, has been led by a bishop quite tolerant of innovation. Given the weakness of diocesan structures, such innovation is most visible at the parish level. A case in point is the parish of La Isabelica. La Isabelica is a relatively new area of government housing, serving middle-class public employees, with about sixty thousand people gathered into a single parish. The parish is staffed by a team of five Maryknoll priests, all foreign (four North Americans and one Chilean). To this setting, a community in formation within a city undergoing very rapid growth, the Maryknoll priests bring a commitment to identify with the community. Their goal is to draw closer to the people of La Isabelica in every possible way.

> Catholic Action groups of the traditional sort are completely dead. They have no meaning to youth today. Now the priest studies the community first, and then offers himself to the community for whatever purposes it seeks or needs . . . we feel that you cannot speak the word of God without being part of the community in which you live and [without] learning to know and love it.[15]

In their work these men express a vision of the Church as the People of God, a living community continually forming and reforming itself through action. Thus, the priests in La Isabelica

[14] Interview 60308, 17 June 1971.
[15] Interview 60403, 8 June 1971, with an official of the Maryknoll order in Venezuela.

seek not to impose a given line of action from above, but rather to develop a new language, a set of symbols attuned to and derived from the life of the community. Such symbols are both external (e.g., a multipurpose room instead of a separate Church, ordinary clothes instead of cassocks or clerical collars, living in apartments instead of in a rectory) and internal, centered on a transformation of Christian symbols in ways that stress their meaning for social commitment.

Working in terms of the needs and desires of the community has involved the Maryknoll team, as participants, in activities ranging from the normal run of baptisms, confessions, and marriages to strikes, demonstrations, and community issues of all kinds.[16] In all this activity they search for the signs of the times, those crucial events which illuminate the faith and in turn are given greater meaning by it.

> The moment has come for the Latin American Church to interpret the signs of the times. What we lack is a language of symbols for this . . . the bishop goes to a factory and blesses it: this is a symbol which says something to the people. We lack a [new] vision of symbols.[17]

In this way, the significance of religious faith and action for daily life is transformed. The stress is on shared experience and identification; the role of the Church is seen as response to and extension of the people's felt needs, *not* as direction.

I believe that in Latin America today there is a great hope for

---

[16] This whole orientation reflects what I called earlier an existential approach to religious life. For these priests, a parish must be active. As one American priest working in a Caracas parish put it, "There is a traditional pastoral strategy which tends to sit back and let the people come to the Church. Here, traditional parish life is centered on the parish buildings, and on an overworked pastor who is really not available most of the time. The contrast to this is a parish life which knows no real limits or boundaries. You have a small center and the rest is a direct effort to enter into the lives of the people, to respond to their needs and to help them take initiatives to deal with their needs themselves. . . . The basic choice here is between a sacramental as opposed to a secular strategy: [between] a strategy which focuses on sacraments (baptism, marriage, death, etc.) and considers that sufficient; and one which seeks a much more dynamic projection out" (Interview 60401, 18 May 1971).

[17] Interview 60320, 16 July 1973.

the Lord, a great desire for the Lord through the great suffering of our people. Latin America is living in a state of vast humiliation, and for this reason there is a great desire to move ahead. And prophetic voices appear, men full of God, men who pray, who believe deeply in God, and who feel very deeply the humiliations of their people and interpret them in the light of the Gospel. Starting from reality....

And the Church is very beautiful in this, because through the Church we are beginning to see prophetic paths. They feel the weight of the humiliation of their people and begin to live as prophets.[18]

Msgr. Lebrún tolerated and even encouraged such orientations. I first went to the diocese in 1971 to interview Msgr. Lebrún. But when I returned in 1973 and visited La Isabelica the diocese had changed hands. The new bishop was seen as much less tolerant of innovation and more determined to maintain traditional lines of hierarchical authority, and the priests of La Isabelica felt isolated, curtailed, and abandoned.

In looking at such changes in orientation in Valencia, however, it is important to realize that the weakness of diocesan structures means that in poor parishes, or in those without the extra resources that groups like the Maryknoll order can call in, opportunities for action are extremely limited, no matter how active the priests. Experimentation may be tolerated, but the obverse of this situation is that little concrete support and help is given it. This was particularly visible in another parish I visited, located in a very poor area known as Barrio La Raya. Little could be done here, and the emphasis (common to many Venezuelan parishes) was on small-scale personal help. In La Raya,

> we stress concrete assistance, small but concrete. For example, here we are close to the hospital, and we help people get beds, transport, etc. In other cases we have insisted to the governor on the need to improve services. But all this is done as we go along; a really well-coordinated plan is difficult in part because here we are marginal along with the marginals, and our petitions don't get attention at higher levels.[19]

[18] Ibid.   [19] Interview 60318, 13 July 1973.

The case of Cali is quite different. I suggested earlier that the mentality of Cali's archbishop, combining structural views of society with a limited vision of change in the Church, would lead to attempts at innovation with a strong, consistent push for central control. Opportunities for innovation have been great, and the archbishop has seized them eagerly, creating a number of well-organized, efficient, and centrally funded and managed institutions. I mentioned CARITAS and the parish centers earlier. Here I shall focus attention on the parish centers, for they illustrate well the kind of relationships being considered.

In Cali a private foundation based on the large Carvajal family fortune was set up in 1960. This foundation has dedicated most of its resources to the establishment and continued financing of four parish centers, each located in marginal neighborhoods and each intended to serve as an example of a new kind of urban parish.[20] The parish centers are innovative in the sense that they consciously provide health care, education, social promotion, recreation, and cooperative purchasing facilities along with the normal range of pastoral and religious services. Furthermore, a major effort is made to incorporate lay participation in the direction and daily operation of each center, through economic contributions and payment for services and also through membership on committees and service in administrative roles. This arrangement is intended to free the parish priest from administrative duties and business responsibilities, allowing him to concentrate on specifically "pastoral" activities. What are the centers like?

I visited one center in Barrio El Guabal in which two priests and two nuns (all foreign) serve a parish of approximately fifty thousand people. The center is physically impressive, and the programs seem well organized and effective. But despite the center's innovations, in many respects the old pattern of waiting for external help and depending on the priest for paternalistic direction remains strong. To some extent this derives from the origin of the center; it simply descended providentially on the neighborhood, whose residents had little say in the formation or organiza-

[20] The financial arrangements involved here are unusual. Rather than grant a lump sum and then have the centers live off the income, the Carvajal Foundation, through its ownership of 40% of the stock of Carvajal & Cia. (one of Colombia's major paper and printing firms), provides *continuing* income to the centers.

tion of its programs. Nevertheless, priests in Barrio El Guabal have indeed managed to withdraw considerably from the direct management of social activities.

> I would say that there is still a big tendency to depend on the priest—not necessarily as a priest, but as an educated person. There is a complex among many of them that they have no background . . . that if we have to protest then the priest must come with us. The first thought is often that. We say, let's have them go with us, not get him to do it for us. This commission I went with last week was typical. A new police station was created for the area, but so far no police have been assigned to it. So the community said, let's send a commission to see the police chief. Our position is that we will help you if you organize to do this first. . . . In a neighboring parish there is a case that is just the opposite. There the priest runs a health center, he himself calls the doctor, he gets on the loudspeaker to talk about prostitution, or if a Protestant mission comes into the area. He is the mayor of the *barrio*; and, of course, since he is of that bent, the people use him.[21]

Cali thus reveals how transformation can begin in local-level relationships that remain linked to strong central control, represented by the energetic figure of the archbishop. Many other innovations have been undertaken in Cali, including a major, broad-ranging program of family-planning education in the parish centers. But the *range* of innovation is more limited than in Valencia, given the archbishop's firm commitment to three points: First, to central lines of control and direction (including finance); second, to a strict separation of lay and clerical roles (reflected in his emphasis on the incorporation of appropriate lay expertise);[22] and third, to making the Church a focal point for unity and action in Cali. Here, despite his surface differences from someone like the archbishop of Manizales, Msgr. Uribe reveals a basic similarity in the assumption of the Church's key unifying role within

---

[21] Interview 80307, 19 Oct. 1972.

[22] The archbishop strongly believes in the need for specialized training and looks to lay people for orientation in economics, sociology, etc. In his view, priests are not properly prepared in these fields and should leave them to lay people.

a "Christian society"—an assumption with little relevance or meaning in Venezuela.

A look at Cumaná and Facatativá completes our survey. Here, the newness (for Facatativá) and extreme weakness (for Cumaná) of diocesan-level structures makes concentration on parish life more fruitful. The major organizational thrust of the bishop of Facatativá was to turn the structures and energies of both diocese and parish toward the creation of vital "base communities"—relatively homogeneous small groups of reflection and action that, working within the formal structure of the parish, would begin the renovation of Church life from below. Efforts have also been made to incorporate lay people into the administration of the parish itself. But the results are mixed. Despite the stress on forming cooperatives, aiding local unions, training leaders, and in general on making people more able and willing to participate, in the parishes I visited in this diocese there is still a considerable tendency for the local population to depend on the priest for general social leadership. Nevertheless, at least the beginnings of a new orientation are present in Facatativá.

In Cumaná, the bishop's orientation encourages both activism and a general rethinking of the meaning of Church structures. The clergy is active and involved. In the several regular publications of the diocese, one can see a regular structure of meetings and participation by priests and religious in the several geographical zones of the diocese, as well as an exceedingly vigorous social stance by the bishop. Almost every number of the diocesan bulletin includes a letter from the bishop to the governor of the state, written after a pastoral visit, detailing the needs of towns and villages visited. The letters are very forthright. For example:

Mister Governor:

[Here] I have done no more than transcribe the petitions which orally or in writing have been presented to me by the inhabitants of the different towns I visited. In many I think they do not even have the slightest glimmer of hope in putting forward these petitions which they believe will be ignored. I was able to see that these towns are tired of having many, so many promises from politicians and governors in electoral years. They lose hope when they see how their rulers, and members of legislative and municipal bodies, are only interested in personal or party matters, and do not stop to think that with the Bs. 200,000—it is a good example—which came from the state treasury for Carnival, not a few rural roads and bridges could have been built; furniture could have been purchased for the rundown schools of many villages; electricity could have been brought to many towns in the state. . . .

For this reason Mr. Governor, in fulfillment of my pastoral mission, I take the liberty of bringing these delicate points to your attention, for we who hold responsibilities before God and before the nation cannot content ourselves simply with the material progress of the people. Instead, we must also strive to secure for them the most absolute and complete moral, cultural, and spiritual liberation.[23]

A good example of the results of rethinking traditional Church structures is the old minor seminary. In Cumaná, as in many small Venezuelan dioceses, the minor seminary operated as an inefficient Church-run boarding school at the secondary level, producing few if any future priests. Both to save money and to integrate the seminary more fully with the realities of local life, the bishop sold the seminary building and converted the whole operation into a youth center with only a few boarding students (primarily those from remote towns). Students were all enrolled in local secondary schools and were encouraged to live with families and work in local activities. The youth center itself took on broad functions of orientation and activism.

But in Cumaná, efforts at transforming the Church have run up against profound limitations. There are few resources, and contact with the people is sparse. For many years this region of Venezuela was practically abandoned by the Church. Elements of traditional religiosity (especially the cult of the dead) remain strong, but contact with the institutional Church has been sporadic. Thus the Church's task often boils down to a simple effort to establish human contact. The parish of San Luis Gonzaga, staffed by Spanish Jesuits, is representative of this situation. This parish spreads over more than 440 square kilometers, holding

[23] *Boletín de la Diocesis de Cumaná*, no. 55, 31 Mar. 1971, p. 6. The sum of 200,000 *bolívares* mentioned in the letter was equal at the time to approximately 50,000 U.S. dollars.

over thirty thousand people in the city of Cumaná and in small towns and villages along the coast and inland. Although the priests here work through the usual apparatus of schools and through a program of cooperatives (sponsored throughout Venezuela by Jesuits), they also try to use any occasion, any meeting of any kind, as a means of establishing friendship and human contact.

> One begins with soccer teams, with the Legion of Mary, which is a somewhat more religious group, and builds from these. A savings and loan cooperative also forms people. Indeed, one of the boys from the soccer team is now treasurer of the cooperative here, and he said spontaneously, "I am happy because, like the fathers, I am working for the good of others."
>
> So if you look only at Mass, at religious attendance, there has been little progress, because attendance is not very great. They do come to funeral masses: the cult of the dead is very strong.[24]

This stress on simple human contact responds to the concrete needs of the people, most of whom come to the parish for very specific reasons. "The majority who come here come for these matters of jobs, loans, and the like. They don't make the distinction that this is not a government, and they come for these things."[25]

There is really no other way in Cumaná, and the effort at building a Church as community necessarily takes precedence over more traditional, ecclesiastically structured organizational forms. The case of Cumaná is important because it reveals a situation where the relatively open mentality of Church leadership is transformed, given the almost total lack of resources, into a kind of activism which matches the situation and dispositions of the population more closely than would a (perhaps) more efficient, large-scale, and centrally run structure.

Earlier I mentioned popular impression, common in both Venezuela and Colombia, to the effect that Church leaders serving in marginal areas and dioceses are more sensitive to social issues. Their experience of poverty is closer and more direct, and as a result (so the common judgment goes) they tend to alter the

[24] Interview 60312, 19 July 1973.   [25] Ibid.

structure and style of Church activities to respond more fully to these needs. Obviously, the relation is too simple and direct as stated. But a major element of truth is nonetheless present. The dynamic processes which lead to different kinds of Church activities are composed of the combined impact of elite mentalities, socioeconomic context, and institutional structures and resources. The following section puts these elements into a broader perspective.

CONCLUSIONS

A number of cases have been presented in this chapter describing the structure, style, and orientation of Church and Church-related organizations. How can we go beyond mere description to draw from this mass of data the kind of analytical points central to the interests of this book?

As a first step, it is important to return to the dialectic of ideas and structures. The national and local cases considered here, and in preceding chapters on organizational change, make it clear that divergent ecclesiologies and concepts of authority are associated with characteristic kinds of organizations and programs within the Church. These basic notions spill over from this limited arena of ecclesiastical structures to shape Catholic activities on a broader social scale. In this way concepts, organizations, and social context are in continuous interaction.

The processes examined here are classic ones in the sociology of knowledge: the dialectical relation between concepts and forms of knowledge, on the one hand, and their institutional location and social context, on the other. Peter Berger and Thomas Luckmann argue for the kind of approach taken here, noting that "Symbolic universes are social products with a history. If one wants to understand their meaning, one has to understand the history of their production."[26] This is a history, of course, with no end. There is no conclusion to it, for the continuing mutual impact of ideas, structures, and situations is central to the very process of change. Moreover, this process does not work in one direction only. There is no unilinear path to follow, no certain or predetermined outcome. In a sense, this uncertainty and flux is our

[26] Berger and Luckmann, *The Social Construction of Reality*, p. 97.

guarantee that the processes really are dialectical. For in the dialectic, after all, the result cannot be known at the outset: the transcendence of all starting points is fundamental to any genuinely dialectical process.[27]

The key terms in this dialectic are ideological and structural. As used here, "ideological" has referred to concepts of authority, visions of the Church, and ideas about the world and about the proper nature of Church activities in it. "Structural" has denoted a combined measure including elements of surrounding society (nature of social classes, economic activities, population stability, literacy, etc.) and factors more specific to the Church, such as numbers of parishes, religious groups and institutions, clergy and the like, and the resources these provide to Church leaders.

The impact of concepts of authority and of the "Church" has already been explored at length in these pages. I shall now take the general models encountered (Church as institution, Church as People of God) and relate them to very specific, day-to-day styles of action. For example, it is clear that the orientations of the archbishop of Manizales and his views on change in the Church strengthen a general disposition to hierarchical control and paternalistic direction, both within the structures of the Church and also in the institution's relations with its members in many areas of life. Moreover, these orientations dovetail neatly with the power structure of a society like Manizales. It is not that one causes or simply reflects the other. Rather, these elements together comprise and reinforce a particular kind of local reality.

The availability of ample resources for the Church fits well in such a context. Yet abundant resources and a dense net of institutions are not an unmixed blessing. Their absence certainly hinders efforts (as in Cumaná), but their presence may have a stifling effect on change. Thus strong traditions and a vision of past strength may inhibit innovations, which are seen as superfluous. This seems to be the case in San Cristobal. Moreover, strong Church structures may create established interests and powers

---

[27] In a recent discussion of Marxism in American political science (see "The Aufhebung of Marxism"), Alfred G. Meyer stresses this point, noting that the very idea of "orthodox Marxism" is a contradiction in terms, since its dependence on the dialectic presupposes a continual process of transformation and transcendence.

that even the most determined bishop cannot crack open.[28] For example, a reform-minded future archbishop of Manizales might have considerable problems putting change into effect.

All in all, the dynamic processes visible at the local level are quite similar to those already described for the bishops and the national Churches as a whole. Table 9.2 sums up the characteristics of the dioceses, and figure 9.1 offers a graphic view of the trends, highlighting the way in which visions of the Church and their associated perceptions and commitments are expressed through the context of opportunities and resources, yielding different patterns of action. The four patterns cited in figure 9.1 are all visible in our cases: central control and a lid on change in Manizales and San Cristobal; identification with the community in Valencia; bureaucratic organization with some innovation in Cali (and occasionally in Facatativá); and simple human contact as stressed in Facatativá and especially in Cumaná.

In sorting out the significance of these types, three factors are of particular importance: first, the issue of structure at the diocesan level; second, the question of linkage from diocese to movement or parish; and third, the general matter of paternalism. Let us consider these in turn.

The issue of structure refers to the way diocese-wide organizations are formed and projected outward to society. In my fieldwork I encountered a striking inverse relation between powerful structures at the diocesan level and a vital active life in movements and parishes. Logically, this should not hold; for one might expect such diocesan structures to stimulate and encourage activities at other levels. But the reverse is often true, and the reason lies in the character of the structures themselves. Either they are holding operations like the Corporation of the Holy Family in Manizales, which in effect coordinates and stands in for the charitable activities of local elites, or else they represent the kind of organizations that traditionally conferred power and prestige, such as San Cristobal's university, radio station, or seminary. These once-powerful structures are much less effective in a milieu where people no longer depend on the kinds of social bonds which support traditional lines of authority and prestige.

[28] Bruneau's discussion of local-level change in the Brazilian Church stresses this point. Cf. *The Political Transformation*, chap. 8.

TABLE 9.2
SIX DIOCESES: SUMMARY CHARACTERISTICS

Dimension	Manizales	Cali	Facatativá	San Cristobal	Valencia	Cumaná
Bishop's orientation (ecclesial and sociopolitical dimensions)	Ecclesiastical moral	Mixed structural	Ecclesial structural	Ecclesiastical mixed	Ecclesial structural	Ecclesial structural
Social context	Stable rural	New urban	Stable changing rural	Stable changing rural	New urban	Unstable rural
Church resources	High	Medium	Low	High	Low	Low
Institutional context (density)	High	Medium	Low	High	Low	Low
Religiosity	High	Low	High	High	Low	Low
Style of action	Central-paternal	Central-bureaucratic	Decentralized/community-identified	Central-paternal	Decentralized/community identified	Decentralized open/simple human contact
Re-Christianization as a goal	Present	Present	Absent	Present	Absent	Absent

FIGURE 9.1
Processes of Change at the Local Level

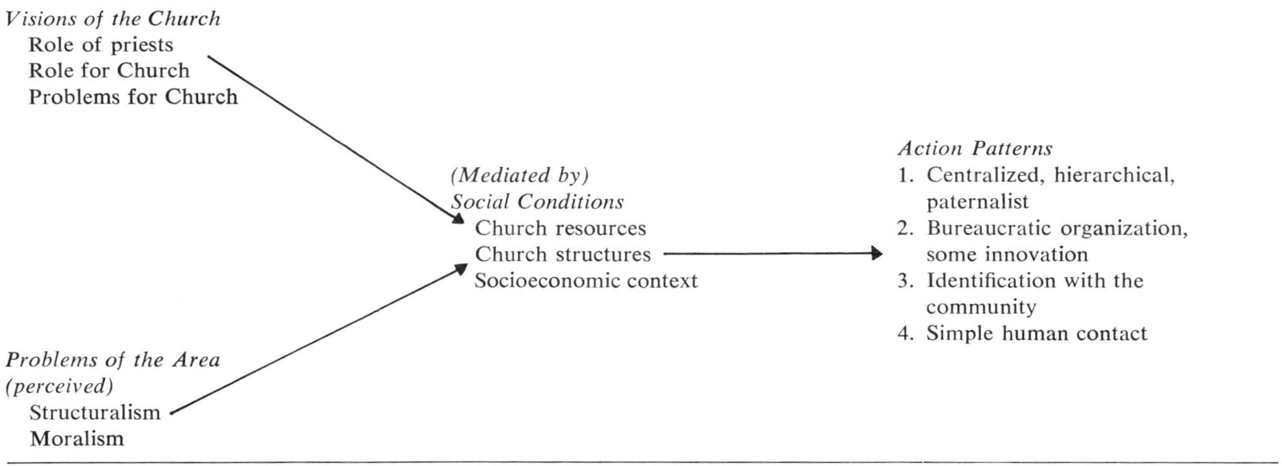

Visions of the Church
Role of priests
Role for Church
Problems for Church

(Mediated by)
Social Conditions
Church resources
Church structures
Socioeconomic context

Problems of the Area
(perceived)
Structuralism
Moralism

Action Patterns
1. Centralized, hierarchical, paternalist
2. Bureaucratic organization, some innovation
3. Identification with the community
4. Simple human contact

STRUCTURE AND STYLE

It is difficult to incorporate lay people into such traditional Church structures, and only where such structures are combined with a conscious, intensive effort to swim *against* the stream, through innovation and deliberate, meaningful incorporation of lay people, can some greater dynamism be lent to the operation. Cali and Facatativá are good examples here.

Structure thus holds many implications beyond the mere concentration of resources and the organization of bureaucratic routines. Certain kinds of structures send a message to their clientele, defining for them their proper place both in the organization itself and, by extension, in society at large. Paulo Freire puts this point in terms of the true meaning of generosity and charity.

> True generosity consists precisely in fighting to destroy the causes which nourish false charity. False charity constrains the fearful and subdued, the "rejects of life," to extend their trembling hands. True generosity lies in striving so that these hands—whether of individuals or entire peoples—need be extended less and less in supplication, so that more and more they become human hands which work and, working, transform the world.[29]

Our second factor, the question of linkage to the parish, is related to diocesan structure. Just as the ties of bishop to priest are paralleled in many cases by those of priest to people, so too a hierarchical, dominant role in one sphere is reflected in a paternalistic, pervasive search for control in others. As we have seen, this question of linkage often goes well beyond explicitly religious questions to include, for example, the priest's taking an authoritative role as intermediary in getting and keeping jobs—certainly a vital point in the lives of ordinary people. In situations of this kind, the meaning of concepts like "dialogue" or the free interchange implied by "collegiality" is hard to imagine. Of course, the terms are often used, but reality is far removed. The power of such implicit styles of action to override explicitly stated commitments is nowhere so visible as in the matter of "paternalism," which is our third factor influencing patterns of action.

Nowadays, it is difficult to find anyone in the Church with a kind word to say for paternalism. Almost without exception,

[29] Freire, *Pedagogy of the Oppressed*, p. 29.

bishops, priests, officers, and rank-and-file members of lay groups all reject paternalism and stress instead their commitment to the creation of viable structures of participation in both Church and society at large. But the reality of this commitment is open to considerable doubt. Part of the problem is surely a staggering lack of clarity. What, after all, *is* paternalism? As commonly used, the term refers to a fatherly or *paternal* role centered on the priest: the priest (traditionally called "father") gives general direction to individuals and communities, securing goods and services for them, and thus often unwittingly maintains them in the status of minor children, unable and unwilling to act or decide for themselves. Even when clearly defined, though, paternalism is hard to eliminate, for several reasons: first, the training and orientation of Church officials continues to promote it; and second, the needs of average Church members are often so urgent as to make demands for immediate help quite overwhelming.

It is hard for priests to shake off old habits and dispositions. I have attended many meetings in parishes which were held up as models of the "absence" of paternalism. What I found, however, was the priest, as ever, at the center of things: urging lay members to make their contribution, prompting and coaxing them, and then presenting all this as the absence of paternalism. It is hard to get rid of paternalism when priests and bishops remain attuned to a general orienting role in the community. Only with a determined, conscious effort (as, for example, in La Isabelica) is it possible to counter this general tendency. But in La Isabelica, it should be recalled, the priests involved were all members of a foreign religious order (Maryknolls) famous for its innovative stance within the Church—not ordinary parish priests by any means!

A second reason for the persistence of paternalism comes from the demands and needs of the average members of the Church. Parishioners often expect their priests to do more in social and economic terms than priests themselves see as proper. In part this is simply a reflection of old expectations and established patterns of behavior. But it is important to realize that in many cases the urge to paternalism is rooted in stark need—as, for example, in many areas in Cumaná or in some extremely poor parishes I visited in Cali. The people there are destitute. Yet they are in contact with an institution which, while not necessarily controlling great wealth, nonetheless can provide points of contact with other institutions and resources in the larger society. For these people the Church's new insistence on getting away from paternalism must occasionally seem self-indulgent and irrelevant.

The three issues just considered—diocesan structure, linkage to parish, and paternalism—are closely related to a fourth, which, I argued earlier, sums up many of the relevant differences between the Venezuelan and Colombian Churches as a whole: Is the re-Christianization of society a central goal? The implicit inclusion of re-Christianization as a goal contributes to the formation and maintenance of hierarchical structures, top-dominant linkages, and paternalistic orientations by de-emphasizing the autonomous value of temporal experience. In seeking to re-Christianize society, clerics and lay people *necessarily* assume that the proper form and model of organization comes from outside society itself and must be imposed from without. The implications of this last point are visible throughout this book, and its broad meaning is considered in detail in the next, concluding part.

Throughout this book I have stressed the central role of politics and the potential ambiguities of a commitment to pastoral action in concrete situations. In the cases presented here, I have deliberately avoided extremes of conflict, for I wanted to give the reader a closer sense of the day-to-day life of these local Churches. Even so, it is easy to see that pastoral action has considerable potential for conflict and that it blends, in imperceptible degrees, with politics—above all in the kind of strategy pursued in La Isabelica. In ecclesiastical environments less hospitable than the Valencia of Msgr. Lebrún, the Facatativá of Msgr. Zambrano, or the Cumaná of Msgr. Parra León, movements in these explicitly political directions must first pass through a screen of ecclesiastical sanctions that make such actions very difficult indeed. As one Manizales priest told me, "There is a saying in Italian: 'I must walk on the razor's edge.' This is what I have to do. I have to work that way."[30]

All in all, the razor's edge is not a bad metaphor for the dilemmas of local-level action. Innovations born from new definitions and images of the Church are hard to put into practice, for they must indeed balance on a thin edge between, on one

[30] Interview 80322, 2 Aug. 1973.

side, the ecclesiastical authorities (not always sympathetic or even able to help much) and, on the other, the surrounding society, whose leaders in *their* structures of power are often openly hostile—they recognize the degree to which new visions of the Church and the transformations of pastoral action, to which the new visions lead, generate new and potentially dangerous forms of social and political activism.

Politics is central to all these developments, and questions about the meaning of politics and about the Church's proper relation to it take center stage, as much in national public debates as in the daily life of poor and isolated dioceses. The centrality of politics in these debates is rooted in the central role politics and power take in forming the world around us. Once the Church redefines itself, and in so doing begins to reshape its proper relation to the world, politics (always present implicitly in the past) becomes a more conscious and prominent part of the equation for Church members. In this way, the goals of action and the proper forms of its exercise—two dimensions which together account for much of the Church's projection into society—change and are transformed together.

Part IV

CONCLUSIONS

10

Further Reflections

THE conclusions this book has to offer are present throughout, woven into the discourse of each succeeding chapter. A formal conclusion thus has little chance of furthering whatever message has not been conveyed already. For these reasons, I take this chapter less as a chance for summary and restatement than as an opportunity to go beyond the findings presented thus far, to confront these data once again with the basic questions shaping the book as a whole.

On reflection, it is clear that we are dealing with something more general than the interaction of "religion" and "politics" alone: religion and politics are examples of the more universal problem of relating thought to action in institutionally circumscribed and historically specific contexts. Religion and politics are the *locations* of our inquiry; the questions are more general. The institutional and historical specificity of the inquiry, closely rooted in the real experiences of communities and nations, is vital to its general validity; for the expression of thought and action is never abstract and general, but is always grounded in concrete human experience. Understanding the richness of human variety is thus essential to grasping the general processes at work in all societies. As Clifford Geertz reminds us, "it is no exaggeration to say, at least so far as the sociology of religion is concerned, that there is no route to generalization save through a dense thicket of particulars."[1]

In addition to exploring further the theoretical bases and implications of the relation of religion and politics, I shall use these conclusions to consider the future of this relation, particularly in Latin America. Looking at the future is difficult and perhaps risky, but informed speculation is worth the effort; it can guide future readers, researchers, and activists alike. In thinking about the future of religion and politics, it is important to maintain

[1] Geertz, *Islam Observed*, p. 22.

CONCLUSIONS

the dynamic, dialectical perspective adopted throughout this book. The future is not solely a matter of static outcomes—for example, a struggle between "religion" and "politics" taken as mutually exclusive or fully formed entities, or between religious as opposed to political priorities of people and institutions. The choice of outcomes is part of the process, and deserves attention; but more is learned by looking at the future in terms of the emergence of new *syntheses* of religion and politics, thought and action, "Church" and "world." New syntheses—innovative ways of knitting the temporal, spiritual, historical, and eschatological dimensions of reality together in concrete social contexts—are what will set the direction and meaning of future events and circumstances as yet unforeseeable.

In going beyond the data, analyses, typologies, and comparisons of earlier chapters, I begin by reflecting on the theoretical and methodological bases of the book as a whole. I then consider the nature of the new symbols being created and their relation to new and continuing structures of action. Finally, I examine religion and politics in terms of alternative syntheses and future projections, both in general and for the specific cases of Venezuela and Colombia.

METHOD AND THEORY: REFLECTIONS

Methods are never neutral. The choice of method always reflects and reinforces theoretical expectations which lie at the heart of any given study. In this book, the interdependence of method and theory is both particularly clear and of central importance to the validity of any assessments of the future. A word, then, on method.

I have stressed the need to take and hold a *phenomenological* and *dialectical* approach. This approach involves seeing religion and politics as a dynamic system of behavior with a clear (if not always explicit) set of internal rules guiding it. These rules can be explicitly stated by the actors and can also be seen as implicit in their overt behavior. To understand both sides of this reality, I have worked with formal statements of belief and orientation as well as with projections from attitudes, values, and observed behavior. External, causal explanation is thus combined with analysis of the meaning of events and actions—analysis which is derived from our understanding of the inner structure and logic of the rules religious people create for themselves when acting in the world.[2]

This approach has several notable implications. First, throughout the book it has led me consistently to pull apart what religious people bring together in the activities of daily life. Thus, spiritual and explicitly religious motivations have been distinguished from temporal understandings and examined separately. Only by pulling apart the mental structure of the individuals, groups, and institutions involved is it possible to get at the sources and direction of the transformations underway. Although such separation is artificial, it is crucial to the ability to understand the different dimensions and then put them together in different combinations—with care and sensitivity. Proceeding in this way, I have tried to get inside the rule structure of the Catholic community—to look at the world from the inside out. Of course, such an approach itself runs the risk of reifying the mental structures of a given period, of assuming that what was once given remains forever valid. But such inner structures are never static; they are constantly changing. Separate attention to the components of this process helps highlight key points of change in individuals and organizations (and helps locate their sources), matching the points of change with the counterpoints of caution so visible, for example, in the role constraints that bishops experience.

These methodological considerations have personal as well as theoretical grounds. Ever since I began working on this research, nearly ten years ago, I have been increasingly struck and moved by the immense impact of experience on the orientations and actions of religious people. The depth of commitment is enormous: all over Latin America, men and women are literally putting their lives on the line in pursuit of goals derived from a particular synthesis of religion with social and political life. To appreciate the full depth and impact of these human commitments, a phenomenological approach is needed. By thus working from the inside out, we see problems and situations less as objec-

[2] This combination of external causal analysis with inner, meaningful analysis is well treated in Rex, *Key Problems*. See also the works on phenomenological analysis and ethnomethodology referred to in note 12, chapter 1, above.

tive "puzzles" to be solved by policy makers than as moments in a creative process of change in which real people and real interests are involved.[3] The researcher gets more involved with and committed to his subject; analysis becomes richer, more humane, and less bloodless and purely "scientific" in orientation. All in all, a phenomenological approach is less a grab bag of methodological tricks than an *attitude* that puts analysis within the context of the rules, perceptions, and lives of the actors themselves.[4]

Finally, these methodological considerations have several implications for the scope and the general validity of the analyses and projections advanced in these pages. As used here, theory and analysis are grounded in particular historical and institutional situations. This means that the use of theory here differs somewhat from the approach common to much recent work in the social sciences. I use theory not to "prove" or "apply" general propositions or hypotheses derived from abstract formulations, but rather as a means of giving form and pattern to the findings. As Geertz puts it, "not to generalize across cases but to generalize within them."[5] My theoretical goals are thus more attuned to depth than breadth, and ever closely tied to specific cases. This point of view joins this study to the more general perspectives of cultural analysis where, in Geertz's words,

> Studies do build on other studies, not in the sense that they take up where the others leave off, but in the sense that, better informed and better conceptualized, they plunge more deeply into the same things. . . . Theoretical formulations hover so low over the interpretations they govern that they don't make much sense or hold much interest apart from them. This is so, not because they are not general (if they are not general, they are not theoretical) but because, stated independently of their applications they seem either commonplace or vacant.[6]

Although the range of generalization is limited, general explanation per se is not debarred. Rather, it must be formulated with great care, and its applications must be firmly rooted in

[3] This point is made very forcefully in Alves, "Christian Realism."
[4] These points are developed more fully in Levine, "Urbanization in Latin America."
[5] Geertz, "Thick Description," p. 26.
[6] Ibid., p. 25.

specific historical processes and in the way in which actors create worlds of meaning within them. These are dialectical processes, and, as Trent Schroyer has pointed out,

> A dialectical relationship is not reducible to a function of an independent variable, but requires a nonformalizable reciprocal relation to other processes. This does not mean, however, that one cannot gain knowledge about dialectical processes, although it does set limits to the range of generalization and the status of the knowledge itself.[7]

These considerations bring us to the process which lies at the heart of this book: the creation, use, and transformation of symbols and structures in religion and politics. The next section explores these issues in greater depth, with particular reference to three points: first, the way religious symbols are created and used;[8] second, the role played in this process by specific institutional structures; and finally, the impact on this process of elements of social (above all national and local) context.

Symbols and Structures

In a sense, Latin America finds itself today in a state of cultural crisis. As we have seen, deep questioning and rapid transformation of the bases, legitimacy, and symbolic expression of religion, politics, and social, cultural, and economic life in general are common throughout the region. Symbols are of central importance to this process, for they are the visible manifestations of changing consciousness, its expression in images that guide understanding, shape emotions, and mold action. What is the content of the new symbols being created?

I have given particular emphasis here to the creation of symbols bridging the temporal and the spiritual sides of life, and

[7] Schroyer, *The Critique of Domination*, p. 130.

[8] A word of explanation may be useful here. I do not propose to explain the creation of symbols in general, or even to deal with the question in any systematic way. Instead, I take the symbols as the starting point for analysis; my attention is directed toward the forms symbols take, the way they shape and are shaped by institutions and interests, and their implications for action. As used here, the "creation" of symbols thus refers to their elaboration and definition by individuals and groups, not to their psychological origins.

thereby creating a basis for new syntheses of religious and secular perspectives and actions. In this process, basic notions of *both* religion and politics have been reshaped, with bridging concepts like pastoral action stretched and expanded in new ways. Concepts like pastoral action are particularly important because they articulate religious motivations in the activities of day-to-day life.[9] Rather than restate my earlier discussions, I prefer to consider these questions here from a somewhat different point of view and at a deeper level.

In his work on cultural transformation, Victor Turner argues that periods of great cultural stress and change (which he labels "liminal") often see a renewed emphasis on symbols of *communitas*—that is, the elaboration of a sense of belonging and identity that has been overshadowed in hitherto accepted routines of daily life.[10] The concern for community and belonging is visible in at least two senses: first, in a stress on community and identity as values over and above structure and order, which is expressed in the creation of islands of community within existing structures; and second, in the search for and creation of ways of life seen as more authentic and natural.[11] Turner's discussion

[9] Weber saw pastoral care as an essential connection between the mystical, charismatic side of religion and its involvement in daily life. "Pastoral care in all its forms is the priest's real instrument of power, particularly over the workaday world, and it influences the conduct of life most powerfully when religion has achieved an ethical character. In fact, the power of ethical religion over the masses parallels the development of pastoral care. Wherever the power of an ethical religion is intact, the pastor will be consulted in all the situations of life by both private individuals and the functionaries of groups" (*The Sociology of Religion*), pp. 75-76.

[10] Victor Turner, *Dramas, Fields, and Metaphors*. Such periods see intense self-questioning and experimentation. New combinations of form, content, and symbols are tried out in an attempt to find categories of analysis and identities which better "fit" the changing pattern of experience, and such reprogramming is central to change. "In the evolution of man's symbolic cultural action, we must seek those processes which correspond to open-endedness in biological evolution. I think we have found them in those liminal, or 'liminoid' (post-industrial-revolution), forms of symbolic action, those genres of free-time activity, in which all previous standards and models are subjected to criticism, and fresh new ways of describing and interpreting sociocultural experience are formulated. The first of these forms are expressed in philosophy and science, the second in art and religion" (p. 15).

[11] For example, as Victor Turner points out (ibid., pp. 265-67), a view of

poses several questions to the analysis presented here. To what degree is such a stress on community, identity, and belonging visible in Latin American Catholicism in general, and in the specific cases considered here? What bearing do such concerns have on the political expressions of religious belief and action?

Clearly, a stress on building or rebuilding community within the structures of the Church and among Catholics in general is very prominent. Much of the thrust of Vatican II, as picked up and amplified in Latin America since Medellín, points in this direction. The visible stress on renewed and simplified styles of life, the restructuring of parishes, the search for less juridical relations within the institutional Church, and the greater identification of clergy with the faithful—all are expressions of a search for community.[12] This is a general phenomenon whose expression varies notably with context. Thus, Venezuelans give relatively more weight to these dimensions than do Colombians. Moreover, in both nations it is clear that the persistence of relatively open social environments offers possibilities of community building *outside of religion* (e.g., in political parties, trade unions, or community groups) that are simply not available in more repressive situations. In cases like Chile or El Salvador, for example, the role of the Church as a central focus of community is magnified even further: it is the only one available to many people.

How is the search for *communitas* expressed in Latin American Catholicism today? Catholicism may be characterized by its continued stress on the necessity and goodness of fusing secular and sacred spheres of action and meaning. Few Catholics (of any ideological persuasion) would differ from this long-standing tradition. Thus the issue is not whether secular and sacred dimensions should be joined, but rather the nature and content of the synthesis itself. Adherents of Liberation Theology and members of TFP groups share a common belief in the fusion of this world and the next, but the content of their respective visions of *communitas* is extremely different.

To get at the roots of these differences, earlier chapters have

---

poverty as somehow a more genuine, real, and natural state of life is common to many different epochs and societies.

[12] Base communities are a good example of the search for community, as are some of the religious orders founded in the Middle Ages, which responded to the same needs at that time.

explored various concepts of authority, of Church, and also the impact of experience on such values and beliefs. To sort these out, it is important to grasp the underlying eschatological dimension of religious views of the world, and the way these eschatological perspectives are worked into the experiences, perceptions, and judgements of daily life. These underlying images of the trans-historical frame of human existence give force and direction to patterns of action whose surface similarities (e.g., in their common fusion of sacred and secular) may mask enormous differences in action. In studying this process, it is important to avoid determinism of any kind: crude materialism and ethereal idealism must be equally shunned. Thought and action are themselves dynamic; neither mere reflections of social conditions nor abstract deductions from ethical symbols, they move forward in continuous interaction, in a process whereby religious beliefs and practical ethics and imperatives influence one another. In Weber's classic formulation,

> Not ideas but material and ideal interests directly govern men's conduct. Yet very frequently the "world images" that have been created by "ideas" have, like switchmen, determined the tracks along which action has been pushed by the dynamics of interest.[13]

The analysis put forward in this book has emphasized the interaction of ideology, context, and structures *as mediated through institutions*. Institutions are taken not only as sets of rules and procedures derived from the past, but also as ways of life—modes of self-perception and self-image which generate particular motivations and styles of action. With a closer look at the institutional mediation in the relation of religion and politics, three dimensions come to the fore: views of the institution of the Church, views of the nature of being religious, and the nature and impact of historical experience as lived within these institutional settings. A review of these three dimensions will clarify the process by which the urge for *communitas* is transformed into patterns of action.

Views of an institution are vital in shaping the kind of community created within its formal boundaries. They shape the

[13] Weber, *From Max Weber*, p. 280.

translation of desires for *communitas* into action through the kind of opportunities and constraints built into the role expectations of leaders and members of the institution. We have already seen how the felt constraints of being leaders of a special kind of institution leads many bishops to shape their actions to fit a leadership role filled with a heavy sense of responsibility to past, present, and future. Further, the idea of the Church as a heterogeneous, broadly defined institution limits action by constraining bishops to ensure unity among its elements. On the other hand, those who see the Church as necessarily involved deeply in the world take seriously the requirements of testimony and witness as guides to action. Faith in this sense leads to active pursuit of justice in this world, which is seen as a necessary step in building the Kingdom of God and as an expression of faith in life itself.[14] Visions of the institution thus provide conceptual and behavioral frameworks for action: in any field, action works out of the central core of religious commitment. Obviously, this sense of the institution is closely related to the basic sense of what being religious is all about in the first place. What is this core of belief, this unified vision of self and world which gives motive force to action, moving the institution (however defined) to act?

The nature of being religious, our second dimension of institutional mediation, is a vast and difficult question.[15] For present purposes, it can be broken into two separate though related questions: the general matter of commitment, and the inner feeling of religious experience as expressed in action. The issue of commitment should be familiar by now. It draws our attention to what are seen as the necessary implications of faith for action, and to the quality of the relation between the two. The sense of commitment is closely tied to the sense of the institution itself, for commitment can take many forms. Three are particularly important

[14] A good example is the experience of Nestor Paz, the Bolivian *guerrillero*; see *My Life for My Friends*. The serious nature and extreme depth of the theological and disciplinary challenge posed by the left to the Church were particularly notable in Chile during the Allende years. For a very complete discussion, see Brian Smith, "The Catholic Church and Political Change in Chile, 1920-1978," especially chapter 8.

[15] On different views of the nature of being religious, see the excellent essay by Birnbaum, "Beyond Marx in the Sociology of Religion." Other useful works include Wallace, *Religion*, and the essays collected in Bellah, *Beyond Belief*.

CONCLUSIONS

in contemporary Latin American Catholicism: commitment to institutional and community preservation, commitment to social action, and commitment to the expression of a particular kind of religious experience in the world.

Commitment to institutional and community preservation runs very deep in the Church. Where more traditional, institutional images of the Church predominate, this commitment leads to a kind of action characterized here as re-Christianization of the world—an attempt to reshape the world in Christian terms. This kind of commitment is separate from the matter of progressive or conservative social attitudes; it can go along with either. Commitment to re-Christianization implies that the Church continue to guide and direct any social process, be it oriented to preservation of the status quo or to thoroughgoing reform. For someone with this commitment, visions of the "inner" order of the Church and its "outer" mission run together in the persistence of a hierarchical, paternalistic orientation to the world.

Unfortunately, commitment to a particular kind of religious experience in the world is often overlooked by social scientists in their concern for more directly social or political issues; but commitment of this kind is not purely ethereal. Rather, the nature of religious experience, and the ongoing transformation of religious meaning into daily life experiences, is what gives continuously renewed richness and motivation to action. The way religious experience is expressed in action is central to the entire process. This has less to do with articulated social analysis or political ideology than with deeply felt experiences and orientations.[16] After all, Christianity is a religion founded on mysteries, and its mystical side takes on central importance here. The mystical and contemplative core of the Christian experience gives constant nurture to the strength to act. Segundo Galilea puts the matter well, arguing that actions for liberation are most profoundly rooted in a commitment to evangelical values expressed in contemplation.

Authentic Christian contemplation, passing through the desert,

[16] A major methodological problem of dealing with religious experience is that one is always dealing with remembered reconstructions of that experience, and not with the experience itself. On this point, cf. Worsley, *The Trumpet Shall Sound*, and Geertz, "Religion as a Cultural System."

transforms contemplatives into prophets and heroes of commitment, and militants into mystics. Christianity achieves the synthesis of the politician and the mystic, the militant and the contemplative, and abolishes the false distinction between the religious-contemplative and the militantly committed. Authentic contemplation, through the encounter with the absolute of God, leads to the absolute of one's neighbors. It is the meeting place for this difficult symbiosis which is so necessary and creative for Latin American Christians committed to the liberation of the poor.[17]

As Galilea sees it, this commitment to the poor has several possible expressions. It may be found in a "straight political option," whereby power is sought to put goals into effect, or in a "prophetic pastoral option," which stresses proclamation of the message of liberation.[18] Galilea's emphasis on the transformative effects of contemplation and prayer points to the deep religious roots of temporal action, to the ways in which contemplative experiences are transformed into action, and to the close and enduring link of the two in the Catholic tradition.[19] In his words, "The message becomes a critical consciousness, and is capable of inspiring the deepest and most decisive liberating transformation. In this sense it has social and political consequences. This option is more charismatic and therefore it is less widespread [than the straight political option].[20]

Religious experience is thus a powerful source of motivation for action in the world. But it is also a value in itself and valued as such by believers. After all, religion is not purely or even primarily instrumental: it seeks more than the accomplishment of specific goals. It is also, and primarily, an *expressive* experience, satisfying in itself by bringing a sense of greater meaning to all aspects of life. In this vein, Illich argues that it is not the specific mission of the Church to make plans for change; these are best left to secular humanist groups. Rather,

[17] Galilea, "Liberation as an Encounter with Politics and Contemplation," p. 28.
[18] Ibid., p. 31.
[19] Gilfeather ("Women Religious") points to the way in which temporal experience affects the practice and meaning of such central religious experiences as prayer and contemplation.
[20] Galilea, "Liberation as an Encounter," p. 31.

CONCLUSIONS

> The specific task of the Church in the modern world is the Christian celebration of the experience of change. . . .
>
> The new era of constant development must not only be enjoyed, it must be brought about. What is the task of the Church in the gestation of the new world? The Church can accelerate time by celebrating its advent, but it is not the Church's task to engineer its shape. She must resist that temptation. Otherwise she cannot celebrate the wondrous surprise of the coming, the advent.[21]

Illich points here to the need to separate the religious, mystical experience from one dedicated to problem solving or planning. He goes on to argue that, with religious awareness and faith,

> We become capable of affirming the autonomy of the ludicrous in the face of the useful, of the gratuitous as opposed to the purposeful, of the spontaneous as opposed to the rationalized and planned, of creative expression made possible by inventive solution.
>
> We will need ideological rationalizations for a long time to achieve purposefully planned inventive solutions to social problems. Let consciously secular ideology assume this task.
>
> I want to celebrate my faith for no purpose at all.[22]

This position does not reject the search for solutions to social and political problems, but refuses to derive them from religious faith. Religious experience is different in kind; it cannot be fully appreciated unless it is liberated from the requirements (both old and new) of achieving things in the world. Achievement will follow, Illich and others like him argue; but it will come out of a general sense of commitment and a broad way of experiencing the world—not from a direct commitment to a particular achievement per se. In this light, the content of religious experience speaks to the dialectics of the whole process being considered here, shaping action as religious people respond to their contact with the world, reworking their own religious values and giving a new sense to both spiritual and secular dimensions of life.

Our third dimension of institutional mediation, the impact of historical experience, has received less emphasis in this book than

[21] Illich, "The Powerless Church," pp. 98, 100.
[22] Ibid., p. 103.

other factors; but a number of points may nonetheless be picked up from earlier chapters. First, the experience of marginality and oppression clearly has a major impact on the commitments brought to action. Threats to the integrity of the Church as an institution have often led to greater involvement in politics, if only in self-defense. In the current political climate of many Latin American countries, such actions typically set off a chain of events leading to expanded conflict, division, and radicalization within the Church. The impact of experience is further visible in the findings of this book at three main points: first, in the impact of career and nation on the personal orientations of the bishops; second, in the experience of organizational change and the evolving relations of lay groups with the hierarchy; and third, in the nature of change at the local level and the evolution of strategies such as "paternalism" or "simple human contact." These points have all been discussed extensively in earlier chapters; rather than review them here, I need only point out that they are all expressions of the same basic process—the impact of experience in shaping the nature of action and the form of action deemed to express the Christian commitment most fully.

In general, the quality and impact of experience is most fully expressed in the close relation of symbols to structures, which together form the community as it is lived. The spillover of religious orientations to social forms and styles of action, which is so central to this analysis, speaks directly to this point. In this regard, one often finds a tendency among Catholic radicals to dismiss the bishops' concern for preserving the institutions of the Church as somehow equivalent to moral cowardice or evasion. This is shortsighted and unfair. Since to committed believers, and above all to leaders of the institution itself, the Church is the whole human community in embryo, bearing a message of salvation and keeping it alive through the centuries, such a concern for institutional preservation is not surprising; for the Church preserves, as institutional bearer of the message, the ultimate possibilities of a fuller life now and in the future. The differences and conflicts so visible here revolve not around the idea of preserving the institution or maintaining unity per se. These are generally accepted. Instead, conflict arises over basic notions of what is to be brought together and what "unity" means in the first place. The answers to these questions, which are raised every day all over Latin America, are located in particular syntheses of the elements reviewed in this section: institutions, commitment, and experience. Catholicism offers unique mixtures of symbols and structures that can lead to a variety of forms and patterns of social and political action. The political implications of this process warrant further reflection, and the following section takes a closer look at the several syntheses of religion and politics now being put forward in Latin America.

RELIGION AND POLITICS: ALTERNATIVE SYNTHESES

In a recent critique of writings on "development," K. H. Silvert and Leonard Reissman argued that much "development theory" concentrates too heavily on institutional differentiation and specialization. These are conceived in general, abstract terms as "a drifting apart of bunches of activities in a way that creates neat clusters and permits heightened freedom of action (or sub-institutional 'autonomy') within each institutional setting."[23] But so exclusive a focus on differentiation makes it hard to give systematic attention to the development of syntheses that give unity to the new and complex forms being created: "A weakness of much social theorizing about institutions and institutional differentiation is that primary attention is put on the growth of social division, while only lip service is paid to the emergence of the new syntheses which must glue together the emergent patterns of differentiation."[24]

Silvert and Reissman argue here that social science must both produce its own synthesis and recognize the many creative syntheses invented in the normal course of social life. A synthesis of both kinds is clearly needed, and I have already pointed to efforts at its construction. How is such a synthesis built? What is it made of? In approaching these questions, we can begin to put back together the dimensions separated earlier, joining ecclesial and sociopolitical sides of reality to get at the way these dimensions fit into a whole: how, why, and when. In creating a synthesis of religion and politics, three sets of factors must be woven together: first, types of authority, visions of the Church, and religious experience; second, types of politics, visions of the

[23] Silvert and Reissman, *Education, Class, and Nation*, p. 21.
[24] Ibid., p. 35.

political, and political experience; and third, the nature of institutional mediation. A final consideration of these elements, each in turn, is now appropriate.

First, on the religious side of the coin, are questions of authority, visions of the Church, and attitude toward experience, which all share an underlying dimension of historicity and openness. A sense of historicity and openness implies awareness of contingency and permanent change, as opposed to the more traditional Catholic position, which saw social developments as the unfolding of set, necessarily limited potentialities.[25] As noted earlier, the gradual move to more open and historically focused positions in Catholicism helped transform the nature and meaning of authority in the Church (by tying it more closely to action); the models of the Church most commonly used (stressing the Church as Pilgrim People of God); and religious experience, which became more closely interwoven with experience in general —no longer kept sheltered and apart as a model of purity for saved and sinners to contemplate.

The second set of factors—the transformation of types of politics, of visions of the political, and of the nature of political experience—is no less deep or important. The underlying dimension at work here is the expansion of "politics" from a narrow identification with partisanship, political parties, and government to a broad and far-reaching concern with *structures* of power and privilege, wherever they may appear. This expansion and transformation has both negative and positive aspects. In negative terms, "politics" is liberated from earlier identifications with specific institutional vehicles, thus opening the way to broader forms and arenas of legitimate political action. In more positive terms, the expansion of politics goes hand in hand with the evolution of a richer vision of freedom. The new vision goes beyond classical liberal freedom from restraint (essentially a negative concept) to see freedom in terms of expanding and fulfilling human potentialities.

The impact of experience is critical to both politics and religion. I have already noted the new dimensions of religious experience. In political terms, it is clear that the experience of conflict, violence, oppression, and poverty has brought new questions

[25] A point of view absorbed into Thomist thought from Aristotelian science.

to the fore for religious people seeking political orientation. The *mix* of political with religious dimensions is central to the entire process of building syntheses, for neither is sufficient by itself. After all, poverty, oppression, violence, and the like are nothing new in Latin America. But consciousness of them, in the light of new and different ideas about the nature of religious community and commitment, has led to the kinds of innovative and dynamic syntheses so visible, for example, in Liberation Theology.

Finally, institutional mediation, the third factor, knits the whole process together. The structure and felt significance of institutions sets the stage for creating new syntheses and sustaining old ones, through provision of organizational linkages which support and shelter action, and further, by placing the entire process of intellectual weaving together of new relations of religion and politics within an ongoing tradition from which strength and a sense of continuity can be drawn. This double function of institutional mediation explains why the link to experience and forms of action is so important in both religion and politics.

Attention to experience and to its institutional and contextual location also helps explain one of the most striking aspects of the data presented here: the powerful impact of nation and the notable shifts in attitudes and patterns of response with a move from the general and abstract to the concrete and the specific. The strong, mutual impact of self-image, organizational form, and styles of action also speaks to this point. Thus, faith and hope for a different kind of future are expressed in religion, the Catholic Church, and politics—not in general terms alone, but, more significantly, within specific historical structures.

What, finally, are the syntheses of religion and politics now competing among Latin American Catholics? Four syntheses are particularly notable: Christendom, Neo-Christendom, Liberation Theology, and the Evangelical-Pastoral position elaborated most fully at the 1979 General Conference of Latin American Bishops in Puebla. Let me review these in turn, paying particular attention to the kind of mixture of religion and politics each advances, and to the organizational structures and programs through which each is expressed.

The ideal of Christendom has few but vocal adherents in Latin America today. Represented primarily among the most traditional, "integrist" wing of the Church and in groups like the

TFP,[26] Christendom looks to a social and political order founded on, guided by, and suffused with Christian principles. In practice this position takes a highly reactionary turn in social and political matters, locating its Christian principles mainly in the most traditional expressions of conservative and corporatist political theory and of Catholic social doctrine.

Neo-Christendom, as expressed primarily by Christian Democratic parties and many progressive Church people, differs sharply in social content, seeking to reform the world and to make it more just through an application of more modern and advanced Catholic social thought. Lay leaders are much more autonomous than with Christendom, and great stress is placed on a distinction of levels between lay and clerical action.

For purposes of this discussion, Christendom and Neo-Christendom can be taken together despite the large gulf in political ideology and social policy which separates their adherents. The two fit together because each in some way looks to the ordering of social reality according to Christian principles. For each, the world is to be recaptured for Christianity and made whole again. I stress the importance of seeing Christian principles as a basis for organizing the world because the goal of re-Christianization is what most clearly sets these two syntheses off from the others. The reader will recall how the salience of this goal set some bishops off in tone and style from those more accepting of the plurality of the world and hence more concerned with building community within it—not remaking it on "Christian lines."

Liberation Theology offers a new synthesis. Like many other positions, this synthesis brings together human history and salvation history, temporal and spiritual dimensions of life, stressing the strong and necessary links between them. But it differs from positions advocating the re-Christianization of the world in its notable stress on history, social context, and experience as guides and starting points for Christian reflection and action. The world is not to be reconquered, but rather *remade*, so that "authentic" community (at once temporal and spiritual) is possible in the first place. Liberation Theology sees history less as a stage on which preexisting potentialities are fulfilled than as an open-ended context for the development of new ways to be human.

[26] Cf. Van Texel, "La ultima escisión del integrismo."

CONCLUSIONS

Thus, despite the many differences between writers often lumped together as representatives of Liberation Theology, "there is," as Segundo points out, "something common and basic for all of them—the view that men, on a political as well as an individual basis, construct the Kingdom of God from within history now."[27]

This perspective leads Liberation Theology to commitments which join spiritual and political motivations and forms of action, while maintaining considerable openness and room for creativity and play on both dimensions. This flexibility is made possible through constant stress on specific historical situations and activities. Thus, as another commentator has pointed out, liberation is never to be taken in the abstract, but always "in regard to this or that situation of oppression to which Christ bears witness. Therefore, it is not only a question of revealing the social and political implications of the gospel in regard to this or that actual situation, but of making effective participation in the process of liberation the occasion for verifying theological discourse."[28] The need for participation, involvement, and action here and now is thus central to the synthesis Liberation Theology offers to contemporary Latin American Catholics.

With notable modifications concerning political action, these themes are also visible in the Evangelical-Pastoral position, which is more or less identical with the "center" position outlined in chapter 2. In that discussion, I suggested that labels like center (and left and right as well) are inadequate and misleading, since they are taken from political milieux and applied directly to religious motivations and circumstances with insufficient attention to the special characteristics of these situations. "Center" is a par-

---

[27] Segundo, "Capitalism-Socialism," p. 112. Brian Smith sums it up well, noting that, for this position, "salvation involves more than personal immortality, but is associated with struggle for liberation from historical patterns of oppression in this world, and Christian love requires solidarity with the poor amidst class conflict to achieve this. Distinctions between sacred and profane spheres of action are eliminated in this new theological framework, as are lines between religious and political responsibility. The locus for grace and redemption is situated in historical movements aiming at greater freedom and equality, and the function of the church is to act as a community of liberation intimately involved with these forces and to articulate from within these movements the deeper religious meaning that they have" ("Church and Political Change in Chile," p. 73).

[28] Geffré, "Editorial," p. 11.

ticularly weak analytical term, for it makes this position seem largely residual, a byproduct of the defense of Church institutions against attacks from radicals and reactionaries alike. By using the term "Evangelical-Pastoral," I want to indicate more precisely the religious sources of its own genuine dynamism, and point more clearly to the kinds of social and political expressions this stance generates. This general perspective on religion and society was well articulated at the Third General Conference of Latin American Bishops, held in Puebla, Mexico, in early 1979. Puebla was intended to review and evaluate the decade since Medellín and chart a course for the future. Hence, a look at Puebla should provide considerable insight into the kind of synthesis of religion and politics now emerging in the central institutions of the Church.[29]

Debates at Puebla were sharp and often divisive, and the documents themselves are occasionally ambiguous and contradictory, but nevertheless a number of central themes emerged there which sharpen the outlines of the Evangelical-Pastoral synthesis. Four points stand out: first, a stress on unity, with action to be contained within the institutional structures of the Church as guided by its authoritative leaders, the bishops; second, a related stress on building community, fraternity, and a sense of belonging in the Church, particularly through the creation of vigorous "ecclesial base communities"; third, a concern for revitalizing the content and delivery of the gospel message; and fourth, disengagement from direct, partisan politics in favor of a more general stress on highlighting and denouncing injustice, creating vital Christian communities and commitments, and thus moving others (primarily lay people) to action. The critical insights into Latin American society and politics developed since Medellín are not rejected, but rather reaffirmed as part of a broad "preferential option for the poor."[30]

[29] The Puebla meetings took place after the research for this book was substantially completed. The analyses and conclusions advanced here are thus independent of Puebla, although I believe they are confirmed by it. This situation, plus limitations of time and space, make any comprehensive review of Puebla impossible here. However, like Medellín, Puebla has generated a vast and growing critical literature. Some useful works include Berryman, "What Happened at Puebla"; Poblete, "From Medellín to Puebla"; Wilde, "Ten Years of Change in the Church"; and Sanders, *The Puebla Conference.*

[30] The ambiguities of Puebla are heightened by the negotiation and com-

CONCLUSIONS

At Puebla, the need for unity in the Church was stressed, and the role of bishops as authoritative leaders—symbols and creators of that unity—was given great emphasis. Bishops give continuity and authenticity to faith and action by linking them directly to the teachings and legacy of Christ and the Apostles. Contemporary issues and experiences are thus fitted into a long Christian tradition. Moreover, maintenance of explicit ties to the bishops ensures that actions by believers will be contained within the institutional structures of the Church. The bishops want to avoid having others act in the name of the Church. Thus, institutional unity is stressed as a way of binding the Catholic community as a whole to central transcendental values while preserving the possibility of a creative and independent participation in social and political affairs.[31]

The Puebla documents are distinctive in their sustained effort to remain sensitive to urgent social and political issues while rooting perspectives in these areas in a renewed sense of religious community and spiritual values. Greater participation, involvement, and an enhanced sense of belonging to the Church as a community are at once goals and means: they are seen as good in themselves, and also as a path to a renewed sense of identity and commitment. In this sense, Puebla takes a new look inward, reaffirming traditional Christian values of fraternity, solidarity, and community in the context of creating new structures to nur-

---

promise during the preparation of the texts. The documents went through several stages: a "predocument" setting out themes and issues was circulated in advance to the national bishops' conferences; a "working document" was then prepared incorporating comments, criticisms, and objections (which were numerous); and the final texts themselves, which are quite different in tone and substance from the original "predocument," were finally published. Berryman ("What Happened at Puebla") argues that the "predocument" represented the thinking of those in control of CELAM, who wanted to pull back from the activism and commitments of the post-Medellín period. Although they controlled the machinery of the conference, these bishops could not head off the modifications proposed at the meetings themselves. The result is a compromise, with acceptance and legitimation of many Liberation Theology themes balanced against a flat, explicit rejection of the categories and positions of more "radical" theologians.

[31] The predocument draws an explicit link between orthodoxy and orthopraxis, tying legitimate forms of thought and faith to their expression in sanctioned modes of action. CELAM, *La evangelización en el presente y en el futuro de America Latina* . . . par. 544, p. 110.

ture and sustain them. Puebla's extensive praise for the ecclesial base communities now rapidly spreading throughout Latin America is a case in point. Such communities are to be promoted and explicitly tied to older Church structures, such as dioceses and parishes. In this way the bishops hope to stimulate the creation of small, homogeneous, and intense islands of community within existing structures and yet ensure that such new groups become primarily communities for living Christian values and for spreading the gospel message, not simply tools for social action or political manipulation.[32]

Despite these cautions, religious faith and the experience of community are not divorced from social and political issues by Puebla. Rather, the commitment to social justice is grounded in a concept of community itself as a structure of sharing, solidarity, and common experience.

> The love of God which gives us basic dignity becomes of necessity a communion of love with all men and of fraternal participation; for us, today, this must take the form of working for justice for the oppressed, liberation of those who need it most. In effect, "One who has no love for the brother he has seen cannot love the God he has not seen" (I John 4, 20). True communion and participation can only exist in this life projected on the very concrete plane of temporal realities. . . . The Gospel should teach us that, in the face of the reality in which we live, in Latin America today one cannot truly love one's brother, and thus love God, without a personal and structural commitment to service to and promotion of the most dispossessed and humiliated groups and strata of society, whatever the consequences which may follow in the realm of these temporal realities.[33]

Evangelization is the great theme of Puebla, and a concern for deepening and spreading the gospel message runs through all the documents. This great stress on evangelization reaffirms the centrality of ethical and spiritual values and more generally reflects

---

[32] Discussion of base communities is scattered throughout the final documents. Some representative discussions are in CELAM, *III Conferencia General del Episcopado Latinoamericano Puebla*, pars. 96-100 (pp. 65-66), and pars. 617-57 (pp. 163-69).

[33] Ibid., par. 327, p. 110.

the bishops' belief that the kind of faith practiced and the quality of community created are central to the ability to fashion authentically liberating and fulfilling forms of action in the first place.

Puebla thus makes community, fraternity, and belonging central to the future of the Latin American Church in a way which helps explain its complex and occasionally ambiguous position on politics. At Puebla, the bishops took an "activation" stance, recognizing the importance of politics but stressing the need for clear and firm distinctions among the roles appropriate for laity and clergy.[34] At least two concepts of politics and political commitment were delineated: a broad politics of the common good and social interest; and a narrow, party politics dedicated to the resolution of particular social, economic, and governmental questions. The Church necessarily joins the first, but must stand apart from the second. Withdrawal from partisan involvement is seen as necessary in order to avoid giving religious legitimacy to political positions and thus "absolutizing" what are limited, debatable issues. Such participation would divide the Christian community along partisan lines.[35]

In this view, power and the making of policy cannot and should not be the goal of Church personnel; such activities should be left to trained and competent lay people. The particular mission and unique qualities of priests and religious find fullest expression in living a faith which allows them to share the situation of the people and in this way help create the solidarity, commitment, and understanding necessary for any common action. This position recalls the stress on contact, sharing, and the identification of secular with religious realities and meanings through shared experience so visible in Cumaná and Valencia. To that stance, Puebla adds a strong sense of Church structure, intended to bind such experiences firmly into the ongoing traditions, organizations, and needs of the Catholic community as a whole.

Ambiguities become apparent with a moment's reflection on the meaning of politics. Although the stress at Puebla was on shared values, experience, and "pastoral action," the bishops

---

[34] "It is especially important in the field of politics to distinguish what corresponds to laity, to religious, and to ministers of the unity of the Church, the bishop and his priests" (ibid., par. 520, p. 143).

[35] Important discussions on politics appear in ibid., pars. 521-30, pp. 144-46.

clearly recognized that "pastoral" and "political" are no longer neatly separable categories: political meaning may be given to pastoral action by those involved and by external observers as well. In such highly charged contexts, the bishops find it particularly important to define an autonomous course for the Church in politics. Automatic identification with any regime, ideology, or public position is to be avoided. Indeed, throughout the documents the bishops consistently reject Marxism, liberal capitalism, and the national security doctrine as alternatives for Latin America. They assert the Church's independent right to denounce injustice and to criticize any social or political situation.[36] Such criticism is grounded on the Church's "preferential option for the poor" (the title of one chapter in the final documents) and expressed through a vision of Latin American society as characterized by "structural conflict"—that is, a society where poverty, misery, and oppression are the inevitable products of the existing structures of power.[37]

This combination of partisan disengagement with positive recognition of the need for commitment and action on behalf of the poor and weak is characteristic of Puebla, and it highlights the complexity of the relation between religion and politics visible throughout this book. Avoiding initiatives which start from explicitly partisan and political motives will allow the Church, in this view, to remain truer to its central message and freer in the long run to pursue its goals. Freedom from explicit ties and commitments thus makes possible a *public* role which, while nonpartisan, is nonetheless political in the broad sense of politics advanced in these pages. The distinction is fine, and many in Latin

---

[36] A good example is the discussion in ibid., pars. 542-49, p. 149. Marxism is especially threatening, given the recent experiences of Christians for Socialism in Chile. The bishops were anxious to avoid seeing religious categories dissolve into political commitments, and they repeat the criticism of Marxist influence in the Church noted in chapter 2, above. Thus, "We must note here the risk of theological reflection becoming ideological, when it is carried out from the basis of a praxis which resorts to Marxist analysis. The consequences are complete politicization of Christian existence, dissolution of the language of faith in that of the social sciences, and the emptying of the transcendental dimension of Christian salvation" (ibid., par. 545, p. 149).

[37] The bishops recognize that this position has brought division, conflict, and criticism to the Church, but see these as the necessary price of genuine commitment. Ibid., pars. 1135-39, pp. 238-39.

America reject it as meaningless. But it must be taken seriously, as it reflects an attempt to chart a creative and autonomous course for the Church. In their *Message to the People of Latin America*, which introduces the Puebla documents, the bishops sum up their perspective, and their unique contribution, as a "word of faith, hope, and charity." They ask:

> What have we to offer you in the midst of the grave and complex problems of our epoch? . . .
>
> Dear brothers: Once again we wish to declare that, in treating social, economic, and political problems, we do so not as masters of the material, as scientists, but from a pastoral perspective, as interpreters for our peoples, confidants of their desires, especially those of the most humble, the great majority of Latin American society. . . . Our hope is to build, day by day, the reality of our true destiny. Thus, the men of this continent, objects of our pastoral concerns, hold an essential significance for the Church, because Jesus Christ assumed humanity in its real conditions, with the exception of sin. And in so doing, He took on as well the immanent and transcendent vocation of all men.
>
> The man who struggles, suffers, and at times despairs is never discouraged and wants, above all, to live the full meaning of his divine filiation. For this, it is important that his rights be recognized, that his life not become an abomination, that nature, the work of God, not be devastated contrary to his legitimate aspirations.
>
> What concerns us as pastors is the integral proclamation of the truth about Jesus Christ, about the nature and mission of the Church, about the dignity and destiny of man.[38]

The four syntheses reviewed here offer Latin American Catholics alternative ways of seeing the world, while advancing a series of concrete proposals about how to act and what to do. Moving from interpretation to action leads me to some final considerations on the future of religion and politics both in Latin America generally and in the specific nations and communities of special concern here.

[38] Ibid., pp. 40-41.

RELIGION AND POLITICS: POSSIBLE FUTURES

The sources, patterns, and likely points of contact between religion and politics can be isolated, in general terms, and projected into the future. In both religion and politics, the processes of change run parallel. On the religious side, the transformation and extension of pastoral action, linked in one of several possible ways to new concerns for social action, will clearly have major political repercussions. This general development would have less notable political consequences were it not for the growth, extension, and hardening of authoritarian ideologies and state machines throughout the area. The heavy stress on security and order so visible in these regimes makes *any* action a political threat. Authoritarian regimes all over Latin America are deeply hostile to any socially oriented pastoral action going beyond traditional charity. Indeed, even charity has become suspect in many cases, if its recipients include "subversives." This pattern of growing conflict is visible throughout Latin America. But what of Venezuela and Colombia?

On the contemporary Latin American scene, Venezuela and Colombia stand out as exceptions to the trend of authoritarianism and military rule. They are relatively free, open societies where social, political, and religious action is, on the whole, untrammeled. Our two nations thus offer a kind of laboratory in the Latin American context in which to examine the way new trends in the Church affect organization and action in democratic settings. What does the future hold here?

Compared with the continent as a whole, Venezuela and Colombia will clearly experience less tension. This means both lower levels of conflict (fewer incidents, though incidents will always occur) and conflicts of a different nature and tone. Since the political process remains relatively open in each country, political issues are less likely to migrate to and be encapsulated by Church-State confrontations. Other outlets are available and will be used. But the new forms of thought and commitment and the new styles of action so visible in the Latin American Church are of course present in both Venezuela and Colombia, and it is interesting to speculate here on the *direction* these forces will take in each case—to give flesh to the "nature and tone" just mentioned.

CONCLUSIONS

In Colombia, the next ten or fifteen years will see the Church push vigorously to regain a position of renewed institutional strength, combined with active social criticism. No one should be misled any longer by the traditional conservative image of the Colombian Catholic Church. Its leaders are actively concerned to promote social change, and these concerns will be expressed in increasingly penetrating social criticism, which forms an integral part of the Church's overall drive for the re-Christianization of Colombia. In my view, the key characteristics of the Colombian case lie not in the *content* of its social position, but rather in the way this position is put forward, and in the overall directing and orienting role the Church seeks. Combining "advanced" social positions with institutional vigor and a renewed insistence on an authoritative role for the Church as commentator and guide on all kinds of issues, the Colombian Church will strive once again for a position of vast social influence and leadership. Institutional strengthening and a stress on more effective delivery of the gospel message are central to this strategy, for they provide a concrete basis (through organizations and through revivified lines of contact between parish, group, and bishop) to ensure that such "influence" is not confined to words alone, but leads rather to action.

The Venezuelan bishops have more modest aspirations. They combine less "advanced" social positions with a much simpler and more open approach to organization, an approach which "fits" the Venezuelan context well. Thus, in most cases the leaders of the Venezuelan Church are content to work for expanded human contact of one kind or another, leaving broad questions of ideological orientation to be set in more conventional terms: the stress will continue to be on practice. Attempts to strengthen the organizational structures of the Venezuelan Church are being made, but their significance is limited both by available resources and because their general goal is more one of internal coordination than renewed, vigorous projection into national life.

The leaders and the structures of the Church in both Colombia and Venezuela are deeply involved in national life, and their current orientation and likely futures reflect a double-edged process of growth and change. On the one hand, each Church moves toward a vision of national society which fits both personal and institutional experience: each works with a vision of national life as a continuum of past, present, and future. Yet while the individual Churches shape their actions to fit the kind of society they see and hope to build, more is involved here than mere reflection of such social images. Religious belief and action are not derivative; they are paradigmatic, reaching out to shape thought and action in all areas of life. Thus, while Venezuelans and Colombians mold their efforts to the society in which they live, at the same time these energies are fitted to a vision of the Church and to a sense of purpose and motivation springing from religious experience and commitment themselves. Religion and politics, society and Church, move and change together, calling believers and activists, leaders and rank and file alike to a life in which Heaven and earth are joined, faith and hope made real.

Bibliography

Abbot, Walter M., ed. *The Documents of Vatican II*. New York: Association Press and America Press, 1966.

Alexander, Robert. *The Venezuelan Democratic Revolution*. New Brunswick: Rutgers University Press, 1964.

Allardt, Erik. "Implications of Within-Nation Variations and Regional Imbalances for Cross-National Research." In R. Merrit and S. Rokkan, eds., *Comparing Nations: The Use of Quantitative Data in Cross-National Research*, pp. 337-48. New Haven: Yale University Press, 1966.

Alonso, Isidoro; Luzardo, Medardo; Garrido, Ginés; and Oriol, José. *La iglesia en Venezuela y Ecuador*. Bogotá: FERES, 1962.

Alves, Rubem. "Christian Realism: Ideology of the Establishment." *Christianity and Crisis* 33:15 (17 Sept. 1973), pp. 173-76.

Antoine, Charles. *Church and Power in Brazil*. Maryknoll: Orbis Books, 1973.

Arenas Reyes, Jaime. *La guerrilla por dentro: análisis del E.L.N. colombiano*. Bogotá: Ediciones Tercer Mundo, 1971.

Assmann, Hugo. *Opresión-liberación desafío a los cristianos*. Montevideo: Tierra Nueva, 1971.

———. "Reflexiones teológicas a nivel táctico-estratégico." In Camilo Moncada, ed., *Liberación en América Latina*, pp. 69-72. Bogotá: Servicio de Comunicación Social, 1971.

———. *Theology for a Nomad Church*. Maryknoll: Orbis Books, 1976.

Avila, Rafael. *La liberación*. Bogotá: Editorial Voluntad, 1971.

———. *Teologia, evangelización, y liberación*. Bogotá: Ediciones Paulinas, 1973.

Avineri, Shlomo. *The Social and Political Thought of Karl Marx*. Cambridge: Cambridge University Press, 1968.

Bachrach, Peter, and Baratz, Morton S. "Decisions and Non-Decisions: An Analytical Framework." *American Political Science Review* 56:3 (Sept. 1963), pp. 632-43.

———. "Two Faces of Power." *American Political Science Review* 56:4 (Dec. 1962), pp. 947-52.

Bailey, David C. *¡Viva Cristo Rey! The Cristero Rebellion and the Church-State Conflict in Mexico*. Austin: University of Texas Press, 1974.

Barreiro, Alvaro. "Catequesis y desarrollo: justificación teológica de una catequesis liberadora." *Encuentro* [Bogotá] 18-19 (1971), pp. 31-43.

Bellah, Robert N. *Beyond Belief: Essays on Religion in a Post-Traditional World* New York: Harper & Row, 1970.

———. "Religious Evolution." In Roland Robertson, ed., *Sociology of Religion*, pp. 262-92. Baltimore: Penguin Books, Pelican, 1969.

Berger, Peter. *The Noise of Solemn Assemblies*. Garden City: Doubleday & Co., 1961.

———. *A Rumor of Angels*. Garden City: Doubleday & Co., 1968.

———. *The Sacred Canopy: Elements of A Sociological Theory of Religion*. Garden City: Doubleday & Co., 1967.

Berger, Peter; Berger, Brigitte; and Kellner, Hansfried. *The Homeless Mind: Modernization and Consciousness*. New York: Random House, Vintage Books, 1974.

Berger, Peter, and Luckmann, Thomas. *The Social Construction of Reality*. New York: Doubleday & Co., Anchor Books, 1967.

Bernal Alarcón, Hernando. *Educación fundamental integral y medios de comunicación social: el uso sistemático de los medios masivos de comunicación en programas de desarrollo*. Bogotá: Editorial los Andes, 1971.

Bernal Escobar, Alejandro; Benoit, Andres; Corredor, Berta; and Wust, Isaac. *La educación en Colombia*. Bogotá: CIS, 1965.

Bernal Jiménez, Rafael. *La cuestión social y la lucha de clases: el liberalismo, el comunismo, el fascismo, y el orden social cristiano*. Bogotá: Editorial Centro, 1940.

Berryman, Phillip. "Latin American Liberation Theology." *Theological Studies* 34:3 (Sept. 1973), pp. 357-95.

———. "What Happened at Puebla." In Daniel H. Levine, ed., *Churches and Politics in Latin America*, pp. 55-86. Beverly Hills: SAGE Publications, 1980.

Bigo, Pierre. "Los integrismos." *Tierra Nueva* 21 (Apr. 1977), pp. 5-9.

Birnbaum, Norman. "Beyond Marx in the Sociology of Religion." In Charles Y. Glock and Phillip E. Hammond, eds., *Beyond the Classics? Essays in the Scientific Study of Religion*, pp. 3-70. New York: Harper & Row, 1973.

Bond, Robert. *Contemporary Venezuela and Its Role in International Affairs*. New York: New York University Press, 1977.

Bonilla, Victor Daniel. *Servants of God or Masters of Men*. Baltimore: Penguin Books, Pelican, 1972.

Broderick, Walter J. *Camilo Torres*. Garden City: Doubleday & Co., 1975.

Bruneau, Thomas C. "Basic Christian Communities in Latin America: Their Nature and Significance (especially in Brazil)." In Daniel H.

Levine, ed., *Churches and Politics in Latin America*, pp. 225-37. Beverly Hills: SAGE Publications, 1980.

——. *The Political Transformation of the Brazilian Catholic Church*. New York: Cambridge University Press, 1974.

——. "Power and Influence: An Analysis of the Church in Latin America and the Case of Brazil." *Latin American Research Review* 8:2 (Summer 1973), pp. 25-52.

——. "Religiosity and Politicization in Brazil: The Church in an Authoritarian Regime." Book MS.

Bühlmann, Walbert. *The Coming of the Third Church*. Maryknoll: Orbis Books, 1976.

Caballero Calderon, Eduardo. *El Cristo de espaldas*. Medellín: Editorial Bedout, n.d.

——. *Historia privada de los colombianos*. Bogotá, 1960.

Cadavid, Ivan. *Los fueros de la iglesia ante el liberalismo y el conservatismo en Colombia*. Medellín: Editorial Bedout, 1955.

Calvo, Roberto. "The Church and the Doctrine of National Security." *Journal of Interamerican Studies and World Affairs* 21:1 (Feb. 1979), pp. 69-88.

Camacho de Pinto, Teresa. *Colombia: el proceso de urbanización y sus factores relacionados*. Tunja: Ediciones La Rana y el Aguila, 1970.

Câmara, Gabriel. *Itinerario de liberación para educadores*. Bogotá: Asociación de Publicaciones Educativas, 1972.

Câmara, Helder. *The Church and Colonialism: The Betrayal of the Third World*. Danville, N.J.: Sheed & Ward, 1969.

——. *Revolution Through Peace*. New York: Harper & Row, Colophon Books, 1972.

Cameron, J. M. *Images of Authority: A Consideration of the Concepts of Regnum and Sacerdotium*. New Haven: Yale University Press, 1966.

Cannon, Mark; Fosler, R. Scott; and Witherspoon, Robert. *Urban Government for Valencia, Venezuela*. New York: Praeger Publishers, 1973.

Caporale, Rocco. *Vatican II: Last of the Councils*. Baltimore: Helicon Press, 1964.

Cardenal, Ernesto. *The Gospel in Solentiname*. 3 vols. Maryknoll: Orbis Books, 1976, 1978, 1979.

Cardona, Ramiro. *Las migraciones internas*. Bogotá: Editorial Andes, 1972.

Cardoso, Fernando Henrique. *Estado y sociedad en América Latina*. Buenos Aires: Ediciones Nueva Visión, 1972.

Castillo Bernal, Gonzalo. "Teófilo escribano de frente." *El Tiempo*. 12 March 1972.

Castrillón, Darío. "Politica y pastoral." *Tierra Nueva* 6 (July 1973), pp. 89-96.

CEDIAL. *Desarrollo y revolución—iglesia y liberación (bibliografía). Primera parte: "desarrollo y revolución"* (*con comentario bibliográfico de R. Jiménez*). *Segunda parte: "iglesia y liberación"* (*con comentario bibliográfico de R. Vekemans*). Bogotá: CEDIAL, 1973.

———. *Seguridad nacional y temas conexos: bibliografía. Documento de trabajo (borrador)*. Bogotá: CEDIAL, 1977.

CELAM. *The Church in the Present Day Transformation of Latin America in the Light of the Council*. 2 vols. Bogotá: CELAM, 1970.

———. *La evangelización en el presente y en el futuro de America Latina, Puebla, México, 1978: preparación documento de consulta a las conferencias episcopales*. Bogotá: CELAM, 1979.

———. *Seminarios*. Bogotá: Secretario Ejecutivo del Denim, 1971.

———. *III Conferencia General del Episcopado Latino Americano, Puebla: documento de trabajo*. Bogotá: CELAM, 1978.

———. *III Conferencia General del Episcopado Latino Americano, Puebla: la evangelización en el presente y en el futuro de América Latina*. Bogotá: CELAM, 1979.

Centro Arquidiocesano de Pastoral Juvenil. "La crisis en la educación media." Mimeographed. Caracas: Centro Arquidiocesano de Pastoral Juvenil, May 1971.

Cetrulo, Ricardo. "Conclusión crítica." In J. J. Rossi, ed., *Iglesia latinoamericana, ¿protesta o profecía?* pp. 403-24. Avellaneda, Argentina: Ediciones Búsqueda, 1969.

Chilean Episcopal Conference. "Our Life as a Nation." *LADOC* 7:6 (July-August, 1977), pp. 1-14.

CISOR. *Anuario de la iglesia católica en Venezuela*. Caracas: CISOR, 1969.

———. *Directorio de la iglesia católica en Venezuela. 1972-1973*. Caracas: CISOR, 1972.

———. *Iglesia y sociedad*. Mimeographed. Caracas: CISOR, 1973.

———. *Religiosidad popular en Venezuela: Estudio Preliminar*. Caracas: CISOR, 1970.

Cobb, Roger; Ross, Jennie Keith; and Ross, Marc H. "Agenda Building as a Comparative Political Process." *American Political Science Review* 70:1 (Mar. 1976), pp. 126-38.

Coleman, John. "Civil Religion and Liberation Theology in North America." In Sergio Torres and John Eagleson, eds., *Theology in the Americas*, pp. 113-38. Maryknoll: Orbis Books, 1976.

Coles, Robert, and Berrigan, Daniel. *The Geography of Faith*. Boston: Beacon Press, 1971.

Colmenares Díaz, Luis. *La espada y el incensario: la iglesia bajo Pérez Jiménez*. Caracas, 1961.

Colombia, República de [Departamento Administrativo Nacional de Estadística]. *Annario general de estadística, 1966-1967: población, asistencia social e higiene, tomo I.* Bogotá: Litografía Colombia.

———. *XIII censo nacional de población resúmen general (15 de julio de 1964).* Bogotá: Imprenta Nacional, 1967.

Comblin, José. *The Church and the National Security State.* Maryknoll: Orbis Books, 1979.

———. "The Church in Latin America After Vatican II." *LADOC* 7:3 (Jan.-Feb. 1977), pp. 1-18.

Comisión Venezolana de Justicia y Paz. *Justicia y paz: el subdesarrollo latinoamericano a la luz de la populorum progressio.* Caracas: Comisión Venezolana de Justicia y Paz, 1968.

Comisiones Episcopales de Educación y Catequesis de Colombia. *Programas nacionales de catequesis para secundaria: guía general.* Bogotá: SPEC, 1971.

Confederación Latinoamericana de Reliosos (CLAR). *Estudio sociográfico de los religiosos y las religosas en América Latina.* Bogotá: Secretariado General de la CLAR, 1971.

———. *La vida religiosa en América Latina: respuestas y compromisos.* Bogotá: Secretariado General de la CLAR, 1969.

Conferencia Episcopal de Colombia. *Conferencias episcopales de Colombia.* Vol. 1, 1908-1953; vol. 2, 1954-1960. Bogotá: Editorial El Catolicismo, 1956, 1960.

———. *Identidad cristiana en la acción por la justicia.* Bogotá: SPEC, 1976.

———. *La iglesia ante el cambio.* Bogotá: SPEC, 1969.

———. *La justicia en el mundo: textos sinodales, aportes de la iglesia colombiana.* Bogotá: SPEC, 1972.

Conferencia Episcopal Venezolana. *Ante la situación social.* Caracas: Secretariado Permanente del Episcopado Venezolano, 1974.

———. *Carta del episcopado venezolano a sus sacerdotes.* Caracas: Secretariado Permanente del Episcopado Venezolano, 1969.

———. *Carta pastoral colectiva del episcopado venezolano: instrucción sobre el primer aniversario de la encíclica "Humanae vitae."* La Macarena—Los Teques: Secretariado Permanente del Episcopado Venezolano, 1969.

———. *Carta pastoral colectiva que el episcopado de Venezuela dirige a su muy venerable clero y amadísimos fieles, en la oportunidad de los nuevos horizontes que se abren a la patria después de la caída del régimen imperante en enero de 1958.* Caracas, 15 June 1958.

———. *Carta pastoral colectiva sobre los problemas planteados a la educación católica en el país: dirigida al pueblo con motivo de las conferencias extraordinarias, celebradas en Caracas, de 25 de agosto a 30 de septiembre de 1947.* Caracas: Editorial Venezuela, 1947.

BIBLIOGRAPHY

Conferencia Episcopal Venezolana. *Conclusiones aprobados en la Conferencia Nacional del Episcopado Venezolano, celebrada en la Ciudad de Los Teques, del día 1 hasta el día 21 del mes de junto de 1966.* Caracas: Secretariado Permanente del Episcopado Venezolano, 1966.

———. *Conclusiones, Declaraciones, y Acuerdos del Episcopado Venezolano, tomados durante la Asamblea Plenaria Ordinaria, celebrada en el Seminario de San José de El Hatillo del 27 de agosto al 5 de septiembre de 1970.* Caracas: Secretariado Permanente del Episcopado Venezolano, 1970.

———. *Iglesia y política.* Caracas: Secretariado Permanente del Episcopado Venezolano, 1973.

———. *Normas para el Movimiento de Cursillos de Cristiandad en Venezuela.* Caracas: Trípode, 1970.

Congar, Yves. "Le développement historique de l'autorité dans l'église: éléments pour la réflexion chrétienne." In J. Todd, ed., *Problèmes de l'autorité*, pp. 145-82. Paris: Editions du Cerf, 1962.

Corrêa de Oliveira, Plinio. *Revolución y contra-revolución.* Buenos Aires: Tradición, Familia, y Propiedad, 1970.

———. *Trasbordo ideológico inadvertido y diálogo.* Madrid: C.I.O., 1971.

Costa Pinto, L. A. *Transición social en Colombia.* Bogotá: Ediciones Tercer Mundo, 1970.

Cox, Harvey. *The Secular City.* Harmondsworth: Penguin Books, 1968.

———. *The Seduction of the Spirit: The Use and Misuse of Peoples' Religion.* New York: Simon & Schuster, 1973.

Crahan, Margaret. "Salvation Through Christ or Marx: Religion in Revolutionary Cuba." *Journal of Interamerican Studies and World Affairs* 21:1 (Feb. 1979), pp. 156-84.

Davies, J. G. *Christians, Politics, and Violent Revolution.* Maryknoll: Orbis Books, 1976.

De Castro Mayer, Antonio; De Proença Sigaud, Geraldo; Corrêa de Oliveira, Plinio; and Mendonça de Freitas, Luis. *Reforma agraria: cuestión de conciencia.* Bogotá: Asociación Colombiana Para la Defensa del Derecho Natural, 1971.

De Kadt, Emmanuel. *Catholic Radicals in Brazil.* New York: Oxford University Press, 1970.

———. "Church, Society, and Development in Latin America." *Journal of Development Studies* 8:1 (Oct. 1971), pp. 23-43.

———. "Paternalism and Populism: Catholicism in Latin America." *Journal of Contemporary History* 2:4 (Oct. 1967), pp. 89-106.

Della Cava, Ralph. "Catholicism and Society in Twentieth Century Brazil." *Latin American Research Review* 11:2 (1976), pp. 7-50.

———. *Miracle at Joaseiro.* New York: Columbia University Press, 1970.

Dent, David W. "Oligarchy and Power Structure in Urban Colombia: The Case of Cali." *Journal of Latin American Studies* 6:1 (May 1974), pp. 113-33.

D'Entrèves, A. P. *The Medieval Contribution to Political Thought.* New York: Humanities Press, 1959.

De Santa Ana, Julio. *El desafío de los pobres a la iglesia.* San José, Costa Rica: EDUCA, 1977.

De Toqueville, Alexis. *Democracy in America.* Vol. 2. New York: Schocken Books, 1961.

Dix, Robert. *Colombia: The Political Dimensions of Change.* New Haven: Yale University Press, 1966.

Dodson, Michael. "The Christian Left in Latin American Politics." *Journal of Interamerican Studies and World Affairs* 21:1 (Feb. 1979), pp. 45-68.

Doyle, Joseph J. "Venezuela 1958: Transition From Dictatorship to Democracy." Ph.D. dissertation, George Washington University, 1967.

Drake, George. "Elites and Voluntary Associations: A Study of Community Power in Manizales, Colombia." Ph.D. dissertation, University of Wisconsin-Madison, 1970.

Dulles, Avery. *Models of the Church.* New York: Doubleday & Co., 1974.

Dussel, Enrique. *Ethics and the Theology of Liberation.* Maryknoll: Orbis Books, 1978.

———. *Hipotesis para una historia de la iglesia en América Latina.* Barcelona: Editorial Estela, 1967.

———. *History and the Theology of Liberation.* Maryknoll: Orbis Books, 1976.

———. "El tercerismo eclesial: táctica política y mecanismo ideológico." In Elsa Támez and Saúl Trinidad, eds., *Capitalismo: Violencia y anti-vida. La opresión de las mayorías y la domesticación de los dioses, Tomo I*, pp. 315-27. San José, Costa Rica: EDUCA, 1978.

Eagleson, John, ed. *Christians and Socialism: Documentation of the Christians for Socialism Movement in Latin America.* Maryknoll: Orbis Books, 1975.

Eagleson, John, and Scharper, Philip, eds. *Puebla and Beyond.* Maryknoll: Orbis Books, 1979.

Eckstein, Susan. *The Poverty of Revolution: The State and the Urban Poor in Mexico.* Princeton: Princeton University Press, 1978.

Einaudi, Luigi; Maullin, Richard; Stepan, Alfred; and Fleet, Michael. *Latin American Institutional Development: The Changing Catholic Church.* Santa Monica: RAND Corporation, 1969.

EPICA. *Reflections and Problems of a Church Being Born Among the*

People. Washington: Ecumenical Program for Interamerican Communication and Action (EPICA), 1978.

Fals-Borda, Orlando. *Subversion and Social Change in Colombia*. New York: Columbia University Press, 1969.

Flora, Cornelia B. *Pentecostalism in Colombia: Baptism by Fire and Spirit*. Rutherford, N.J.: Fairleigh Dickinson University Press, 1976.

Floridi, Alexis, and Stiefbold, Annette. *The Uncertain Alliance: The Catholic Church and Organized Labor in Latin America*. Miami: Center for Advanced International Studies, 1973.

Forman, Shepard. *The Brazilian Peasantry*. New York: Columbia University Press, 1975.

———. "The Significance of Participation: Peasants in the Politics of Brazil." In John Booth and Mitchell Seligson, eds., *Political Participation in Latin America. Volume II: Politics and the Poor*, pp. 36-50. New York: Holmes & Meier Publishers, 1979.

Freire, Paulo. *Education for a Critical Consciousness*. New York: Seabury Press, 1974.

———. *Las iglesias, la educación, y el proceso de liberación humana en la historia*. Buenos Aires: Asociación Editorial La Aurora, 1974.

———. *Pedagogy of the Oppressed*. New York: Seabury Press, 1968.

Gaitán, Aquilino. *Por qué cayó el Partido Conservador*. Bogotá: Talleres "Mundo al Día," 1935.

Galilea, Segundo. *¿A los pobres se les anuncia el evangelio?* Bogotá: CELAM, 1972.

———. "Liberation as an Encounter with Politics and Contemplation." In Claude Geffré and Gustavo Gutierrez, eds., *The Mystical and Political Dimensions of the Christian Faith*, pp. 19-33. New York: Herder & Herder.

Garces, Joan. "La continuidad del sistema a través del cambio: el sistema bipartidista de Colombia." *Revista latinoamericana de sociología* 6:1 (Mar. 1970), pp. 7-59.

García Márquez, Gabriel. *One Hundred Years of Solitude*. New York: Avon Books, 1971.

Geertz, Clifford. *The Interpretation of Cultures*. New York: Basic Books, 1973.

———. *Islam Observed: Religious Development in Morocco and Indonesia*. Chicago: University of Chicago Press, Phoenix Books, 1973.

———. "Religion as a Cultural System." In M. Banton, ed., *Anthropological Approaches to the Study of Religion*, pp. 1-46. London: Travistock, 1968.

———. "Thick Description: Toward an Interpretive Theory of Culture." In Clifford Geertz, *The Interpretation of Cultures*, pp. 3-22. New York: Basic Books, 1973.

Geffré, Claude. "Editorial: A Prophetic Theology." In Claude Geffré and Gustavo Gutierrez, eds., *The Mystical and Political Dimensions of the Christian Faith*, pp. 7-15. New York: Herder & Herder, 1974.

Geffré, Claude, and Gutierrez, Gustavo, eds. *The Mystical and Political Dimensions of the Christian Faith*. New York: Herder & Herder, 1974.

Gheerbrant, Alain, ed. *The Rebel Church in Latin America*. Baltimore: Penguin Books, 1974.

Gilfeather, Katherine A. "Women Religious, the Poor, and the Institutional Church in Chile." *Journal of Interamerican Studies and World Affairs* 21:1 (Feb. 1979), pp. 129-55.

Gilhodes, Pierre. "Agrarian Struggles in Colombia." In Rodolfo Stavehagen, ed., *Agrarian Problems and Peasant Movements in Latin America*, pp. 407-52. Garden City: Doubleday & Co., Anchor Books, 1970.

Glock, Charles, and Hammond, Phillip E. *Beyond the Classics? Essays in the Scientific Study of Religion*. New York: Harper & Row, 1973.

Gómez, Laureano. *Desde el Exilio*. N.p., n.d.

Gómez Hurtado, Enrique. *Respuestas*. Bogotá: Editorial Revista Colombiana, 1971.

Gott, Richard. *Guerrillas in Latin America*. Garden City: Doubleday & Co., Anchor Books, 1972.

Gremillion, Joseph, ed. *The Gospel of Peace and Justice: Catholic Social Teaching Since Pope John*. Maryknoll: Orbis Books, 1976.

Gutierrez, Gustavo. "Liberation, Theology, and Proclamation." In Claude Geffré and Gustavo Gutierrez, eds., *The Mystical and Political Dimensions of the Christian Faith*, pp. 57-77. New York: Herder & Herder, 1974.

———. *A Theology of Liberation: History, Politics, and Salvation*. Maryknoll: Orbis Books, 1973.

Guzmán Campos, German. *La violencia en Colombia: parte descriptiva*. Cali: Ediciones Progreso, 1968.

Havens, A. Eugene, and Flinn, William L. *Internal Colonialism and Structural Change in Colombia*. New York: Praeger Publishers, 1970.

Hebblethwaite, Peter. *The Runaway Church: Post-Conciliar Growth or Decline*. New York: Seabury Press, 1975.

Henríquez, Luis Eduardo. *Evangelización y pastoral popular*. Caracas: Publicaciones Pastorales, 1969.

———. "Pastoral Care of the Masses and the Elites." In CELAM, *The Church in the Present Day Transformation of Latin America in the Light of the Council*, vol. 1, pp. 179-240. Bogotá: CELAM, 1970.

———. *Testigos de la palabra de Dios*. Madrid: Ediciones Paulinas, 1971.

Hervas, Juan. *Manual de dirigentes de Cursillos de Cristiandad.* Madrid: La Editorial Católica, 1968.
Hinkelammert, Franz J. *Las armas ideológicas de la muerte. El discernimiento de los fetiches: capitalismo y cristianismo.* San José, Costa Rica: EDUCA, 1977.
―――. *Ideología del sometimiento: la iglesia católica chilena frente al golpe, 1973-1974.* San José, Costa Rica: EDUCA, 1977.
Hoskin, Gary. "Power Structure in a Venezuelan Town: The Case of San Cristobal." In Hans-Dieter Evers, ed., *Case Studies in Social Power,* pp. 28-47. Leiden: E. J. Brill, 1969.
Houtart, François, and Rousseau, André. *The Church and Revolution.* Maryknoll: Orbis Books, 1971.
Houtart, François, and Pin, Emile. *The Church and the Latin American Revolution.* New York: Sheed & Ward, 1965.
ICODES. *Aspectos de la religiosidad popular en Colombia.* Bogotá: ICODES, 1970.
Illich, Ivan. "The Powerless Church." In Ivan Illich, *Celebration of Awareness,* pp. 95-104. New York: Doubleday & Co., 1970.
―――. "The Vanishing Clergyman." In Ivan Illich, *Celebration of Awareness,* pp. 69-94. New York: Doubleday & Co., 1970.
Jaramillo Salazar, Pablo. *Epítome de la Ley Concha.* Bogotá: Editorial Pax, 1972.
Jaramillo Uribe, Jaime. *El pensamiento colombiano en el siglo XIX.* Bogotá: Editorial Temis, 1964.
Jiménez, Roberto. *Seguridad nacional y temas conexos: comentario a la bibliografía disponible en América Latina. Documento de trabajo* (borrador). Bogotá: CEDIAL, 1977.
Jiménez Cadena, Gustavo. *Sacerdote y cambio social.* Bogotá: Ediciones Tercer Mundo, 1967.
Jóvenes de Acción. "El joven y la renovación en la iglesia, sociedad, educación: conclusiones finales de la Asamblea General de Jóvenes de Acción." Mimeographed. Caracas, 1970.
―――. "Reflexiones alrededor de la expulsión del P. Francisco Wuytack, por el movimiento 'Jóvenes de Acción.' " Mimeographed, n.d.
Kahl, Joseph. *Modernization, Exploitation, and Dependency in Latin America: Germani, González Casanova, and Cardoso.* New Brunswick, N.J.: Transaction Books, 1976.
Kennedy, John J. "The Legal Status of the Church in Latin America: Some Recent Developments." In Henry Landsberger, ed., *The Church and Social Change in Latin America,* pp. 157-72. Notre Dame: University of Notre Dame Press, 1970.
Kung, Hans. *The Church.* Garden City: Doubleday & Co., 1976.
―――. *Truthfulness: The Future of the Church.* New York: Sheed & Ward, 1968.

Landsberger, Henry, ed. *The Church and Social Change in Latin America*. Notre Dame: University of Notre Dame Press, 1970.

Legión de María. *Informe especial*. Caracas: Senatus de Caracas, Consejo Nacional, 1969.

Leñero Otero, Luis, ed. *Población, iglesia, y cultura: sistemas en conflicto*. Mexico City: IMES-FERES, 1970.

Levine, Daniel H. "Authority in Church and Society: Latin American Models." *Comparative Studies in Society and History* 20:4 (Oct. 1978), pp. 517-44.

―――. "Church Elites in Venezuela and Colombia: Context, Background, and Beliefs." *Latin American Research Review* 14:1 (Spring 1979), pp. 51-79.

―――. *Conflict and Political Change in Venezuela*. Princeton: Princeton University Press, 1973.

―――. "Democracy and the Church in Venezuela." *Journal of Interamerican Studies and World Affairs* 18:1 (Feb. 1976), pp. 3-22.

―――. "Issues in the Study of Culture and Politics: A View From Latin America." *Publius* 4:2 (Spring 1974), pp. 77-104.

―――. "Religion and Politics, Politics and Religion: An Introduction." *Journal of Interamerican Studies and World Affairs* 21:1 (Feb. 1979), pp. 5-29.

―――. "Religion and Politics: Recent Works." *Journal of Inter- Studies and World Affairs* 16:4 (Nov. 1974), pp. 497-507.

―――. "Urbanization in Latin America: Changing Perspectives." *Latin American Research Review* 14:1 (Spring 1979), pp. 170-83.

―――. "Urbanization, Migrants, and Politics in Venezuela." *Journal of Interamerican Studies and World Affairs* 17:3 (Aug. 1975), pp. 358-72.

Levine, Daniel H., ed., *Churches and Politics in Latin America*. Beverly Hills: SAGE Publications, 1980.

Levine, Daniel H., and Wilde, Alexander W. "The Catholic Church, 'Politics,' and Violence: The Colombian Case." *The Review of Politics* 39:2 (Apr. 1977), pp. 220-39.

Lewy, Guenter. *Religion and Revolution*. New York: Oxford University Press, 1974.

Lieuwin, Edwin. *Generals vs. Presidents: Neo-Militarism in Latin America*. New York: Praeger Publishers, 1964.

Linz, Juan, and De Miguel, Amando. "Within-Nation Differences and Comparisons: The Eight Spains." In Richard Merritt and Stein Rokkan, eds., *Comparing Nations: The Use of Quantitative Data in Cross-National Research*, pp. 267-320. New Haven: Yale University Press, 1966.

Lipset, Seymour M., and Rokkan, Stein, eds. *Party Systems and Voter Alignments*. New York: Free Press, 1968.

Londoño, Fernando. *Situación de la educación en Colombia 1971*. Bogotá: CIAS, 1971.
López Trujillo, Alfonso. "A los 10 años de la populorum progressio." *Tierra Nueva* 22 (July 1977), pp. 81-96.
———. "Análisis marxista y liberación cristiana." *Tierra Nueva* 4 (Jan. 1973), pp. 5-43.
———. "El compromiso politico del sacerdote." *Tierra Nueva* 14 (July 1975), pp. 17-53.
———. "El cristiano ante la política." *El Catolicismo* [Bogotá] (Feb. 27, 1972).
———. "La liberación y las liberaciones." *Tierra Nueva* 1 (Apr. 1972), pp. 5-26.
Mabry, Donald J. *Mexico's Acción Nacional: A Catholic Alternative to Revolution*. Syracuse: Syracuse University Press, 1973.
McKenzie, John. *Authority in the Church*. New York: Sheed & Ward, 1966.
Maduro, Otto. *Revelación y revolución*. Mérida, Venezuela: Ediciones del Rectorado, Universidad de los Andes, 1970.
Marcuse, Herbert. "Repressive Tolerance." In Robert P. Wolff et al., *A Critique of Pure Tolerance*, pp. 81-123. Boston: Beacon Press, 1965.
Maritain, Jacques. *True Humanism*. New York: Charles Scribner's Sons, 1938.
Martz, John. *Acción Democrática: Evolution of a Modern Political Party in Venezuela*. Princeton: Princeton University Press, 1966.
———. *Colombia: A Contemporary Political Survey*. Chapel Hill: University of North Carolina Press, 1962.
Martz, John, and Baloyra, Enrique. *Political Attitudes in Venezuela: Societal Cleavages and Political Opinion*. Austin: University of Texas Press, 1979.
Mecham, J. Lloyd. *Church and State in Latin America*. Rev. ed. Chapel Hill: University of North Carolina Press, 1966.
Meissner, William. *The Assault on Authority: Dialogue or Dilemma*. Maryknoll: Orbis Books, 1971.
Merton, Thomas. *Faith and Violence: Christian Teaching and Christian Practice*. Notre Dame: University of Notre Dame Press, 1968.
Methol Ferré, Alberto. "Sobre la actual ideología de la seguridad nacional." In *Dos ensayos sobre seguridad nacional*, 2 vols. Santiago, Chile: Vicaría de Solidaridad, 1977.
Metz, Johannes B. "Prophetic Authority." In J. Moltmann et al., *Religion and Political Society*, pp. 171-209. New York: Harper & Row, 1974.
Meyer, Alfred G. "The Aufhebung of Marxism." *Social Research* 43:2 (Summer 1976), pp. 199-219.

Meyer, Jean. *La cristiada. 1: la guerra de los cristeros. 2: el conflicto entre la iglesia y el estado—1926/1929. 3: los cristeros.* Mexico: Siglo XXI Editores, 1973-74.

Míguez Bonino, José. *Christians and Marxists: The Mutual Challenge to Revolution.* Grand Rapids: William B. Eerdmans Publishing Co., 1976.

Mills, C. Wright. *The Sociological Imagination.* New York: Oxford University Press, 1959.

Miranda, José. *Marx and the Bible: A Critique of the Philosophy of Repression.* Maryknoll: Orbis Books, 1974.

Molina, Gerardo. *Las ideas liberales en Colombia—1849-1914.* Bogotá: Ediciones Tercer Mundo, 1971.

Moncada, Camilo, ed. *Aportes para la liberación.* Bogotá: Editorial Presencia, 1970.

———. *Liberación en América Latina encuentro teológico.* Bogotá: Servicio Colombiano de Comunicación Social, 1971.

Montgomery, Tommie Sue. "Latin American Evangelicals: Oaxtepec and Beyond." In Daniel H. Levine, ed., *Churches and Politics in Latin America,* pp. 87-107. Beverly Hills: SAGE Publications, 1980.

Moreno, Fernando. "Jacques Maritain y la América Latina." *Tierra Nueva* 13 (Apr. 1975), pp. 57-70.

Musto, Stefan A. et al. *Los medios de comunicación social al servicio del desarrollo rural: analisis de eficiencia de "Acción Cultural Popular"—Radio Sutatenza, Colombia.* Bogotá: Editorial los Andes, 1971.

Mutchler, David E. *The Church as a Political Factor in Latin America With Particular Reference to Colombia and Chile.* New York: Praeger Publishers, 1971.

Nieto Rojas, José María. *La batalla contra el comunismo en Colombia.* Bogotá: Empresa Nacional de Publicaciones, 1956.

Ocampo, José Fernando. *Dominio de clase en la ciudad colombiana.* Bogotá: Editorial la Oveja Negra, 1972.

O'Dea, Thomas F. *The Catholic Crisis.* Boston: Beacon Press, 1968.

———. *The Sociology of Religion.* Englewood Cliffs: Prentice-Hall, 1966.

O'Donnell, Guillermo. *Modernization and Bureaucratic Authoritarianism: Studies in South American Society.* Berkeley: Institute of International Studies, 1973.

Parsons, James J. *Antioqueño Colonization in Western Colombia.* Berkeley and Los Angeles: University of California Press, 1968.

Payne, James. *Patterns of Conflict in Colombia.* New Haven: Yale University Press, 1968.

Paz, Nestor. *My Life For My Friends: The Guerrilla Journal of Nestor Paz, Christian.* Maryknoll: Orbis Books, 1975.

Peattie, Lisa R. *The View From the Barrio*. Ann Arbor: University of Michigan Press, 1968.
Pérez, Gustavo. *El problema sacerdotal en Colombia*. Bogotá: CIS, 1962.
Pérez, Gustavo, and Wust, Isaac. *La iglesia en Colombia: estructuras eclesiásticas*. Bogotá: CIS, 1961.
Pérez Morales, Ovidio. *Diaconado permanente: notas acerca de su restauración en Venezuela*. Caracas: Publicaciones Pastorales, 1969.
———. *Fé y desarrollo*. Caracas: Ediciones Paulinas, 1971.
———. *La iglesia: sacramento de unificación universal*. Salamanca: Ediciones Sígueme, 1971.
———. *Liberación-Iglesia-Marxismo*. Caracas: Oficina Latinoamericana de Cursillos de Cristiandad, 1973.
Peruvian Bishops' Commission for Social Action. *Between Honesty and Hope*. Maryknoll: Orbis Books, 1970.
Pierce, Roy. *Contemporary French Political Thought*. New York: Oxford University Press, 1966.
Pineda, Virginia G. de. *Estructura, función, y cambio de la familia en Colombia, Tomo I*. Bogotá: ASCOFAME, 1975.
Pironio, Eduardo. *Iglesia, pueblo de Dios*. Bogotá: Indo America Press Service, 1970.
———. *La iglesia que nace entre nosotros*. Bogotá: Indo America Press Service, 1970.
Poblete, Renato. "From Medellín to Puebla: Notes for Reflection." *Journal of Interamerican Studies and World Affairs* 21:1 (Feb. 1979), pp. 31-44.
Poggi, Gianfranco. *Catholic Action in Italy*. Stanford: Stanford University Press, 1971.
Pope, Liston. *Millhands and Preachers: A Study of Gastonia*. New Haven: Yale University Press, 1942.
Powell, John D. *Political Mobilization of the Venezuelan Peasant*. Cambridge: Harvard University Press, 1971.
Pro Mundi Vita. *Basic Communities in the Church*. Brussels: Pro Mundi Vita Bulletin 62, Sept. 1976.
Putnam, Robert D. *The Beliefs of Politicians*. New Haven: Yale University Press, 1973.
Rabinow, Paul, and Sullivan, William M. *Interpretive Social Science: A Reader*. Berkeley and Los Angeles: University of California Press, 1979.
Ray, Talton. *The Politics of the Barrios of Venezuela*. Berkeley and Los Angeles: University of California Press, 1969.
Restrepo Posada, José. *Dos momentos difíciles de la iglesia en la historia patria*. Bogotá, 1972.

Reuther, Rosemary. *The Radical Kingdom: The Western Experience of Messianic Hope*. New York: Paulist Press, 1970.
Rex, John. *Key Problems of Sociological Theory*. London: Routledge & Kegan Paul, 1961.
Robertson, Roland, ed. *Sociology of Religion*. Baltimore: Penguin Books, 1969.
Rodríguez, Jaime. *Educación católica y secularización en Colombia*. Bogotá CIEC, 1970.
Rodríguez Iturbe, José. *Iglesia y estado en Venezuela, 1824-1964*. Caracas: Imprenta Universitaria, 1968.
Roncagliolo, Rafael, and Reyes Matta, Fernando. *Iglesia, prensa, y militares: el caso Riobamba y los obispos latinoamericanos*. Mexico: Instituto Latinoamericano de Estudios Transnacionales, 1978.
Rossi, Juan José, ed., *Iglesia latinoamericana, ¿protesta o profecía?* Avellaneda, Argentina: Ediciones Búsqueda, 1969.
Ruddle, K., and Hamour, M., eds. *Statistical Abstract of Latin America*. Los Angeles: University of California Latin American Center, 1972.
Sabine, George. *A History of Political Theory*. 3d ed. New York: Holt, Rinehart & Winston, 1963.
Sanders, Thomas G. *Catholic Innovation in a Changing Latin America*. Cuernavaca: CIDOC, 1968.
―――. *The Chilean Episcopate: An Institution in Transition*. American Universities Field Staff Reports, West Coast South America Series, vol. 15, no. 3. New York: American Universities Field Staff, 1968.
―――. "The New Latin American Catholicism." In D. E. Smith, ed., *Religion and Political Modernization*, pp. 282-302. New Haven: Yale University Press, 1974.
―――. "The Priests of the People." Letter to the Institute of Current World Affairs, New York. TGS-11. 24 Mar. 1968.
―――. *Protestant Concepts of Church and State: Historical Backgrounds and Approaches for the Future*. New York: Holt, Rinehart & Winston, 1964.
―――. "Religion and Modernization: Some Reflections." Letter to the Institute of Current World Affairs, New York. TGS-14. 4 Aug. 1968.
―――. "The Theology of Liberation: Christian Utopianism." *Christianity and Crisis* 33:15 (17 Sept. 1973), pp. 167-73.
―――. "A Typology of Catholic Elites." Letter to the Institute of Current World Affairs, New York. TGS-10. 21 Feb. 1968.
―――. *The Puebla Conference*. American Universities Field Staff Reports, South America Series, no. 30. New York: American Universities Field Staff, 1979.

Sanders, Thomas G., and Smith, Brian. *The Chilean Catholic Church During the Allende and Pinochet Regimes.* American Universities Field Staff Reports, West Coast South America Series, vol. 23, no. 1. New York: American Universities Field Staff, 1976.

Sanks, T. Howard. *Authority in the Church: A Study in Changing Paradigms.* Missoula, Mont.: Scholar's Press, 1974.

Schattschneider, E. E. *The Semi-Sovereign People: A Realist's View of America.* New York: Holt, Rinehart & Winston, 1960.

Schroyer, Trent. *The Critique of Domination: The Origins and Development of Critical Theory.* Boston: Beacon Press, 1975.

Schwan, Hubert. *Directorio de la iglesia católica en Colombia, 1969.* Bogotá: Varios Servicios, 1969.

Schwan, Hubert, and Ugalde, Antonio. "Orientations of the Bishops of Colombia Toward Social Development, 1930-1970." *Journal of Church and State* 16:3 (Autumn 1974), pp. 473-92.

Searing, Donald D., and Edinger, Lewis J. "Social Background in Elite Analysis: A Methodological Inquiry." *American Political Science Review* 51:2 (June 1967), pp. 428-45.

Segundo, J. L. "Capitalism-Socialism: A Theological Crux." In C. Geffré and G. Gutierrez, eds., *The Mystical and Political Dimensions of the Christian Faith*, pp. 105-26. New York: Herder & Herder. 1974.

———. *The Community Called Church.* Vol. 1. A Theology for Artisans of a New Humanity. Maryknoll: Orbis Books, 1973.

———. *Evolution and Guilt.* Vol. 5. A Theology for Artisans of a New Humanity. Maryknoll: Orbis Books, 1974.

———. *Grace and the Human Condition.* Vol. 2. A Theology for Artisans of a New Humanity. Maryknoll: Orbis Books, 1973.

———. *The Liberation of Theology.* Maryknoll: Orbis Books, 1976.

———. *Our Idea of God.* Vol. 3. A Theology for Artisans of a New Humanity. Maryknoll: Orbis Books, 1974.

———. *The Sacraments Today.* Vol. 4. A Theology for Artisans of a New Humanity. Maryknoll: Orbis Books, 1974.

Segura, Luis B. *Wuytack: el evangelio como única ley.* Caracas: Ediciones Centauro, 1970.

Sharpless, Richard E. *Gaitán of Colombia: A Political Biography.* Pittsburgh: University of Pittsburgh Press, 1978.

Silvert, Kalman H., ed. *Churches and States: The Religious Institution and Modernization.* New York: American Universities Field Staff, 1967.

Silvert, K. H., and Reissman, Leonard. *Education, Class, and Nation: The Experiences of Chile and Venezuela.* New York: Elsevier Scientific Publishing Co., 1976.

Smith, Brian. "The Catholic Church and Political Change in Chile, 1920-1978." Ph.D. dissertation, Yale University, 1979.

———. "Churches and Human Rights in Latin America: Recent Trends in the Subcontinent." *Journal of Interamerican Studies and World Affairs* 21:1 (Feb. 1979), pp. 89-128.

———. "Religion and Social Change: Classical Theories and New Formulations in the Context of Recent Developments in Latin America." *Latin American Research Review* 10:2 (Summer 1975), pp. 3-34.

Smith, Brian, and Sanks, T. Howard. "Liberation Ecclesiology: Praxis, Theory, and Praxis." *Theological Studies* 38:1 (Mar. 1977), pp. 3-38.

Smith, Donald E., ed. *Religion and Political Development.* Boston: Little, Brown & Co. 1970.

Stepan, Alfred. *The Military in Politics: Changing Patterns in Brazil.* Princeton: Princeton University Press, 1971.

Támez, Elsa, and Trinidad, Saúl, eds. *Capitalismo: violencia y anti-vida. La opresión de las mayorías y la domesticación de los dioses.* 2 vols. San José, Costa Rica: EDUCA, 1978.

Taylor, Phillip. *The Venezuelan Golpe de Estado of 1958: The Fall of Marcos Pérez Jiménez.* Washington: Institute for the Comparative Study of Political Systems, 1968.

Torres, Camilo. *Cristianismo y revolución.* Mexico: Ediciones Era, 1970.

———. *Father Camilo Torres, Revolutionary Writings.* New York: Harper & Row, Colophon Books, 1972.

———. *La revolución: imperativo cristiano.* N.p., n.d.

Torres, Sergio, and Fabella, Virginia. *The Emergent Gospel: Theology from the Underside of History.* Maryknoll: Orbis Books, 1978.

Torres, Sergio, and Eagleson, John, eds. *Theology in the Americas.* Maryknoll: Orbis Books, 1976.

Tugwell, Franklin. *The Politics of Oil in Venezuela.* Stanford: Stanford University Press, 1975.

Turner, Frederick. *Catholicism and Political Development in Latin America.* Chapel Hill: University of North Carolina Press, 1971.

Turner, Roy. *Ethnomethodology: Selected Readings.* Baltimore: Penguin Books, 1974.

Turner, Victor. *Dramas, Fields, and Metaphors: Symbolic Action in Human Society.* Ithaca: Cornell University Press, 1974.

Ullmann, Walter. *A History of Political Thought in the Middle Ages.* Rev. ed. Baltimore: Penguin Books, 1970.

United States Catholic Conference. *Basic Christian Communities.* LADOC Keyhole Series, no. 14. Washington, D.C.: Latin America Documentation, 1976.

———. *Latin American Bishops Discuss Human Rights.* LADOC

Keyhole Series, nos. 15-16. Washington, D.C.: Latin American Documentation, 1978.

Urrutia, Miguel. *The Development of the Colombian Labor Movement.* New Haven: Yale University Press, 1969.

Utz, Arthur. "Ojeada sobre la evolución de la doctrina social de la iglesia." *Tierra Nueva* 22 (July 1977), pp. 5-19.

Vallier, Ivan. *Catholicism, Social Control, and Modernization in Latin America.* Englewood Cliffs: Prentice-Hall, 1970.

———. "Comparative Studies of Roman Catholicism: Dioceses as Strategic Units." *Social Compass* 16:2 (1969), pp. 147-84.

———. "Extraction, Insulation, and Re-entry: Towards a Theory of Religious Change." In H. Landsberger, ed., *The Church and Social Change in Latin America*, pp. 9-35. Notre Dame: University of Notre Dame Press, 1970.

———. "Radical Priests and the Revolution." In D. Chalmers, ed., *Changing Latin America: New Interpretations of its Politics and Society*, pp. 15-26. New York: Academy of Political Science, 1972.

———. "Religious Elites: Differentiations and Developments in Roman Catholicism." In Seymour M. Lipset and A. Solari, eds., *Elites in Latin America*, pp. 190-232. New York: Oxford University Press, 1967.

Van Texel, Hendrik. "La ultima escisión del integrismo." *Tierra Nueva* 20 (Jan. 1977), pp. 71-75.

Vekemans, Roger. *¿Agonía o resurgimiento? Reflexiones teológicas acerca de la "contestación" en la iglesia.* Barcelona: Editorial Herder, 1972.

———. *Caesar and God: The Priesthood and Politics.* Maryknoll: Orbis Books, 1972.

———. "La iglesia en el proceso de liberación." *Tierra Nueva* 19 (Sept. 1976), pp. 80-86.

———. "Iglesia y cambio social en América Latina." *Tierra Nueva* 11 (Oct. 1974), pp. 36-64.

———. "Unidad y pluralismo en la iglesia." *Tierra Nueva* 5 (Apr. 1973), pp. 45-50.

Velásquez, Ramón J. *La caída del liberalismo amarillo.* Caracas, 1973.

Venezuela, República de. *X censo de población y vivienda: resúmen nacional características generales.* 2 vols. Caracas: Dirección General de Estadística y Censos Nacionales, Ministerio de Fomento, Taller gráfico, 1974.

Vidales, Raúl. *La iglesia latinoamericana y la política después de Medellín*, Bogotá: CELAM, 1972.

Vivas Dorado, Raúl. *Diagnóstico de la educación privada.* Bogotá: CONACED, 1970.

Wallace, Anthony F. C. *Religion: An Anthropological View*. New York: Random House, 1966.

Watters, Mary. *A History of the Church in Venezuela, 1810-1933*. Chapel Hill: University of North Carolina Press, 1933.

Weber, Max. *From Max Weber: Essays in Sociology*. Edited by Hans Gerth and C. Wright Mills. New York: Oxford University Press, 1958.

―――. *The Methodology of the Social Sciences*. Edited by Henry Finch and Edward Shils. Glencoe: Free Press, 1949.

―――. *The Sociology of Religion*. Boston: Beacon Press, 1963.

Wienert, Richard. "Violence in Pre-Modern Societies: Rural Colombia." *American Political Science Review* 60:2 (June 1966), pp. 340-47.

Wilde, Alexander W. "Ten Years of Change in the Church: Puebla and the Future." In Daniel H. Levine, ed., *Churches and Politics in Latin America*, pp. 267-81. Beverly Hills: SAGE Publications, 1980.

―――. "A Traditional Church and Politics: Colombia." Ph.D. dissertation, Columbia University, 1972.

Willems, Emilio. *Followers of the New Faith*. Nashville: Vanderbilt University Press, 1967.

Wills, Gary. *Bare, Ruined Choirs: Doubt, Prophecy, and Radical Religion*. New York: Dell Publishing Co., Delta Paperbacks, 1974.

Wilson, Bryan R. *Magic and the Millennium: A Sociological Study of Religious Movements of Protest Among Tribal and Third World Peoples*. London: Heinemann Educational Books, 1973.

Wolf, Donald J., ed. *Toward Consensus: Catholic-Protestant Interpretations of Church and State*. Garden City: Doubleday & Co., Anchor Books, 1968.

Worsley, Peter. *The Trumpet Shall Sound: A Study of 'Cargo' Cults in Melanesia*. 2d ed., augmented. New York: Schocken Books, 1968.

Xavier da Silveira, Fabio Vigdal. *Frei: el Kerensky chileno*. Caracas: Grupo Tradicionalista de Jóvenes Cristianos Venezolanos, 1968.

Yinger, J. Milton. *The Scientific Study of Religion*. London: Macmillan Co., 1970.

Zago, Angela. *Aquí no ha pasado nada*. Caracas: Síntesis Dos Mil, 1973.

Zapata Isaza, Gilberto. *¿Patricios o asesinos?* Bogotá: Editorial y Tipografía Ital Torino, 1969.

Zuluaga, Francisco. *Estructuras eclesiásticas de Colombia*. Bogotá: CIAS, 1971.

Index

Acción Cultural Popular (ACPO), 220n, 228-31, 251; finances of, 231; and Peasant Institutes, 230; relations of, to Church, 229-30; technical criteria of, 230-31
activation, 139, 140, 179-80, 310
activism, 27, 139, 140, 180, 181, 191; association of, with violence, 181, 191-201; reasons for rejection of, 181; witness, 180
Adveniat, 114
Allende, Salvador, 48, 52
Alvarez Restrepo, Msgr. Baltasar, profile of, 117-20
Andrade, Father Vicente, 225
Argentina, 51
Assmann, Hugo, 45
authority, 36, 37, 143, 145, 152, 158, 302; ecclesial, 217; ecclesiastical, 217; exercise of, 144; and legitimacy, 143; patriarchal, 145; and role of laity, 180; sources of, in Church, 144, 148; witness, 145. *See also* models of the Church

base communities, 253n, 274, 295
Berger, Peter, 23, 277
Berrigan, Daniel, 10n
birth control, 54
bishops: age, 100; career patterns, 100, 102, 104, 105; contacts with government, 109; daily routine, 106-10; education, 100, 102, 103, 106; and local Church organization, 111; and local Church planning, 110; pastoral visits, 112-13; profiles, 117-31; regional origins, 100; relations with clergy, 110, 154; relations with laity, 154; social background, 100; status as notables, 108; style, 118, 123; types, 117. *See also* Colombian bishops' public views, Venezuelan bishops' public views
body-soul metaphor, 21
Brazil, 8, 30, 51, 196, 200n
Builes, Msgr. Miguel Angel, 64

Caldas, 256
Cali, 257-58, 279; Barrio El Guabal in, 272, 273; bishop's orientation, 262; and CARITAS, 272; innovation in, 262, 264; organizational pattern of, 272; parish centers in, 272-73
Caracas, 196
Cardenal, Ernesto, 19
Carvajal Foundation, 272
Castrillón, Msgr. Darío, 199
Castro, Cipriano, 60
catechism, 218, 248; innovations in, 241-43; methodologies of, 243, 246; and political issues, 241, 244; and relations to Liberation Theology, 244
Catholic Action, 74, 133, 213, 218, 222, 223, 233, 250; in Colombia, 74; organizational traits of, 150; origins of, 31; in Venezuela, 74
Cauca Valley, 258
charity, 39, 42, 282
Chile, 8, 30, 38, 48, 51, 196, 295, 311n
Chilean bishops, 51; and Christians for Socialism, 51; and Marxism, 185; and the military, 52; and politics, 51
Christendom, 21, 33-34, 139, 206, 304, 305
Christian Democracy, 33, 34, 137, 305
Christian Family Movement, 218
Christian Identity in Actions for Justice, 89, 92-94

337

INDEX

Christian-Marxist alliances, 38, 48, 51, 140
Christians for Socialism, 48, 49, 51, 53, 311n
Church: in agrarian societies, 21; in conflicts with state, 27; distinguished from sect, 36; established status of, 31; as minority, 162; national structures of, 9, 16, 57
Church Facing Change, The, 89-90, 232
Church organizations: legal status, 70-71; resources, 72; structures, 73-74
Church roles: defined, 176-77
CIAS, 222n
clergy: community roles of, 161, 267, 282; foreign, 111; as moral advisers, 118, 168n, 225, 232; scarcity of, 118, 167
clericalism, 171. *See also* models of the Church
CODESA, 235
Coleman, John, 44n
collegiality, 37, 147, 148, 149, 168, 169; relation of, to oligarchy, 168
Colombian bishops' public views: anticommunism, 90; Church-State separation, 87; clergy-laity distinction, 87-88; ideal of Christendom, 84; identification of Church with nation, 87; liberalism, 83, 84; Liberation Theology, 93, 94; Marxism, 84; partisanship, 86; politics, 83; poverty, 85; property, 85; social problems, 86; triumphalism, 90
commitment, 297
communitas, 294-96
community, 153, 163, 294, 295, 307, 308
CONACED, 245
Concha Córdoba, Msgr. Luis, 64
concientización, 47-48, 171
Concordat, 70, 71
Conservative party, 32, 58, 64, 84, 154
COPEI, 78, 235

corporatism, 32
Counter-Reformation, 143
Cumaná, 258-59, 278, 279; bishop's orientation, 262; organizational pattern of, 274-75; resource limitations of, 275; San Luis Gonzaga Parish in, 275; simple human contact in, 276; stress on community in, 276
curia, 100
Cursillos de Cristiandad, 126, 218, 220, 228, 233, 237; membership selection for, 236; origins of, 235; relation to bishops, 236; in Venezuela, 235-36

De Toqueville, Alexis, 144
democracy, 8, 76; attitude of Venezuelan bishops toward, 76-79
Democratic Action (Acción Democrática), 67, 68, 76, 190
Denuncia, 245, 246, 247
dependency, 37, 45, 169, 244
development theory, 302; and Christian Democrats, 38; and Latin American Catholics, 38; in Medellín Conference, 38n; in Vatican II, 37. *See also* modernization theory
dioceses, 9, 16, 56; clergy-laity relations in, 282; links to parishes, 282
distinction of levels, 214
Drake, George, 266
Duque Villegas, Msgr. Arturo, 259

ecclesial, 138, 139
ecclesiastical, 138, 139
ecclesiology, 146; and activism, 147; and authority, 146; and collegiality, 147; organizational consequences of, 149-50; and participation, 147; and sources of values, 150-51. *See also* authority, models of the Church
ekklesia, 139
El Salvador, 8, 30, 196, 295

338

Encuentro, 245, 246
Evangelical-Pastoral positions, 304, 306-12
evangelization, 161, 307, 309
evolutionism, 6, 10
experience, 139, 301, 302; historical, 146, 215, 300; religious, 297, 298-300; shared, 146

Facatativá, 258-59; bishop's orientation, 263; organizational pattern of, 274
FANAL, 224, 225, 226
fascism, 32
Fernandez Feo, Msgr. Alejandro, 260
Freire, Paulo, 47, 282
functionalism, 132
future, 161-64; context of perceptions of, 163, 206-7

Gaitán, Jorge Eliécer, 62, 84
Galilea, Segundo, 176, 298
Gaudium et Spes, 154
Geertz, Clifford, 5n, 9, 143, 289, 292
generalization, 292
Gilfeather, Katherine, 37n, 299n
Golconda, 247
Gómez, Juan Vicente, 60, 66
Gómez, Laureano, 63
Gregorian University, 103
Gutierrez, Gustavo, 38n, 43, 44, 214n

Hervas, Bishop Juan B., 236
human promotion, 89-90

IDES, 22, 222, 231
Illich, Ivan, 143, 299, 300
institutions, mediating role, 304

Jesuits, 16
JOC, 222, 224, 250
Jóvenes de Acción, 250-52
just war, 189-99
Justice in the World, 89-91
Juventud Católica Feminina Venezolana, 250
Juventud Católica Venezolana, 249

La Vega, 196
laity: participation, 148; role, 148, 153, 239
Law of Ecclesiastical Patronage, 71
lay organizations: areas of action, 218-19; in Colombia, 220-33; favored by bishops, 218-19; relation to concepts of authority, 253; in Venezuela, 234-39
Lebrún Moratinos, Msgr. Alí, 261, 264, 271, 284
Legion of Mary, 151, 218, 220, 228, 233; origins of, 237; in Venezuela, 237-38
Liberación, La, 242, 245, 247
liberal analysis, 3, 4, 24
Liberal party (Colombia), 84, 154
Liberal party (Venezuela), 59
liberation: defined, 45-46, 46n
Liberation Theology, 28, 43-49, 51, 140, 244, 295, 304-6; and change, 45; and dependency, 45; and development, 45; historicity in, 303; Latin American focus of, 43; and love, 44; and Marxism, 44; method of, 43; primacy of politics in, 47; praxis of, 46-47; and the proletariat, 44; rejection of, in Colombia, 93-94
liminal, 39n
López Trujillo, Msgr. Alfonso, 182
Louvain University, 41, 63
Luckmann, Thomas, 277

McKenzie, John, 145
Manatí, 195
Manizales, 117, 118, 256, 278, 279; barrio centers in, 265; bishop's orientation, 259; Corporation of the Holy Family in, 265, 279; Minitas Parish in, 265-66; organizational pattern of, 265-66; Parish Councils in, 267; Pastoral Councils in, 267; Priests' Councils in, 267
Maritain, Jacques, 33, 140
Márquez Gómez, Msgr. Tomás Enrique, profile of, 124-27

INDEX

Marxism, 54, 120, 123, 127, 130, 182-86, 190, 311
Marxist categories, 3, 4; in Catholic thought, 37
Maryknoll, 269, 270, 283
meaning, analysis of, 11
Medellín, 35, 38, 40, 88, 144, 176, 182, 197, 295, 312; compared with Vatican II, 38n; and conflict, 38, 40; and development, 38n; and poverty, 39, 40; and sin, 39; and violence, 38, 39, 41
Mérida, 117, 120, 131
Metz, J. B., 145
Mexico, 30; *cristero* wars in, 31n
Meyer, Alfred G., 278n
Míguez Bonino, José, 29n
military. *See* national security doctrine
Mills, C. Wright, 14, 99n
Miserior, 114
mission territories, 16n, 71
models of the Church, 35, 142, 146, 302; clericalism and, 165-66; institutional, 35, 146, 213; People of God, 35, 36, 44, 146, 151, 302; ties to action of, 278
modernization theory, 6, 7, 24
modus vivendi, 71
Montoya, Father Hernán, 266, 267
Mounier, Emmanuel, 33, 34
Movement of Base Education (Brazil), 231n

National Coordination for Social Action, 133
National Front, 63, 65
National Secretariat for Social Pastoral, 169
national security doctrine, 28, 49, 50, 54, 169, 311
nations as units of analysis, 8, 9, 16
neo-Christendom, 33, 34, 304, 305
neo-Thomism, 32-33
neutrality. *See* politics
Nicaragua, 8

obedience, 36, 37. *See also* authority

ordinations, 72-73
organizations: content, 215; relations to hierarchy, 216; structure, 215; style, 215-16. *See also* lay organizations
Ostpolitik, 185

Paraguay, 30
Parish Councils, 267
parishes, 16
Parra León, Msgr. José Mariano, 262, 284
participation, 147, 149, 153, 169. *See also* collegiality, laity
pastoral action, 26, 161, 311, 313; expansion of, 25, 171, 194, 294; in dioceses, 265-77, 284; relation to politics of, 194, 200
Pastoral Councils, 110, 167, 267
paternalism, 283, 301
Patria y Libertad, 49n
Paul VI (pope), 39, 193, 197
Paz, Nestor, 297n
Perdomo, Msgr. Ismael, 64
Pereira, 117, 118
Pérez Cisneros, Msgr. Angel, profile of, 120-23
Pérez Jiménez, Marcos, 67, 78
Pérez Morales, Msgr. Ovidio, 80
personalism, 34
petroleum, impact on Venezuela of, 59-60
phenomenological approaches, 12, 290-91, 292, 293
Pius XII (pope), 247
political parties, 58, 60, 63
politics, 25, 26, 140, 169, 294, 302, 311; as agenda setting, 194, 200; broad concepts of, 172, 178, 194, 199; and the Colombian Church, 65, 94, 193; narrow concepts of, 172, 194; and neutrality, 27, 172, 178; primacy of, 47, 51, 94; surrogate role for Church in, 53; and violence, 191-201
poverty, 39, 39n, 40, 304; redefined, 39-40
praxis, 37, 44, 46, 47, 147n, 182

340

Priests' Councils, 110, 128, 167, 267
Proaño, Msgr. Leonidas, 46n
proletariat, 40
prophetic positions, 8
Protestant Reformation, 21-22, 24
Puebla, 35, 306-12

Radio Sutatenza. *See* Acción Cultural Popular
re-Christianization, 200, 284, 298, 305, 314
Reissman, Leonard, 302
religion: defined, 19, 25, 294ff. *See also* experience, religious
Religion, La, 28, 228
religion and politics, 54; Christendom as a synthesis of, 304-5; current syntheses of, 302-12; Evangelical-Pastoral synthesis of, 306-12; future paths of, 313-14; Liberation Theology as a synthesis of, 305-6; medieval views of, 21, 21n; neo-Christendom as a synthesis of, 305; problems of, for one another, 22-23, 27. *See also* pastoral action, politics
religious orders, 16
República, La, 248
resources, implications in dioceses of, 278
Reuther, Rosemary, 5n
Roman School, 104, 106, 144n, 157
Romanitas, 104

Salcedo, Msgr. José Joaquin, 229, 230
Salesians, 16
San Cristobal, 256, 278, 279; bishop's orientation, 260; organizational pattern of, 268
San Felipe, 117, 124
Sanders, Thomas G., 131, 136, 137, 139; criticism of, 138; typology of Catholic elites by, 136-38

Sanks, T. Howard, 103, 104, 144n, 146
Santander, Jaime, 195, 198
Schroyer, Trent, 293
Second Vatican Council. *See* Vatican II
secularization, 4-5n, 20
Segundo, Juan Luis, 300
SETRAC, 222, 223, 225, 226, 227n
Siglo, El, 247
signs of the times, 147, 148, 150. *See also* authority, models of the Church
Silvert, K. H., 302
simple human contact, 276, 301
simplicity, 149, 153
Sincelejo, 117, 127, 128, 136
Smith, Brian H., 53, 146, 306n
sociological language, 10, 113, 176
sociologism, 89
Solentiname, 18
solidarity, 25, 171, 308. *See also* authority, experience, models of the Church, pastoral action, poverty, witness
Sonsón, 117
SPEC, 221, 232
structuralism: defined, 173-74; language of, 113, 188
structure: defined, 215-16; implications of, 282; in dioceses, 279
style: defined, 215-16
symbols, 291; relations of, to structure, 301
syntheses, 302ff. *See also* religion and politics

Táchira, 256, 268
Teilhard de Chardin, Pierre, 33, 34
testimony, 25, 36, 146, 169
TFP, 28, 49, 136, 295, 305
Torres, Camilo, 28, 41, 44, 63, 69, 88, 137, 178n, 198, 247; and activism, 42; and charity, 42; and faith, 41; and politics, 42; relations of, to Marxism, 42; and violence, 42

341

INDEX

Torres Parra, Msgr. Félix María, profile of, 128-30
Turner, Victor, 39n, 294
two swords doctrine, 21
typologies, 131-41; dimensions of, 138-40; by Sanders, 136-38; uses of, 131; by Vallier, 131-36

United Front, 41
unity, 301, 307, 308; in clergy, 121; in Colombian Church, 93, 193, 193n
urbanization, 58, 60
Uribe Urdaneta, Msgr. Alberto, 262, 264, 273
Uruguay, 51
UTC, 223, 224, 225, 226
utilitarian thought, 24
Utz, Arthur, 181

Valencia, 258, 279; Barrio La Raya in, 271; bishop's orientation, 261, 271; innovation in, 261-62, 269; La Isabelica Parish in, 269, 271, 283; organizational pattern of, 264
Vallier, Ivan, 30, 100, 131, 132, 133, 217; concept of influence held by, 132, 136n; criticism of, 135-36; functionalist models by, 132, 135; typology of Catholic elites by, 133-35
Vatican II, 9, 34-38, 40, 88, 119, 121, 136, 157, 163, 167, 172, 176, 247, 261, 295; compared with Medellín, 37, 38n, 40; concepts of authority in, 35-38, 143-46; and concern for development, 37; and models of the Church, 35-36, 146-48; and openness to historical change, 35-36
Vekemans, Roger, 147
Velásquez, Ramón J., 60
Venezuelan Bishops' Conference, 74
Venezuelan bishops' public views, 75-82; on celibacy, 82; on definition of the Church, 81; on democracy, 76-79; on educational policy, 76-77; political neutrality, 80; on poverty, 79; radical critiques of, 80; relations of, with military, 77-78; on role of priests, 82
Violence, The (La Violencia—Colombia), 62-65, 191; impact of, on the Church, 62-64, 84, 191-96

Weber, Max, 11, 294n, 296
witness, 25, 36, 146, 169
Worsely, Peter, 27, 29n
Wuytack, Father Francis, 196-98, 252

Young Colombian Workers, 227n
Youth Central, 227
Youth organizations, 218, 220; in Venezuela, 249-50

Zambrano Camader, Msgr. Raúl, 263, 284

Library of Congress Cataloging in Publication Data

Levine, Daniel H
   Religion and politics in Latin America.

   Bibliography: p.
   Includes index.
   1. Catholic Church in Venezuela. 2. Catholic Church in Colombia. 3. Venezuela—Politics and government—1830- 4. Colombia—Politics and government—1940- 5. Christianity and politics. 6. Venezuela—Church history. 7. Colombia—Church history. I. Title.
BX1488.2.L48   282'.861   80-20110
ISBN 0-691-07624-3
ISBN 0-691-02200-3 (pbk.)

Daniel H. Levine is Associate Professor of Political Science at the University of Michigan and the author of *Conflict and Political Change in Venezuela* (Princeton)